Jailed for Freedom

ALICE PAUL

Jailed for Freedom

DORIS STEVENS

Introduction by Janice Law Trecker

Studies in the Life of Women
General Editor: Gerda Lerner

SCHOCKEN BOOKS · NEW YORK

First published by SCHOCKEN BOOKS 1976

Introduction copyright © 1976 by Schocken Books Inc.

Library of Congress Cataloging in Publication Data

Stevens, Doris, 1892–
 Jailed for freedom.

 Reprint, with a new introd., of the 1920 ed.
published by Boni and Liveright, New York.
 Includes bibliographical references.
 1. Women—Suffrage—United States. I. Title.
JK1901.S85 1976   324'.3'0973   75-36494

Manufactured in the United States of America

INTRODUCTION

by Janice Law Trecker

BETWEEN JUNE 1917 and the spring of 1919, over five hundred American women were arrested for carrying banners demanding the right to vote. Almost one hundred and seventy of these women served prison sentences, and they, along with their colleagues who escaped imprisonment, were attacked by mobs, subjected to official harassment and vilified in the press. These women were persecuted by officials of the District of Columbia and the federal government not when women suffrage was a radical and improbable demand, but when the belief in votes for women was rapidly becoming a political reality. On appeal, the suffragists' convictions were dismissed, and even at the height of the controversy influential citizens both inside and outside of the government pointed out that the actions against the "suffrage pickets" were without legal foundation. Yet women were brought out of the infamous Occoquan Workhouse half dead of starvation; they were force fed, beaten and subjected to all sorts of physical neglect and psychological pressures for "obstructing traffic" and "blocking sidewalks." Their sentences for these trifling crimes ran as high as seven months. At the same time, no charges were ever filed against members of the mobs who attacked the suffragists, destroyed their banners and broke up their marches.

The picketing campaign of the Woman's Party and the federal government's brutal response to it created the most dramatic moment of the long effort to secure the ballot. The crisis provoked by the militants served to focus national interest on the vote and demonstrated the undeniable determination of American women to secure their political rights. When Doris Stevens wrote *Jailed for Freedom,* she was confident that the final struggle for the vote would be identified with the story of the Woman's Party and that the party's picketing campaign would be seen as the major force in securing suffrage. Half a century later, few Americans know that there was any struggle for the vote at all, and fewer still that the pursuit of the ballot eventually involved protest, confrontation, violence and imprisonment. While books, articles and even a popular television series have illustrated the horrors and triumphs of the British suffragette movement, knowledge of our own suffrage militants is still rare. People are surprised and horrified to learn that in the United States, as well as the United Kingdom, getting the vote required not only dedication and moral stamina but also physical courage.

The popular image of the suffrage campaigns is an undramatic one, and even scholarly works have usually stressed the organizations and achievements of the more conventional suffrage organizations. As for the average history text, when such works give space to the story of the vote, they tend to allot it to two figures, Susan B. Anthony and Carrie Chapman Catt. The image presented is one of dogged determination, extraordinary patience and thorough organization. Success, it is frequently hinted, came because American men chivalrously "gave" women the vote in recognition of female service in World War I. The vote was a reasonable request, granted, after prudent delay, by reasonable men. Anthony, who was admittedly ahead of her time, and Catt, who emerged at precisely the right moment, are presented as calm, statesmanlike and rational leaders who gradually educated the nation to the wisdom of woman suffrage.

Even a cursory reading of *Jailed for Freedom* will indicate that the Woman's Party does not easily fit into this account of suffrage. The Woman's Party and its predecessor, the Congressional Union, might also revere Susan B. Anthony—but as a radical agitator, not as that kindly American institution, "Aunt Susan." The party might stress thorough organization and discipline as much as Mrs.

Catt's National American Woman Suffrage Association. Its membership, like NAWSA's, was undeniably persistent, frequently ladylike and sometimes politically astute; but when all is said and done, it did not see itself in the same way as did other women's organizations. Doris Stevens and the rest of its historians did not regard the campaign for the vote as a polite, purely political exercise which would, in due course, be rewarded by chivalrous statesmen. They saw it as a battle, not only for the vote but for emancipation, and as a deadly struggle, not only against certain recalcitrant Congressmen but against unimaginative stupidities and outmoded male privileges. Eventually, their view was vindicated. Thrown into District Jail and Occoquan Workhouse on the flimsiest pretexts, the imprisoned militants came close to martyrdom. Despite similarities between the Woman's Party and other female organizations of the time, the party's sense of identity, origins, methods and, above all, its experiences at the hands of the Washington establishment, distinguish it from other women's groups. The Woman's Party has not fitted the image of the suffrage struggle, and it is perhaps fair to say that, beyond any assessment of its successes or failures, it is the party's lack of conformity which has kept the history of the militants obscure.

The neglect of the Woman's Party and the obscurity of major sources like *Jailed for Freedom* represents an omission in the history of American feminism—and in social and political history as well. Stevens' book presents strikingly interesting information on the militant women of her era and on the organization, tactics and attitudes of the suffrage movement. It also illuminates the social attitudes and the political climate of the war years, raises the issue of American political prisoners and traces the genesis of a political technique which has since served the civil rights, peace, student and modern feminist movements: nonviolent confrontation.

The militant suffragists of the Woman's Party developed the techniques of nonviolent protest and confrontation which have become increasingly prominent. Alice Paul and her colleagues learned how to stage events which would stir the popular imagination as well as provoke the government officials who were their immediate targets. In recent years, technological developments in television and film have made it much easier for militant groups to gain a hearing, and the voracious appetites of the media have made current society an even more responsive setting for the types of protest and confrontation the Woman's Party pioneered.

Of course, the picketing campaign has only rarely been recognized as the first major nonviolent militancy in this country. When Dr. Martin Luther King and other black leaders began the modern civil rights movement, they looked back to Mohandas Gandhi's drive for independence in colonial India. Gandhi's ideas, however, owed a debt not only to his religious convictions but to the American feminists' British ancestor, the WSPU, the Women's Social and Political Union. Gandhi studied the WSPU's methods and observed its success in swaying the public with militant activity. Like Dr. King and others since, the Indian leader was impressed by the potential that militant, but nonviolent, activities offered to groups without conventional means of power.

The WSPU and later nonviolent movements challenged the hypocrisy of the democratic governments they confronted and conferred moral authority upon their own members. When faced with repression, violence, even martyrdom, militant leaders have used a variety of appeals to prevent their followers from the retaliation which might produce disaster. Religion, a strong sense of discipline and moral superiority, and an abhorrence of violence were all important in maintaining order. These factors seem to have been significant to the feminists as well. Alice Paul, for example, was a Quaker, and the Woman's Party (although not the WSPU) had a strongly pacifistic tinge. For the women's groups, adherence to a nonviolent stance was perhaps encouraged by the traditional picture of women as the more peaceful, less violent sex. There is evidence in the histories of both the British and the American militants that while rejecting stereotyped limitations, the radical women did not reject the "female virtues." They show a positive pride in being women; rather than trying to copy men's tactics, they proudly asserted their own value and uniqueness. They believed themselves more peaceful than men and less aggressive. Unlike some modern feminists, they most emphatically did not view either trait as a weakness or a limitation. In the opinion of both groups of militants, women were more intelligent, sensible and imaginative than men and considerably more stable emotionally. It would have come as a surprise to their male opponents to know that the women considered them predictably bombastic, dull-witted and insecure: in short, no match for determined women despite their masculine strength.

Besides their introduction of new techniques to the political arena, the Congressional Union and the Woman's Party had important roles in redirecting the energies of the suffrage movement and in stirring the larger NAWSA to regroup and refocus its forces. *Jailed for Freedom* relates how Paul and Burns reawakened interest in the federal route to suffrage, and how their skillful organization, plus the District of Columbia's disastrous handling of the first big Washington suffrage parade, put the vote back in the headlines. From then on, the Congressional Union's aggressive organization not only directed attention to the constitutional amendment but acted as a rebuke to the faction-torn NAWSA. The eventual reorganization of the NAWSA thus owed a debt, if indirectly, to the militants. Dislike of the partisan political philosophy of Alice Paul, Lucy Burns and Mrs. O. H. P. Belmont aroused the more moderate suffragists to the need for an alternative to the British-style militant activity.

Finally, as Eleanor Flexner and Anne and Andrew Scott have noted, the smaller Woman's Party was, for conservative suffragists and politicians alike, a look at the shape of things to come. Not only did Woman's Party militancy indicate that the suffrage struggle might escalate dangerously as it had in Britain, but the party's partisan political activites might be, and in fact were, followed by NAWSA's increasing involvement in political campaigns.

The Woman's Party's policies were a forecast of work by larger, more conservative women's organizations; its experiences with the Washington, D.C., police served as a political barometer for other radical groups. The militant suffragists were the first victims of the Red Scare, and their treatment was a sign that a new wave of conservative reaction was on the horizon. It is interesting that in 1917, conservatives associated the militant feminists with socialism and pacificism — two increasingly unpopular "isms" in the militaristic climate. In November, *The New York Times,* which was also carrying exposés of the suffragists' treatment in Occoquan and District Jail, editorialized against the Woman's Party and carried hostile accounts of local party rallies. Thus, on November 12, an article assailed the New York committee formed to fight the suffragists' imprisonment, declaring the group was "stampeded for socialism and propaganda" by the organizers. An editorial of November 27 not only connected the militants with both socialism and the peace movement, but described the latest delegation to Washington as an attempt

> to filch the time when Congressmen owe to the country and the war, to distract their attention, to cajole or menace, to interfere with the vital work of the nation at the greatest hour of its history.
> Plain speaking is best. It is but a disguised, more dangerous form of picketing which these sorely misguided women are about to undertake.

During the war years, the stigma of disloyalty was applied to all who dared differ with received opinion — whether they actually supported the war (like NAWSA, which did not escape criticism despite its war work) or took no stand on the war in policy (like the Woman's Party). If the militants' sex and status enabled them to escape the horrors of deportation, lynching, mutilation and murder, their severe sentences for "traffic violations" must still be rated as barbarous, especially since there was no evidence that they were armed or dangerous. So harmless did they appear that the government did not even charge them with conspiracy or try to indict them under the new Espionage Act, although this was threatened. It was clear even to the Justice Department that there was no case against Paul, Burns and their colleagues, and while the famous "Kaiser Wilson" banner was provocative, in fact no one had been arrested for carrying it. Treason indictments for women who quoted President Woodrow Wilson's opinions on democracy were too Kafkaesque even for wartime Washington. The charges against the women were trumped up from first to last, and their experiences should have warned other dissidents that the things which happened to the respectable and, in some cases, prominent militants—and worse—could happen to others.

The manner and purpose of their arrests and the prison conditions they encountered had an effect on the suffragists. The Woman's Party rapidly became interested in prison reform; after securing some elementary decencies, it made special demands for its members as political prisoners. Stevens not only defends these claims for special treatment, but includes an appendix which offers definitions of political offenders and their treatment in other countries. Her narrative makes it abundantly clear that the militants were imprisoned for their beliefs.

Because the Woman's Party members were unarmed, and there is no record of their resorting to violence, the imprisoning of the militants offers a clear example of the manner in which the American government can deal with political dissidents. Woodrow Wilson instructed his aide Joseph Tumulty on the proper reply to a NAWSA suffragist indignant about the sentences. In doing so, he summed up both the rationale for and the method of silencing political dissidents, while denying them the dignity of that title. Tell her, he said, "that these ladies cannot in any sense be regarded as political prisoners. We have no political prisoners and could have none under the law. They offended against an ordinance of the District and are undergoing the punishment appropriate in the circumstances." In this statement the President was supported by sentiment, not logic. It is a curiously unimaginative philosophy which claims that a democratic system cannot produce political offenders, although, by and large, our political offenders have not been opponents of true democratic philosophy. The militant suffragists are a classic case of Americans of democratic impulse who were arrested for exercising basic rights of free speech and free assembly. Their crime was not to oppose democratic government, but to wish to extend the system to their own group. Wilson was therefore politically correct, if quite wrong, in seeking to deny that the women were political prisoners. To admit them to be political offenders would have necessitated a discussion of their crime. And their crime, free speech, was a guaranteed constitutional right.

Jailed for Freedom is thus of considerable interest even beyond its importance as a record of feminist and suffragist activity. For contemporary women, however, its most interesting aspect may be the picture it presents of emancipated women and of the way in which the sacrifices and exertions of the suffrage campaign illustrated that emancipation and increased it. In her tribute to Alice Paul, Stevens writes:

> She called a halt to further pleading, wheedling, proving, praying. It was as if she had bidden women stand erect, with confidence in themselves and in their own judgments, and compelled them to be self-respecting enough to dare to put their freedom first, and so determine for themselves the day when they would be free. Those who had a taste of begging under the old regime and who abandoned it for demanding, know how fine and strong a thing it is to realize that you must take what is yours and not waste your energy proving that you are . . . worthy of a gift of power from your masters.

She speaks of freeing oneself to fight for freedom and points out that Paul's great gift lay in strengthening the sense of inner freedom and spiritual emancipation in her followers.

The women who were attracted to Paul and to the Woman's Party formed a remarkable group, as Stevens' narrative and her bibliographical appendix on the prisoners attest. In addition to being a notably well-educated group, the suffrage prisoners included medical personnel like Lavinia Dock, social workers like Mrs. Lawrence Lewis, teachers, journalists, a pioneer woman flyer, artists, union organizers and munitions workers. Several came from well-known families, the daughters of Senators, Congressmen and ambassadors, women whose menfolk had accepted and, indeed, expected the exercise of political power. At least some had strong support from their husbands and families, as *Jailed for Freedom* plainly illustrates.

It is clear from the character and quality of the women attracted to the Woman's Party standard that the charges that the militants were "unstable" and "fanatical" were without foundation. Nor does the evidence suggest, as their opponents maintained, that they sought martyrdom. *Jailed for Freedom,* Agnes Irwin's *The Story of the Woman's Party,* news reports, and the reminiscences of the surviving members of the militant corps all point to the opposite conclusion: that the militant suffragists expected to succeed, they planned to succeed, and they considered neither failure nor martyrdom. True, the willingness to risk death—especially for the older and less sturdy pickets—was a prerequisite for entering on the long terms at Occoquan and the District Jail, but the militants accepted this as one of the fortunes of war. All evidence suggests that the militant suffragists persisted in their campaign in the face of escalating severity for two reasons: because they sincerely believed such pressure was necessary for the passage of the constitutional amendment and because they were free women, who having determined the conditions of the conflict, could only retire with victory.

The latter sentiment has been glossed over by many commentators or interpreted as masochism, fanaticism, inflexibility and the like, or admired as splendid, if misguided, valor. This may be the case, but Stevens' passage on the spiritual necessity of demanding rather than pleading seems more nearly an explanation. Militancy was, in the end, more than one tactic among others, and it had a value for its participants and, they believed, for other women beyond its undoubted efficacy. The ability to demand, the willingness to suffer for an ideal, the capacity for militancy (and distinctly feminine militancy) was the very badge of emancipation. Confidence, gallantry, self-control, assertiveness, idealism: these were the new ingredients of femininity, and their demonstration was important. The militants never forgot the other means of working for the vote—they continued conventional lobbying and speaking and demonstrations. But they also felt the need to show that they were free—rather, they felt impelled to act what they in fact were: emancipated.

The Woman's Party was a remarkable organization which at its peak had an impact out of all proportion to either its numbers or its resources. This strength came out of two traditions. The party imitated the organization of and was inspired by the militant British suffragette movement; but the base of its strength was drawn from the legacy of nearly seventy years of work, organization and agitation by American feminists.

The American suffrage campaign is usually dated from 1848 when a small group of women at a convention in Seneca Falls, New York, presented a list of demands, including the right to the ballot, to an astonished public. From Seneca Falls on, the idea of woman suffrage was spread by the brilliant orators and reformers of the early feminist movement, along with such basic demands as changes in the property laws, equal educational and employment opportunities, and abolition of the many customs and traditions inimical to women. The vote was one demand among many, and in the early years the pursuit of the ballot took the form of an educational campaign. The intrepid women who traveled by stage, train, sleigh and riverboat to speak for suffrage were feminine John the Baptists, preparing the way for later political organization.

After the Civil War the more radical and militant feminists, led by Elizabeth Cady Stanton and Susan B. Anthony, added legal challenges, political action and demonstrations to the activities of the movement. These suffragists believed that women deserved the vote in recognition of their valuable services during the war. They also believed that the constitutional changes being planned to secure civil rights and the vote for black men could be enlarged to secure rights for all women. Instead, male politicians and reformers alike told the feminists that this was "the Negro's hour" and passed the Fourteenth Amendment, which did not enlarge female rights but itself raised doubts about the very citizenship of women.

The hostility which the Stanton-Anthony faction showed to the form of the Fourteenth Amendment and their campaign for woman suffrage in Kansas where Negro suffrage was also at issue aroused hostility from reformers anxious to secure the liberties of the newly freed slaves. The ensuing controversy not only alienated old friends but split the suffrage movement into the more radical, women-only National Woman Suffrage Association, and the more conservative American Woman Suffrage Association, led by Lucy Stone and Julia Ward Howe. The schism was not healed until 1890 when, with advancing age and changing attitudes, both groups had become more conventional and respectable.

By the time of their merger, the smaller, less active American Woman Suffrage Association had seen its attitudes and policies triumph. The suffrage movement focused narrowly on the vote and on state referendums as the means of its attainment. In the

1870's, however, when Stanton and Anthony were in their prime, the National Woman Suffrage Association was quite different. Militant and controversial, these radical suffragists were interested in a wide range of women's problems and concerns. They decided to force passage of a constitutional amendment rather than to fritter away time and energy in the unending state campaigns.

This concentration on the federal route to the vote was one of the things which the Woman's Party admired about Susan B. Anthony. The other was her militancy. With Stanton, she was outspoken on a variety of issues. She took part in the voting demonstrations of the seventies, and she was the defendant in a celebrated suffrage trial in 1872, one of the cases which closed off the possibility of obtaining the ballot through court action. When neither demonstrations nor the existing Constitution provided an avenue for the vote, Anthony and other radical feminists turned to the possiblity of a constitutional amendment. They pursued this goal energetically until the time the two suffrage groups merged under the new name, National American Woman Suffrage Association, NAWSA.

Between the heyday of the National Association in the 1870's and the so-called doldrums of the movement in 1896–1910, vast social changes had taken place—in feminism as well as in society at large. Without doubt, the women in the later suffrage movement were more cautious and conventional than their predecessors. By the close of the century, the courageous leaders of the early movement were dead, in semi-retirement, or set aside like Stanton, who saw her radical views repudiated. Women were more highly educated, better organized, freer in many ways than they had been, yet it was obvious that the feminist movement in general and the vote in particular were stagnating. Only Colorado and Idaho had joined the pioneering suffrage states, Wyoming and Utah, and the state-by-state route to the ballot was meeting increasingly heavy opposition from such entrenched interests as the brewers, the railroads and the large manufacturers. Big money interests in the North and conservative politicians in the South joined hands in opposing an innovation which might upset their political and economic calculations.

Against such opposition the suffrage forces lacked resources and, more importantly, leadership. The great figures of the past were gone, leaving the movement to the timid and the conventional or, in the case of Anthony's "heir," Anna Howard Shaw, a woman with every good gift except patience and administrative skill. In the first decade of the twentieth century, the American suffrage movement was bereft of imaginative leadership and a sense of over-all strategy. State organizations muddled through arduous and doomed referendums, while the national organization was rent with dissension. The American suffrage movement needed new leadership, new techniques and fresh spirit.

A parallel situation had occurred in Britain where the movement had flowered in mid-century, then declined. The end of the status quo for British feminism came in 1903 with the formation of the Woman's Social and Political Union by Emmeline Pankhurst and her daughters, Cristabel and Sylvia. Beginning in Manchester as an attempt to organize working women within the Independent Labor Party, the WSPU found its way to militancy almost by accident. In 1905, following ancient British custom, the WSPU sent a couple of its members to question Sir Edward Grey at an important Liberal Party meeting in Free Trade Hall, Manchester. When the women were refused an answer, dragged from the hall and arrested, the long press boycott on suffrage was broken. The WSPU had found its weapon.

From then on, the Pankhursts and their supporters developed protest and dramatic confrontation to a fine art. They heckled members of Parliament, they held open-air meetings, they organized parades, fairs and deputations to the prime minister. They made suffrage pageants with beautiful banners and decorations, and they used the utmost ingenuity to get their message across to reluctant and evasive politicians and to the public. The WSPU had an instinct for publicity, and in Mrs. Pankhurst they possessed a charismatic speaker and a dynamic leader. Their techniques of nonviolent confrontation and protest and their dramatic ability to mobilize public opinion enabled the British militants to convert their very weaknesses into strengths.

Outside the political system, economically weak, untrained in the skills of physical combat every schoolboy picks up in the playground, the members of the WSPU found a way to shorten the odds against them. They provoked and challenged the government until it was pushed into acting foolishly and brutally. The women responded magnificently. They went to jail, they went on hunger strikes, they resisted force feeding. The jails, the courts and Parliament made martyrs, and the martyrs converted their particular sufferings into an emblem of oppressed womanhood. Ray Strachey, herself a suffragist, wrote that women "read into the Cause not only what lay upon the surface, but all the discontents which they, as women, were suffering; their economic dependence, their conventional limitations and all the multitude of trifles which made them hate being women and long to have been men; and they saw in the suffrage movement a symbol of their release from all these evils." In this spirit, British women fought. Hundreds went to jail, thousands more marched and protested, and sympathetic, as well as curious, members of the public made the WSPU's Hyde Park rallies the largest in British history.

The British struggle became both bitter and dangerous, with vandalism and then arson added to the WSPU's nonviolent techniques. Only the onset of war prevented disaster for both sides in the conflict. The suspension of militancy for the duration and the conspicuous and essential service rendered by British women during the conflict gave politicians a graceful way to concede and made the ballot at war's end a foregone conclusion.

There were dangers, obviously, in the tactics and approach of the British militants, but so great was their gallantry, so irresistible the glamor of their activities that visiting American suffragists were dazzled. In England, in contrast to the moribund American organizations, was a dynamic, vigorous and creative approach. As early as 1907, Harriot Stanton Blatch, the daughter of Elizabeth Cady Stanton, was lamenting the total lack of imagination in the old suffrage movement in New York. Drawing on her knowledge of the WSPU campaign, then still in its early nonviolent stages, she formed the Equality League of Self Supporting Women and introduced such novelties as open-air meetings, parades, visits by prominent British suffragists, new campaign methods and work with trade unions and working women. Other groups were also to import British techniques, but it remained for two young veterans of British jails and WSPU battles, Alice Paul and Lucy Burns, to create a real militant party in the American suffrage campaign. Paul and Burns not only borrowed the methods of the Pankhursts, they transmitted the suffragettes' political views and their analysis of political activity. The Congressional Union (later the Woman's Party) shared technique, philosophy and spirit with the British militants.

Paul and Burns had encountered the WSPU while they were studying and practicing social work in Britain in 1909. They did organizational work for the Union in both England and Scotland, and took their turn at heckling government ministers and M.P.'s, including the young Winston Churchill. Jailed in London following a disruption at the Lord Mayor's banquet, Paul refused food and was force-fed, an ordeal which not only gave her a great terror of the feeding operation but which also severely damaged her health. Weak and emaciated, she sailed back to the United States in January of 1910. Soon Paul was at work in the American movement, and in January 1913, she and Burns were appointed to the NAWSA's long dormant Congressional Committee to work for the federal suffrage amendment. The two young women went to Washington where their zeal, their organizational skills and their knack for securing financial contributions soon refocused interest on the federal route to the ballot and led to a split with the more conventional parent organization. While the NAWSA floundered with intraparty disputes until the inspired selection of Carrie Chapman Catt as president in 1915, the new Woman's Party became the main effective force for suffrage. *Jailed for Freedom* includes an account of the party's activities, the techniques it employed, and the manner in which it mobilized its forces even before it turned to militancy.

Militancy, exemplified by the picketing of President Wilson and the Congress, is the most obvious difference between the two suffrage groups, but it was only one of the things which marked the split between the two organizations. More basic than the question of whether agitation was useful were the differing strategies and divergent analyses of the political situation. Differences in political approach had already split the parties in 1914— well before the first pickets appeared. By its over-all approach, as well as in its adoption of militancy, the Woman's Party showed its debt to the earlier Pankhurst organization.

From the first days of the NAWSA Congressional Committee, Paul and her supporters had emphasized the federal amendment and they were not to be distracted even by such blandishments as the Shaffroth-Palmer Act, which promised an "easier" state-by-state route to the vote. They insisted that there be no compromise on efforts to secure the constitutional amendment, a position which the larger NAWSA found difficult to adopt. As Catt pointed out in her "winning plan" of 1916, the NAWSA had the necessity of coping with those Southern suffragists who opposed the federal route on the grounds that it infringed states' rights. By strenuous efforts, Catt managed to keep these women within the fold. The Woman's Party, smaller and more centralized, was not under the same pressure to compromise.

Insistence on one approach to suffrage, and friction with state suffrage organizations, made Paul's group an irritant within NAWSA. More serious were what the older organization considered the party's reckless political adventures. These were based on the fundamental tenet of the WSPU: the party in power was to be held responsible for the failure to secure the ballot. In the period under consideration, the majority party was the Democratic Party, and after the Congressional Union broke with NAWSA in 1914, it immediately entered the lists against Democratic candidates in the Western woman suffrage states. The Union's aim was to persuade women voters to vote against the Democrats in reprisal for the party's failure to push the Susan B. Anthony Amendment through the Congress. While NAWSA regarded this procedure with horror because it sometimes meant working against good suffragists, the Union was unconcerned. All representatives from suffrage states should be suffragists, the Union said, and therefore the voters could punish the Democrats without hurting the cause. The more conservative NAWSA disagreed and Catt and her organization came to list the Woman's Party among their many crosses. This hostility was only increased when the Union carried its analysis one step further and began direct attacks on President Wilson as head of the party responsible for blocking the vote. While NAWSA courted Wilson assiduously, the Woman's Party began a series of British-style protests which led, within six months, to confrontation, arrest, and a long stretch of what can only be called official brutality.

Some historians feel that the politics which Paul and Burns imported from Britain were not really applicable to the American situation. In Britain, a small group of politicians blocked a reform which a majority of the public and Parliament favored. The record of manipulation of parliamentary technicalities, of broken promises, and outright deception practiced by British prime ministers and their most powerful supporters is a long and shameful story. There is no doubt that a few prominent men blocked the vote, and the WSPU rightly concentrated their fire on them.

The situation in the United States was less clear. While the Woman's Party was correct in thinking that President Wilson could have done more sooner for the vote had he been sincerely interested, the later history of the suffrage fight, as well as the tragic failure of the League of Nations, showed that his power was not as great as the Woman's Party strategists assumed. Nor was the party correct in its optimistic projection that Western women would form a voting bloc. Although the party managed to inject suffrage into the Western campaigns of 1914, the extent of the success of its tactics is debatable. The predictable drop off in votes in a nonpresidential year and the fact that men's and women's votes were not separately tabulated weakened the party's claim that women had defeated twenty-three of forty-two Western Democrats. In 1916, when the Woman's Party campaigned against Wilson, the President was nonetheless returned in ten of the twelve suffrage stages. The party had to face the facts that it was too small to be more than a political nuisance and that women voters were already behaving remarkably like their male counterparts: that is, they were voting along party and special-interest lines, not merely as women.

Still, if the Woman's Party had not proved itself a major political force, it did succeed in making suffrage a part of the campaigns in both 1914 and 1916. The national publicity it garnered no doubt aided in the continued resurgence of suffrage interest, a resurgence which began to pay important dividends with the addition of five states to the suffrage column, including all-important New York in 1917. Even more significantly, the Woman's Party was regarded as bellwether for the much larger NAWSA. Politicians were nervous enough over the Woman's Party's modest efforts in 1914 to question the party's policies and intentions in Congressional hearings. By fall 1917, with the new suffrage states and the big suffrage margin in New York, politicians had, as Eleanor Flexner has written, "a good deal to ponder." When the NAWSA met in convention that year it, too, decided that partisan political activity might be necessary. If the Sixty-fifth Congress failed to pass the amendment, NAWSA declared itself ready to oppose a sufficient number of senators and congressmen to change the balance of political power in the House and Senate. With politically astute Catt at the helm, with its membership and excellent grassroots organization, NAWSA promised to be a formidable opponent. But in political activity of this sort, as in the earlier revitalization of the federal amendment and, indeed, of the entire suffrage movement, the small Congressional Union and the Woman's Party had led the way.

Jailed for Freedom provides a record of the militants' suffrage activities, an explanation of tactics and strategy, an account of personalities and, equally interesting, a reflection of the spirit and attitudes of the suffragists. Doris Stevens, active in state campaigns as well as in the final drama in Washington, was one of the party's leaders. She worked closely with Alice Paul and acted in a variety of capacities. *Jailed for Freedom* is clearly the work of a knowledgeable, but not unbiased, observer. Written at the close of the campaign in Washington and dedicated to Alice Paul, *Jailed for Freedom* is uncritical and frequently intemperate. It could scarcely be otherwise. It was the product of an active partisan struggle, and it would be unrealistic to expect a completely dispassionate account. Memoirs of the NAWSA figures, if more temperate in tone, are no more even-handed when it comes to dealing with the rival suffrage organization. In reading either group's account, it is well to remember that there were two important organizations in the field, as well as many state and local groups which also did valuable work.

Jailed for Freedom makes large claims for the Woman's Party and its adherents, and the early sections of the book are marred by a condescending and mocking tone toward the opposition. Stevens, and probably other militants as well, identified herself not only with the true spirit of feminism but with youth and revolt. At various points in the narrative the militants are referred to as "young Amazons" or as "the lions." They were conscious of being in the vanguard of a great movement, and they drew strength and confidence from the very strength of their opposition. As Stevens wrote of one deputation to Wilson:

> His irritation only serves to awaken in every woman a new strength. It is a wonderful experience to feel strength take posses-sion of your being in a contest of ideas. No amount of trappings, no amount of authority, no number of plainclothes men, nor the glamour of the gold-braided attachés, nor the vastness of the great reception hall, nor the dazzle of the lighted chandeliers, and above all not the mind of your opponent can cut in on your slim, hard strength. You are more than invincible.

This spirit, this sense of being exceptional people in exceptional circumstances was important in sustaining the militants through some dangerous and unglamorous experiences. It was just as surely one of the things that made them seem provocative and difficult, not only to President Wilson, who harbored reservations about women's intellectual and political capacities, but also to their conservative suffrage colleagues. As Anne and Andrew Scott have written, "The constant emphasis upon the youth and vigor of the Congressional Union women contributed to the friction be-tween the two groups. Neither Mrs. Park in her late thirties nor Mrs. Catt in her fifties felt themselves ready to be put out to pasture."

If the militants sometimes seem lacking in moderation and modesty in the early stages of *Jailed for Freedom,* their sufferings in Occoquan Workhouse and District Jail are treated with dignity and presented with surprising detachment. Stevens selected material from the many narratives and affidavits now in the *Woman's Party Papers* in the Library of Congress, and the imprisoned suffragists speak for themselves with courage and even humor. The appalling conditions of the penal institutions are amply documented, and the record is enriched with accounts of the complicated behind-the-scenes maneuvering of the prison authorities, the government and the Woman's Party attorneys.

Although *Jailed for Freedom* does include material on the Congressional Union's early, premilitant days, the focus is clearly on the more dramatic moments of the campaign. So bitter did the struggle become that what began as a modestly scaled and dignified protest almost ended in tragedy. A woman of seventy-three, Mrs. Mary Nolan, was confined to the Workhouse, Lucy Burns manacled to the bars of her cell and held down by five persons to be force-fed, and Alice Paul forcibly fed and threatened with commitment as a mental case. These were by any standards excessive reactions from a secure and powerful government. How did a man of Woodrow Wilson's intelligence manage such a blunder?

The answer lies not only in Wilson's own attitudes toward women but also in the neglected affairs of the District of Columbia. It will not surprise anyone interested in prison history that Washington's penal institutions were in poor shape or that such dubious practices as committing prisoners across District lines to the Occoquan Workhouse were tolerated. The clientele of the prisons were the poor, the outcast and the friendless, both black and white. Congress and the political appointees charged with District affairs had little interest in prisoners or in their treatment. Any incident which committed able, vigorous and intelligent persons with powerful friends to such institutions guaranteed a scandal. The militants saw that one was speedily provided.

President Wilson, naturally, maintained that the suffragists were well treated and denied all charges regarding prison conditions. While he may not have known the facts initially, his denials were certainly disingenuous after the first prisoners were released on presidential pardons. His own friends, like Alison Hopkins, were jailed. One of his loyal and trusted associates, Dudley Field

Malone, not only resigned as Collector of the Port of New York in protest, but became counsel for the militants. The newspapers carried full accounts of the shocking conditions and of the force feeding. Further, published Wilson memoranda and letters reveal that the President took steps, not to improve the prisons, but to "clean up" the suffrage news, as a memo of July 20, 1917 attests. Wilson almost immediately recognized that Commissioner Louis Brownlow had mishandled the first suffrage arrests. He pardoned the women and ordered the commissioners not to permit further arrests without his knowledge. The President, as well as the District commissioners and minor officials, therefore, must bear responsibility for the subsequent actions against the militants.

The suffragists were correct in seeing Wilson's hand behind their persecution, but the President's letters and papers indicate that the militants underestimated his efforts for the cause after he had become convinced of its validity. This, to be sure, was late in the day. Given the President's long equivocation, it is not surprising that his appeals for votes to individual Congressmen and Senators and even his eloquent address to the Senate in September 1918 were insufficient to secure immediate passage. But although Wilson did not declare suffrage a war measure until his Senate speech, it is clear in hindsight (if not to the militants at the time) that he was deeply concerned over the fate of the ballot at least a year before. His correspondence with Mrs. Catt and other NAWSA leaders shows that he was hopeful that the upcoming state referendums would pass and that he was concerned lest militant activity cost suffrage votes.

Of course, it was Wilson's and the District commissioners' own mishandling of the situation that had made the pickets national news. Had the government and the police continued to treat the women with courteous indifference, the pickets might have remained a Washington, D.C., tourist attraction; they would scarcely have become a major story. The government chose to use the police, the prisons, and, through force feeding and the psychopathic ward, terror against the women for two reasons, one psychological, one purely political.

Wilson, and other conservatives, saw even the mild militancy of the Woman's Party as so unfeminine as to indicate serious mental aberration. His correspondence refers to the women as "unstable," and he speculates that the "less sane" among them might be provoked to violence. There is little doubt that he found the pickets personally offensive. Such an attitude may be one reason he assented in treatment he knew was not only cruel but totally without legal foundation.

Political considerations were even more important. The militant suffragists, in Wilson's view, posed a double threat. He felt, now that he had become a convert to woman suffrage, that their activities threatened the success of the federal amendment. Some of his hostility came, therefore, from the very success of the long campaign to "educate" him to the necessity of the ballot. Further, once imprisoned, the suffragists raised a more serious and delicate question: that of being political offenders. In demanding to be treated as political prisoners, which they most certainly were, they uncovered a nest of difficulties. In the tense wartime situation, the last thing the President wanted was a group demanding special treatment as political offenders. That Wilson was presenting himself not only to the nation but to all Europe as the leader of democracy increased the embarrassment caused by the suffragists. The treatment of the Woman's Party pickets, which to modern eyes seems scarcely credible, grew out of a complex tangle of psychological attitudes, wartime tensions and political necessities.

Although writers on the Woman's Party have recognized the responsibility the government must bear for the disgraceful handling of the militants, emphasis has been placed on the pickets and, in particular, on whether the picketing was a wise strategy or not. Eleanor Flexner points out that earlier historians have underestimated the party's contributions and ignored its status as the first victim of the Red scare by concentrating on debates about the wisdom of militant tactics. Very much the same thing is evident in discussions of the WSPU. While it is certainly legitimate to try to identify the most useful political methods, one cannot help feeling that the militants on both sides of the Atlantic are objects of a historical double standard. Accounts of male movements and political activities only very rarely raise the question of whether violence (never mind mere picketing) was justified. The picketing, the watchfires, the demonstrations of both the Woman's Party and its predecessor, the WSPU, were striking to contemporary observers and to historians because they were so "unfeminine." Activities which would scarcely have merited attention if carried on by men had great impact and interest simply because the actors were women. Obviously this impact and attention could be either positive or negative, but historians like William L. O'Neill, who dismisses the picketing as totally counterproductive, seem unduly harsh. True, picketing annoyed President Wilson and exasperated NAWSA. True, the Woman's Party files indicate numerous cancellations of memberships. But it is also true that the party received sizable financial contributions during its militant time, gained enormous publicity for suffrage, attracted some of the ablest women in the nation and illustrated once and for all that American women wanted the vote enough to go to prison for it and perhaps to die for it.

A more balanced assessment of the contributions of the conservative and radical wings of the suffrage struggle appears in *One Half of the People* by Anne and Andrew Scott. They write, "Nervousness about what the radical women might do next encouraged both Congress and the president to make concessions and to embrace the more conservative suffragists as the lesser evil. The sequence here, as elsewhere, illustrates the usefulness of a radical faction in a reform movement." This contention is supported by the ever-increasing pace of suffrage activity in 1917–1919 and by the rapid evolution of President Wilson's ideas — under militant pressure as well as NAWSA persuasion. The either/or tone of the memoirs and propaganda of suffragists from both sides has clouded the fact that the movement was not monolithic and that there was ample room for a variety of methods and approaches.

The history of the Woman's Party leaves open the question of whether equally rapid progress would have occurred had pressure been confined to conventional means. The Woman's Party activity does show the dependence of successful militancy upon a wide base of popular support. Given a small group of able and highly motivated people, an organization like the Woman's Party can have a disproportionate effect on public opinion. Success, however, clearly depends on access to the media and on gaining the sympathies of the public. The militants were able to focus attention on the vote and even to moderate the draconic prison conditions at Occoquan and the District Jail not simply because they were intelligent and brave but because they had friends in the press, as well as influential contacts in the government. It does not take too much imagination to see what would have happened had the Occoquan regulars mounted a similar protest. Although imprisoned members of the Woman's Party took sizable risks, they had organized legal, financial and moral support "outside." These were the fruits of their long and careful pre-militant organizing work, of the growth of suffrage sentiment and, although they never admitted it, of the revitalization of NAWSA.

The importance of a base of popular support for militancy is clearly illustrated by the Woman's Party's history post-suffrage. Unlike NAWSA, which transformed itself into the nonpartisan and highly respectable League of Women Voters, the Woman's Party maintained a distinct and aggressively feminist position. Despite their sacrifices for the ballot, Alice Paul and her followers were without illusions about the work still to be done. The party continued to examine women's legal status and to urge changes. Within three years, it had launched a drive for yet another constitutional amendment, the still-controversial Equal Rights, or Lucretia Mott, Amendment (ERA). By the time this legislation was approved by Congress in 1972, the party had been working for its adoption for almost fifty years.

Although ERA has long been the main issue of the Woman's Party, it was by no means their only interest. One of the Woman's Party's earlier successes came with the passage of the Cable Act in 1922, which protected the citizenship of American woman married to foreigners. Along with their efforts for a new constitutional amendment, Woman's Party members worked to open federal service to women on a nondiscriminatory basis, to secure state equal rights amendments and to publicize and change the myriad of laws and practices harmful to women. When they began this work in the 1920's, the feminists of the Woman's Party hoped that the spirit fostered by the long suffrage struggle would forge a real political force. For the next decade, despite frustration of ERA and increasingly bitter quarrels with more moderate feminists, the Woman's Party was optimistic.

Their hopes, however, were to be rudely disappointed. The grass roots support they had hoped for did not materialize and, interestingly, the Woman's Party did not attempt a militant action to dramatize ERA. The party leadership knew that the time was not right. Nor did prospects improve. By the 1930's, the tide of feminism had subsided. Depression, the conservativism of the 1920's and its Red scare, divisions within the feminist movement over ERA and protective labor laws all took their toll. By the end of the decade, the militant feminists were clearly on the defensive, fighting off a series of measures designed to limit the right to work of married women. By the 1940's, the Woman's Party was only a shadow of its former vigorous self, and not only the party but organized feminism was divided and weakened.

For some of these divisions, the inflexibility of the Woman's Party leadership was responsible. While Paul and her supporters were correct in thinking that further constitutional guarantees would have helped women's status, the stress on ERA introduced devastating conflict into feminist ranks. Many good feminists saw the passage of ERA as a threat to hard-won protective labor laws. Labor leaders, as well, saw the amendment as a threat to the slender gains in regulating wages, hours and working conditions. Fifty years later both labor organizers and feminists have come to agree that labor laws that "protect" women only may be used to deny equal opportunity and to fix women on the lowest rungs of the work scale. But in the 1920's and 1930's, regulation of women's working conditions was the best bargain labor and socially concerned feminists could strike. That Paul was theoretically correct does not change the fact that her inflexible determination, so necessary in the militant suffrage campaign, engendered destructive conflicts within feminism. The inflexibility, the unwillingness to compromise and, as important, the often provocative stance of the Woman's Party not only damaged the party's reputation and credibility but cut off an important and charismatic leader from popular support.

Of course, had the climate of opinion been different, the Woman's Party might have continued to score gains. The chief factors in its continued decline and retrenchment were beyond the feminists' control. The fear of radicalism, so strong in the 1920's, threatened their public support. The economic devastation of the Depression made women's claims for economic justice, however justified, seem petty and self-seeking. World War II provided another crisis that pushed aside concern for women's issues and submerged women's rights in another kind of national crusade. Against this background, the Woman's Party and the feminist movement in general found it increasingly difficult to mobilize support for women's goals. Moreover, young women came to seem increasingly indifferent to feminism as an ideology. In the popular mind the celebrated new woman of the World War I era was replaced by the Flapper and, later, by the suburban supermom of the 1950's and early 1960's.

Commentators have offered a number of reasons why the triumphant suffragists were unable to inspire the next generation of young women with feminist ideals. The conservativism of women, flaws in the feminist ideology, even Freudian psychology have been suggested. More convincing, however, are analyses such as William L. O'Neill's and William Chafe's which point to the severe economic, legal and political difficulties that confronted women even after the vote. Women had asked for equality with suffrage, but the nation settled for the vote and tokenism. While new educational and economic opportunities had opened for the truly exceptional (and lucky) woman, there remained many restrictions. Thus the promise implied by the brilliant group of militant feminists was denied. There were women doctors imprisoned at Occoquan, but, even after suffrage, women were admitted to medical schools only on a quota basis and denied internships in all but a handful of hospitals. More women than ever before entered college and took degrees in the 1920's, yet jobs such as college teaching, available to their male colleagues, were in short supply for women. Women continued to enter the job market and, especially during and after World War II, the numbers increased rapidly and steadily. Women continued to be paid less even for equal work, however, and at every level, in every trade and profession, female workers were kept by custom, policy and law in the more poorly compensated jobs. The skilled trades, as well as the better jobs in industry, were closed to women, and female workers remained concentrated in such traditional "women's work" as domestic service, clerical positions and lower-level schoolteaching. Nor were women's economic disabilities simply related to their low pay scales and limited opportunities. Even in World War II, when the nation asked for women workers, policy makers and popular opinion refused to sanction the support services necessary to free homemakers, and especially mothers, for productive employment. In the absence of day care, household assistance and equitable tax policies, it is not surprising that all but the most privileged of employed women saw work as drudgery, not emancipation.

There were other causes as well for the rejection of feminism in the post-suffrage era. The concentration by the more radical feminists on new legal rights did not gain them the sympathy of the less well-educated, less fortunate and more oppressed segments of the female population. Nor did the sense of mission and sacrifice which had drawn young women to the picket line and to prison remain attractive. In the time of the militant suffragists, true emancipation and freedom had too often to be bought at the price of celibacy and the denial of the human satisfactions, such as lovers, homes and children. That many of the suffragists in both camps were wives and mothers as well as emancipated did not change the fact that a career or a profession—achievement in the male world — required enormous amounts of energy, luck and talent if it were to be combined with marriage and a family. Given the worsening economic climate and the spirit of reaction and conservativism that swept the country, young women began to question their elders' code of service, reform and confrontation. The rewards of emancipation began to look too slender to be worth the great struggles of 1917 and 1918. The generation which received the benefits had not also received the joys and gains of the struggle itself, and it sensed a certain sterility in the New Woman. Nor were they alone.

Emma Goldman, a liberated woman by any standard, wrote eloquently not only of the difficulties facing the average working woman but also of what she called the "tragedy" of woman's emancipation. This she saw not only in the deadening and low paid work offered women but also in "the narrowness of the existing conception of woman's independence and emancipation; the dread of love for a man who is not her social equal; the fear that love will rob her of her freedom and independence." Goldman concluded that "the tragedy of the self-supporting or economically free woman does not lie in too many, but in too few experiences." The women of the following decades sought to remedy this lack, not through feminism, but through the successful ideals of sexual freedom and motherhood. These retreats from feminist goals and ideology do not necessarily mean that the older suffragists were wrong, only that society had not reached the point where it could, or would, support the legitimate aspirations of women. Only as more and more women entered the labor force, as law and custom began to change in attitudes toward women and as women again became discontented with their roles could there be a revival of feminism.

Despite the lack of enthusiasm shown by the post-suffrage generation for the Woman's Party ideals, despite the party's own stagnation, and despite the controversy which surrounded its militant campaign, the history of events outlined in *Jailed for Freedom* remains worthy of examination and study. Doris Stevens' book is a document which contributes to both the social and political histories of the World War I era and to any consideration of the decade's feminist activities. Furthermore, *Jailed for Freedom* possesses an interest and a relevance for the contemporary reader aside from its historical importance. Modern women may have a different set of concerns than their suffragist predecessors — in part because the earlier feminists secured many important and basic changes. They have added new women to the feminist pantheon: freeswinging thinkers like Elizabeth Cady Stanton, abolitionists like the Grimkes and Sojourner Truth, sexual and intellectual rebels like Victoria C. Woodhull, Frances Wright and Emma Goldman have joined the Woman's Party's patron saint, Susan B. Anthony. But the inner goal, what Stevens defined as the achievement of self-respect and self-determination, remains the same. Beyond its other merits, beyond the light it sheds on suffrage and wartime political issues, *Jailed for Freedom* is valuable for its portrait of independent women, the ideals they held, and the uses they made of their freedom.

January, 1976

TO

ALICE PAUL

THROUGH WHOSE BRILLIANT
AND DEVOTED LEADERSHIP
THE WOMEN OF AMERICA HAVE
BEEN ABLE TO CONSUMMATE
WITH GLADNESS AND GALLANT
COURAGE THEIR LONG STRUG-
GLE FOR POLITICAL LIBERTY,
THIS BOOK IS AFFECTIONATELY
DEDICATED

PREFACE

This book deals with the intensive campaign of the militant suffragists of America [1913-1919] to win a solitary thing—the passage by Congress of the national suffrage amendment enfranchising women. It is the story of the first organized militant political action in America to this end. The militants differed from the pure propagandists in the woman suffrage movement chiefly in that they had a clear comprehension of the forces which prevail in politics. They appreciated the necessity of the propaganda stage and the beautiful heroism of those who had led in the pioneer agitation, but they knew that this stage belonged to the past; these methods were no longer necessary or effective.

For convenience sake I have called Part II "Political Action," and Part III "Militancy," although it will be perceived that the entire campaign was one of militant political action. The emphasis, however, in Part II is upon political action, although certainly with a militant mood. In Part III dramatic acts of protest, such as are now commonly called militancy, are given emphasis as they acquired a greater importance during the latter part of the campaign. This does not mean that all militant deeds were not committed for a specific political purpose. They were. But militancy is as much a state of mind, an approach to a task, as it is the commission of deeds of protest. It is the state of mind of those who is their fiery idealism do not lose sight of the real springs of human action.

There are two ways in which this story might be told. It might be told as a tragic and harrowing tale of martyrdom. Or it might be told as a ruthless enterprise of compelling a hostile administration to subject women to martyrdom in order to hasten its surrender. The truth is, it has elements of both ruthlessness and martyrdom. And I have tried to make them appear in a true proportion. It is my sincere hope that you will understand and appreciate the martyrdom involved, for it was the conscious voluntary gift of beautiful, strong .and young hearts. *But it was never martyrdom for its own sake. It was martyrdom used for a practical purpose.*

The narrative ends with the passage of the amendment by Congress. The campaign for ratification, which extended over fourteen months, is a story in itself. The ratification of the amendment by the 36th and last state legislature proved as difficult to secure from political leaders as the 64th and last vote in the United States Senate.

This book contains my interpretations, which are of course arguable. But it is a true record of events.

DORIS STEVENS.

New York, August, 1920.

CONTENTS

CONTENTS

ILLUSTRATIONS

"*I do pray, and that most earnestly and constantly, for some terrific shock to startle the women of the nation into a self-respect which will compel them to see the absolute degradation of their present position; which will compel them to break their yoke of bondage and give them faith in themselves; which will make them proclaim their allegiance to women first. . . . The fact is, women are in chains, and their servitude is all the more debasing because they do not realize it. O to compel them to see and feel and to give them the courage and the conscience to speak and act for their own freedom, though they face the scorn and contempt of all the world for doing it!*"

SUSAN B. ANTHONY, 1872.

PART I
LEADERSHIP

CHAPTER 1

S USAN B. ANTHONY was the first militant suffragist. She has been so long proclaimed only as the magnificent pioneer that few realize that she was the first woman to defy the law for the political liberty of her sex.

The militant spirit was in her many early protests. Sometimes these protests were supported by one or two followers; more often they were solitary protests. Perhaps it is because of their isolation that they stand out so strong and beautiful in a turbulent time in our history when all those about her were making compromises.

It was this spirit which impelled her to keep alive the cause of the enfranchisement of women during the passionate years of the Civil War. She held to the last possible moment that no national exigency was great enough to warrant abandonment of woman's fight for independence. But one by one her followers deserted her. She was unable to keep even a tiny handful steadfast to this position. She became finally the only figure in the nation appealing for the rights of women when the rights of black men were agitating the public mind. Ardent abolitionist as she was, she could not tolerate without indignant protest the exclusion of women in all discussions of emancipation. The suffrage war policy of Miss Anthony can be compared to that of the militants a half century later when confronted with the problem of this country's entrance into the world war.

The war of the rebellion over and the emancipation of the

3

negro man written into the constitution, women contended they
had a right to vote under the new fourteenth amendment. Miss
Anthony led in this agitation, urging all women to claim the
right to vote under this amendment. In the national election
of 1872 she voted in Rochester, New York, her home city, was
arrested, tried and convicted of the crime of "voting without
having a lawful right to vote."

I cannot resist giving a brief excerpt from the court records
of this extraordinary case, so reminiscent is it of the cases of
the suffrage pickets tried nearly fifty years later in the courts
of the national capital.

After the prosecuting attorney had presented the government's case, Judge Hunt read his opinion, said to have been
written before the case had been heard, and directed the jury
to bring in a verdict of guilty. The jury was dismissed without deliberation and a new trial was refused. On the following
day this scene took place in that New York court room.

JUDGE HUNT (Ordering the defendant to stand up)—Has
the prisoner anything to say why sentence shall not be pronounced?

MISS ANTHONY—Yes, your Honor, I have many things to
say; for in your ordered verdict of guilty, you have trampled
under foot every vital principle of our government. My nat-
ural rights, my civil rights, my political rights, my judicial
rights, are all alike ignored. Robbed of the fundamental privilege of citizenship, I am degraded from the status of a citizen
to that of a subject; and not only myself individually, but all
my sex are, by your Honor's verdict doomed to political subjection under this so-called republican form of government.

JUDGE HUNT—The Court cannot listen to a rehearsal of
argument which the prisoner's counsel has already consumed
three hours in presenting.

MISS ANTHONY—May it please your Honor, I am not argu-
ing the question, but simply stating the reasons why sentence

cannot in justice be pronounced against me. Your denial of my citizen's right to vote, is the denial of my right of consent as one of the governed, the denial of my right of representation as one taxed, the denial of my right to a trial by jury of my peers as an offender against law; therefore, the denial of my sacred right to life, liberty, property, and——

JUDGE HUNT—The Court cannot allow the prisoner to go on.

MISS ANTHONY—But, your Honor will not deny me this one and only poor privilege of protest against this high-handed outrage upon my citizen's rights. May it please the Court to remember that since the day of my arrest last November this is the first time that either myself or any person of my disfranchised class has been allowed a word of defense before judge or jury——

JUDGE HUNT—The prisoner must sit down, the Court cannot allow it.

MISS ANTHONY—Of all my persecutors from the corner grocery politician who entered the complaint, to the United States marshal, commissioner, district attorney, district judge, your Honor on the bench, not one is my peer, but each and all are my political sovereigns. . . . Precisely as no disfranchised person is entitled to sit upon the jury and no woman is entitled to the franchise, so none but a regularly admitted lawyer is allowed to practice in the courts, and no woman can gain admission to the bar—hence, jury, judge, counsel, all must be of superior class.

JUDGE HUNT—The Court must insist—the prisoner has been tried according to the established forms of law.

MISS ANTHONY—Yes, your Honor, but by forms of law, all made by men, interpreted by men, administered by men, in favor of men and against women; and hence your Honor's ordered verdict of guilty, against a United States citizen for the exercise of the "citizen's right to vote," simply because that citizen was a woman and not a man. . . . As then the slaves who got their freedom had to take it over or under or through the unjust forms of the law, precisely so now must women take it to get their right to a voice in this government; and I have taken mine, and mean to take it at every opportunity.

JUDGE HUNT—The Court orders the prisoner to sit down. It will not allow another word.

MISS ANTHONY—When I was brought before your Honor for trial I hoped for a broad interpretation of the constitution and its recent amendments, which should declare all United States citizens under its protecting ægis. . . . But failing to get this justice, failing even to get a trial by a jury—not of my peers—I ask not leniency at your hands but rather the full rigor of the law.

JUDGE HUNT—The Court must insist (here the prisoner sat down). The prisoner will stand up. (Here Miss Anthony rose again.) The sentence of the Court is that you pay a fine of $100.00 and the costs of the prosecution.

MISS ANTHONY—May it please your Honor, I will never pay a dollar of your unjust penalty. . . . And I shall earnestly and persistently continue to urge all women to the practical recognition of the old Revolutionary maxim, "Resistance to tyranny is obedience to God."

JUDGE HUNT—Madam, the Court will not order you stand committed until the fine is paid.

Miss Anthony did not pay her fine and was never imprisoned. I believe the fine stands against her to this day.

On the heels of this sensation came another of those dramatic protests which until the very end she always combined with political agitation. The nation was celebrating its first centenary of the signing of the Declaration of Independence at Independence Square, Philadelphia. After women had been refused by all in authority a humble half moment in which to present to the Centennial the Women's Declaration of Rights,

Miss Anthony insisted on being heard. Immediately after the Declaration of Independence had been read by a patriot, she led a committee of women, who with platform tickets had slipped through the military, straight down the center aisle of the platform to address the chairman, who pale with fright and powerless to stop the demonstration had to accept her document. Instantly the platform, graced as it was by national dignitaries and crowned heads, was astir. The women retired, distributing to the gasping spectators copies of their Declaration. Miss Anthony had reminded the nation of the hollowness of its celebration of an independence that excluded women.

Susan B. Anthony's aim was the national enfranchisement of women. As soon as she became convinced that the constitution would have to be specifically amended to include woman suffrage, she set herself to this gigantic task. For a quarter of a century she appealed to Congress for action and to party conventions for suffrage endorsement. When, however, she saw that Congress was obdurate, as an able and intensely practical leader she temporarily directed the main energy of the suffrage movement to trying to win individual states. With women holding the balance of political power, she argued, the national government will be compelled to act. She knew so well the value of power. She went to the West to get it.

She was a shrewd tactician; with prophetic insight, without compromise. To those women who would yield to party expediency as advised by men, or be diverted into support of other measures, she made answer in a spirited letter to Lucy Stone:

"So long as you and I and all women are political slaves, it ill becomes us to meddle with the weightier discussions of our sovereign masters. It will be quite time enough for us, with self-respect, to declare ourselves for or against any party upon

the intrinsic merit of its policy, when men shall recognize us as
their political equals. . . .

"If all the suffragists of all the States could see eye to eye
on this point, and stand shoulder to shoulder against every
party and politician not fully and unequivocally committed to
'Equal Rights for Women,' we should become at once the
moral balance of power which could not fail to compel the
party of highest intelligence to proclaim woman suffrage the
chief plank of its platform. . . . Until that good day comes,
I shall continue to invoke the party in power, and each party
struggling to get into power, to pledge itself to the emancipation of our enslaved half of the people. . . ."

She did not live to see enough states grant suffrage in the
West to form a balance of power with which to carry out this
policy. She did not live to turn this power upon an unwilling
Congress. But she stood to the last, despite this temporary
change of program, the great dramatic protagonist of national freedom for women and its achievement through rebellion and practical strategy.

With the passing of Miss Anthony and her leadership,
the movement in America went conscientiously on endeavoring
to pile up state after state in the "free column." Gradually
her followers lost sight of her aggressive attack and her objective—the enfranchisement of women by Congress. They did
not sustain her tactical wisdom. This reform movement, like
all others when stretched over a long period of time, found
itself confined in a narrow circle of routine propaganda. It
lacked the power and initiative to extricate itself. Though it
had many eloquent agitators with devoted followings, it lacked
generalship.

The movement also lost Miss Anthony's militant spirit, her
keen appreciation of the fact that the attention of the nation
must be focussed on minority issues by dramatic acts of protest.

Susan B. Anthony's fundamental objective, her political attitude toward attaining it, and her militant spirit were revived in suffrage history in 1913 when Alice Paul, also of Quaker background, entered the national field as leader of the new suffrage forces in America.

CHAPTER 2

A MILITANT GENERAL—ALICE PAUL

MOST people conjure up a menacing picture when a person is called not only a general, but a militant one. In appearance Alice Paul is anything but menacing. Quiet, almost mouselike, this frail young Quakeress sits in silence and baffles you with her contradictions. Large, soft, gray eyes that strike you with a positive impact make you feel the indescribable force and power behind them. A mass of soft brown hair, caught easily at the neck, makes the contour of her head strong and graceful. Tiny, fragile hands that look more like an X-ray picture of hands, rest in her lap in Quakerish pose. Her whole atmosphere when she is not in action is one of strength and quiet determination. In action she is swift, alert, almost panther-like in her movements. Dressed always in simple frocks, preferably soft shades of purple, she conforms to an individual style and taste of her own rather than to the prevailing vogue.

I am going recklessly on to try to tell what I think about Alice Paul. It is difficult, for when I begin to put it down on paper, I realize how little we know about this laconic person, and yet how abundantly we feel her power, her will and her compelling leadership. In an instant and vivid reaction, I am either congealed or inspired; exhilarated or depressed; sometimes even exasperated, but always *moved*. I have seen her very presence in headquarters change in the twinkling of an eye the mood of fifty people. It is not through their affections

10

that she moves them, but through a naked force, a vital force which is indefinable but of which one simply cannot be unaware. Aiming primarily at the intellect of an audience or an individual, she almost never fails to win an emotional allegiance.

I shall never forget my first contact with her. I tell it here as an illustration of what happened to countless women who came in touch with her to remain under her leadership to the end. I had come to Washington to take part in the demonstration on the Senate in July, 1913, en route to a much-needed, as I thought, holiday in the Adirondacks.

"Can't you stay on and help us with a hearing next week?" said Miss Paul.

"I'm sorry," said I, "but I have promised to join a party of friends in the mountains for a summer holiday and . . ."

"Holiday?" said she, looking straight at me. Instantly ashamed at having mentioned such a legitimate excuse, I murmured something about not having had one since before entering college.

"But can't you stay?" she said.

I was lost. I knew I would stay. As a matter of fact, I stayed through the heat of a Washington summer, returned only long enough at the end of the summer to close up my work in state suffrage and came back to join the group at Washington. And it was years before I ever mentioned a holiday again.

Frequently she achieved her end without even a single word of retort. Soon after Miss Paul came to Washington in 1913, she went to call on a suffragist in that city to ask her to donate some funds toward the rent of headquarters in the Capital. The woman sighed. "I thought when Miss Anthony died," she said, "that all my troubles were at an end. She used to come to me for money for a federal amendment and I always told her it was wrong to ask for one, and that besides we would never get it. But she kept right on coming. Then when she died we didn't hear any more about an amendment. And now you come again saying the same things Miss Anthony said."

Miss Paul listened, said she was sorry and departed. Very shortly a check arrived at headquarters to cover a month's rent.

A model listener, Alice Paul has unlimited capacity for letting the other person relieve herself of all her objections without contest. Over and over again I have heard this scene enacted.

"Miss Paul, I have come to tell you that you are all wrong about this federal amendment business. I don't believe in it. Suffrage should come slowly but surely by the states. And although I have been a life-long suffragist, I just want to tell you not to count on me, for feeling as I do, I cannot give you any help."

A silence would follow. Then Miss Paul would say ingenuously, "Have you a half hour to spare?"

"I guess so," would come slowly from the protestant. "Why?"

"Won't you please sit down right here and put the stamps on these letters? We have to get them in the mail by noon."

"But I don't believe . . ."

"Oh, that's all right. These letters are going to women probably a lot of whom feel as you do. But some of them will want to come to the meeting to hear our side."

By this time Miss Paul would have brought a chair, and that ended the argument. The woman would stay and humbly proceed to stick on endless stamps. Usually she would come back, too, and before many days would be an ardent worker for the cause against which she thought herself invincible.

Once the state president of the conservative suffrage forces in Ohio with whom I had worked the previous year wrote me a letter pointing out what madness it was to talk of winning the amendment in Congress "this session," and adding that "nobody but a fool would ever think of it, let alone speak of it publicly." She was wise in politics; we were nice, eager, young girls, but pretty ignorant—that was the gist of her remonstrance. My vanity was aroused. Not wishing to be called "mad" or "foolish" I sat down and answered her in a friendly spirit, with the sole object of proving that we were wiser than she imagined. I had never discussed this point with anybody, as I had been in Washington only a few months and it had never occurred to me that we were not right to talk of getting the amendment in that particular session. But I answered my patronizing friend, in effect, that of course we were not fools, that we knew we would not get the amendment that session, but we saw no reason for not demanding it at once and taking it when we got it.

When Miss Paul saw the carbon of that letter she said quietly, pointing to the part where I had so nobly defended our sagacity, "You must never say that again and never put it on paper." Seeing my embarrassment, she hastened to explain. "You see, we *can* get it this session if enough women care sufficiently to demand it now."

Alice Paul brought back to the fight that note of immediacy which had gone with the passing of Miss Anthony's leadership. She called a halt on further pleading, wheedling, proving, praying. It was as if she had bidden women stand erect, with confidence in themselves and in their own judgments, and compelled them to be self-respecting enough to dare to put their freedom first, and so determine for themselves the day when they should be free. Those who had a taste of begging under the old régime and who abandoned it for demanding, know how fine and strong a thing it is to realize that you must take what is yours and not waste your energy proving that you are or will some day be worthy of a gift of power from your masters. On that glad day of discovery you have first freed yourself to fight for freedom. Alice Paul gave to thousands of women the essence of freedom.

And there was something so cleansing about the way in which she renovated ideas and processes, emotions and instincts. Her attack was so direct, so clear, so simple and unafraid. And her resistance had such a fine quality of strength.

Sometimes it was a roaring politician who was baffled by this non-resistant force. I have heard many an irate one come into her office in the early days to tell her how to run the woman's campaign, and struggle in vain to arouse her to combat. Having begun a tirade, honor would compel him to see it through even without help from a silent adversary. And so he would get more and more noisy until it would seem as if one lone shout from him might be enough to blow away the frail object of his attack. Ultimately he would be forced to retire, perhaps in the face of a serene smile, beaten and angered that he had been able to make so little impression. And many the delicious remark and delightful quip afterward at his expense!

Her gentle humor is of the highest quality. If only her opponents could have seen her amusement at their hysteria. At the very moment they were denouncing some plan of action and calling her "fanatical" and "hysterical" she would fairly beam with delight to see how well her plan had worked. Her intention had been to arouse them to just that state of mind, and how admirably they were living up to the plan. The hysteria was all on their side. She coolly sat back in her chair and watched their antics under pressure.

"But don't you know," would come another thundering one, "that this will make the Democratic leaders so hostile that . . ."

The looked-for note of surprise never came. She had counted ahead on all this and knew almost to the last shade the reaction that would follow from both majority and minority leaders. All this had been thoroughly gone over, first with herself, then with her colleagues. All the "alarms" had been rung. The male politician could not understand why his well-meaning and generously-offered advice caused not a ripple and not a change in plan. Such calm unconcern he could not endure. He was accustomed to emotional panics. He was not accustomed to a leader who had weighed every objection, every attack and counted the cost accurately.

Her ability to marshal arguments for keeping her own followers in line was equally marked. A superficial observer would rush into headquarters with, "Miss Paul, don't you think it was a great tactical mistake to force President Wilson at this time to state his position on the amendment? Will it not hurt our campaign to have it known that he is against us?"

"It is the best thing that could possibly happen to us. If he is against us, women should know it. They will be aroused to greater action if he is not allowed to remain silent upon something in which he does not believe. It will make it easier for us to campaign against him when the time comes."

And another time a friend of the cause would suggest, "Would it not have been better not to have tried for planks in party platforms, since we got such weak ones?"

"Not at all. We can draw the support of women with greater ease from a party which shows a weak hand on suffrage, than from one which hides its opposition behind silence."

She had always to combat the fear of the more timid ones who felt sure with each new wave of disapproval that we would be submerged. "Now, I have been a supporter of yours every step of the way," a "fearful" one would say, "but this is really going a little too far. I was in the Senate gallery to-day when two suffrage senators in speeches denounced the pickets and their suffrage banners. They said that we were setting suffrage back and that something ought to be done about it."

"Exactly so," would come the ready answer from Miss Paul. "And they *will* do something about it only if we continue to make them uncomfortable enough. Of course even suffrage senators will object to our pickets and our banners because they do not want attention called to their failure to compel the Administration to act. They know that as friends of the measure their responsibility is greater." And the "fearful" one was usually convinced and made stronger.

I remember so well when the situation was approaching its final climax in Washington. Men and women, both, came to Miss Paul with, "This is terrible! Seven months' sentence is impossible. You must stop! You cannot keep this up!"

With an unmistakable note of triumph in her voice Miss Paul would answer, "Yes, it is terrible for us, but not nearly so terrible as for the government. The Administration has fired its heaviest gun. From now on we shall win and they will lose."

Most of the doubters had by this time banished their fears and had come to believe with something akin to superstition that she could never be wrong, so swiftly and surely did they see her policies and her predictions on every point vindicated before their eyes.

She has been a master at concentration, a master strategist—a great general. With passionate beliefs on all important social questions, she resolutely set herself against being seduced into other paths. Far from being naturally an ascetic, she has disciplined herself into denials and deprivations, cultural and recreational, to pursue her objective with the least possible waste of energy. Not that she did not want above all else to do this thing. She did. But doing it she had to abandon the easy life of a scholar and the aristocratic environment of a cultured, prosperous, Quaker family, of Moorestown, New Jersey, for the rigors of a ceaseless drudgery and frequent imprisonment. A flaming idealist, conducting the fight with the sternest kind of realism, a mind attracted by facts, not fancies, she has led fearlessly and with magnificent ruthlessness. Thinking, thinking day and night of her objective and never retarding her pace a moment until its accomplishment, I know no modern woman leader with whom to compare her. I think she must possess many of the same qualities that Lenin does, according to authentic portraits of him—cool, practical, rational, sitting quietly at a desk and counting the consequences, planning the next move before the first one is finished. And if she has demanded the ultimate of her followers, she has given it herself. Her ability to get women to work and never to let them stop is second only to her own unprecedented capacity for work.

Alice Paul came to leadership still in her twenties, but with a broad cultural equipment. Degrees from Swarthmore, the University of Pennsylvania, and special study abroad in English universities had given her a scholarly background in history, politics, and sociology. In these studies she had specialized, writing her doctor's thesis on the status of women. She also did factory work in English industries and there acquired first hand knowledge of the industrial position of women. In the midst of this work the English militant movement caught her imagination and she abandoned her studies temporarily to join that movement and go to prison with the English suffragists.

Convinced that the English women were fighting the battle for the women of the world, she returned to America fresh from their struggle, to arouse American women to action. She came bringing her gifts and concentration to this one struggle. She came with that inestimable asset, youth, and, born of youth, indomitable courage to carry her point in spite of scorn and misrepresentation.

Among the thousands of telegrams sent Miss Paul the day the amendment finally passed Congress was this interesting message from Walter Clark, Chief Justice of the Supreme

Court of North Carolina, Southern Democrat, Confederate
Veteran and distinguished jurist:

"Will you permit me to congratulate you upon the great
triumph in which you have been so important a factor? Your
place in history is assured. Some years ago when I first met
you I predicted that your name would be written 'on the dusty
roll the ages keep.' There were politicians, and a large degree
of public sentiment, which could only be won by the methods
you adopted. . . . It is certain that, but for you, success
would have been delayed for many years to come."

Part II

POLITICAL ACTION

CHAPTER 1

W HERE are the people?" This was Woodrow Wilson's
first question as he arrived at the Union Station in
Washington the day before his first inauguration to
the Presidency in March, 1913.

"On the Avenue watching the suffragists parade," came the
answer.

The suffrage issue was brought oftenest to his attention
from then on until his final surrender. It lay entirely with
him as to how long women would be obliged to remind him of
this issue before he willed to take a hand.

"The people" were on the Avenue watching the suffragists
parade. The informant was quite right. It seemed to those
of us who attempted to march for our idea that day that the
whole world was there—packed closely on Pennsylvania
Avenue.

The purpose of the procession was to dramatize in numbers
and beauty the fact that women wanted to vote—that women
were asking the Administration in power in the national government to speed the day. What politicians had not been able
to get through their minds we would give them through their
eyes—often a powerful substitute. Our first task seemed
simple—actually to show that thousands of women wanted immediate action on their long delayed enfranchisement. This
we did.

This was the first demonstration under the leadership of
Alice Paul, at that time chairman of the Congressional Com-

mittee of the National American Woman Suffrage Association. It was also the beginning of Woodrow Wilson's liberal education.

The Administration, without intending it, played into the hands of the women from this moment. The women had been given a permit to march. Inadequate police protection allowed roughs to attack them and all but break up the beautiful pageant. The fact of ten thousand women marching with banners and bands for this idea was startling enough to wake up the government and the country, but not so startling as ten thousand women man-handled by irresponsible crowds because of police indifference.

An investigation was demanded and a perfunctory one held. The police administration was exonerated, but when the storm of protest had subsided the Chief of Police was quietly retired to private life.

It was no longer a secret that women wanted to vote and that they wanted the President and Congress to act.

A few days later the first deputation of suffragists ever to appear before a President to enlist his support for the passage of the national suffrage amendment waited upon President Wilson.[1] Miss Paul led the deputation. With her were Mrs. Genevieve Stone, wife of Congressman Stone of Illinois, Mrs. Harvey W. Wiley, Mrs. Ida Husted Harper, and Miss Mary Bartlett Dixon of Maryland. The President received the deputation in the White House Offices. When the women entered they found five chairs arranged in a row with one chair in front, like a class-room. All confessed to being frightened when the President came in and took his seat at the head of the class. The President said he had no opinion on the subject of woman suffrage; that he had never given it any thought;[2]

[1] There had been individual visits to previous presidents.
[2] At Colorado Springs in 1911, when Mr. Wilson was Governor of New Jersey and campaigning for the Presidential nomination, a delegation of Colorado women asked him his position on woman suffrage. He said.

and that above all it was his task to see that Congress concentrated on the currency revision and the tariff reform. It is recorded that the President was somewhat taken aback when Miss Paul addressed him during the course of the interview with this query, "But Mr. President, do you not understand that the Administration has no right to legislate for currency, tariff, and any other reform without first getting the consent of women to these reforms?"

"Get the consent of women?" It was evident that this course had not heretofore occurred to him.

"This subject will receive my most careful consideration," was President Wilson's first suffrage promise.

He was given time to "consider" and a second deputation went to him, and still a third, asking him to include the suffrage amendment in his message to the new Congress assembling in extra session the following month. And still he was obsessed with the paramount considerations of "tariff" and "currency." He flatly said there would be no time to consider suffrage for women. But the "unreasonable" women kept right on insisting that the liberty of half the American people was paramount to tariff and currency.

President Wilson's first session of Congress came together April 7th, 1913. The opening day was marked by the suffragists' second mass demonstration. This time women delegates representing every one of the 435 Congressional Districts in the country bore petitions from the constituencies showing that the people "back home" wanted the amendment passed. The delegates marched on Congress and were received with a warm welcome and their petitions presented to Congress. The same day the amendment which bears the name of Susan B. Anthony, who drafted it in 1875, was reintroduced into both houses of Congress.

"Ladies, this is a very arguable question and my mind is in the midst of the argument."

The month of May saw monster demonstrations in many cities and villages throughout the country, with the direct result that in June the Senate Committee on Suffrage made the first favorable report made by that committee in *twenty-one years*, thereby placing it on the Senate calendar for action.

Not relaxing the pressure for a day we organized the third great demonstration on the last of July when a monster petition signed by hundreds of thousands of citizens was brought to the Senate asking that body to pass the national suffrage amendment. Women from all parts of the country mobilized in the countryside of Maryland where they were met with appropriate ceremonies by the Senate Woman Suffrage Committee. The delegation motored in gaily decorated automobiles to Washington and went direct to the Senate, where the entire day was given over to suffrage discussion.

Twenty-two senators spoke in favor of the amendment in presenting their petitions. Three spoke against it. For the first time in *twenty-six years* suffrage was actually debated in Congress. That day was historic.

Speeches? Yes. Greetings? Yes. Present petitions from their constituencies? Gladly. Report it from the Senate Committee? They had to concede that. But passage of the amendment? That was beyond their contemplation.

More pressure was necessary. We appealed to the women voters, of whom there were then four million, to come into action.

"Four million women voters are watching you," we said to Congress. We might as well have said, "There are in the South Sea Islands four million heathens."

It was clear that these distant women voters had no relation in the senatorial mind to the realism of politics. We decided to bring some of these women voters to Washington. Having failed to get the Senate to act by August, we invited the Council of Women Voters to hold its convention in Washington that Congress might learn this simple lesson: women did vote; there were four million of them; they had a voters' organization; they cared about the enfranchisement of all American women; they wanted the Senate to act; suffrage was no longer a moral problem; it could be made a practical political problem with which men and parties would have to reckon.

Voting women made their first impression on Congress that summer.

Meanwhile the President's "paramount issues"—tariff and currency—had been disposed of. With the December Congress approaching, he was preparing another message. We went to him again. This time it was the women from his own home state, an influential deputation of seventy-three women, including the suffrage leaders from all suffrage organizations in New Jersey. The women urged him to include recommendation of the suffrage resolution in his message to the new Congress. He replied:

"I am pleased, indeed, to greet you and your adherents here, and I will say to you that I was talking only yesterday with several members of Congress in regard to a Suffrage Committee in the House. The subject is one in which I am deeply interested, and you may rest assured that I will give it my earnest attention."

In interesting himself in the formation of a special committee to sit on suffrage in the House, the President was doing the smallest thing, to be sure, that could be done, but he was doing something. This was a distinct advance. It was our task to press on until all the maze of Congressional machinery had been used to exhaustion. Then there would be nothing left to do but to pass the amendment.

A fourth time that year the determination of women to secure the passage of the amendment was demonstrated. In December, the opening week of the new Congress, the annual convention of the National American Woman Suffrage Association was held in Washington. Miss Lucy Burns, vice chairman of its Congressional Committee and also of the Congressional Union, was applauded to the echo by the whole convention when she said:

"The National American Woman Suffrage Association is assembled in Washington to ask the Democratic Party to enfranchise the women of America.

"Rarely in the history of the country has a party been more powerful than the Democratic Party is to-day. It controls the Executive Office, the Senate and more than two-thirds of the members of the House of Representatives. It is in a position to give us effective and immediate help.

"We ask the Democrats to take action now. Those who hold power are responsible to the country for the use of it. They are responsible not only for what they do, but for what they do not do. Inaction establishes just as clear a record as does a policy of open hostility.

"We have in our hands to-day not only the weapon of a just cause; we have the support of ten enfranchised states— states comprising one-fifth of the United States Senate, one-seventh of the House of Representatives, and one-sixth of the electoral vote. More than 3,600,000 women have a vote in Presidential elections. It is unthinkable that a national government which represents women, and which appeals periodically for the suffrages of women, should ignore the issue of the right of all women to political freedom.

"We cannot wait until after the passage of scheduled Administration reforms. . . . Congress is free to take action on our question in the present session. We ask the Administration to support the woman suffrage amendment in Congress with its whole strength."

This represented the attitude of the entire suffrage movement toward the situation in the winter of 1913. At no time did the militant group deviate from this position until the amendment was through Congress.

It was difficult to make the Administration believe that the women meant what they said, and that they meant to use everything in their power and resourcefulness to see it carried out.

Men were used to having women ask them for suffrage. But they were disconcerted at being asked for it now; at being threatened with political chastisement if they did not yield to the demand.

In spite of the repeated requests to President Wilson that he include support of the measure in his message to Congress, he delivered his message December 2nd while the convention was still in session, and failed to make any mention of the suffrage amendment. He recommended self-government for Filipino men instead.

Immediately Miss Paul organized the entire convention into a fifth deputation to protest against this failure and to urge support in a subsequent message. Dr. Anna Howard Shaw led the interview. In reply to her eloquent appeal for his assistance, the President said in part: "I am merely the spokesman of my party. . . . I am not at liberty to urge upon Congress in messages, policies which have not had the organic consideration of those for whom I am spokesman. I am by my own principles shut out, in the language of the street, from 'starting anything.' I have to confine myself to those things which have been embodied as promises to the people at an election."

I shall never forget that day. Shafts of sunlight came in at the window and fell full and square upon the white-haired leader who was in the closing days of her power. Her clear, deep, resonant voice, ringing with the genuine love of liberty, was in sharp contrast to the halting, timid, little and technical answer of the President. He stooped to utter some light pleasantry which he thought would no doubt please the "ladies." It did not provoke even a faint smile. Dr. Shaw had dramatically asked, "Mr. President, if *you* cannot speak for us and your party will not, who then, pray, is there to speak for us?"

"You seem very well able to speak for yourselves, ladies," with a broad smile, followed by a quick embarrassment when no one stirred.

"We mean, Mr. President, who will speak for us with *authority?*" came back the hot retort from Dr. Shaw.

The President made no reply. Instead he expressed a desire to shake the hands of the three hundred delegates. A few felt that manners compelled them to acquiesce; the others filed out without this little political ceremony.

Alice Paul's report to the national convention for her year's work as Chairman of the Congressional Committee of the National American Woman Suffrage Association, and as Chairman also of the Congressional Union for Woman Suffrage, showed that a budget of twenty-seven thousand dollars had been raised and expended under her leadership as against *ten dollars* spent during the previous year on Congressional work. At the beginning of the year there was no interest in work with Congress. It was considered hopeless. At the close of the year 1913 it had become a practical political issue. Suffrage had entered the national field to stay.

At this point the Congressional Union for Woman Suffrage was obliged to become an independent body in order to continue this vigorous policy which the conservative suffrage leaders were unwilling to follow.

Hearings, deputations to the President, petitions to Congress, more persistent lobbying, all these things continued during the following year under Miss Paul's leadership with the result that a vote in the Senate was taken, though at an inopportune moment,—the first vote in the Senate since 1887. The vote stood 36 to 34—thereby failing by 11 votes of the necessary two-thirds majority. This vote, nevertheless, indicated that a new strength in the suffrage battle had forced Congress to take some action.

In the House, the Rules Committee on a vote of 4 to 4

refused to create a suffrage committee. We appealed to the
Democratic caucus to see if the party sustained this action.
We wished to establish their party responsibility, one way or
another, and by securing the necessary signatures to a petition,
we compelled the caucus to meet. By a vote of 123 to 57 the
caucus declared " . . . that the question of woman suffrage
is a state and not a federal question," as a substitute for the
milder resolution offered, providing for the creation of a committee on woman suffrage. If this had left any doubt as to
how the Democratic Party, as a party, stood, this doubt was
conveniently removed by Representative Underwood, the Majority Leader of the House, when he said on the floor of the
House the following day: "The Democratic Party last night
took the distinctive position that it was not in favor of this
legislation because it was in favor of the states controlling the
question of suffrage. . . . I not only said I was opposed to it,
but I said the Party on this side of the Chamber was opposed
to it, and the Party that has control of the legislation in Congress certainly has the right to say that it will not support a
measure if it is not in accordance with its principles."

Meanwhile the President had said to a deputation of work-
ingwomen who waited upon him in February, "Until the Party,
as such, has considered a matter of this very supreme importance, and taken its position, I am not at liberty to speak for
it; and yet I am not at liberty to speak for it as an individual,
for I am not an individual."

"But we ask you to speak *to* your party, not *for* it," answered Mrs. Glendower Evans, Chairman of the deputation,
amid evident presidential embarrassment.

Those women who had been inclined perhaps to accept the
President's words as true to fact, entertained doubts when a
few days later he demanded of his party in Congress the repeal
of the free tolls provision in the Panama Canal tolls act. In
so doing, he not only recommended action not endorsed by his

party, but he demanded action which his party had specifically declared against.

It was necessary to appeal again to the nation. We called for demonstrations of public approval of the amendment in every state on May 2. Thousands of resolutions were passed calling for action in Congress. These resolutions were made the center of another great demonstration in Washington, May 9, when thousands of women in procession carried them to the Capitol where beautiful and impressive ceremonies were held on the Capitol steps. The resolutions were formally received by members of Congress and the demonstration ended dramatically with a great chorus of women massed on the steps singing "The March of the Women" to the thousands of spectators packed closely together on the Capitol grounds.

And still the President withheld his support.

Under our auspices five hundred representative club women of the country waited upon him in another appeal for help.[1] To them he explained his "passion for local self-government," which led to his conviction "that this is a matter for settlement by the states [2] and not by the federal government. . . ."

Women had to face the fact that the 63rd Congress had made a distinctly hostile record on suffrage. The President, as leader of his party, had seven times refused all aid; the Democratic Party had recorded its opposition through an adverse vote in the Senate and a caucus vote in the House forbidding even consideration of the measure.

It became clear that some form of political action would have to be adopted which would act as an accelerator to the Administration. This feeling was growing momentarily among many women, but it was conspicuously strong in the mind of Mrs. Oliver H. P. Belmont, recognized as one of the ablest

[1] 7th deputation to the President, June 30, 1914.
[2] This amounted to virtual opposition because of the great difficulties, (some of them almost insuperable) involved in amending many state constitutions.

suffrage leaders in the country. Anticipating the unfriendly
record made by the Democrats in the 63rd Congress, Mrs.
Belmont had come to Miss Paul and to her vice-chairman,
Miss Lucy Burns, to urge the formulation of a plan whereby
we could strike at Administration opposition through the
women voters of the West. Miss Paul had the same idea and
welcomed the support of this plan by so able a leader.

Mrs. Belmont was impatient to do nationally what she had
already inaugurated in New York State suffrage work—make
suffrage an election issue. She was the first suffragist in
America to be "militant" enough to wage a campaign against
office-seekers on the issue of woman suffrage. She was roundly
denounced by the opposition press, but she held her ground.
It is interesting to record that she defeated the first candidate
for the New York Assembly ever campaigned against on this
issue.

She had associated herself with the Pankhursts in England
and was the first suffrage leader here publicly to commend the
tactics of the English militants. Through her, Mrs. Pankhurst made her first visits to America, where she found a sympathetic audience. Even among the people who understood
and believed in English tactics, the general idea here was that
only in the backward country of England was "militancy"
necessary. In America, men would give women what women
wanted without a struggle.

Mrs. Belmont was the one suffrage leader who foresaw a
militant battle here whenever women should determine to ask
for their freedom immediately. In a great measure she prepared the way for that battle.

Since the movement had not even advanced to the stage of
political action at that time, however, Mrs. Belmont realized
that political action would have to be exhausted before attempting more aggressive tactics. Not knowing whether Miss
Paul had contemplated inaugurating political action in the

national field, she sought out the new leader and urged her to begin at once to organize the women's power for use in the approaching national elections.

Those interested in the woman's movement are fairly familiar with Mrs. Belmont's early state suffrage work and her work with the militants in England, but they do not know as much about her national work. It is not easy for a woman of vast wealth to be credited with much else in America than the fact of generosity in giving money to the cause in which she believes. Wealth dazzles us and we look no further. Mrs. Belmont has given hundreds of thousands of dollars to suffrage, both state and national, but she has given greater gifts in her militant spirit, her political sagacity and a marked tactical sense. She was practically the only leader formerly associated with the conservative forces who had the courage to extricate herself from the old routine propaganda and adventure into new paths. She always approached the struggle for liberty in a wholesome revolutionary mood. She was essentially a leader, and one who believed in action—always action.

Until the movement in America regained its militant spirit, her heart was primarily with the English women, because she thought their fight so magnificent that it would bring suffrage to women in England sooner than our slow-going methods would bring it to us. In 1910, when English militancy was at its height, Mrs. Belmont gave out an interview in London, in which she predicted that English women would have the suffrage before us. She even went so far as to say that we in America would have to create an acute situation here, probably a form of militancy, before we could win. At the same time the President of the International Suffrage Alliance said in London: "The suffrage movement in England resembles a battle. It is cruel and tragic. Ours in America is an evolution—less dramatic, slow but more *sure*." Facts sustained Mrs. Belmont's prophecy. Facts did not sustain the other

Mrs. O. H. P. Belmont

Democrats Hire Messenger Boys to Display Posters in an Attempt to Counteract Woman's Party Campaign

INEZ MILHOLLAND BOISSEVAIN

Scene of Memorial Service—Statuary Hall, The Capitol

SCENES ON THE PICKET LINE

Top—"We Shall Fight" Banner*
Silent Sentinel—Joy Young
Middle—Picketing in the Rain
Bottom—Working Women March to White House*
Pickets in June

* © *Harris & Ewing.*

Section of Picket Circling White House in Rain   "They Marched and Waited—Waited and Marched"

prediction. English women got the vote in 1918. American women were not enfranchised nationally until August, 1920.

The following is the political theory and program approved by Mrs. Belmont and submitted to the Congressional Union, by its chairman, Alice Paul, at a conference of the organization at the home of Mrs. Belmont in Newport in August, 1914:

The dominant party (at that time the Democratic Party) is responsible for all action and therefore for action on suffrage.

This party's action had been hostile to this measure.

The dominant party in the approaching election must be convinced, and through it all other parties, that opposition to suffrage is inexpedient.

All parties will be convinced when they see that their opposition costs them votes.

Our fight is a political one.

We must appeal for support to the constituency which is most friendly to suffrage, that constituency being the voting women.

An attempt must be made, no matter how small, to organize the women's vote.

An appeal must be made to the women voters in the nine suffrage states to withhold their support from the Democrats nationally, until the national Democratic Party ceases to block the suffrage amendment.

This is non-partisanship in the highest degree, as it calls upon women to forego previous allegiance to a party. If they are Democrats in this instance, they must vote against their party. If the Republican Party were in power and pursued a similar course, we would work against that party.

The party which sees votes falling away will change its attitude.

After we have once affected by this means the outcome of a national election, even though slightly, every party will hesitate to trifle with our measure any longer.

All candidates from suffrage states are professing suffragists, and therefore we have nothing to lose by defeating a member of the dominant party in those states. Another suffragist will take his place.

Men will object to being opposed because of their party responsibility in spite of their friendliness individually to suffrage. But women certainly have a right to further through the ballot their wishes on the suffrage question, as well as on other questions like currency, tariff, and what not.

This can only be done by considering the Party record, for as the individual record and individual pledges go, all candidates are practically equal.

We, as a disfranchised class, consider our right to vote, preëminently over any other issue in any party's program.

Political leaders will resent our injecting our issue into their campaign, but the rank and file will be won when they see the loyalty of women to women.

This policy will be called militant and in a sense it is, being strong, positive and energetic.

If it is militant to appeal to women to use their vote to bring suffrage to this country, then it is militant to appeal to men or women to use their vote to any good end.

To the question of "How will we profit if another party comes in?" our answer will be that adequate political chastisement of one party for its bad suffrage record through a demonstration of power by women voters affecting the result of the national election, will make it easier to get action from any party in power.

Amidst tremendous enthusiasm this plan was accepted by the little conference of women at Newport, and $7,000 pledged in a few moments to start it. There was a small group of women, an infinitely small budget with which to wage a campaign in nine states, but here was also enthusiasm and resolute determination.

A tiny handful of women—never more than two, more often only one to a state—journeyed forth from Washington into the nine suffrage states of the West to put before the voting women this political theory, and to ask them to support it.

CHAPTER 2

"IT can't be done." "Women don't care about suffrage." "Once they've got it, it is a dead issue." "To talk of arousing the Western women to protest against the Congressional candidates of the National Democratic Party in the suffrage states, when every one of them is a professing suffragist, is utter folly." So ran the comment of the political wiseacres in the autumn of 1914.

But the women had faith in their appeal.

It is impossible to give in a few words any adequate picture of the anger of Democratic leaders at our entrance into the campaign. Six weeks before election they woke up to find the issue of national suffrage injected into a campaign which they had meant should be no more stirring than an orderly and perfunctory endorsement of the President's legislative program.

The campaign became a very hot one during which most of the militancy seemed to be on the side of the political leaders. Heavy fists came down on desks. Harsh words were spoken. Violent threats were made. In Colorado, where I was campaigning, I was invited politely but firmly by the Democratic leader to leave the state the morning after I had arrived. "You can do no good here. I would advise you to leave at once. Besides, your plan is impracticable and the women will not support it."

"Then why do you object to my being here?" I asked.

"You have no right to ask women to do this. . . ."

Some slight variation of this experience was met by every

35

woman who took part in this campaign. Of course, the Democratic leaders did not welcome an issue raised unexpectedly,
and one which forced them to spend an endless amount of time
apologizing for and explaining the Democratic Party's record.
Nor did they relish spending more money publishing more literature, in short, adding greatly to the burdens of their campaign. The candidates, a little more suave than the party
leaders, proved most eloquently that they had been suffragists
"from birth." One candidate even claimed a suffrage inheritance from his great-grandmother.

This first entry of women into a national election on the
suffrage amendment was little more than a quick, brilliant
dash. With all its sketchiness, however, it had immediate
political results, and when the election was over, there came
tardily a general public recognition that the Congressional
Union had made a real contribution to these results. In the
nine suffrage states women voted for 45 members of Congress.
For 43 of these seats the Democratic Party ran candidates.
We opposed in our campaign all of these candidates. Out of
the 43 Democratic candidates running, only 20 were elected.
While it was not our primary aim to defeat candidates it was
generally conceded that we had contributed to these defeats.

Our aim in this campaign was primarily to call to the
attention of the public the bad suffrage record of the Democratic Party. The effect of our campaign was soon evident
in Congress. The most backward member realized for the first
time that women had voted. Even the President perceived that
the movement had gained new strength, though he was not yet
politically moved by it. He was still "tied to a conviction" [1]
which he had had all his life that suffrage "ought to be brought
about state by state."

Enough strength and determination among women had

---

[1] Statement to Deputation of Democratic women (eighth deputation)
at the White House, Jan. 6, 1915.

been demonstrated to the Administration, however, to make them want to do something "just as good" as the thing we asked. The Shafroth-Palmer [1] Resolution was introduced, providing for a constitutional amendment permitting a national initiative and referendum on suffrage in the states, thereby forcing upon women the very course we had sought to circumvent. This red herring drawn across the path had been accepted by the conservative suffragists evidently in a moment of hopelessness, and their strength put behind it, but the politicians who persuaded them to back it knew that it was merely an attempt to evade the issue.

This made necessary a tremendous campaign throughout the country by the Congressional Union, with the result that the compromise measure was eventually abandoned. During its life, however, politicians were happy in the opportunity to divide their support between it and the original amendment, which was still pending. To offset this danger and to show again in dramatic fashion the strength and will of the women voters to act on this issue, we made political work among the western women the principal effort of the year 1915, the year preceding the presidential election. Taking advantage of the Panama-Pacific Exposition in San Francisco, we opened suffrage headquarters in the Palace of Education on the exposition grounds. From there we called the first Woman Voters' Convention ever held in the world for the single purpose of attaching political strength to the movement. Mrs. O. H. P. Belmont was chairman of the committee which signed the convention call.

Women from all the voting states assembled in a mass convention September 14, 15 and 16. There is not time to describe

---

[1] This resolution was introduced in the Senate by Senator Shafroth of Colorado, Democrat; in the House by Representative A. Mitchell Palmer of Pennsylvania, Democrat, later Attorney General in President Wilson's Cabinet. Both men, although avowed supporters of the original Susan B. Anthony amendment, backed this evil compromise.

the beauty of the pageantry which surrounded that gathering, nor of the emotional quality which was at high pitch throughout the sessions. These women from the deserts of Arizona, from the farms of Oregon, from the valleys of California, from the mountains of Nevada and Utah, were in deadly earnest. They had answered the call and they meant to stay in the fight until it was won. The convention went on record unanimously for further political action on behalf of national suffrage and for the original amendment without compromise, and pledged itself to use all power to this end without regard to the interests of any existing political party.

Two emissaries, Sara Bard Field and Frances Joliffe, both of California, were commissioned by women voters at the final session, when more than ten thousand people were present, to go to the President and Congress bearing these resolutions and hundreds of thousands of signatures upon a petition gathered during the summer. They would speak directly to the President lest he should be inclined to take lightly the women voters' resolutions.

The envoys, symbolic of the new strength that was to come out of the West, made their journey across continent by automobile. They created a sensation all along the way, received as they were by governors, by mayors, by officials high and low, and by the populace. Thousands more added their names to the petition and it was rolled up to gigantic proportions until in December when unrolled it literally stretched over miles as it was borne to the Capitol with honor escorts.

The action of the convention scarcely cold, and the envoys mid-way across the continent, the President hastened to New Jersey to cast his vote for suffrage in a state referendum. He was careful to state that he did so as a private citizen, "not as the leader of my party in the nation." He repeated his position, putting the emphasis upon his opposition to national suffrage, rather than on his belief in suffrage for his state.

"I believe that it (suffrage) should be settled by the states and not by the national government, and that in no circumstances should it be made a party question; and my view has grown stronger at every turn of the agitation." He knew women were asking the powerful aid of the President of the United States, not the aid of Mr. Wilson of Princeton, New Jersey. The state amendment in New Jersey was certain to fail, as President Wilson well knew. Casting a vote for it would help his case with women voters, and still not bring suffrage in the East a step nearer.

The envoys' reception at the Capitol was indeed dramatic. Thousands of women escorted them amid bands and banners to the halls of Congress, where they were received by senators and representatives and addressed with eloquent speeches. The envoys replied by asking that their message be carried by friends of the measure to the floor of the Senate and House, and this was done.

The envoys waited upon the President at the White House. This visit of the representatives of women with power marked rather an advance in the President's position. He listened with an eager attention to the story of the new-found power and what women meant to do with it. For the first time on record, he said he had "an open mind" on the question of national suffrage, and would confer with his party colleagues.

The Republican and Democratic National Committees heard the case of the envoys. They were given a hearing before the Senate Suffrage Committee and before the House Judiciary in one of the most lively and entertaining inquisitions in which women ever participated.

No more questions on mother and home! No swan song on the passing of charm and womanly loveliness! Only agile scrambling by each committee member to ask with eagerness and some heat, "Well, if this amendment has not passed Congress by then, what will you do in the elections of 1916?" It was with difficulty that the women were allowed to tell their story, so eager was the Committee to jump ahead to political consequences. "Sirs, that depends upon what you gentlemen do. We are asking a simple thing——" But they never got any further from the main base of their interest.

"If President Wilson comes out for it and his party does not," from a Republican member, "will you——"

"I object to introducing partisan discussions here," came shamelessly from a Democratic colleague. And so the hearing passed in something of a verbal riot, but with no doubt as to the fact that Congressmen were alarmed by the prospect of women voting as a protest group.

The new year found the Senate promptly reporting the measure favorably again, but the Judiciary Committee foot-balled it to its sub-committee, back to the whole committee, postponed it, marked time, dodged without a blush, and finally defeated it.

The problem of neutrality toward the European war was agitating the minds of political leaders. Nothing like suffrage for women must be allowed to rock the ship even slightly! Oh, no, indeed; it was men's business to keep the nation out of war. Men never had shown marked skill at keeping nations out of war in the history of the world. But never mind! Logic must not be pressed too hard upon the "reasoning" sex. This time, men *would* do it.

The exciting national election contest was approaching. Party conventions were scheduled to meet in June while the amendment languished at the Capitol. It was clear that more highly organized woman-power would have to be called into action before the national government would speed its pace. To the women voters the Eastern women went for decisive assistance. A car known as the "Suffrage Special," carrying distinguished Eastern women and gifted speakers, made an extensive tour of the West and under the banner of the Congressional Union called again upon the women voters to come to Chicago on June 5th to form a new party,—The Woman's Party [1]—to serve as long as should be necessary as the balance of power in national contests, and thus to force action from the old parties.

The instant response which met this appeal surpassed the most optimistic hopes. Thousands of women assembled in Chicago for this convention, which became epoch-making not only in the suffrage fight but in the whole woman movement. *For the first time in history, women came together to organize their political power into a party to free their own sex.* For the first time in history representatives of men's political parties came to plead before these women voters for the support of their respective parties.

The Republican Party sent as its representatives John Hays Hammond and C. S. Osborn, formerly Governor of Michigan. The Democrats sent their most persuasive orator, President Wilson's friend, Dudley Field Malone, Collector of the Port of New York. Allan Benson, candidate for the Presidency on the Socialist ticket, represented the Socialist Party. Edward Polling, Prohibition leader, spoke for the Prohibition Party, and Victor Murdock and Gifford Pinchot for The Progressive Party.

All laid their claims for suffrage support before the women with the result that the convention resolved itself into another political party—The Woman's Party. A new party with but one plank—the immediate passage of the federal suffrage amendment—a party determined to withhold its support from all existing parties until women were politically free, and to punish politically any party in power which did not use its

---

[1] The Woman's Party started with a membership of all Congressional Union members in suffrage states. Anne Martin of Nevada was elected chairman.

power to free women; a party which became a potent factor
of protest in the following national election.

This first step towards the solidarity of women quickly
brought results. The Republican National Convention, meeting immediately•after the Woman's Party Convention, and the
Democratic National Convention the week following, both included suffrage planks in their national platforms for the first
time in history. To be sure, they were planks that failed to
satisfy us. But the mere hint of organized political action on
suffrage had moved the two dominant parties to advance a
step. The new Woman's Party had declared suffrage a national political issue. The two major parties acknowledged
the issue by writing it into their party platforms.

The Republican platform was vague and indefinite on
national suffrage. The Democratic Party made its suffrage
plank specific against action by Congress. It precisely said,
"We recommend the extension of the franchise to the women
of the country *by the states* upon the same terms as men." It
was openly stated at the Democratic Convention by leading
Administration Democrats that the President himself had
written this suffrage plank. If the Republicans could afford
to write a vague and indefinite plank, the President and his
party could not. They as the party in power had been under
fire and were forced to take sides. They did so. The President chose the plank and his subordinates followed his lead.
It may be remarked in passing that this declaration so solidified the opposition within the President's party that when the
President ultimately sought to repudiate it, he met stubborn
resistance.

Protected by the President's plank, the Democratic Congress continued to block national suffrage. It would not
permit it even to be reported from the Judiciary Committee.
The party platform was written. The President, too, found
it easy to hide behind the plank which he had himself written,

counting on women to be satisfied. To Mrs. D. E. Hooker of Richmond, Virginia, who as a delegate from the Virginia Federation of Labor, representing 60,000 members, went to him soon after to ask his support of the amendment, the President said, "I am opposed by conviction and political traditions to federal action on this question. Moreover, after the plank which was adopted in the Democratic platform at St. Louis, I could not comply with the request contained in this resolution even if I wished to do so."

President Wilson could not act because the party plank which he had written prevented him from doing so!

Meanwhile the women continued to protest.

Miss Mabel Vernon of Delaware, beloved and gifted crusader, was the first member of the Woman's Party to commit a "militant" act. President Wilson, speaking at the dedication services of the Labor Temple in Washington, was declaring his interest in all classes and all struggles. He was proclaiming his beliefs in the abstractions of liberty and justice, when Miss Vernon, who was seated on the platform from which he was speaking, said in her powerful voice, "Mr. President, if you sincerely desire to forward the interests of all the people, why do you oppose the national enfranchisement of women?" Instant consternation arose, but the idea had penetrated to the farthest corner of the huge assembly that women were protesting to the President against the denial of their liberty.

The President found time to answer, "That is one of the things which we will have to take counsel over later," and resumed his speech. Miss Vernon repeated her question later and was ordered from the meeting by the police.

As the summer wore on, women realized that they would have to enter the national contest in the autumn. Attention was focussed on the two rival presidential candidates, Woodrow Wilson and Charles Evans Hughes, the Republican nominee, upon whom the new Woman's Party worked diligently for prompt statements of their position on the national amendment.

The next political result of the new solidarity of women was Mr. Hughes' declaration on August 1st, 1916: "My view is that the proposed amendment should be submitted and ratified and the subject removed from political discussion."

The Democratic Congress adjourned without even reporting the measure to that body for a vote, and went forthwith to the country to ask reëlection.

We also went to the country. We went to the women voters to lay before them again the Democratic Party's record— now complete through one Administration. We asked women voters again to withhold their support nationally from President Wilson and his party.

The President accepted at once the opportunity to speak before a convention of suffragists at Atlantic City in an effort to prove his great belief in suffrage. He said poetically, "The tide is rising to meet the moon. . . . You can afford to wait." Whatever we may have thought of his figure of speech, we disagreed with his conclusion.

The campaign on, Democratic speakers throughout the West found an unexpected organized force among women, demanding an explanation of the past conduct of the Democratic Party and insisting on an immediate declaration by the President in favor of the amendment. Democratic orators did their utmost to meet this opposition. "Give the President time. He can't do everything at once." "Trust him once more; he will do it for you next term." "He kept us out of war. He is the best friend the mothers of the nation ever had." "He stood by you. Now you women stand by him." "What good will votes do you if the Germans come over here and take your country?" And so on. Enticing doctrine to women—the peace lovers of the human race.

Although we entered this contest with more strength than

we had had in 1914, with a budget five times as large and with piled-up evidence of Democratic hostility, we could not have entered a more difficult contest. The people were excited to an almost unprecedented pitch over the issue of peace versus war. In spite of the difficulty of competing with this emotional issue which meant the immediate disposal of millions of lives, it was soon evident that the two issues were running almost neck and neck in the Western territory.

No less skilled a campaigner than William Jennings Bryan took the stump in the West against the Woman's Party. At least a third of each speech was devoted to suffrage. He urged. He exorted. He apologized. He explained. He pleaded. He condemned. Often he was heckled. Often he saw huge "VOTE AGAINST WILSON! HE KEPT US OUT OF SUFFRAGE!" banners at the doors of his meetings. One woman in Arizona, who, unable longer to listen in patience to the glory of "a democracy where only were governed those who consented," interrupted him. He coldly answered, "Madam, you cannot pick cherries before they are ripe." By the time he got to California, however, the cherries had ripened considerably, for Mr. Bryan came out publicly for the national amendment.

What was true of Mr. Bryan was true of practically every Democratic campaigner. Against their wills they were forced to talk about suffrage, although they had serenely announced at the opening of the campaign that it was "not an issue in this campaign." Some merely apologized and explained. Others, like Dudley Field Malone, spoke for the federal amendment, and promised to work to put it through the next Congress, "if only you women will stand by Wilson and return him to power."

Space will not permit in this book to give more than a hint of the scope and strength of our campaign. If it were possible to give a glimpse of the speeches made by men in that campaign, you would agree that it was not peace alone that was the dominant issue, but peace and suffrage. It must be made perfectly clear that the Woman's Party did not attempt to elect Mr. Hughes. It did not feel strong enough to back a candidate in its first battle, and did not conduct its fight affirmatively at all. No speeches were made for Mr. Hughes and the Republican Party. The appeal was to vote a vote of protest against Mr. Wilson and his Congressional candidates, because he and his party had had the power to pass the amendment through Congress and had refused to do so. That left the women free to choose from among the Republicans, Socialists and Prohibitionists. It was to be expected that the main strength of the vote taken from Mr. Wilson would go to Mr. Hughes, as few women perhaps threw their votes to the minority parties. But just as the Progressive Party's protest had been effective in securing progressive legislation without winning the election, so the Woman's Party hoped its protest would bring results in Congress without attempting to win the election.

History will never know in round numbers how many women voted against the President and his party at this crisis, for there are no records kept for men and women separately, except in one state, in Illinois. The women there voted two to one against Mr. Wilson and for Mr. Hughes.

Men outnumber women throughout the entire western territory; in some states, two and three to one; in Nevada, still higher. But, whereas, in the election of 1912, President Wilson got 69 electoral votes from the suffrage states, in the 1916 election, when the whole West was aflame for him because of his peace policy, he got only 57. Enthusiasm for Mr. Hughes in the West was not sufficiently marked to account entirely for the loss of these 12 electoral votes. Our claim that Democratic opposition to suffrage had cost many of them was never seriously denied.

The Democratic Judiciary Committee of the House which
had refused to report suffrage to the House for a vote, had
only one Democratic member from a suffrage state, Mr. Taggart of Kansas, standing for reëlection. This was the only
spot where women could strike out against the action of this
committee—and Mr. Taggart. They struck with success. He
was defeated almost wholly by the women's votes.

With a modest campaign fund of slightly over fifty thousand dollars, raised almost entirely in small sums, the women
had forced the campaign committee of the Democratic Party
to assume the defensive and to practically double expenditure
and work on this issue. As much literature was used on suffrage as on peace in the suffrage states.

Many Democrats although hostile to our campaign said
without qualification that the Woman's Party protest was the
only factor in the campaign which stemmed the western tide
toward Wilson, and which finally made California the pivotal
state and left his election in doubt for a week.

Again, with more force, national suffrage had been injected
into a campaign where it was not wanted, where the leaders
had hoped the single issue of "peace" would hold the center
of the stage. Again many women had stood together on this
issue and put woman suffrage first. And the actual reëlection
of President Wilson had its point of advantage, too, for it
enabled us to continue the education of a man in power who
had already had four years of lively training on the woman
question.

CHAPTER 3

O F the hundreds of women who volunteered for the last Western campaign, perhaps the most effective in their appeal were the disfranchised Eastern women.

The most dramatic figure of them all was Inez Milholland Boissevain, the gallant and beloved crusader who gave her life that the day of women's freedom might be hastened. Her last words to the nation as she fell fainting on the platform in California were, "Mr. President, how long must women wait for liberty?" Her fiery challenge was never heard again. She never recovered from the terrific strain of the campaign which had undermined her young strength. Her death touched the heart of the nation; her sacrifice, made so generously for liberty, lighted anew the fire of rebellion in women, and aroused from inertia thousands never before interested in the liberation of their own sex.

Memorial meetings were held throughout the country at which women not only paid radiant tribute to Inez Milholland, but reconsecrated themselves to the struggle and called again upon the reëlected President and his Congress to act.

The most impressive of these memorials was held on Christmas Day in Washington. In Statuary Hall under the dome of the Capitol—the scene of memorial services for Lincoln and Garfield—filled with statues of outstanding figures in the struggle for political and religious liberty in this country, the first memorial service ever held in the Capitol to honor a woman, was held for this gallant young leader.

Boy choristers singing the magnificent hymn

"Forward through the darkness
Leave behind the night,
Forward out of error,
Forward into light"

led into the hall the procession of young girl banner-bearers.
Garbed in simple surplices, carrying their crusading banners
high above their heads, these comrades of Inez Milholland
Boissevain seemed more triumphant than sad. They seemed
to typify the spirit in which she gave her life.

Still other young girls in white held great golden banners
flanking the laurel-covered dais, from which could be read the
inscriptions: "Greater love hath no man than this, that he
lay down his life for his friend" . . . "Without extinction is
liberty; Without retrograde is equality" . . . "As He died to
make men holy let us die to make men free" . . .

From behind the heavy velvet curtains came the music of
voices and strings, and the great organ sounded its tragic
and triumphant tones.

Miss Maud Younger of California was chosen to make the
memorial address on this occasion. She said in part:

"We are here to pay tribute to Inez Milholland Boissevain,
who was our comrade. We are here in the nation's capital, the
seat of our democracy, to pay tribute to one who gave up her
life to realize that democracy. . . .

"Inez Milholland walked down the path of life a radiant
being. She went into work with a song in her heart. She went
into battle with a laugh on her lips. Obstacles inspired her,
discouragement urged her on. She loved work and she loved
battle. She loved life and laughter and light, and above all
else she loved liberty. With a loveliness beyond most, a kindli-
ness, a beauty of mind and soul, she typified always the best
and noblest in womanhood. She was the flaming torch that
went ahead to light the way—the symbol of light and freedom. . . .

"Symbol of the woman's struggle, it was she who carried to the West the appeal of the unenfranchised, and carrying it, made her last appeal on earth, her last journey in life.

"As she set out upon her last journey, she seems to have had the clearer vision, the spiritual quality of one who has already set out for another world. With infinite understanding and intense faith in her mission, she was as one inspired. Her meetings were described as 'revival meetings,' her audiences as 'wild with enthusiasm.' Thousands acclaimed her, thousands were turned away unable to enter. . . .

"And she made her message very plain.

"She stood for no man, no party. She stood only for woman. And standing thus she urged:

" 'It is women for women now and shall be until the fight is won! Together we shall stand shoulder to shoulder for the greatest principle the world has ever known, the right of self-government.

" 'Whatever the party that has ignored the claims of women we as women must refuse to uphold it. We must refuse to uphold any party until all women are free.

" 'We have nothing but our spirits to rely on and the vitality of our faith, but spirit is invincible.

" 'It is only for a little while. Soon the fight will be over. Victory is in sight.'

"Though she did not live to see that victory, it is sweet to know that she lived to see her faith in women justified. In one of her last letters she wrote:

" 'Not only did we reckon accurately on women's loyalty to women, but we likewise realized that our appeal touched a certain spiritual, idealistic quality in the western woman voter, a quality which is yearning to find expression in political life. At the idealism of the Woman's Party her whole nature flames into enthusiasm and her response is immediate. She gladly transforms a narrow partisan loyalty into loyalty to a principle, the establishment of which carries with it no personal advantage to its advocate, but merely the satisfaction of achieving one more step toward the emancipation of mankind. . . . We are bound to win. There never has been a fight yet where interest was pitted against principle that principle did not triumph!'

" . . . The trip was fraught with hardship. Speaking day and night, she would take a train at two in the morning to arrive at eight; then a train at midnight to arrive at five in the morning. Yet she would not change the program; she would not leave anything out. . . .

"And so . . . her life went out in glory in the shining cause of freedom.

"And as she had lived loving liberty, working for liberty, fighting for liberty, so it was that with this word on her lips she fell. 'How long must women wait for liberty?' she cried and fell—as surely as any soldier upon the field of honor—as truly as any who ever gave up his life for an ideal.

"As in life she had been the symbol of the woman's cause so in death she is the symbol of its sacrifice. The whole daily sacrifice, the pouring out of life and strength that is the toll of woman's prolonged struggle.

"Inez Milholland is one around whom legends will grow up. Generations to come will point out Mount Inez and tell of the beautiful woman who sleeps her last sleep on its slopes.

"They will tell of her in the West, tell of the vision of loveliness as she flashed through on her last burning mission, flashed through to her death—a falling star in the western heavens.

"But neither legend nor vision is liberty, which was her life. Liberty cannot die. No work for liberty can be lost. It lives on in the hearts of the people, in their hopes, their aspirations, their activities. It becomes part of the life of the nation. What Inez Milholland has given to the world lives on forever.

"We are here to-day to pay tribute to Inez Milholland Boissevain, who was our comrade. Let our tribute be not words which pass, nor song which flies, nor flower which fades. Let it be this: that we finish the task she could not finish; that with new strength we take up the struggle in which fighting beside us she fell; that with new faith we here consecrate ourselves to the cause of woman's freedom until that cause is won; that with new devotion we go forth, inspired by her sacrifice, to the end that her sacrifice be not in vain, for dying she shall bring to pass that which living she could not achieve—full freedom for women, full democracy for the nation.

"Let this be our tribute, imperishable, to Inez Milholland Boissevain."

Miss Anne Martin of Nevada, chairman of the Woman's Party, presided over the services. Other speakers were Honorable George Sutherland, United States Senator from Utah, representing the United States Congress; and Honorable Rowland S. Mahany, former member of Congress and lifelong friend of the Milholland family.

Mrs. William Kent of California, wife of Representative Kent, presented two resolutions which the vast audience approved by silently rising. One resolution, a tribute of rare beauty, prepared by Zona Gale, a friend of Inez Milholland, was a compelling appeal to all women to understand and to reverence the ideals of this inspiring leader. The other was an appeal to the Administration for action.

The pageantry of surpliced choristers and the long line of girl standard-bearers retired to the strains of the solemn recessional. The great audience sat still with bowed heads as the voices in the distance dropped in silence. Instantly the strains of the Marseillaise, filling the great dome with its stirring and martial song of hope, were taken up by the organ and the strings, and the audience was lifted to its feet singing as if in anticipation of the triumph of liberty.

The women were in no mood merely to mourn the loss of a comrade-leader. The government must be shown again its share of responsibility. Another appeal must be made to the President who, growing steadily in control over the people and over his Congress, was the one leader powerful enough to direct his party to accept this reform. But he was busy gathering his power to lead them elsewhere. Again we would have to compete with pro-war anti-war sentiment. But it was no time to relax.

Following the holiday season a deputation of over three hundred women carried to the White House the Christmas Day memorial for Inez Milholland and other memorials from similar services. The President was brought face to face with the new protest of women against the continued waste of physical and spiritual energy in their battle. There is no better way to picture the protest than to give you something verbatim from the speeches made that memorable day. This was the first meeting of suffragists with the President since the campaign against him in the previous autumn. It was only because of the peculiar character of the appeal that he consented to hear them.

Miss Younger presented the national memorial to him and introduced Mrs. John Winters Brannan, who made no plea to the President but merely gave him the New York memorial which read as follows:

"This gathering of men and women, assembled on New Year's day in New York to hold a memorial service in honor of Inez Milholland Boissevain, appeals to you, the President of the United States, to end the outpouring of life and effort that has been made for the enfranchisement of women for more than seventy years in this country. The death of this lovely and brave women symbolizes the whole daily sacrifice that vast numbers of women have made and are making for the sake of political freedom. It has made vivid the 'constant unnoticed tragedy of this prolonged effort for a freedom that is acknowledged just, but still denied.'

"It is not given to all to be put to the supreme test and to accept that test with such gallant gladness as she did. The struggle, however, has reached the point where it requires such intensity of effort—relentless and sustained—over the whole vast country, that the health of thousands of noble women is being insidiously undermined. If this continues, and it will continue until victory is won, we know only too surely that many women whom the nation can ill spare will follow in the footsteps of Inez Milholland.

"We desire to make known to you, Mr. President, our deep sense of wrong being inflicted upon women in making them spend their health and strength and forcing them to abandon other work that means fuller self-expression, in order to win freedom under a government that professes to believe in democracy.

"There is only one cause for which it is right to risk health and life. No price is too high to pay for liberty. So long as lives of women are required, these lives will be given.

"But we beg of you, Mr. President, so to act that this ghastly price will not have to be paid. Certainly it is a grim irony that a Republic should exact it. Upon you at this moment rests a solemn responsibility; for with you it rests to decide whether the life of this brilliant, dearly-loved woman whose glorious death we commemorate to-day, shall be the *last* sacrifice of life demanded of American women in their struggle for self-government.

"We ask you with all the fervor and earnestness of our souls to exert your power over Congress in behalf of the national enfranchisement of women in the same way you have so successfully used it on other occasions and for far less important measures.

"We are confident that if the President of the United States decides that this act of justice shall be done in the present session of Congress, it will be done. We know further that if the President does not urge it, it will not be done. . . ."

A fraction of a moment of silence follows, but it is long enough to feel strongly the emotional state of mind of the President. It plainly irritates him to be so plainly spoken to. We are conscious that his distant poise on entering is dwindling to petty confusion. There is something inordinately cool about the fervor of the women. This too irritates him. His irritation only serves to awaken in every woman new strength. It is a wonderful experience to feel strength take possession of your being in a contest of ideas. No amount of trappings, no amount of authority, no number of plainclothes men, nor the glamour of the gold-braided attaches, nor the vastness of the great reception hall, nor the dazzle of the lighted crystal chandeliers, and above all not the mind of your opponent can cut in on your slim, hard strength. You are more than invincible. Your mind leaps ahead to the infinite liberty of which yours is only a small part. You feel his strength in authority, his weakness in vision. He does not follow. He feels sorrow for us. He patronizes us. He must temper his irritation at our undoubted fanaticism and unreason. We, on the other hand, feel so superior to him. Our strength to demand is so much greater than his power to withhold. But he does not perceive this.

In the midst of these currents the serene and appealing voice of Sara Bard Field came as a temporary relief to the President—but only temporary. She brought tears to the eyes of the women as she said in presenting the California memorial resolutions:

"Mr. President, a year ago I had the honor of calling upon you with a similar deputation. At that time we brought from my western country a great petition from the voting women urging your assistance in the passage of the federal amendment for suffrage. At that time you were most gracious to us. You showed yourself to be in line with all the progressive leaders by your statement to us that you could change your mind and would consider doing so in connection with this amendment. We went away that day with hope in our hearts, but neither the hope inspired by your friendly words nor the faith we had in you as an advocate of democracy kept us from working day and night in the interest of our cause.

"Since that day when we came to you, Mr. President, one of our most beautiful and beloved comrades, Inez Milholland, has paid the price of her life for this cause. The untimely death of a young woman like this—a woman for whom the world has such bitter need—has focussed the attention of the men and women of the nation on the fearful waste of women which this fight for the ballot is entailing. The same maternal instinct for the preservation of life—whether it be the physical life of a child or the spiritual life of a cause—is sending women into this battle for liberty with an urge which gives them no rest night or day. Every advance of liberty has demanded its quota of human sacrifice, but if I had time I could show you that we have paid in a measure that is running over. In the

light of Inez Milholland's death, as we look over the long backward trail through which we have sought our political liberty,
we are asking how long must this struggle go on.

"Mr. President, to the nation more than to women alone
is this waste of maternal force significant. In industry such
a waste of money and strength would not be permitted. The
modern trend is all toward efficiency. Why is such waste permitted in the making of a nation?

"Sometimes I think it must be very hard to be a President,
in respect to his contacts with people as well as in the great
business he must perform. The exclusiveness necessary to a
great dignitary holds him away from that democracy of com-
munion, necessary to a full understanding of what the people
are really thinking and desiring. I feel that this deputation
to-day fails in its mission if, because of the dignity of your
office and the formality of such an occasion, we fail to bring
you the throb of woman's desire for freedom and her eagerness to ally herself when once the ballot is in her hand, with all
those activities to which you, yourself, have dedicated your
life. Those tasks which this nation has set itself to do are her
tasks as well as man's. We women who are here to-day are
close to this desire of women. We cannot believe that you are
our enemy or indifferent to the fundamental righteousness of
our demand.

"We have come here to you in your powerful office as our
helper. We have come in the name of justice, in the name of
democracy, in the name of all women who have fought and died
for this cause, and in a peculiar way with our hearts bowed
in sorrow, in the name of this gallant girl who died with the
word 'liberty' on her lips. We have come asking you this day
to speak some favorable word to us that we may know that
you will use your good and great office to end this wasteful
struggle of women."

The highest point in the interview had been reached. Before the President began his reply, we were aware that the high
moment had gone. But we listened.

"Ladies, I had not been apprised that you were coming here
to make any representations that would issue an appeal to me.

I had been told that you were coming to present memorial resolutions with regard to the very remarkable woman whom your cause has lost. I, therefore, am not prepared to say anything further than I have said on previous occasions of this sort.

"I do not need to tell you where my own convictions and my own personal purpose lie, and I need not tell you by what circumscriptions I am bound as leader of a party. As the leader of a party my commands come from that party and not from private personal convictions.

"My personal action as a citizen, of course, comes from no source but my own conviction and, therefore, my position has been so frequently defined, and I hope so candidly defined, and it is so impossible for me until the orders of my party are changed, to do anything other than I am doing as a party leader, that I think nothing more is necessary to be said.

"I do want to say this: I do not see how anybody can fail to observe from the utterances of the last campaign that the Democratic Party is more inclined than the opposition to assist in this great cause, and it has been a matter of surprise to me, and a matter of very great regret that so many of those who were heart and soul for this cause seemed so greatly to misunderstand and misinterpret the attitude of parties. *In this country*, as in every other self-governing country, *it is really through the instrumentality of parties that things can be accomplished. They are not accomplished by the individual voice but by concerted action, and that action must come only so fast as you can concert it.* I have done my best and shall continue to do my best to concert it in the interest of a cause in which I personally believe."

Dead silence. The President stands for a brief instant at the end of his words as if waiting for some faint stir of approval which does not come. He has the baffled air of a disappointed actor who has failed to "get across." Then he turns abruptly on his heel and the great doors swallow him up. Silently the women file through the corridor and into the fresh air.

The women returned to the spacious headquarters across

the park all of one mind. How little the President knew about
women! How he underestimated their intelligence and penetra-
tion of things political! Was it possible that he really thought
these earnest champions of liberty would merely carry resolutions of sorrow and regret to the President?

But this was not the real irony. How lightly he had
shifted the responsibility for getting results to his party. With
what coldness he had bade us "concert opinion," a thing which
he alone could do. That was pretty hard to bear, coming as it
did when countless forms of appeal had been exhausted by
which women without sufficient power could "concert" anything. The movement was almost at the point of languish-
ing so universal was the belief in the nation that suffrage for
women was inevitable. And yet he and his party remained
immovable.

The three hundred women of the memorial deputation
became on their return to headquarters a spirited protest
meeting.

Plans of action in the event the President refused to help
had been under consideration by Miss Paul and her executive
committee for some time, but they were now presented for the
first time for approval. There was never a more dramatic
moment at which to ask the women if they were ready for
drastic action.

Harriot Stanton Blatch, daughter of Elizabeth Cady Stanton and a powerful leader of women, voiced the feeling of the
entire body when she said, in a ringing call for action:

"We have gone to Congress, we have gone to the President
during the last four years with great deputations, with small
deputations. We have shown the interest all over the country
in self-government for women—something that the President
as a great Democrat ought to understand and respond to
instantly. Yet he tells us to-day that we must win his party.
He said it was strange that we did not see before election that

his party was more favorable to us than the Republican party.
How did it show its favor?   How did he show his favor to-
day to us?   He says we have got to convert his party . . .
Why?   Never before did the Democratic Party lie more in the
hands of one man than it lies to-day in the hands of President
Wilson. Never did the Democratic Party have a greater leader,
and never was it more susceptible to the wish of that leader,
than is the Democratic Party of to-day to President Wilson.
He controls his party, and I don't think he is too modest to
know it.   He can mould it as he wishes and he has moulded it.
He moulded it quickly before election in the matter of the
eight-hour law.   Was that in his party platform?   He had to
crush and force his party to pass that measure.   Yet he is not
willing to lay a finger's weight on his party to-day for half the
people of the United States. . . . Yet to-day he tells us that
we must wait more—and more.

"We can't organize bigger and more influential deputations.   We can't organize bigger processions.   We can't, women, do anything more in that line.   We have got to take a
new departure.   We have got to keep the question before him
all the time.   We have got to begin and begin immediately.

"Women, it rests with us.   We have got to bring to the
President, individually, day by day, week in and week out, the
idea that great numbers of women want to be free, *will* be free,
and want to know what he is going to do about it.

"Won't you come and join us in standing day after day at
the gates of the White House with banners asking, 'What will
you do, Mr. President, for one-half the people of this nation?'
Stand there as sentinels—sentinels of liberty, sentinels of self-
government—silent sentinels.   Let us stand beside the gateway
where he must pass in and out, so that he can never fail to
realize that there is a tremendous earnestness and insistence
back of this measure.   Will you not show your allegiance to-
day to this ideal of liberty?   Will you not be a silent sentinel
of liberty and self-government?"

Deliberations continued.   Details were settled.   Three
thousand dollars was raised in a few minutes among these
women, fresh from the President's rebuff.   No one suggested

waiting until the next Presidential campaign. No one even mentioned the fact that time was precious, and we could wait no longer. Every one seemed to feel these things without troubling to put them into words. Volunteers signed up for sentinel duty and the fight was on.

Part III

MILITANCY

"*I will write a song for the President, full of menacing signs,
And, back of it all, millions of discontented eyes.*"
WALT WHITMAN.

CHAPTER 1

WHEN all suffrage controversy has died away it will be the little army of women with their purple, white and gold banners, going to prison for their political freedom, that will be remembered. They dramatized to victory the long suffrage fight in America. The challenge of the picket line roused the government out of its half-century sleep of indifference. It stirred the country to hot controversy. It made zealous friends and violent enemies. It produced the sharply-drawn contest which forced the surrender of the government in the second Administration of President Wilson.

The day following the memorial deputation to the President, January 10th, 1917, the first line of sentinels, a dozen in number, appeared for duty at the White House gates. In retrospect it must seem to the most inflexible person a reasonably mild and gentle thing to have done. But at the same time it caused a profound stir. Columns of front page space in all the newspapers of the country gave more or less dispassionate accounts of the main facts. Women carrying banners were standing quietly at the White House gates "picketing" the President; women wanted President Wilson to put his power behind the suffrage amendment in Congress. That did not seem so shocking and only a few editors broke out into hot condemnation.

When, however, the women went back on the picket line the next day and the next and the next, it began to dawn upon the excited press that such persistence was "undesirable" . . .

"unwomanly" . . . "dangerous." Gradually the people most
hostile to the idea of suffrage in any form marshaled forth the
fears which accompany every departure from the prescribed
path. Partisan Democrats frowned. Partisan Republicans
chuckled. The rest remained in cautious silence to see how
"others" would take it. Following the refrain of the press,
the protest-chorus grew louder.

"Silly women" . . . "unsexed" . . . "pathological" . . .
"They must be crazy" . . . "Don't they know anything about
politics?" . . . "What can Wilson do? He does not have to
sign the constitutional amendment." . . . So ran the comment
from the wise elderly gentlemen sitting buried in their cush-
ioned chairs at the gentlemen's club across the Park, watching eagerly the "shocking," "shameless" women at the gates
of the White House. No wonder these gentlemen found the
pickets irritating! This absorbing topic of conversation, we
are told, shattered many an otherwise quiet afternoon and
broke up many a quiet game. Here were American women before their very eyes daring to shock them into having to think
about liberty. And what was worse—liberty for women. Ah
well, this could not go on,—this insult to the President. They
could with impunity condemn him and gossip about his affairs.
But that women should stand at his gates asking for liberty,—
that was a sin without mitigation.

Disapproval was not confined merely to the gentlemen in
their Club. I merely mention them as an example, for they
were our neighbors, and the strain on them day by day, as
our beautiful banners floated gaily out from our headquarters
was, I am told, a heavy one.

Yet, of course, we enjoyed irritating them. Standing on
the icy pavement on a damp, wintry day in the penetrating
cold of a Washington winter, knowing that within a stone's
throw of our agony there was a greater agony than ours—
there was a joy in that!

There were faint rumblings also in Congress, but like so many of its feelings they were confined largely to the cloak rooms. Representative Emerson of Ohio did demand from the floor of the House that the "suffrage guard be withdrawn, as it is an insult to the President," but his protest met with no response whatever from the other members. His oratory fell on indifferent ears. And of course there were always those in Congress who got a vicarious thrill watching women do in their fight what they themselves had not the courage to do in their own. Another representative, an anti-suffrage Democrat, inconsiderately called us "Iron-jawed angels," and hoped we would retire. But if by these protests these congressmen hoped to arouse their colleagues, they failed.

We were standing at the gates of the White House because the American Congress had become so supine that it could not or would not act without being compelled to act by the President. They knew that if they howled at us it would only afford an opportunity to retort—"Very well then, if you do not like us at the gates of your leader; if you do not want us to 'insult' the President, end this agitation by taking the matter into your own hands and passing the amendment." Such a suggestion would be almost as severe a shock as our picketing. The thought of actually initiating legislation left a loyal Democratic follower transfixed.

The heavy dignity of the Senate forbade their meddling much in this controversy over tactics. Also they were more interested in the sporting prospect of our going into the world war. There was no appeal to blood-lust in the women's fight. There were no shining rods of steel. There was no martial music. We were not pledging precious lives and vast billions in our crusade for liberty. The beginning of our fight did indeed seem tiny and frail by the side of the big game of war, and so the senators were at first scarcely aware of our presence.

But the intrepid women stood their long vigils, day

by day, at the White House gates, through biting wind and driving rain, through sleet and snow as well as sunshine, waiting for the President to act. Above all the challenges of their banners rang this simple, but insistent one:

MR. PRESIDENT!
HOW LONG MUST WOMEN WAIT FOR LIBERTY?

The royal blaze of purple, white and gold—the Party's tricolored banners—made a gorgeous spot of color against the bare, blacklimbed trees.

There were all kinds of pickets and so there were all kinds of reactions to the experience of picketing. The beautiful lady, who drove up in her limousine to do a twenty minute turn on the line, found it thrilling, no doubt. The winter tourist who had read about the pickets in her home paper thought it would be "so exciting" to hold a banner for a few minutes. But there were no illusions in the hearts of the women who stood at their posts day in and day out. None of them will tell you that they felt exalted, ennobled, exhilarated, possessed of any rare and exotic emotion. They were human beings before they were pickets. Their reactions were those of any human beings called upon to set their teeth doggedly and hang on to an unpleasant job.

"When *will* that woman come to relieve me? I have stood here an hour and a half and my feet are like blocks of ice," was a more frequent comment from picket to picket than "Isn't it glorious to stand here defiantly no matter what the stupid people say about us?"

"I remember the thousand and one engaging things that would come to my mind on the picket line. It seemed that anything but standing at a President's gate would be more diverting. But there we stood.

And what were the reflections of a President as he saw the indomitable little army at his gates? We can only venture to say from events which happened. At first he seemed amused and interested. Perhaps he thought it a trifling incident staged by a minority of the extreme "left" among suffragists and anticipated no popular support for it. When he saw their persistence through a cruel winter his sympathy was touched. He ordered the guards to invite them in for a cup of hot coffee, which they declined. He raised his hat to them as he drove through the line. Sometimes he smiled. As yet he was not irritated. He was fortified in his national power.

With the country's entrance into the war and his immediate elevation to world leadership, the pickets began to be a serious thorn in his flesh. His own statements of faith in democracy and the necessity for establishing it throughout the world left him open to attack. His refusal to pay the just bill owed the women and demanded by them brought irritation.

What would *you* do if you owed a just bill and every day some one stood outside your gates as a quiet reminder to the whole world that you had not paid it?

You would object. You would get terribly irritated. You would call the insistent one all kinds of harsh names. You might even arrest him. But the scandal would be out.

Rightly or wrongly, your sincerity would be touched; faith in you would be shaken a bit. Perhaps even against your will you would yield.

But you *would* yield. And that was the one important fact to the women.

This daily sight, inspiring, gallant and impressive, escaped no visitor to the national capital. Distinguished visitors from the far corners of the earth passed by the pickets on those days which made history. Thousands read the compelling messages on the banners, and literally hundreds of thousands learned the story, when the visitors got "back home."

Real displeasure over the sentinels by those who passed was negligible. There was some mirth and joking, but the vast

majority were filled with admiration, either silent or expressed.
"Keep it up." . . . "You are on the right track." . . .
"Congratulations." . . . "I certainly admire your pluck—
stick to it and you will get it." . . . This last from a military
officer. . . . "It is an outrage that you women should have to
stand here and beg for your rights. We gave it to our women
in Australia long ago." . . . This from a charming gentleman
who bowed approvingly.

Often a lifted hat was held in sincere reverence over the
heart as some courteous gentleman passed along the picket line.
Of course there were some who came to try to argue with the
pickets; who attempted to dissuade them from their persistent
course. But the serene, good humor and even temper of the
women would not allow heated arguments to break in on the
military precision of their line. If a question was asked, a
picket would answer quietly. An occasional sneer was easy
to meet. That required no acknowledgment.

A sweet old veteran of the Civil War said to one of my
comrades: "Yous all right; you gotta fight for your rights
in this world, and now that we are about to plunge into another
war, I want to tell you women there'll be no end to it unless
you women get power. We can't save ourselves and we need
you. . . . I am 84 years old, and I have watched this fight
since I was a young man. Anything I can do to help, I want
to do. I am living at the Old Soldiers' Home and I ain't got
much money, but here's something for your campaign. It's
all I got, and God bless you, you've gotta win." He spoke the
last sentence almost with desperation as he shoved a crumpled
$2.00 bill into her hand. His spirit made it a precious gift.

Cabinet members passed and repassed. Congressmen by the
hundreds came and went. Administration leaders tried to conceal under an artificial indifference their sensitiveness to our
strategy.

And domestic battles were going on inside the homes

throughout the country, for women were coming from every
state in the Union, to take their place on the line. For the
first time good "suffrage-husbands" were made uncomfortable.
Had they not always believed in suffrage? Had they not always been uncomplaining when their wife's time was given to
suffrage campaigning? Had they not, in short, been good
sports about the whole thing? There was only one answer.
They had. But it had been proved that all the things that
women had done and all the things in which their menfolk had
coöperated, were not enough. Women were called upon for
more intensive action. "You cannot go to Washington and
risk your health standing in front of the White House. I
cannot have it."

"But the time has come when we have to take risks of health
or anything else."

"Well, then, if you must know, I don't believe in it. Now
I am a reasonable man and I have stood by you all the way
up to now, but I object to this. It isn't ladylike, and it will do
the cause more harm than good. You women lay yourselves
open to ridicule."

"That's just it—that's a fine beginning. As soon as men
get tired laughing at us, they will do something more about it.
They won't find our campaign so amusing before long."

"But I protest. You've no right to go without considering
me."

"But if your country called you in a fight for democracy,
as it is likely to do at any moment, you'd go, wouldn't you?"

"Why, of course."

"Of course you would. You would go to the front and
leave me to struggle on as best I could without you. That is
the way you would respond to your country's call, whether it
was a righteous cause or not. Well, I am going to the front
too. I am going to answer the women's call to fight for democracy. I would be ashamed of myself if I were not willing to

join my comrades. I am sorry that you object, but if you will just put yourself in my place you will see that I cannot do otherwise."

It must be recorded that there were exceptional men of sensitive imaginations who urged women against their own hesitancy. They are the handful who gave women a hope that they would not always have to struggle alone for their liberation. And women passed by the daily picket line as spectators, not as participants. Occasionally a woman came forward to remonstrate, but more often women were either too shy to advance or so enthusiastic that nothing could restrain them. The more kind-hearted of them, inspired by the dauntless pickets in the midst of a now freezing temperature, brought mittens, fur pieces, golashes, wool-lined raincoats; hot bricks to stand on, coffee in thermos bottles and what not.

Meanwhile the pickets became a household word in Washington, and very soon were the subject of animated conversation in practically every corner of the nation. The Press cartoonists, by their friendly and satirical comments, helped a great deal in popularizing the campaign. In spite of the bitter editorial comment of most of the press, the humor of the situation had an almost universal appeal.

At the Washington dinner of the Gridiron Club, probably the best known press club in the world,—a dinner at which President Wilson was a guest,—one of the songs sung for his benefit was as follows:

"We're camping to-night on the White House grounds
    Give us a rousing cheer;
Our golden flag we hold aloft, of cops we have no fear.
    Many of the pickets are weary to-night,
Wishing for the war to cease; many are the chilblains and
    frost-bites too;
    It is no life of ease.

Camping to-night, camping to-night,
Camping on the White House grounds."

The White House police on duty at the gates came to treat the picketers as comrades.

"I was kinda worried," confessed one burly officer when the pickets were five minutes late one day. "We thought perhaps you weren't coming and we would have to hold down this place alone."

The bitter-enders among the opponents of suffrage broke into such violent criticism that they won new friends to the amendment.

People who had never before thought of suffrage for women had to think of it, if only to the extent of objecting to the way in which we asked for it. People who had thought a little about suffrage were compelled to think more about it. People who had believed in suffrage all their lives, but had never done a stroke of work for it, began to make speeches about it, if only for the purpose of condemning us.

Some politicians who had voted for it when there were not enough votes to carry the measure loudly threatened to commit political suicide by withdrawing their support. But it was easy to see at a glance that they would not dare to run so great a political risk on an issue growing daily more important.

As soon as the regular picket line began to be accepted as a matter of course, we undertook to touch it up a bit to sustain public interest. State days were inaugurated, beginning with Maryland. The other states took up the idea with enthusiasm. There was a College Day, when women representing 15 American colleges stood on the line; a Teachers' Day, which found the long line represented by almost every state in the Union, and a Patriotic Day, when American flags mingled with the party's banners carried by representatives of the Women's Reserve Corps, Daughters of the Revolution and other patriotic organizations. And there were professional days when women doctors, lawyers and nurses joined the picket appeal.

Lincoln's birthday anniversary saw another new feature.

A long line of women took out banners bearing the slogans:

LINCOLN STOOD FOR WOMAN SUFFRAGE 60 YEARS AGO.
MR. PRESIDENT, WHY DO YOU BLOCK THE NATIONAL
SUFFRAGE AMENDMENT TO-DAY?

WHY ARE YOU BEHIND LINCOLN?

and another:

AFTER THE CIVIL WAR, WOMEN ASKED FOR POLITICAL
FREEDOM. THEY WERE TOLD TO WAIT—THIS WAS THE
NEGRO'S HOUR. IN 1917 AMERICAN WOMEN STILL ASK
FOR FREEDOM.
WILL YOU, MR. PRESIDENT, TELL THEM TO WAIT—
THAT THIS IS THE PORTO RICAN'S HOUR? [1]

A huge labor demonstration on the picket line late in February brought women wage earners from office and factory throughout the Eastern States.

A special Susan B. Anthony Day on the anniversary of the birth of that great pioneer, served to remind the President who said, "You can afford to wait," that the women had been waiting and fighting for this legislation to pass Congress since the year 1878.

More than one person came forward to speak with true religious fervor of the memory of the great Susan B. Anthony. Her name is never mentioned nor her words quoted without finding such a response.

In the face of heavy snow and rain, dozens of young women stood in line, holding special banners made for this occasion. Thousands of men and women streaming home from work in the early evening read words of hers spoken during the Civil

[1] President Wilson had just advocated self-government for Porto Rican men.

War, so completely applicable to the policy of the young banner-bearers at the gates.

WE PRESS OUR DEMAND FOR THE BALLOT AT THIS
TIME IN NO NARROW, CAPIOUS OR SELFISH SPIRIT, BUT
FROM PUREST PATRIOTISM FOR THE HIGHEST GOOD OF
EVERY CITIZEN, FOR THE SAFETY OF THE REPUBLIC
AND AS A GLORIOUS EXAMPLE TO THE NATIONS OF THE
EARTH.

AT THIS TIME OUR GREATEST NEED IS NOT MEN OR
MONEY, VALIANT GENERALS OR BRILLIANT VICTORIES,
BUT A CONSISTENT NATIONAL POLICY BASED UPON THE
PRINCIPLE THAT ALL GOVERNMENTS DERIVE THEIR
JUST POWERS FROM THE CONSENT OF THE GOVERNED.

THE RIGHT OF SELF-GOVERNMENT FOR ONE-HALF OF
ITS PEOPLE IS OF FAR MORE VITAL CONSEQUENCE TO
THE NATION THAN ANY OR ALL OTHER QUESTIONS.

During the reunion week of the Daughters and Veterans of the Confederacy, the picket line was the center of attraction for the sight-seeing veterans and their families. For the first time in history the troops of the Confederacy had crossed the Potomac and taken possession of the capital city. The streets were lined with often tottering but still gallant old men, white-haired and stooped, wearing their faded badges on their gray uniforms, and carrying their tattered flags.

It seemed to the young women on picket duty during those days that not a single veteran had failed to pay his respects to the pickets. They came and came; and some brought back their wives to show them the guard at the gates.

One old soldier with tears in his dim eyes came to say, "I've done sentinel duty in my time. I know what it is. . . .

And now it's your turn. You young folks have the strength and the courage to keep it up. . . . You are going to put it through!"

One sweet old Alabamian came shyly up to one of the pickets and said, "I say, Miss, this *is* the White House, isn't it?"

Before she could answer, he added: "We went three times around the place and I told the boys, the big white house in the center was the White House, but they wasn't believing me and I wasn't sure, but as soon as I saw you girls coming with your flags, to stand here, I said, 'This *must* be the White House. This is sure enough where the President lives; here are the pickets with their banners that we read about down home.'" A note of triumph was in his frail voice.

The picket smiled, and thanked him warmly, as he finished with, "You are brave girls. You are bound to get him"— pointing his shaking finger toward the White House.

President Wilson's second inauguration was rapidly approaching. Also war clouds were gathering with all the increased emotionalism that comes at such a crisis. Some additional demonstration of power and force must be made before the President's inauguration and before the excitement of our entry into the war should plunge our agitation into obscurity. This was the strategic moment to assemble our forces in convention in Washington.

Accordingly, the Congressional Union for Woman Suffrage and the Woman's Party, that section of the Congressional Union in suffrage states made up of women voters, convened in Washington and decided unanimously to unite their strength, money and political power in one organization, and called it the National Woman's Party.

The following officers were unanimously elected to direct the activities of the new organization: Chairman of the National Woman's Party, Miss Alice Paul, New Jersey; vice-

chairman, Miss Anne Martin, Nevada; secretary, Miss Mabel
Vernon, Nevada; treasurer, Miss Gertrude Crocker, Illinois;
executive members, Miss Lucy Burns, Mrs. O. H. P. Belmont,
Mrs. John Winters Brannan, New York; Mrs. Gilson Gardner,
Illinois; Mrs. Robert Baker, Washington, D. C.; Mrs. William
Kent and Miss Maud Younger, California; Mrs. Florence
Bayard Hilles, Delaware; Mrs. Donald Hooker, Maryland;
Mrs. J. A. H. Hopkins, New Jersey; Mrs. Lawrence Lewis,
Pennsylvania, and Miss Doris Stevens, Nebraska.

The convention came to a close on the eve of inauguration,
culminating in the dramatic picket line made up of one thousand delegates who sought an interview with the President.
The purpose of the interview was to carry to him the resolutions of the convention, and further plead with him to open his
second administration with a promise to back the amendment.

In our optimism we hoped that this glorified picket-pageant
might form a climax to our three months of picketing. The
President admired persistence. He said so. He also said he
appreciated the rare tenacity shown by our women. Surely
"now" he would be convinced! No more worrying persistence
would be needed! The combined political strength of the
western women and the financial strength of the eastern
women would surely command his respect and entitle us to a
hearing.

What actually happened?

It was a day of high wind and stinging, icy rain, that
March 4th, 1917, when a thousand women, each bearing a
banner, struggled against the gale to keep their banners erect.
It is always impressive to see a thousand people march, but
the impression was imperishable when these thousand women
marched in rain-soaked garments, hands bare, gloves roughly
torn by the sticky varnish from the banner poles and the
streams of water running down the poles into the palms of
their hands. It was a sight to impress even the most hardened

spectator who had seen all the various forms of the suffrage agitation in Washington. For more than two hours the women circled the White House—the rain never ceasing for an instant—hoping to the last moment that at least their leaders would be allowed to take in to the President the resolutions which they were carrying.

Long before the appointed hour for the march to start, thousands of spectators sheltered by umbrellas and raincoats lined the streets to watch the procession. Two bands whose men managed to continue their spirited music in spite of the driving rain led the march playing "Forward Be Our Watchword"; "The Battle Hymn of the Republic"; "Onward Christian Soldiers"; "The Pilgrim's Chorus" from Tannhäuser; "The Coronation March" from Le Prophēte, the Russian Hymn and "The Marsellaise."

Miss Vida Milholland led the procession carrying her sister's last words, "Mr. President, how long must women wait for liberty?" She was followed by Miss Beulah Amidon of North Dakota, who carried the banner that the beloved Inez Milholland carried in her first suffrage procession in New York.

The long line of women fell in behind.

Most extraordinary precautions had been taken about the White House. Everything had been done except the important thing. There were almost as many police officers as marchers. The Washington force had been augmented by a Baltimore contingent and squads of plainclothes men. On every fifty feet of curb around the entire White House grounds there was a policeman. About the same distance apart on the inside of the tall picket-fence which surrounds the grounds were as many more.

We proceeded to the main gate. Locked! I was marshalling at the head of the line and so heard first hand what passed between the leaders and the guards. Miss Anne Martin addressed the guard—

"We have come to present some important resolutions to the President of the United States."

"I have orders to keep the gates locked, Ma'am."

"But there must be some mistake. Surely the President does not mean to refuse to see at least . . ."

"Those are my only orders, Ma'am."

The procession continued on to the second gate on Pennsylvania Avenue. Again locked. Before we could address the somewhat nervous policeman who stood at the gates, he hastened to say, "You can't come in here; the gates are locked."

"But it is imperative; we are a thousand women from all States in the Union who have come all the way to Washington to see the President and lay before him . . ."

"No orders, Ma'am."

The line made its way to the third and last gate—the gate leading to the Executive offices. As we came up to this gate a small army of grinning clerks and secretaries manned the windows of the Executive offices, evidently amused at the sight of the women struggling in the wind and rain to keep their banners intact. Miss Martin, Mrs. William Kent of California, Mrs. Florence Bayard Hilles of Delaware, Miss Mary Patterson of Ohio, niece of John C. Patterson of Dayton, Mrs. J. A. H. Hopkins of New Jersey, Miss Eleanor Barker of Indiana, and Mrs. Mary Darrow Weible of North Dakota,—the leaders —stayed at the gate, determined to get results from the guard, while the women continued to circle the White House.

"Will you not carry a message to the President's Secretary asking him to tell the President that we are here waiting to see him?"

"Can't do that, Ma'am."

"Will you then take our cards to the Secretary to the President, merely announcing to him that we are here, so that he may send somebody to carry in our resolutions?"

Still the guard hesitated. Finally he left the gate and

carried the message a distance of a few rods into the Executive offices. He had scarcely got inside when he rushed back to his post. When we sought to ascertain what had happened to the cards—had they been given and what the answer was—he quietly confided to us that he had been reprimanded for even attempting to bring them in and informed us that the cards were still in his pocket.

"I have orders to answer no questions and to carry no messages. If you have anything to leave here you might take it to the entrance below the Executive offices, and when I go off my beat at six o'clock I will leave it as I go by the White House."

We examined this last entrance suggested. It did not strike us as the proper place to leave an important message for the President.

"What is this entrance used for?" I asked the guard.

"It's all right, lady. If you've got something you'd like to leave, leave it with me. It will be safe."

I retorted that we were not seeking safety for our message, but speed in delivery.

The guard continued: "This is the gate where Mrs. Wilson's clothes and other packages are left."

It struck us as scarcely fitting that we should leave our resolutions amongst "Mrs. Wilson's clothes and other packages," so we returned to the last locked gate to ask the guard if he had any message in the meantime for us. He shook his head regretfully.

Meanwhile the women marched and marched, and the rain fell harder and as the afternoon wore on the cold seemed almost unendurable.

The white-haired grandmothers in the procession—there were some as old as 84—were as energetic as the young girls of 20. What was this immediate hardship compared to eternal subjection! Women marched and waited—waited and marched, under the sting of the biting elements and under the worse sting of the indignities heaped upon them. It was impossible to believe that in democratic America they could not see the President to lay before him their grievance.

It was only when they saw the Presidential limousine, in the late afternoon, roll luxuriously out of the grounds, and through the gates down Pennsylvania Avenue, that the weary marchers realized that President Wilson had deliberately turned them away unheard!

The car for an instant, as it came through the gates, divided the banner-bearers on march. President and Mrs. Wilson looked straight ahead as if the long line of purple, white and gold were invisible.

All the women who took part in that march will tell you what was burning in their hearts on that dreary day. Even if reasons had been offered—and they were not—genuine reasons why the President could not see them, it would not have cooled the women's heat. Their passionate resentment went deeper than any reason could possibly have gone.

This one single incident probably did more than any other to make women sacrifice themselves. Even something as thin as diplomacy on the part of President Wilson might have saved him many restless hours to follow, but he did not take the trouble to exercise even that.

The women returned to headquarters and there wrote a letter which was dispatched with the resolutions to President Wilson. In a letter to the National Woman's Party, acknowledging the receipt of them, he concluded by saying: "May I not once more express my sincere interest in the cause of woman suffrage?"

Three months of picketing had not been enough. We must not only continue on duty at his gates but also at the gates of Congress.

CHAPTER 2

THE SUFFRAGE WAR POLICY

P RESIDENT WILSON called the War Session of the Sixty-fifth Congress on April 2, 1917.

On the opening day of Congress not only were the pickets again on duty at the White House, but another picket line was inaugurated at the Capitol. Returning senators and congressmen were surprised when greeted with great golden banners reading:

RUSSIA AND ENGLAND ARE ENFRANCHISING THEIR WOMEN IN WAR-TIME. HOW LONG MUST AMERICAN WOMEN WAIT FOR THEIR LIBERTY?

The last desperate flurries in the pro-war and anti-war camps were focused on the Capitol grounds that day. There swarmed about the grounds and through the buildings pacifists from all over the country wearing white badges, and advocates of war, wearing the national colors. Our sentinels at the Capitol stood strangely silent, and almost aloof, strong in their dedication to democracy, while the peace and war agitation circled about them.

With lightning speed the President declared that a state of war existed. Within a fortnight following, Congress declared war on Germany and President Wilson voiced his memorable, "We shall fight for the things we have always carried nearest our hearts—for democracy—for the right of those who submit to authority to have a voice in their own government." Inspiring words indeed! The war message concluded with still another defense of the fight for political liberty: "To such a task we can dedicate our lives and our fortunes, everything that we are and everything that we have, with the pride of those who know that the day has come when America is privileged to spend her blood and her might for the principles that gave her birth and happiness and the peace which she has treasured. God helping her, she can do no less."

Now that the United States was actually involved in war, we were face to face with the question, which we had considered at the convention the previous month, when war was rumored, as to what position we, as an organization, should take in this situation.

The atmosphere of that convention had been dramatic in the extreme. Most of the delegates assembled had been approached either before going to Washington or upon arriving, and urged to use their influence to persuade the organization to abandon its work for the freedom of women and turn its activities into war channels. Although war was then only rumored, the hysterical attitude was already prevalent. Women were asked to furl their banners and give up their half century struggle for democracy, to forget the liberty that was most precious to their hearts.

"The President will turn this Imperialistic war into a crusade for democracy." . . . "Lay aside your own fight and help us crush Germany, and you will find yourselves rewarded with a vote out of the nation's gratitude," were some of the appeals made to our women by government officials high and low and by the rank and file of men and women. Never in history did a band of women stand together with more sanity and greater solidarity than did these 1000 delegates representing thousands more throughout the States.

As our official organ, *The Suffragist*, pointed out editorially, in its issue of April 21st, 1917: Our membership was made up of women who had banded together to secure political freedom for women. We were united on no other subject. Some would offer passive resistance to the war; others would become devoted followers of a vigorous military policy. Between these, every shade of opinion was represented. Each was loyal to the ideas which she held for her country. With the character of these various ideals, the National Woman's Party, we maintained, had nothing to do. It was concerned only with the effort to obtain for women the opportunity to give effective expression, through political power, to their ideals, whatever they might be.

The thousand delegates present at the convention, though differing widely on the duty of the individual in war, were unanimous in voting that in the event of war, the National Woman's Party, *as an organization,* should continue to work for political liberty for women and for that alone, believing as the convention stated in its resolutions, that in so doing the organization "serves the highest interest of the country." They were also unanimous in the opinion that all service which *individuals* wished to give to war or peace should be given through groups organized for such purposes, and not through the Woman's Party, a body created, according to its constitution, for one purpose only—"to secure an amendment to the United States Constitution enfranchising women."

We declared officially through our organ that this held "as the policy of the Woman's Party, whatever turn public events may take."

Very few days after we were put upon a national war basis it became clear that never was there greater need of work for internal freedom in the country. Europe, then approaching her third year of war, was increasing democracy in the midst of the terrible conflict. In America at that very moment women were being told that no attempt at electoral reform had any place in the country's program "until the war is over." The Democrats met in caucus and decided that only "war measures" should be included in the legislative program, and announced that no subjects would be considered by them, unless the President urged them as war measures.

Our task was, from that time on, to make national suffrage a war measure.

We at once urged upon the Administration the wisdom of accepting this proposed reform as a war measure, and pointed out the difficulty of waging a war for democracy abroad while democracy was denied at home. But the government was not willing to profit by the experience of its Allies in extending suffrage to women, without first offering a terrible and brutal resistance.

We must confess that the problem of dramatizing our fight for democracy in competition with the drama of a world-war, was most perplexing. Here were we, citizens without power and recognition, with the only weapons to which a powerless class which does not take up arms can resort. We could not and would not fight with men's weapons. Compare the methods women adopted to those men use in the pursuit of democracy,—bayonets, machine guns, poison gas, deadly grenades, liquid fire, bombs, armored tanks, pistols, barbed wire entanglements, submarines, mines—every known scientific device with which to annihilate the enemy!

What did we do?

We continued to fight with our simple, peaceful, almost quaint device—a banner. A little more fiery, perhaps; pertinent to the latest political controversy, but still only a banner inscribed with militant truth!

Just as our political strategy had been to oppose, at elections, the party in power which had failed to use its power to free women, so now our military strategy was based on the military doctrine of concentrating all one's forces on the enemy's weakest point. To women the weakest point in the

Administration's political lines during the war was the inconsistency between a crusade for world democracy and the denial of democracy at home. This was the untenable position of President Wilson and the Democratic Administration, from which we must force them to retreat. We could force such a retreat when we had exposed to the world this weakest point.

Just as the bluff of a democratic crusade must be called, so must the knight-leader of the crusade be exposed to the critical eyes of the world. Here was the President, suddenly elevated to the position of a world leader with the almost pathetic trust of the peoples of the world. Here was the champion of their democratic aspirations. Here was a kind of universal Moses, expected to lead all peoples out of bondage— no matter what the bondage, no matter of how long standing.

The President's elevation to this unique pinnacle of power was at once an advantage and a disadvantage to us. It was an advantage to us in that it made our attack more dramatic. One supposed to be impeccable was more vulnerable. It was a disadvantage to have to overcome this universal trust and world-wide popularity. But this conflict of wits and brains against power only enhanced our ingenuity.

On the day the English mission headed by Mr. Balfour, and the French mission headed by M. Viviani, visited the White House, we took these inscriptions to the picket line:

WE SHALL FIGHT FOR THE THINGS WE HAVE ALWAYS CARRIED
NEAREST OUR HEARTS

DEMOCRACY SHOULD BEGIN AT HOME

WE DEMAND JUSTICE AND SELF-GOVERNMENT IN OUR OWN LAND

Embarrassing to say these things before foreign visitors? We hoped it would be. In our capacity to embarrass Mr. Wilson in his Administration, lay our only hope of success. We had to keep before the country the flagrant inconsistency of the President's position. We intended to know why, if democracy were so precious as to demand the nation's blood and treasure for its achievement abroad, its execution at home was so undesirable.

Meanwhile:—

"I tell you solemnly, ladies and gentlemen, we cannot any longer postpone justice in these United States"—President Wilson.

"I don't wish to sit down and let any man take care of me without my at least having a voice in it, and if he doesn't listen to my advice, I am going to make it as unpleasant as I can."—President Wilson,—and other challenges were carried on banners to the picket line.

Some rumblings of political action began to be heard. The Democratic majority had appointed a Senate Committee on Woman Suffrage whose members were overwhelmingly for federal action. The chairman, Senator Andreas Jones of New Mexico, promised an early report to the Senate. There were scores of gains in Congress. Representatives and Senators were tumbling over each other to introduce similar suffrage resolutions. We actually had difficulty in choosing the man whose name should stamp our measure.

A minority party also was moved to act. Members of the Progressive Party met in convention in St. Louis on April 12, 13 and 14 and adopted a suffrage plank which demanded "the nation-wide enfranchiseemnt of women. . . ."

In addition to this plank they adopted a resolution calling for the establishment of democracy at home "at a time when the United States is entering into an international war for democracy" and instructing the chairman of the convention "to request a committee consisting of representatives of all liberal groups to go to Washington to present to the President and the Congress of the United States a demand for immediate submission of an amendment to the United States constitution enfranchising women."

They appointed a committee from the convention to carry these resolutions to the President. The committee included Mr. J. A. H. Hopkins of the Progressive Party, as chairman; Dr. E. A. Rumley of the Progressive-Republican Party and Vice President of the New York *Evening Mail;* Mr. John Spargo of the Socialist Party; Mr. Virgil Hinshaw, chairman of the Executive Committee of the Prohibition Party; and Miss Mabel Vernon, Secretary of the National Woman's Party. It was the first suffrage conference with the President after the declaration of war, and was the last deputation on suffrage by minority party leaders. The conference was one of the utmost informality and friendliness.

The President was deeply moved, indeed, almost to the point of tears, when Miss Mabel Vernon said, "Mr. President, the feelings of many women in this country are best expressed by your own words in your war message to Congress. . . . To every woman who reads that message must come at once this question: If the right of those who submit to authority to have a voice in their own government is so sacred a cause to foreign people as to constitute the reason for our entering the international war in its defense, will you not, Mr. President, give immediate aid to the measure before Congress demanding self-government for the women of this country?"

The President admitted that suffrage was constantly pressing upon his mind for reconsideration. He added, however, that the program for the session was practically complete and intimated that it did not include the enfranchisement of women.

He informed the Committee that he had written a letter to Mr. Pou, Chairman of the Rules Committee of the House, expressing himself as favoring the creation of a Woman Suffrage Committee in that body. While we had no objection to having the House create a Suffrage Committee, we were not primarily interested in the amplification of Congressional machinery, unless this amplification was to be followed by the passage of the amendment. The President could as easily have written the Senate Committee on Suffrage or the Judiciary Committee of the House, advising an immediate report on the suffrage resolution, as have asked for the creation of another committee to report on the subject.

He made no mention of his state-by-state conviction, however, as he had in previous interviews, and the Committee of Progressives understood him to have at least tacitly accepted federal action.

The House Judiciary Committee continued to refuse to act and the House Rules Committee steadily refused to create a Suffrage Committee.

Hoping to win back to the fold the wandering Progressives who had thus demonstrated their allegiance to suffrage and seeing an opportunity to embarrass the Administration, the Republicans began to interest themselves in action on the amendment. In the midst of Democratic delays, Representative James R. Mann, Republican leader of the House, moved to discharge the Judiciary Committee from further consideration of the suffrage amendment. No matter if the discussion which followed did revolve about the authorization of an expenditure of $10,000 for the erection of a monument to a dead President as a legitimate war measure. It was clear from the partisan attitude of those who took part in the debate that we were advancing to that position where we were as good political material to be contested over by opposing political groups as was a monument to a dead President. And if the Democrats could defend such an issue as a war measure, the Republicans wanted to know why they should ignore suffrage for women as a war measure. And it was encouraging to find ourselves thus suddenly and spontaneously sponsored by the Republican leader.

The Administration was aroused. It did not know how far the Republicans were prepared to go in their drive for action, so on the day of this flurry in the House the snail-like Rules Committee suddenly met in answer to the call of its chairman, Mr. Pou, and by a vote of 6 to 5 decided to report favorably on the resolution providing for a Woman Suffrage Committee in the House *"after all pending war measures have been disposed of."*

Before the meeting, Mr. Pou made a last appeal to the Woman's Party to remove the pickets. . . . "We can't possibly win as long as pickets guard the White House and Capitol," Mr. Pou had said. The pickets continued their vigil and the motion carried.

Still uncertain as to the purposes of the Republicans, the Democrats were moved to further action.

The Executive Committee of the Democratic National Committee, meeting in Washington a few days later, voted 4 to 2 to "officially urge upon the President that he call the two Houses of Congress together and recommend the immediate submission of the Susan B. Anthony amendment." This action which in effect reversed the plank in the Democratic platform evidently aroused protests from powerful quarters. Also the Republicans quickly subsided when they saw the Democrats making an advance. And so the Democratic Executive Committee began to spread abroad the news that its act was not really official, but merely reflected the "personal conviction" of the members present. It extracted the official flavor, and so of course no action followed in Congress.

And so it went—like a great game of chess. Doubtless the politicians believed they were moved from their own true and noble motives. The fact was that the pickets had moved the Democrats a step. The Republicans had then attempted to take two steps, whereupon the Democrats must continue to move more rapidly than their opponents. Behind this matching of political wits by the two parties stood the faithful pickets compelling them both to act.

Simultaneously with these moves and counter-moves in political circles, the people in all sections of this vast country began to speak their minds. Meetings were springing up everywhere, at which resolutions were passed backing up the picket line and urging the President and Congress to act. Even the South, the Administration's stronghold, sent fiery telegrams demanding action. Alabama, South Carolina, Texas, Maryland, Mississippi, as well as the West, Middle West, New England and the East—the stream was endless.

Every time a new piece of legislation was passed,—the war tax bill, food conservation or what not,—women from unexpected quarters sent to the Government their protest against the passage of measures so vital to women without women's consent, coupled with an appeal for the liberation of women. Club women, college women, federations of labor,—various kinds of organizations sent protests to the Administration leaders. The picket line, approaching its sixth month of duty, had aroused the country to an unprecedented interest in suffrage; it had rallied widespread public support to the amendment as a war measure, and had itself become almost universally accepted if not universally approved. And in the midst of picketing and in spite of all the prophecies and fears that "picketing" would "set back the cause," within one month, Michigan, Nebraska and Rhode Island granted Presidential suffrage to women.

The leaders were busy marshaling their forces behind the President's war program, which included the controversial Conscription and Espionage Bills, then pending, and did not relish having our question so vivid in the public mind. Even when the rank and file of Congress gave consideration to questions not

in the war program, they had to face a possible charge of inconsistency, insincerity or bad faith. The freedom of Ireland, for
example, was not in the program. And when 132 members of
the House cabled Lloyd George that nothing would do more
for American enthusiasm in the war than a settlement of the
Irish question, we took pains to ascertain the extent of the
belief in liberty at home of these easy champions of Irish liberty. When we found that of the 132 men only 57 believed in
liberty for American women, we were not delicate in pointing
out to the remaining 75 that their belief in liberty for Ireland
would appear more sincere if they believed in a democratic
reform such as woman suffrage here.

The manifestations of popular approval of suffrage, the
constant stream of protests to the Administration against its
delay nationally, and the shame of having women begging at
its gates, could result in only one of two things. The Administration had little choice. It must yield to this pressure from
the people or it must suppress the agitation which was causing
such interest. It must pass the amendment or remove the
troublesome pickets.

It decided to remove the pickets.

CHAPTER 3

THE Administration chose suppression. They resorted to force in an attempt to end picketing. It was a policy doomed to failure as certainly as all resorts to force to kill agitation have failed ultimately. This marked the beginning of the adoption by the Administration of tactics from which they could never extricate themselves with honor. Unfortunately for them they were entering upon this policy toward women which savored of czarist practices, at the very moment they were congratulating the Russians upon their liberation from the oppression of a Czar. This fact supplied us with a fresh angle of attack.

President Wilson sent a Mission to Russia to add America's appeal to that of the other Allies to keep that impoverished country in the war. Such was our democratic zeal to persuade Russia to continue the war and to convince her people of its democratic purposes, and of the democratic quality of America, that Elihu Root, one of the President's envoys, stated in Petrograd that he represented a republic where "universal, direct, equal and secret suffrage obtained." We subjected the President to attack through this statement.

Russia also sent a war mission to our country for purposes of coöperation. This occasion offered us the opportunity again to expose the Administration's weakness in claiming complete political democracy while women were still denied their political freedom.

It was a beautiful June day when all Washington was agog

with the visit of the Russian diplomats to the President. As the car carrying the envoys passed swiftly through the gates of the White House there stood on the picket line two silent sentinels, Miss Lucy Burns of New York and Mrs. Lawrence Lewis of Philadelphia, both members of the National Executive Committee, with a great lettered banner which read:

TO THE RUSSIAN ENVOYS

PRESIDENT WILSON AND ENVOY ROOT ARE DECEIVING RUSSIA WHEN THEY SAY "WE ARE A DEMOCRACY, HELP US WIN THE WORLD WAR SO THAT DEMOCRACY MAY SURVIVE."

WE THE WOMEN OF AMERICA TELL YOU THAT AMERICA IS NOT A DEMOCRACY. TWENTY-MILLION AMERICAN WOMEN ARE DENIED THE RIGHT TO VOTE. PRESIDENT WILSON IS THE CHIEF OPPONENT OF THEIR NATIONAL ENFRANCHISEMENT.

HELP US MAKE THIS NATION REALLY FREE. TELL OUR GOVERNMENT IT MUST LIBERATE ITS PEOPLE BEFORE IT CAN CLAIM FREE RUSSIA AS AN ALLY.

Rumors that the suffragists would make a special demonstration before the Russian Mission had brought a great crowd to the far gate of the White House; a crowd composed almost entirely of men.

Like all crowds, this crowd had its share of hoodlums and roughs who tried to interfere with the women's order of the day. There was a flurry of excitement over this defiant message of truth, but nothing that could not with the utmost ease have been settled by one policeman.

There was the criticism in the press and on the lips of men that we were embarrassing our Government before the eyes of foreign visitors. In answering the criticism, Miss Paul publicly stated our position thus: "The intolerable conditions against which we protest can be changed in the twinkling of an eye. The responsibility for our protest is, therefore, with the Administration and not with the women of America, if the lack of democracy at home weakens the Administration in its fight for democracy three thousand miles away."

This was too dreadful. A flurry at the gates of the Chief of the nation at such a time would never do. Our allies in the crusade for democracy must not know that we had a day-by-day unrest at home. Something must be done to stop this exposé at once. Had these women no manners? Had they no shame? Was the fundamental weakness in our boast of pure and perfect democracy to be so wantonly displayed with impunity?

Of course it was embarrassing. We meant it to be. The truth must be told at all costs. This was no time for manners.

Hurried conferences behind closed doors! Summoning of the military to discuss declaring a military zone around the White House! Women could not advance on drawn bayonets. And if they did . . . What a picture! Common decency told the more humane leaders that this would never do. I daresay political wisdom crept into the reasoning of others.

Closing the Woman's Party headquarters was discussed. Perhaps a raid! And all for what? Because women were holding banners asking for the precious principle at home that men were supposed to be dying for abroad.

Finally a decision was reached embodying the combined wisdom of all the various conferees. The Chief of Police, Major Pullman, was detailed to "request" us to stop "picketing" and to tell us that if we continued to picket, we would be arrested.

"We have picketed for six months without interference," said Miss Paul. *"Has the law been changed?"*

"No," was the reply, "but you must stop it."

"But, Major Pullman, we have consulted our lawyers and know we have a legal right to picket."

"I warn you, you will be arrested if you attempt to picket again."

The following day Miss Lucy Burns and Miss Katherine Morey of Boston carried to the White House gates "We shall fight for the things we have always held nearest our hearts, for democracy, for the right of those who submit to authority to have a voice in their own government," and were arrested.

News had spread through the city that the pickets were to be arrested. A moderately large crowd had gathered to see the "fun." One has only to come into conflict with prevailing authority, whether rightly or wrongly, to find friendly hosts vanishing with lightning speed. To know that we were no longer wanted at the gates of the White House and that the police were no longer our "friends" was enough for the mob mind.

Some members of the crowd made sport of the women. Others hurled cheap and childish epithets at them. Small boys were allowed to capture souvenirs, shreds of the banners torn from non-resistant women, as trophies of the sport.

Thinking they had been mistaken in believing the pickets were to be arrested, and having grown weary of their strenuous sport, the crowd moved on its way. Two solitary figures remained, standing on the sidewalk, flanked by the vast Pennsylvania Avenue, looking quite abandoned and alone, when suddenly without any warrant in law, they were arrested on a completely deserted avenue.

Miss Burns and Miss Morey upon arriving at the police station, insisted, to the great surprise of all the officials, upon knowing the charge against them. Major Pullman and his entire staff were utterly at a loss to know what to answer. The Administration had looked ahead only as far as threatening arrest. They doubtless thought this was all they would have to do. People could not be arrested for picketing. Picketing is a guaranteed right under the Clayton Act of

Congress. Disorderly conduct? There had been no disorderly conduct. Inciting to riot? Impossible! The women had stood as silent sentinels holding the President's own eloquent words.

Doors opened and closed mysteriously. Officials and sub-officials passed hurriedly to and fro. Whispered conversations were heard. The book on rules and regulations was hopefully thumbed. Hours passed. Finally the two prisoners were pompously told that they had "obstructed the traffic" on Pennsylvania Avenue, were dismissed on their own recognizance, and never brought to trial.

The following day, June 23rd, more arrests were made; two women at the White House, two at the Capitol. All carried banners with the same words of the President. There was no hesitation this time. They were promptly arrested for "obstructing the traffic." They, too, were dismissed and their cases never tried. It seemed clear that the Administration hoped to suppress picketing merely by arrests. When, however, women continued to picket in the face of arrest, the Administration quickened its advance into the venture of suppression. It decided to bring the offenders to trial.

On June 26, six American women were tried, judged guilty on the technical charge of "obstructing the traffic," warned by the court of their "unpatriotic, almost treasonable behavior," and sentenced to pay a fine of twenty-five dollars or serve three days in jail.

"Not a dollar of your fine will we pay," was the answer of the women. "To pay a fine would be an admission of guilt. We are innocent."

The six women who were privileged to serve the first terms of imprisonment for suffrage in this country, were Miss Katherine Morey of Massachusetts, Mrs. Annie Arneil and Miss Mabel Vernon of Delaware, Miss Lavinia Dock of Pennsylvania, Miss Maud Jamison of Virginia, and Miss Virginia Arnold of

North Carolina. "Privileged" in spite of the foul air, the rats, and the mutterings of their strange comrades in jail!

*   *   *   *

Independence Day, July 4, 1917, is the occasion for two demonstrations in the name of liberty. Champ Clark, late Democratic speaker of the House, is declaiming to a cheering crowd behind the White House, "Governments derive their just powers from the consent of the governed." In front of the White House thirteen silent sentinels with banners bearing the same words, are arrested. It would have been exceedingly droll if it had not been so tragic. Champ Clark and his throng were not molested. The women with practically a deserted street were arrested and served jail terms for "obstructing traffic."

The trial of this group was delayed to give the jail authorities time to "vacate and tidy up," as one prisoner confided to Miss Joy Young. It developed that "orders" had been received at the jail immediately after the arrests and before the trial, "to make ready for the suffragettes." What did it matter that their case had not yet been heard? To jail they must go.

Was not the judge who tried and sentenced them a direct appointee of President Wilson? Were not the District Commissioners who gave orders to prepare the cells the direct appointees of President Wilson? And was not the Chief of Police of the District of Columbia a direct appointee of these same commissioners? And was not the jail warden who made life for the women so unbearable in prison also a direct appointee of the commissioners?

It was all a merry little ring and its cavalier attitude toward the law, toward justice, and above all toward women was of no importance. The world was on fire with a grand blaze. This tiny flame would scarcely be visible. No one would notice a few "mad" women thrown into jail. And if the world should find it out, doubtless public opinion would agree that the women ought to stay there. And even if it should not agree,

OFFICER ARRESTS PICKETS
Miss Catherine Flanagan, Mrs. William U. Watson

© *Harris & Ewing.*

WOMEN PUT INTO POLICE PATROL

SUFFRAGISTS IN PRISON COSTUME*

Left to Right:—†Miss Doris Stevens; ‡Mrs. J. A. H. Hopkins:
*Mrs. John Winters Brannan

SEWING ROOM AT OCCOQUAN WORKHOUSE

© Harris & Ewing.

RIOTOUS SCENES ON PICKET LINE WHEN HOODLUMS WERE PERMITTED TO ATTACK WOMEN

DUDLEY FIELD MALONE

LUCY BURNS

this little matter could all be explained away before another election.

Meanwhile the President could proclaim through official channels his disinterestedness. Observe the document, of which I give the substance, which he caused or allowed to be published at this time, through his Committee on Public Information.

"OFFICIAL BULLETIN"

"Published Daily under order of the President of the United States, by the Committee on Public Information.

GEORGE CREEL, Chairman.

"Furnished without charge to all newspapers, post offices, government officials and agencies of a public character for the dissemination of official news of the United States Government."

* * * *

"Washington, July 3, 1917. No. 46—Vol. i."

There follows a long editorial [1] which laments the public attention which has centered on the militant campaign, appeals to editors and reporters not to "encourage" us in our peculiar conduct by printing defies to the President of the United States even when "flaunted on a pretty little purple and gold banner" and exhorts the public to control its thrills. The official bulletin concludes with:

"It is a fact that there remains in America one man who has known exactly the right attitude to take and maintain toward the pickets. A whimsical smile, slightly puckered at the roots by a sense of the ridiculous, a polite bow—and for the rest a complete ignoring of their existence. He happens to be the man around whom the little whirlwind whirls—the President of the United States." And finally with an admonition that "the rest of the country . . . take example from him in its emotional reaction to the picket question."

[1] From the *Woman Citizen.*

The Administration pinned its faith on jail—that institution of convenience to the oppressor when he is strong in power and his weapons are effective. When the oppressor miscalculates the strength of the oppressed, jail loses its convenience.

CHAPTER 4

IT is Bastille Day, July fourteenth. Inspiring scenes and tragic sacrifices for liberty come to our minds. Sixteen women march in single file to take their own "Liberty, Equality, Fraternity" to the White House gates. It is the middle of a hot afternoon. A thin line of curious spectators is seen in the park opposite the suffrage headquarters. The police assemble from obscure spots; some afoot, others on bicycles. They close in on the women and follow them to the gates.

The proud banner is scarcely at the gates when the leader is placed under arrest. Her place is taken by another. She is taken. Another, and still another steps into the breach and is arrested.

Meanwhile the crowd grows, attracted to the spot by the presence of the police and the patrol wagon. Applause is heard. There are cries of "shame" for the police, who, I must say, did not always act as if they relished carrying out what they termed "orders from higher up." An occasional hoot from a small boy served to make the mood of the hostile ones a bit gayer. But for the most part an intense silence fell upon the watchers, as they saw not only younger women, but white-haired grandmothers hoisted before the public gaze into the crowded patrol, their heads erect, their eyes a little moist and their frail hands holding tightly to the banner until wrested from them by superior brute force.

This is the first time most of the women have ever seen a

police station, and they are interested in their surroundings. They are not interested in helping the panting policeman count them over and identify them. Who arrested whom? That becomes the gigantic question.

"Will the ladies please tell which officer arrested them?"

They will not. They do not intend to be a party to this outrage. Finally the officers abandon their attempt at identification. They have the names of the arrestees and will accept bail for their appearance Monday.

"Well girls, I've never seen but one other court in my life and that was the Court of St. James. But I must say they are not very much alike," was the cheery comment of Mrs. Florence Bayard Hilles, [1] as we entered the court room on Monday.

The stuffy court room is packed to overflowing. The fat, one-eyed bailiff is perspiring to no purpose. He cannot make the throng "sit down." In fact every one who has anything to do with the pickets perspires to no purpose. Judge Mullowny takes his seat, looking at once grotesque and menacing on his red throne.

"Silence in the court room," from the sinister-eyed bailiff. And a silence follows so heavy that it can be heard.

Saturday night's disorderlies—both black and white—are tried first. The suffrage prisoners strain their ears to hear the pitiful pleas of these unfortunates, most of whom come to the bar without counsel or friend. Scraps of evidence are heard.

JUDGE: "You say you were not quarreling, Lottie?"

LOTTIE: "I sho' do yo' hono'. We wuz jes singin'—we wuz sho' nuf, sah."

JUDGE: "Singing, Lottie? Why your neighbors here testify to the fact that you were making a great deal of noise—so much that they could not sleep."

---

[1] Mrs. Hilles is the daughter of the late Thomas Bayard, formerly America's ambassador to Great Britain, and Secretary of State in President Cleveland's cabinet.

LOTTIE: "I tells yo' honor' we wuz jes singin' lak we allays do."

JUDGE: "What were you singing?"

LOTTIE: "Why, hymns, sah."

The judge smiles cynically.

A neatly-attired white man with a wizened face again takes the stand against Lottie. Hymns or no hymns he could not sleep. The judge pronounces a sentence of "six months in the workhouse," for Lottie.

And so it goes on.

The suffrage prisoners are the main business of the morning. Sixteen women come inside the railing which separates "tried" from "untried" and take their seats.

"Do the ladies wish the government to provide them with counsel?"

They do not.

"We shall speak in our own behalf. We feel that we can best represent ourselves," we announce. Miss Anne Martin and I act as attorneys for the group.

The same panting policemen who could not identify the people they had arrested give their stereotyped, false and illiterate testimony. The judge helps them over the hard places and so does the government's attorney. They stumble to an embarrassed finish and retire.

An aged government clerk, grown infirm in the service, takes the stand and the government attorney proves through him that there is a White House; that it has a side-walk in front of it, and a pavement, and a hundred other overwhelming facts. The pathetic clerk shakes his dusty frame and slinks off the stand. The prosecuting attorney now elaborately proves that we walked, that we carried banners, that we were arrested by the aforesaid officers while attempting to hold our banners at the White House gates.

Each woman speaks briefly in her own defense. She denounces the government's policy with hot defiance. The blame is placed squarely at the door of the Administration, and in unmistakable terms. Miss Anne Martin opens for the defense:

"This is what we are doing with our banners before the White Hosue, petitioning the most powerful representative of the government, the President of the United States, for a redress of grievances; we are asking him to use his great power to secure the passage of the national suffrage amendment.

"As long as the government and the representatives of the government prefer to send women to jail on petty and technical charges, we will go to jail. Persecution has always advanced the cause of justice. The right of American women to work for democracy must be maintained. . . . We would hinder, not help, the whole cause of freedom for women, if we weakly submitted to persecution now. Our work for the passage of the amendment must go on. It *will* go on."

Mrs. John Rogers, Jr., descendant of Roger Sherman, one of the signers of the Declaration of Independence, speaks: "We are not guilty of any offence, not even of infringing a police regulation. We know full well that we stand here because the President of the United States refuses to give liberty to American women. We believe, your Honor, that the wrong persons are before the bar in this Court. . . ."

"I object, your Honor, to this woman making such a statement here in Court," says the District Attorney.

"We believe the President is the guilty one and that we are innocent."

"Your Honor, I object," shouts the Government's attorney.

The prisoner continues calmly: "There are votes enough and there is time enough to pass the national suffrage amendment through Congress at this session. More than 200 votes in the House and more than 50 in the Senate are pledged to this amendment. The President puts his power behind all measures in which he takes a genuine interest. If he will say one frank word advocating this measure it will pass as a piece of war emergency legislation."

Mrs. Florence Bayard Hilles speaks in her own defense: "For generations the men of my family have given their services to their country. For myself, my training from childhood has been with a father who believed in democracy and who belonged to the Democratic Party. By inheritance and connection I am a Democrat, and to a Democratic President I went with my appeal. . . . What a spectacle it must be to the thinking people of this country to see us urged to go to war for democracy in a foreign land, and to see women thrown into prison who plead for that same cause at home.

"I stand here to affirm my innocence of the charge against me. This court has not proven that I obstructed traffic. My presence at the White House gate was under the constitutional right of petitioning the government for freedom or for any other cause. During the months of January, February, March, April and May picketing was legal. In June it suddenly becomes illegal. . . .

"My services as an American woman are being conscripted by order of the President of the United States to help win the world war for democracy. . . . 'for the right of those who submit to authority to have a voice in their own government.' I shall continue to plead for the political liberty of American women—and especially do I plead to the President, since he is the one person who . . . can end the struggles of American women to take their proper places in a true democracy."

There is continuous objection from the prosecutor, eager advice from the judge, "you had better keep to the charge of obstructing traffic." But round on round of applause comes from the intent audience, whenever a defiant note is struck by the prisoners, and in spite of the sharp rapping of the gavel confusion reigns. And how utterly puny the "charge" is! If it were true that the prisoners actually obstructed the traffic, how grotesque that would be. The importance of their demand, the purity of their reasoning, the nobility and gentle quality of the prisoners at the bar; all conspire to make the charge against them, and the attorney who makes it, and the judge who hears it, petty and ridiculous.

But justice must proceed.

Mrs. Gilson Gardner of Washington, D. C., a member of the Executive Committee of the National Woman's party, and the wife of Gilson Gardner, a well-known Liberal and journalist, speaks:

"It is impossible for me to believe that we were arrested because we were obstructing traffic or blocking the public highway.

"We have been carrying on activities of a distinctly political nature, and these political activities have seemingly disturbed certain powerful influences. Arrests followed. I submit that these arrests are purely political and that the charge of an unlawful assemblage and of obstructing traffic is a political subterfuge. Even should I be sent to jail which, I could not, your Honor, anticipate, I would be in jail, not because I obstructed traffic, but because I have offended politically, because I have demanded of this government freedom for women."

It was my task to sum up for the defense. The judge sat bored through my statement. "We know and I believe the Court knows also," I said, "that President Wilson and his Administration are responsible for our being here to-day. It is a fact that they gave the orders which caused our arrest and appearance before this bar.

"We know and you know, that the District Commissioners are appointed by the President, that the present commissioners were appointed by President Wilson. We know that you, your Honor, were appointed to the bench by President Wilson, and that the district attorney who prosecutes us was appointed by the President. These various officers would not dare bring us here under these false charges without the policy having been decided upon by the responsible leaders.

"What is our real crime? What have these distinguished and liberty-loving women done to bring them before this court of justice? Why, your Honor, their crime is that they peacefully petitioned the President of the United States for liberty. What must be the shame of our nation before the world when it becomes known that here we throw women into jail who love liberty and attempt to peacefully petition the President for it? These women are nearly all descended from revolutionary ancestors or from some of the greatest libertarian statesmen this country has produced. What would these men say now if they could see that passion for liberty which was in their own hearts rewarded in the twentieth century with foul and filthy imprisonment!

"We say to you, this outrageous policy of stupid and brutal punishment will not dampen the ardor of the women. Where sixteen of us face your judgment to-day there will be sixty to-morrow, so great will be the indignation of our colleagues in this fight."

The trial came to an end after a tense two days. The packed court-room sat in a terrible silence awaiting the judge's answer.

There were distinguished men present at the trial—men who also fight for their ideals. There was Frederic C. Howe, then Commissioner of Immigration of the Port of New York, Frank P. Walsh, International labor leader, Dudley Field Malone, then Collector of the Port of New York, Amos Pinchot, liberal leader, John A. H. Hopkins, then liberal-progressive leader in New Jersey who had turned his organization to the support of the President and become a member of the President's Campaign Committee, now chairman of the Committee of Forty-eight and whose beautiful wife was among the prisoners, Allen McCurdy, secretary of the Committee of Forty-eight and many others. One and all came forward to protest to us during the adjournment. "This is monstrous." . . . "Never have I seen evidence so disregarded." . . . "This is a tragic farce." . . . "He will never dare sentence you." . . .

It was reported to us that the judge used the interim to telephone to the District building, where the District Commissioners sit. He returned to pronounce, "Sixty days in the workhouse in default of a twenty-five dollar fine."

The shock was swift and certain to all the spectators. We would not of course pay the unjust fine imposed, for we were not guilty of any offense.

The judge attempted persuasion. "You had better decide to pay your fines," he ventured. And "you will not find jail a pleasant place to be." It was clear that neither he nor his confreres had imagined women would accept with equanimity so drastic a sentence. It was now their time to be shocked. Here were "ladies"—that was perfectly clear—"ladies" of unusual distinction. Surely they would not face the humiliation of a workhouse sentence which involved not only imprisonment but penal servitude! The Administration was wrong again.

"We protest against this unjust sentence and conviction," we said, "but we prefer the workhouse to the payment of a fine imposed for an offense of which we are not guilty." We filed into the "pen," to join the other prisoners, and wait for the "black maria" to carry us to prison.

*   *   *   *

We are all taken to the District Jail, where we are put through the regular catechism: "Were you ever in prison before?—Age—birthplace—father—mother—religion and what not?" We are then locked up,—two to a cell. What will happen next?

The sleek jailer, whose attempt to be cordial provokes a certain distrust, comes to our corridor to "turn us over" to our next keeper—the warden of Occoquan. We learn that the workhouse is not situated in the District of Columbia but in Virginia.

Other locked wagons with tiny windows up near the driver now take us, side by side with drunks and disorderlies, prostitutes and thieves, to the Pennsylvania Station. Here we embark for the unknown terrors of the workhouse, filing through crowds at the station, driven on by our "keeper," who resembles Simon Legree, with his long stick and his pushing and shoving to hurry us along. The crowd is quick to realize that we are prisoners, because of our associates. Friends try to bid us a last farewell and slip us a sweet or fruit, as we are rushed through the iron station gates to the train.

Warden Whittaker is our keeper, thin and old, with a cruel mouth, brutal eyes and a sinister birthmark on his temple. He guards very anxiously his "dangerous criminals" lest they try to leap out of the train to freedom! We chat a little and attempt to relax from the strain that we have endured since Saturday. It is now late in the afternoon of Tuesday.

The dusk is gathering. It is almost totally dark when we alight at a tiny station in what seems to us a wilderness. It is a deserted country. Even the gayest member of the party, I am sure, was struck with a little terror here.

More locked wagons, blacker than the dusk, awaited us. The prison van jolted and bumped along the rocky and hilly road. A cluster of lights twinkled beyond the last hill, and we knew that we were coming to our temporary summer residence. I can still see the long thin line of black poplars against the smouldering afterglow. I did not know then what tragic things they concealed.

*   *   *   *

We entered a well-lighted office. A few guards of ugly demeanor stood about. Warden Whittaker consulted with the hard-faced matron, Mrs. Herndon, who began the prison routine. Names were called, and each prisoner stepped to the desk to get her number, to give up all jewelry, money, hand-bags, letters, eye-glasses, traveling bags containing toilet necessities, in fact everything except the clothes on her body.

From there we were herded into the long bare dining room where we sat dumbly down to a bowl of dirty sour soup. I say dumbly—for now began the rule of silence. Prisoners are punished for speaking to one another at table. They cannot even whisper, much less smile or laugh. They must be conscious always of their "guilt." Every possible thing is done to make the inmates feel that they are and must continue to be anti-social creatures.

We taste our soup and crust of bread. We try so hard to eat it for we are tired and hungry, but no one of us is able to get it down. We leave the table hungry and slightly nauseated.

Another long march in silence through various channels into a large dormitory and through a double line of cots! Then we stand, weary to the point of fainting, waiting the next ordeal. This seemed to be the juncture at which we lost all that is left us of contact with the outside world,—our clothes.

An assistant matron, attended by negress prisoners, relieves us of our clothes. Each prisoner is obliged to strip naked without even the protection of a sheet, and proceed across what seems endless space, to a shower bath. A large tin bucket stands on the floor and in this is a minute piece of dirty soap, which is offered to us and rejected. We dare not risk the soap used by so many prisoners. Naked, we return from the bath to receive our allotment of coarse, hideous prison clothes, the outer garments of which consist of a bulky mother-hubbard wrapper, of bluish gray ticking and a heavy apron of the same dismal stuff. It takes a dominant personality indeed to survive these clothes. The thick unbleached muslin undergarments are of designs never to be forgotten! And the thick stockings and forlorn shoes! What torture to put on shoes that are alike for each foot and made to fit just anybody who may happen along.

Why are we being ordered to dress? It is long past the bed-time hour.

Our suspense is brief. All dressed in cloth of "guilt" we are led into what we later learn is the "recreation" room. Lined up against its wall, we might any other time have bantered about the possibility of being shot, but we are in no mood to jest. The door finally opens and in strides Warden Whittaker with a stranger beside him.

He reviews his latest criminal recruits, engaging the stranger meanwhile in whispered conversation. There are short, uncertain laughs. There are nods of the head and more whispers.

"Well, ladies, I hope you are all comfortable. Now make yourselves at home here. I think you will find it healthy here. You'll weigh more when you go out than when you came in. You will be allowed to write one letter a month—to your family. Of course we open and read all letters coming in and going out. To-morrow you will be assigned your work. I hope you will sleep well. Good night!"

We did not answer. We looked at each other.

News leaked through in the morning that the stranger had been a newspaper reporter. The papers next morning were full of the "comfort" and "luxury" of our surroundings. The "delicious" food sounded most reassuring to the nation. In fact no word of the truth was allowed to appear.

The correspondent could not know that we went back to our cots to try to sleep side by side with negro prostitutes. Not that we shrank from these women on account of their color, but how terrible to know that the institution had gone out of its way to bring these prisoners from their own wing to the white wing in an attempt to humiliate us. There was plenty of room in the negro wing. But prison must be made so unbearable that no more women would face it. That was the policy attempted here.

We tried very hard to sleep and forget our hunger and weariness. But all the night through our dusky comrades padded by to the lavatory, and in the streak of bright light which shot across the center of the room, startled heads could be seen bobbing up in the direction of a demented woman in the end cot. Her weird mutterings made us fearful. There was no sleep in this strange place.

Our thoughts turn to the outside world. Will the women care? Will enough women believe that through such humiliation all may win freedom? Will they believe that through our imprisonment their slavery will be lifted the sooner? Less philosophically, will the government be moved by public protest? Will such protest come?

The next morning brought us a visitor from suffrage headquarters. The institution hoped that the visitor would use her persuasion to make us pay our fines and leave and so she was admitted. We learned the cheering news, that immediately after sentence had been pronounced by the Court, Dudley Field Malone had gone direct to the White House to protest to the President. His protest was delivered with heat. The President said that he was "shocked" at the sixty day sentence, that he did not know it had been done, and made other evasions. Mr. Malone's report of his interview with the President is given in full in a subsequent chapter.

Following Mr. Malone, Mr. J. A. H. Hopkins went to the White House. "How would you like to have your wife sleep in a dirty workhouse next to prostitutes?" was his direct talk to the President. Again the President was "shocked." No wonder! Mr. and Mrs. Hopkins had been the President's dinner guests not very long before, celebrating his return to power. They had supported him politically and financially in New Jersey. Now Mrs. Hopkins had been arrested at his gate and thrown into prison.

In reporting the interview, Mr. Hopkins said:

"The President asked me for suggestions as to what might be done, and I replied that in view of the seriousness of the present situation the only solution lay in immediate passage of the Susan B. Anthony amendment."

Gilson Gardner also went to the White House to leave his hot protest. And there were others.

Telegrams poured in from all over the country. The press printed headlines which could not but arouse the sympathy of thousands. Even people who did not approve of picketing the White House said, "After all, what these women have done is certainly not 'bad' enough to merit such drastic punishment."

And women protested. From coast to coast there poured in at our headquarters copies of telegrams sent to Administration leaders. Of course not all women by any means had approved this method of agitation. But the government's action had done more than we had been able to do for them. It had made them feel sex-conscious. Women were being unjustly treated. Regardless of their feelings about this particular procedure, they stood up and objected.

For the first time, I believe, our form of agitation began to seem a little more respectable than the Administration's handling of it. But the Administration did not know this fact yet.

*   *   *   *

"Everybody in line for the work-room!"

We were thankful to leave our inedible breakfast. We were unable to drink the greasy black coffee. The pain in the tops of our heads was acute.

"What you all down here for?" asked a young negress, barely out of her teens, as she casually fingered her sewing material.

"Why, I held a purple, white and gold banner at the gates of the White House."

"You don' say so! What de odders do?"

"Same thing. We all held banners at the White House gates asking President Wilson to give us the vote."

"An' yo' all got sixty days fo' *dat?*"

"Yes. You see the President thought it would be a good idea to send us to the workhouse for asking for the vote. You know women want to vote and have wanted to for a long time in our country."

"O—Yass'm, I know. I seen yo' parades, an' meetin's, an' everythin'. I know whah yo' all live, right near the White House. You's alright. I hopes yo' git it, fo' women certainly do need protextion against men like Judge Mullowny. He has us allatime picked up an' sen' down here.

"They sen' yo' down here once, an' then yo' come out without a cent, and try to look fo' a job, an' befo' yo' can fin' one a cop walks up an' asks yo' whah yo' live, an' ef yo' haven't got a place yet, becaus' yo' ain' got a cent to ren' one with, he says, 'Come with me, I'll fin' yo' a home,' an' hustles yo' off to the p'lice station an' down heah again, an' you're called a 'vag' (vagrant). What chanct has we niggahs got, I ask ya? I hopes yo' all gits a vote an' fixes up *somethings* for women!"

"You see that young girl over there?" said another prisoner, who in spite of an unfortunate life had kept a remnant of her early beauty. I nodded.

"Well, Judge Mullowny gave her thirty days for her first offense, and when he sentenced her, she cried out desperately, 'Don't send me down there, Judge! If you do, I'll kill myself!' What do you think he said to that?—'I'll give you six months in which to change your mind!'"

I reflected. The judge that broke this pale-faced, silent girl was the appointee of the President. It was the task of such a man to sentence American women to the workhouse for demanding liberty.

Conversing with the "regulars" was forbidden by the

wardress, but we managed, from time to time, to talk to our
fellow prisoners with stealthiness.

"We knew somethin' was goin' to happen," said one negro
girl, "because Monday the close we had on wer' took off us an'
we were giv' these old patched ones. We wuz told they wanted
to take 'stock,' but we heard they wuz bein' washed fo' you-all
suff"agettes."

The unpleasantness at wearing the formless garments of
these unfortunates made us all wince. But the government's
calculation aroused our hot indignation. We were not convicted until Tuesday and our prison garments were ready
Monday!

"You must not speak against the President," said the
servile wardress, when she discovered we were telling our story
to the inmates. "You know you will be thrashed if you say
anything more about the President; and don't forget you're on
Government property and may be arrested for treason if it
happens again."

We doubted the seriousness of this threat of thrashing until
one of the girls confided to us that such outrages happened
often. We afterward obtained proof of these brutalities.[1]

"Old Whittaker beat up that girl over there just last week
and put her in the 'booby' house on bread and water for five
days."

"What did she do?" I asked.

"Oh, she an' another girl got to scrapping in the black-
berry patch and she didn't pick enough berries. . . ."

"All put up your work, girls, and get in line." This from
the wardress, who sped up the work in the sewing room. It was
lunch time, and though we were all hungry we dreaded going
to the silence and the food in that gray dining room with the
vile odors. We were counted again as we filed out, carrying
our heavy chairs with us as is the workhouse custom.

[1] See affidavit of Mrs. Bovee, page 144.

"Do they do this all the time?" I asked. It seemed as though needless energy was being spent counting and recounting our little group.

"Wouldn't do anybody any good to try to get away from here," said one of the white girls. "Too many bloodhounds!"

"Bloodhounds!" I asked in amazement, for after all these women were not criminals but merely misdemeanants.

"Oh, yes. Just a little while ago three men tried to get away and they turned bloodhounds after them and shot them dead—and they weren't bad men either."

* * * *

When our untasted supper was over that night we were ordered into the square, bare-walled "recreation" room, where we and the other prisoners sat, and sat, and sat, our chairs against the walls, a dreary sight indeed, waiting for the forty-five minutes before bedtime to pass. The sight of two negro girl prisoners combing out each other's lice and dressing their kinky hair in such a way as to discourage permanently a return of the vermin did not produce in us exactly a feeling of "recreation." But we tried to sing. The negroes joined in, too, and soon outsang us, with their plaintive melodies and hymns. Then back to our cells and another attempt to sleep.

* * * *

A new ordeal the next morning! Another of the numberless "pedigrees" is to be taken. One by one we were called to the warden's office.

"Were your father or mother ever insane?"

"Are you a confirmed drunkard, chronic or moderate drinker?"

"Do you smoke or chew or use tobacco in any form?"

"Married or single?"

"Single."

"How many children?"

"None."

"What religion do you profess?"

"Christian."

"What *religion* do you profess?" in a higher pitched voice.

I did not clearly comprehend. "Do you mean 'Am I a Catholic or a Protestant?' I am a Christian."

But it was of no avail. She wrote down, "None."

I protested. "That is not accurate. I insist that I am a Christian, or at least I *try* to be one."

"You must learn to be polite," she retorted almost fiercely, and I returned to the sewing room.

For the hundredth time we asked to be given our tooth-brushes, combs, handkerchiefs and our own soap. The third day of imprisonment without any of these essentials found us depressed and worried over our unsanitary condition. We plead also for toilet paper. It was senseless to deny these necessities. It is enough to imprison people. Why seek to degrade them utterly?

*　　*　　*　　*

The third afternoon we were mysteriously summoned into the presence of Superintendent Whittaker. He seemed warm and cordial. We were ordered drawn up in a semi-circle.

"Ladies, there is a rumor that you may be pardoned," he began.

"By whom?" asked one.

"For what?" asked another. "We are innocent women. There is nothing to pardon us for."

"I have come to ask you what you would do if the President pardoned you."

"We would refuse to accept it," came the ready response from several.

"I shall leave you for a while to consider this. Mind! I have not yet received information of a pardon, but I have been asked to ascertain your attitude."

Our consultation was brief. We were of one mind. We

were unanimous in wishing to reject a pardon for a crime
which we had never committed. We said so with some spirit
when Mr. Whittaker returned for our decision.

"You have no choice. You are obliged to accept a pardon."

That settled it, and we waited. That the protest on the
outside had been strong enough to precipitate action from the
government was the subject of our conversation. Evidently it
had not been strong enough to force action on the suffrage
amendment, but it was forcing action, and that was important.

Mr. Whittaker returned triumphant.

"Ladies, you are pardoned by the President. You are free
to go as soon as you have taken off your prison clothes and
put on your own."

It was sad to leave the other prisoners behind. Especially
pathetic were the girls who helped us with our clothes. They
whispered such eager appeals in our ears, telling us of their
drastic sentences for trifling offenses and of the cruel punishments. It was hard to resist digressing into some effort at
prison reform. That way lay our instincts. Our reason told
us that we must first change the status of women.

As we were leaving the workhouse to return to Washington
we had an unexpected revelation of the attitude of officialdom
toward our campaign. Addressing Miss Lucy Burns, who had
arrived to assist us in getting on our way, Superintendent
Whittaker, in an almost unbelievable rage, said, "Now that you
women are going away, I have something to say and I want to
say it to *you*. The next lot of women who come here won't be
treated with the same consideration that these women were."
I will show later on how he made good this terrible threat.

*   *   *   *

Receiving a Presidential pardon through the Attorney
General had its amusing aspect. My comrades shared this
amusement when I told them the following incident.

On the day after our arrest, I was having tea at the Chevy

Chase Country Club in Washington. Quite casually a gentleman introduced me to Mr. Gregory, the Attorney General.

"I see you were mixed up with the suffragettes yesterday," was the Attorney General's first remark to the gentleman. And before the latter could explain that he had settled accounts quietly but efficiently with a hoodlum who was attempting to trip the women up on their march, the *chief law officer* of the United States contributed this important suggestion: "You know what I'd do if I was those policemen. I'd just take a hose out with me and when the women came out with their banners, why I'd just squirt the hose on 'em. . . ."

"But Mr. Gregory . . ."

"Yes, sir! If you can just make what a woman does look ridiculous, you can sure kill it. . . ."

"But, Mr. Attorney General, what right would the police have to assault these or any other women?" the gentleman managed finally to interpolate.

"Hup—hup——" denoting great surprise, came from the Attorney General, as he looked to me for reassurance.

His expectant look vanished when I said, "Mr. Gregory, did it ever occur to you that it might make the government look ridiculous instead of the women?"

You can imagine how the easy manner of one who is sure of his audience melted from his face.

"This is one of the women arrested yesterday," continued the gentleman, while the Attorney General smothered a "Well, I'll be . . ."

"I am out on bail," I said. "To-morrow we go to jail. It is all prearranged, you understand. The trial is merely a matter of form."

The highest law officer of the land fled gurgling.

* * * *

The day following our release Mrs. J. A. H. Hopkins carried a picket banner to the gates of the White House to test the validity of the pardon. Her banner read, "We do not ask pardon for ourselves but justice for all American women." A curious crowd, as large as had collected on those days when the police arrested women for "obstructing traffic," stood watching the lone picket. The President passed through the gates and saluted. The police did not interfere.

Daily picketing was resumed and no arrests followed for the moment.

It was now August, three months since the Senate Suffrage Committee authorized its chairman, Mr. Jones, to report the measure to the Senate for action. Mr. Jones said, however, that he was too busy to make a report; that he wanted to make a particularly brilliant one, one that would "be a contribution to the cause"; that he did not approve of picketing, but that he would report the measure "in a reasonable time." So much for the situation in the Senate!

From the House we gathered some interesting evidence. We reminded Mr. Webb, Chairman of the Judiciary Committee, that out of a total membership of twenty-one men on his committee, twelve were Democrats, two-thirds of whom were opposed to the measure; we reminded him that the Republicans on the committee were for action. Mr. Webb wrote in answer:

"The Democratic caucus passed a resolution that only war emergency measures would be considered during this extra session, and that the President might designate from time to time special legislation which he regarded as war legislation, and such would be acted on by the House. The President, not having designated woman suffrage and national prohibition so far as war measures, the judiciary committee up to this time has not felt warranted under the caucus rule, in reporting either of these measures. If the President should request either or both of them as war measure, then I think the Committee would attempt to take some action on them promptly. *So you see after all it is important to your cause to make the*

President see that woman suffrage comes within the rules laid down." [1]

Here was a frank admission of the assumption upon which women had gone to jail—that the President was responsible for action on the amendment.

Now that we were again allowed to picket the White House, the Republicans seized the opportunity legitimately to embarrass their opponents by precipitating a bitter debate.

Senator Cummins of Iowa, Republican member of the Suffrage Committee, moved, as had Mr. Mann in the House at an earlier date, to discharge the Suffrage Committee for failing to make the report authorized by the entire Committee. Mr. Cummins said, among other things:

". . . I look upon the resolution as definitely and certainly a war measure. There is nothing that this country could do which would strengthen it more than to give the disfranchised women . . . the opportunity to vote. . . .

"Last week . . . I went to the Chairman of the Committee and told him that . . . we had finished the hearings, reached a conclusion and that it was our bounden duty to make the report to the Senate. . . . I asked him if he would not call a meeting of the Committee. He said that it would be impossible, that he had some other engagements which would prevent a meeting of the Committee."

Senator Cummins explained that he finally got the promise of the Chairman that a meeting of the Committee would be called on a given date. When it was not called he made his motion.

Chairman Jones made some feeble remarks and some evasive excuses which meant nothing, and which only further aroused Republican friends of the measure on the Committee.

Senator Gronna of North Dakota, Republican, interrupted

[1] Italics are mine.

him with the direct question, "I ask the chairman of this committee *why* this joint resolution has not been reported? The Senator, who is chairman of the committee, I suppose, knows as well as I do that the people of the entire country are anxious to have this joint resolution submitted and to be given an opportunity to vote upon it. . . ."

Senator Johnson of California, Republican, proposed that Chairman Jones consent to call the Committee together to consider reporting out the bill, which Senator Jones flatly refused to do.

Senator Jones of Washington, another Republican member of the Committee, added:

"I agree with the Senator from Iowa that this is a war measure and ought to be considered as such at this time. I do not see how we can very consistently talk democracy while disfranchising the better half of our citizenship—*I may not approve of the action of the women picketing the White House, but neither do I approve of what I consider the lawless action toward these women in connection with the picketing.* . . ."

"I do not want to think the chairman does not desire to call the committee together because of some influence outside of Congress as some have suggested. . . ."

At this point Senator Hollis of New Hampshire, Democrat, arose to say:

"There is a small but very active group of women suffragists who have acted in such a way that some who are ardently in favor of woman suffrage believe that their action should not be encouraged by making a favorable report at this time."

Senator Johnson protested at this point, but Senator Hollis continued:

"*To discharge the committee would focus the attention of the country upon the action and would give undue weight to what has been done by the active group of woman suffragists.*"

I think that any student of psychology will acknowledge that our picketing had stimulated action in Congress, and that what was now needed was some still more provocative action from us.

CHAPTER 5

IMPRISONING women had met with considerable public disapproval, and attendant political embarrassment to the Administration. That the presidential pardon would end this embarrassment was doubtless the hope of the Administration. The pickets, however, returned to their posts in steadily increasing numbers. Their presence at the gates was desired by the Administration no more now than it had been before the arrests and imprisonments. But they had found no way to rid themselves of the pickets. And as another month of picketing drew to an end the Administration ventured to try other ways to stop it and with it the consequent embarrassment. Their methods became physically more brutal and politically more stupid. Their conduct became lawless in the extreme.

Meanwhile the President had drafted the young men of America in their millions to die on foreign soil for foreign democracy. He had issued a special appeal to women to give their work, their treasure and their sons to this enterprise. At the same time his now gigantic figure stood obstinately across the path to our main objective. It was our daily task to keep vividly in his mind that objective. It was our responsibility to compel decisive action from him.

Using the return of Envoy Root from his mission to Russia

122

as another dramatic opportunity to speak to the President we took to the picket line these mottoes:

TO ENVOY ROOT

YOU SAY THAT AMERICA MUST THROW ITS MANHOOD TO THE SUPPORT OF LIBERTY.

WHOSE LIBERTY?

THIS NATION IS NOT FREE. TWENTY MILLION WOMEN ARE DENIED BY THE PRESIDENT OF THE UNITED STATES THE RIGHT TO REPRESENTATION IN THEIR OWN GOV-ERNMENT.

TELL THE PRESIDENT THAT HE CANNOT FIGHT AGAINST LIBERTY AT HOME WHILE HE TELLS US TO FIGHT FOR LIBERTY ABROAD.

TELL HIM TO MAKE AMERICA SAFE FOR DEMOCRACY BEFORE HE ASKS THE MOTHERS OF AMERICA TO THROW THEIR SONS TO THE SUPPORT OF DEMOCRACY IN EUROPE.

ASK HIM HOW HE CAN REFUSE LIBERTY TO AMERICAN CITIZENS WHEN HE IS FORCING MILLIONS OF AMERICAN BOYS OUT OF THEIR COUNTRY TO DIE FOR LIBERTY.

At no time during the entire picketing was the traffic on Pennsylvania Avenue so completely obstructed as it was for the two hours during which this banner made its appearance on the line. Police captains who three weeks before were testifying that the police could not manage the crowds, placidly looked on while these new crowds increased.

We did not regard Mr. Wilson as *our* President. We felt that he had neither political nor moral claim to our allegiance. War had been made without our consent. The war would be finished and very likely a bad peace would be written without our consent. Our fight was becoming increasingly difficult—I might almost say desperate. Here we were, a band of women fighting with banners, in the midst of a world armed to the teeth. And so it was not very difficult to understand how high spirited women grew more resentful, unwilling to be a party to the President's hypocrisy, the hypocrisy so eager to sacrifice life without stint to the vague hope of liberty abroad, while refusing to assist in the peaceful legislative steps which would lead to self-government in our own country. As a matter of fact the President's constant oratory on freedom and democracy moved them to scorn. They were stung into a protest so militant as to shock not only the President but the public. We inscribed on our banner what countless American women had long thought in their hearts.

The truth was not pleasant but it had to be told. We submitted to the world, through the picket line, this question:

KAISER WILSON

HAVE YOU FORGOTTEN HOW YOU SYMPATHIZED WITH THE POOR GERMANS BECAUSE THEY WERE NOT SELF-GOVERNED?

20,000,000 AMERICAN WOMEN ARE NOT SELF-GOVERNED.

TAKE THE BEAM OUT OF YOUR OWN EYE.

We did not expect public sympathy at this point. We knew that not even the members of Congress who had occasionally in debate, but more frequently in their cloak rooms, and often to us privately, called the President "autocrat"—"Kaiser"—"Ruler"—"King"—"Czar"—would approve our telling the truth publicly.

Nor was it to be expected that eager young boys, all agog to fight Germans, would be averse to attacking women in the meantime. They were out to fight and such was the public hysteria that it did not exactly matter whom they fought.

And so those excited boys of the Army and Navy attacked the women and the banner. The banner was destroyed. Another was brought up to take its place. This one met the same fate. Meanwhile a crowd was assembling in front of the White House either to watch or to assist in the attacks. At the very moment when one banner was being snatched away and destroyed, President and Mrs. Wilson passed through the gates on their way to a military review at Fort Myer. *The President saw American women being attacked, while the police refused them protection.*

Not a move was made by the police to control the growing crowd. Such inaction is always a signal for more violence on the part of rowdies. As the throng moved to and fro between the White House and our Headquarters immediately opposite, so many banners were destroyed that finally Miss Lucy Burns, Miss Virginia Arnold and Miss Elizabeth Stuyvesant took those remaining to the second and third floor balconies of our building and hung them out. At this point there was not a picket left on the street. The crowd was clearly obstructing the traffic, but no attempt was made to move them back or to protect the women, some of whom were attacked by sailors on their own doorsteps. The two police officers present watched without interference while three sailors brought a ladder from the Belasco Theater in the same block, leaned it against the side of the Cameron House, the Headquarters, climbed up to the second floor balcony, mounted the iron railing and tore down all banners and the American flag. One sailor administered a severe blow in the face with his clenched fist upon Miss Georgina Sturgis of Washington.

"Why did you do that?" she demanded.

The man halted for a brief instant in obvious amazement and said, "I don't know." And with a violent wrench he tore the banner from her hands and ran down the ladder.

The narrow balcony was the scene of intense excitement.

But for Miss Burns' superb strength she would have been dragged over the railing of the balcony to be plunged to the ground. The mob watched with fascination while she swayed to and fro in her wrestle with two young sailors. And still no attempt by the police to quell the riot!

The climax came when in the late afternoon a bullet was fired through one of the heavy glass windows of the second floor, embedding itself in the ceiling. The bullet grazed past the head of Mrs. Ella Morton Dean of Montana. Captain Flather of the 1st Precinct, with two detectives, later examined the holes and declared they had been made by a 38 caliber revolver, but no attempt was ever made to find the man who had drawn the revolver.

Meanwhile eggs and tomatoes were hurled at our fresh banners flying from the flag poles on the building.

Finally police reserves were summoned and in less than five minutes the crowd was pushed back and the street cleared. Thinking now that they could rely on the protection of the police, the women started with their banners for the White House. But the police looked on while all the banners were destroyed, a few paces from Headquarters. More banners went out,—purple, white and gold ones. They, too, were destroyed before they reached the White House.

This entire spectacle was enacted on August 14, within a stone's throw of the White House.

Miss Paul summed up the situation when she said:

"The situation now existing in Washington exists because President Wilson permits it. Orders were first handed down to the police to arrest suffragists. The clamor over their imprisonments made this position untenable. The police were then ordered to protect suffragists. They were then ordered to attack suffragists. They have now been ordered to encourage irresponsible crowds to attack suffragists. No police head would dare so to besmirch his record without orders from his responsible chief. The responsible chief in the National Capital is the President of the United States."

Shortly after the incident of the "Kaiser banner" I was speaking in Louisville, Kentucky. The auditorium was packed and overflowing with men and women who had come to hear the story of the pickets.

Up to this time we had very few members in Kentucky and had anticipated in this Southern State, part of President Wilson's stronghold, that our Committee would meet with no enthusiasm and possibly with warm hostility.

I had related briefly the incidents leading up to the picketing and the Government's suppressions. I was rather cautiously approaching the subject of the "Kaiser banner," feeling timid and hesitant, wondering how this vast audience of Southerners would take it. Slowly I read the inscription on the famous banner, "Kaiser Wilson, have you forgotten how you sympathized with the poor Germans because they were not self-governed? Twenty million American women are not self-governed. Take the beam out of your own eye."

I hardly reached the last word, still wondering what the intensely silent audience would do, when a terrific outburst of applause mingled with shouts of "Good! Good! He is, he is!" came to my amazed ears. As the applause died down there was almost universal good-natured laughter. Instead of the painstaking and eloquent explanation which I was prepared to offer, I had only to join in their laughter.

A few minutes later a telegram was brought to the platform announcing further arrests. I read:

"Six more women sentenced to-day to 30 days in Occoquan workhouse."

Instant cries of "Shame! Shame! It's an outrage!" Scores of men and two women were on their feet calling for the passage of a resolution denouncing the Administration's policy of persecution. The motion of condemnation was put. It seemed as if the entire audience seconded it. It went through instantly, unanimously, and again with prolonged shouts and applause.

The meeting continued and I shall never forget that audience. It lingered to a late hour, almost to midnight, asking questions, making brief "testimonials" from the floor with almost evangelical fervor. Improvised collection baskets were piled high with bills. Women volunteered for picket duty and certain imprisonment, and the following day a delegation left for Washington.

I cite this experience of mine because it was typical. Every one who went through the country telling the story had similar experiences at this time. Indignation was swift and hot. Our mass meetings everywhere became meetings of protest during the entire campaign.

And resolutions of protest which always went immediately by wire from such meetings to the President, his cabinet and to his leaders in Congress, of course created increasing uneasiness in Democratic circles.

On August 15th the pickets again attempted to take their posts on the line.

On this day one lettered banner and fifty purple, white and gold flags were destroyed by a mob led by sailors in uniform. Alice Paul was knocked down three times by a sailor in uniform and dragged the width of the White House sidewalk in his frenzied attempt to tear off her suffrage sash.

Miss Katharine Morey of Boston was also knocked to the pavement by a sailor, who took her flag and then darted off into the crowd. Miss Elizabeth Stuyvesant was struck by a soldier in uniform and her blouse torn from her body. Miss Maud Jamison of Virginia was knocked down and dragged along the sidewalk. Miss Beulah Amidon of North Dakota was knocked down by a sailor.

In the midst of these riotous scenes, a well-known Washington correspondent was emerging from the White House, after an interview with the President. Dr. Cary Grayson, the President's physician, accompanying him to the door, advised:

"You had better go out the side entrance. Those damned women are in the front."

In spite of this advice the correspondent made his exit through the same gate by which he had entered, and just in time to ward off an attack by a sailor on one of the frailest girls in the group.

The Administration, in its desperation, ordered the police to lawlessness. On August 16th, fifty policemen led the mob in attacking the women. Hands were bruised and arms twisted by police officers and plainclothes men. Two civilians who tried to rescue the women from the attacks of the police were arrested. The police fell upon these young women with more brutality even than the mobs they had before encouraged. Twenty-five lettered banners and 123 Party flags were destroyed by mobs and police on this afternoon.

As the crowd grew more dense, the police temporarily retired from the attack. When their activities had summoned a sufficiently large and infuriated mob, they would rest.

And so the passions of the mob continued unchecked upon these irrepressible women, and from day to day the Administration gave its orders.

Finding that riots and mob attacks had not terrorized the pickets, the Administration decided again to arrest the women in the hope of ending the agitation. Having lost public sympathy through workhouse sentences, having won it back by pardoning the women, the Administration felt it could afford to risk losing it again, or rather felt that it had supplied itself with an appropriate amount of stage-setting.

And so on the third day of the riotous attacks, when it was clear that the pickets would persist, the Chief of Police called at headquarters to announce to Miss Paul that "orders have been changed and henceforth women carrying banners will be arrested."

Meanwhile the pickets heard officers shout to civilian friends as they passed—"Come back at four o'clock."

Members of the daily mob announced at the noon hour in various nearby restaurants that "the suffs will be arrested to-day at 4 o'clock."

Four o'clock is the hour the Government clerks begin to swarm homewards. The choice of this hour by the police to arrest the women would enable them to have a large crowd passing the White House gates to lend color to the fiction that "pickets were blocking the traffic."

Throughout the earlier part of the afternoon the silent sentinels stood unmolested, carrying these mottoes:

ENGLAND AND RUSSIA ARE ENFRANCHISING WOMEN IN
WAR-TIME.

HOW LONG MUST WOMEN WAIT FOR LIBERTY?

THE GOVERNMENT ORDERS OUR BANNERS DESTROYED
BECAUSE THEY TELL THE TRUTH.

At four o'clock the threatened arrests took place. The women arrested were Miss Lavinia Dock of Pennsylvania, Miss Edna Dixon of Washington, D. C., a young public school teacher; Miss Natalie Gray of Colorado, Mrs. Wm. Upton Watson and Miss Lucy Ewing of Chicago, and Miss Catherine Flanagan of Connecticut.

Exactly forty minutes were allowed for the trial of these six women. One police officer testified that they were "obstructing traffic."

None of the facts of the hideous and cruel manhandling by the mobs and police officers was allowed to be brought out. Nothing the women could say mattered. The judge pronounced: "Thirty days in Occoquan workhouse in lieu of a $10.00 fine."

And so this little handful of women, practically all of them tiny and frail of physique, began the cruel sentence of 30 days in the workhouse, while their cowardly assailants were not even reprimanded, nor were those who destroyed over a thousand dollars' worth of banners apprehended.

The riots had attracted sufficient attention to cause some anxiety in Administration circles. Protests against us and others against the rioters pressed upon them. Congress was provoked into a little activity; activity which reflected some doubt as to the wisdom of arresting women without some warrant in law.

Two attempts were made, neither of which was successful, to give the Administration more power and more law.

Senator Culberson of Texas, Democrat, offered a bill authorizing President Wilson at any time to prohibit any person from approaching or entering any place—in short a blanket authority granting the President or his officials limitless power over the actions of human beings. Realizing that this could be used to prohibit picketing the White House we appeared before a committee hearing on the bill and spoke against it. The committee did not have the boldness to report such a bill.

Senator Myers of Montana, an influential member of the Democratic majority, introduced into the Senate a few days later a resolution making it illegal to picket the White House. The shamelessness of admitting to the world that acts for which women had been repeatedly sentenced to jail, and for which women were at that moment lying in prison, were so legal as to make necessary a special act of Congress against them, was appalling. The Administration policy seemed to be "Let us put women in jail first—let us enact a law to keep them there afterwards."

This tilt between Senator Brandegee, of Connecticut, anti-suffrage Republican, and Senator Myers, suffrage Democrat, took place when Mr. Myers presented his bill:

MR. BRANDEGEE: . . . Was there any defect in the legal proceedings by which these trouble makers were sentenced and put in jail a few weeks ago?

MR. MYERS: None that I know of. I am not in a position to pass upon that. I do not believe any was claimed. . . .

MR. BRANDEGEE: Inasmuch as the law was sufficient to land them in jail . . . I fail to see why additional legislation is necessary on the subject.

MR. MYERS: There seems to be a doubt in the mind of some whether the present law is sufficient and I think it ought to be put beyond doubt. I think . . . the laws are not stringent or severe enough. . . .

MR. BRANDEGEE: They were stringent enough to land the malefactors in jail. . . .

In spite of Senator Myers' impassioned appeal to his colleagues, he was unable to command any support for his bill. I quote this from his speech in the Senate August 18, 1917:

MR. MYERS: Mr. President, I wish to say a few words about the bill I have just introduced. It is intended for the enactment of better and more adequate legislation to prevent the infamous, outrageous, scandalous, and, I think, almost treasonable actions that have been going on around the White House for months past, which have been a gross insult to the President of the United States and to the people of the United States; I mean the so-called picketing of the White House. . . . These disgusting proceedings have been going on for months, and if there is no adequate law to stop them, I think there ought to be.

"I believe the President, in the generosity of his heart, erred when he pardoned some of the women who have been conducting these proceedings, after they had been sentenced to

60 days in the workhouse. I believe they deserved the sentence, and they ought to have been compelled to serve it. . . .

"I for one am not satisfied longer to sit here idly day by day and submit to having the President of the United States insulted with impunity before the people of the country and before all the world. It is a shame and reproach.

"I hope this bill . . . will receive careful consideration and that it may be enacted into law and may be found an adequate preventive and punishment for such conduct."

This bill, which died a well-deserved death, is so amusing as to warrant reproduction. Although lamenting our comparison between the President and the Kaiser, it will be seen that Senator Myers brought forth a thoroughly Prussian document:

A BILL

For the better protection and enforcement of peace and order and the public welfare in the District of Columbia.

Be it enacted by the Senate and House of Representatives of the United States of America in Congress assembled, That when the United States shall be engaged in war it shall be unlawful for any person or persons to carry, hold, wave, exhibit, display, or have in his or her possession in any public road, highway, alley, street, thoroughfare, park, or other public place in the District of Columbia, any banner, flag, streamer, sash, or other device having thereon any words or language with reference to the President or the Vice President of the United States, or any words or language with reference to the Constitution of the United States, or the right of suffrage, or right of citizenship, or any words or language with reference to the duties of any executive official or department of the United States, or with reference to any proposed amendment to the Constitution of the United States, or with reference to any law or proposed law of the United States, calculated to bring the President of the United States or the Government of the United States into contempt, or which may tend to cause confusion, or excitement, or obstruction of the streets or sidewalks thereof, or any passage in any public place.

Sec. 2. That any person committing any foregoing described offense shall, upon conviction thereof, for each offense
be fined not less than $100 nor more than $1,000 or imprisoned not less than thirty days nor more than one year, or by
both such fine and imprisonment.

Voices were raised in our behalf, also, and among them
I note the following letter written to Major Pullman by Gilson
Gardner: [1]

Mr. Raymond Pullman,
    Chief of Police,
        Washington, D. C.
My dear Pullman,—
    I am writing as an old friend to urge you to get right in
this matter of arresting the suffrage pickets. Of course the
only way for you to get right is to resign. It has apparently
become impossible for you to stay in office and do your duty.
The alternative is obvious.
    You must see, Pullman, that you cannot be right in what
you have done in this matter. You have given the pickets
adequate protection; but you have arrested them and had them
sent to jail and the workhouse; you have permitted the crowd
to mob them, and then you have had your officers do much the
same thing by forcibly taking their banners from them. In
some of the actions you must have been wrong. If it was right
to give them protection and let them stand at the White House
for five months, both before and after the war, it was not
right to do what you did later.
    You say that it was not right when you were "lenient" and
gave them protection. You cannot mean that. The rightness
or wrongness must be a matter of law, not of personal discretion, and for you to attempt to substitute your discretion is
to set up a little autocracy in place of the settled laws of the
land. This would justify a charge of "Kaiserism" right here
in our capital city.
    The truth is, Pullman, you were right when you gave these
women protection. That is what the police are for. When

[1] The distinguished journalist who went to Africa to meet Theodore
Roosevelt and accompanied him on his return journey to America.

there are riots they are supposed to quell them, not by quelling the "proximate cause," but by quelling the rioters.

I know your police officers now quite well and know that they are most happy when they are permitted to do their duty. They did not like the dirty business of permitting a lot of sailors and street rifraff to rough the girls. All that went against the grain, but when you let them protect the pickets, as you did March third, when a thousand women marched around and around the White House, the officers were as contented as they were efficient.

Washington has a good police force and there has never been a minute when they could not have scattered any group gathered at the White House gates and given perfect protection to the women standing there.

You know why they did not do their duty.

In excusing what you have done, you say that the women carried banners with "offensive" inscriptions on them. You refer to the fact that they have addressed the President as "Kaiser Wilson." As a matter of fact not an arrest you have made—and the arrests now number more than sixty—has been for carrying one of those "offensive" banners. The women were carrying merely the suffrage colors or quotations from President Wilson's writings.

But, suppose the banners were offensive. Who made you censor of banners? The law gives you no such power. Even when you go through the farce of a police court trial the charge is "obstructing traffic"; which shows conclusively that you are not willing to go into court on the real issue.

No. As Chief of Police you have no more right to complain of the sentiments of a banner than you have of the sentiments in an editorial in the Washington *Post*, and you have no more right to arrest the banner-bearer than you have to arrest the owner of the Washington *Post*. . . . Congress refused to pass a press censorship law. There are certain lingering traditions to the effect that a people's liberties are closely bound up with the right to talk things out and those who are enlightened know that the only proper answer to words is words. When force is opposed to words there is ground for the charge of "Kaiserism." . . .

There was just one thing for you to have done, Pullman,

and that was to give full and adequate protection to these women, no matter what banners they carried or what ideas their banners expressed. If there is any law that can be invoked against the wording of the banners it was the business of others in the government to start the legal machinery which would abate them. It was not lawful to abate them by mob violence, or by arrests. And if those in authority over you were not willing that you thus do your duty, it was up to you to resign.

After all it would not be such a terrible thing, Pullman, for you to give up being Chief of Police, particularly *when you are not permitted to be chief of police, but must yield your judgment to the district commissioners who have yielded their judgment to the White House.* Being Chief of Police under such circumstances can hardly be worth while. You are a young man and the world is full of places for young men with courage enough to save their self-respect at the expense of their jobs. You did that once,—back in the Ballinger-Pinchot days. Why not now?

Come out and help make the fight which must be made to recover and protect the liberties which are being filched from us here at home. There is a real fight looming up for real democracy. You will not be alone. There are a lot of fine young men, vigorous and patriotic, in and out of the Administration who are preparing for this fight. Yours will not be the only resignation. But why not be among the first? Don't wait. Let them have your resignation now and let me be the first to welcome and congratulate you.

Sincerely,
(Signed) GILSON GARDNER.

Representative John Baer of North Dakota, having witnessed for himself the riotous scenes, immediately introduced into the House a resolution [1] demanding an investigation of conditions in the Capital which permitted mobs to attack women. This, too, went to certain death. Between the members who did not dare denounce the Administration and the others who did dare denounce the women, we had to stand quite

[1] See Appendix 3 for full text of resolution.

solidly on our own program, and do our best to keep them nervous over the next step in the agitation.

The press throughout the entire country at this time protested against mob violence and the severe sentences pronounced upon the women who had attempted to hold their banners steadfast.

The Washington (D. C.) *Herald*, August 19, printed the following editorial:

There is an echo of the President's phrase about the "firm hand of stern repression" in the arrest, conviction and jailing of the six suffragists; a touch of ruthlessness in their incarceration at Occoquan along with women of the street, pickpockets and other flotsam and jetsam. Still, the suffragists are not looking for sympathy, and it need not be wasted upon them.

The police have arrived at a policy, although no one knows whether it will be sufficiently stable and consistent to last out the week. . . . Washington is grateful that the disgraceful period of rioting and mob violence in front of the White House is at an end, and another crisis in the militant crusade to bring the Susan B. Anthony amendment before Congress has been reached.

What is the next step? No one knows. Picketing doubtless will continue, or an effort will be made to continue it; and militancy, if the police continue to arrest, instead of giving the women protection, will pass into a new phase. The suffragists as well as the public at large are thankful that the police department has finally determined to arrest the pickets, instead of allowing them to be mobbed by hoodlums.

. . . The public eye will be on Occoquan for the next few weeks, to find out how these women bear up under the Spartan treatment that is in store for them. If they have deliberately sought martyrdom, as some critics have been unkind enough to suggest, they have it now. And if their campaign, in the opinion of perhaps the great majority of the public, has been misguided, admiration for their pluck will not be withheld.

The Boston *Journal* of August 20, 1917, said in an editorial written by Herbert N. Pinkham, Jr.:

That higher authorities than the Washington police were responsible for the amazing policy of rough house employed against the suffrage pickets has been suspected from the very beginning. Police power in Washington is sufficient to protect a handful of women against a whole phalanx of excited or inspired government clerks and uniformed hoodlums, if that power were used.

. . . In our nation's capital, women have been knocked down and dragged through the streets by government employees—including sailors in uniform. The police are strangely absent at such moments, as a rule, and arrive only in time to arrest a few women. . . .

Perhaps the inscriptions on the suffrage banners were not tactful. It is sometimes awkward indeed to quote the President's speeches after the speeches have "grown cold." Also a too vigorous use of the word "democracy" is distasteful to some government dignitaries, it seems. But right or wrong, the suffragists at Washington are entitled to police protection, even though in the minds of the Administration they are not entitled to the ballot.

Perhaps, even in America, we must have a law forbidding people to carry banners demanding what they consider their political rights. Such a law would, of course, prohibit political parades of all kinds, public mass meetings and other demonstrations of one set of opinions against another set. Such a law has been proposed by Senator Myers of Montana, the author of the latest censorship and anti-free speech bill. It may be necessary to pass the law, if it is also necessary that the public voice be stilled and the nation become dumb and subservient.

But until there is such a law . . . people must be protected while their actions remain within the law. If their opinions differ from ours, we must refrain from smashing their faces, if a certain number of people believe that they have the right to vote we may either grant their claim or turn them sadly away, but we may not roll them into the gutter; if they see fit to tell us our professions of democracy are empty, we may smile sorrowfully and murmur a prayer for their ignorance but we may not pelt them with rotten eggs and fire a shot through the window of their dwelling; if, denied a properly dignified hearing, they insist upon walking through the streets with printed words on a saucy banner, we may be amazed at their zeal and pitiful of their bad taste, but even for the sake of keeping their accusations out of sight of our foreign visitors (whom we have trained to believe us perfect) we may not send them to jail. . . .

All this suffrage shouting in Washington has as its single object the attainment of President Wilson's material support for equal suffrage. . . .

President Wilson's word would carry the question into Congress. . . .

Would there be any harm in letting Congress vote on a suffrage resolution? That would end the disturbance and it would make our shield of national justice somewhat brighter.

It looks like President Wilson's move.

Between these opposing currents of protest and support, the Administration drifted helplessly. Unwilling to pass the amendment, it continued to send women to prison.

On the afternoon of September 4th, President Wilson led his first contingent of drafted "soldiers of freedom" down Pennsylvania Avenue in gala parade, on the first lap of their journey to the battlefields of France. On the same afternoon a slender line of women—also "soldiers of freedom"—attempted to march in Washington.

As they attempted to take up their posts, two by two, in front of the Reviewing Stand, opposite the White House, they were gathered in and swept away by the police like common street criminals—their golden banners scarcely flung to the breeze.

MR. PRESIDENT, HOW LONG MUST WOMEN BE DENIED A VOICE IN A GOVERNMENT WHICH IS CONSCRIPTING THEIR SONS?

was the offensive question on the first banner carried by Miss Eleanor Calnan of Massachusetts and Miss Edith Ainge of New York.

The Avenue was roped off on account of the parade. There was hardly any one passing at the time; all traffic had been temporarily suspended, so there was none to obstruct. But the Administration's policy must go on. A few moments and Miss Lucy Branham of Maryland and Mrs. Pauline Adams of Virginia marched down the Avenue, their gay banners waving joyously in the autumn sun, to fill up the gap of the two comrades who had been arrested. They, too, were shoved into the police automobile, their banners still high and appealing, silhouetted against the sky as they were hurried to the police station.

The third pair of pickets managed to cross the Avenue, but were arrested immediately they reached the curb. Still others advanced. The crowd began to line the ropes and to watch eagerly the line of women indomitably coming, two by two, into the face of certain arrest. A fourth detachment was arrested in the middle of the Avenue on the trolley tracks. But still they came.

A few days later more women were sent to the workhouse for carrying to the picket line this question:

"President Wilson, what did you mean when you said: 'We have seen a good many singular things happen recently. We have been told there is a deep disgrace resting upon the origin of this nation. The nation originated in the sharpest sort of criticism of public policy. We originated, to put it in the vernacular, in a kick, and if it be unpatriotic to kick, why then the grown man is unlike the child. We have forgotten the very principle of our origin if we have forgotten how to object, how to resist, how to agitate, how to pull down and build up, even to the extent of revolutionary practices, if it be necessary to readjust matters. I have forgotten my history if that be not true history.' "

The Administration had not yet abandoned hope of removing the pickets. They persisted in their policy of arrests and longer imprisonments.

CHAPTER 6

D URING all this time the suffrage prisoners were enduring the miserable and petty tyranny of the government workhouse at Occoquan. They were kept absolutely incommunicado. They were not allowed to see even their nearest relatives, should any be within reach, until they had been in the institution two weeks.

Each prisoner was allowed to write one outgoing letter a month, which, after being read by the warden, could be sent or withheld at his whim.

All incoming mail and telegrams were also censored by the Superintendent and practically all of them denied the prisoners. Superintendent Whittaker openly boasted of holding up the suffragists' mail: "I am boss down here," he said to visitors who asked to see the prisoners, or to send in a note. "I consider the letters and telegrams these prisoners get are treasonable. They cannot have them." He referred to messages commending the women for choosing prison to silence, and bidding them stand steadfast to their program.

Of course all this was done in the hope of intimidating not only the prisoners, but also those who came wanting to see them.

It was the intention of the women to abide as far as possible by the routine of the institution, disagreeable and unreasonable as it was. They performed the tasks assigned to them. They ate the prison food without protest. They wore the coarse prison clothes. But at the end of the first week of detention they became so weak from the shockingly bad food that they began to wonder if they could endure such a system. The petty tyrannies they could endure. But the inevitable result of a diet of sour bread, half-cooked vegetables, rancid soup with worms in it, was serious.

Finally the true condition of affairs trickled to the outside world through the devious routes of prison messengers.

Senator J. Hamilton Lewis, of Illinois, Democratic whip in the Senate, heard alarming reports of two of his constituents, Miss Lucy Ewing, daughter of Judge Ewing, niece of Adlai Stevenson, Vice-President in Cleveland's Administration, niece of James Ewing, minister to Belgium in the same Administration, and Mrs. William Upton Watson of Chicago. He made a hurried trip to the workhouse to see them. The fastidious Senator was shocked—shocked at the appearance of the prisoners, shocked at the tale they told, shocked that "ladies" should be subjected to such indignities. "In all my years of criminal practice," said the Senator to Gilson Gardner, who had accompanied him to the workhouse, "I have never seen prisoners so badly treated, either before or after conviction." He is a gallant gentleman who would be expected to be uncomfortable when he actually saw ladies suffer. It was more than gallantry in this instance, however, for he spoke in frank condemnation of the whole "shame and outrage" of the thing.

It is possible that he reported to other Administration officials what he had learned during his visit to the workhouse for very soon afterwards it was announced that an investigation of conditions in the workhouse would be held. That was, of course, an admirable manoeuvre which the Administration could make. "Is the President not a kind man? He pardoned some women. Now he investigates the conditions under which others are imprisoned. Even though they are lawless women, he wishes them well treated."

It would sound "noble" to thousands.

Immediately the District Commissioners announced this investigation, Miss Lucy Burns, acting on behalf of the National Woman's Party, sent a letter to Commissioner Brownlow. After summing up the food situation Miss Burns wrote:

When our friends were sent to prison, they expected the food would be extremely plain, but they also expected that . . . enough eatable food would be given them to maintain them in their ordinary state of health. This has not been the case.

The testimony of one of the prisoners, Miss Lavinia Dock, a trained nurse, is extremely valuable on the question of food supplied at Occoquan. Miss Dock is Secretary of the American Federation of Nurses. She has had a distinguished career in her profession. She assisted in the work after the Johnstown flood and during the yellow fever epidemic in Florida. During the Spanish war she organized the Red Cross work with Clara Barton. 'I really thought,' said Miss Dock, when I last saw her, 'that I could eat everything, but here I have hard work choking down enough food to keep the life in me.'

I am sure you will agree with me that these conditions should be instantly remedied. When these and other prisoners were sentenced to prison they were sentenced to detention and not to starvation or semi-starvation.

The hygienic conditions have been improved at Occoquan since a group of suffragists were imprisoned there. But they are still bad. The water they drink is kept in an open pail, from which it is ladled into a drinking cup. The prisoners frequently dip the drinking cup directly into the pail.

The same piece of soap is used for every prisoner. As the prisoners in Occoquan are sometimes seriously afflicted with disease, this practice is appallingly negligent.

Concerning the general conditions of the person, I am enclosing with this letter, affidavit of Mrs. Virginia Bovee, an ex-officer of the workhouse. . . . The prisoners for whom I am counsel are aware that cruel practices go on at Occoquan. On one occasion they heard Superintendent Whittaker kicking a woman in the next room. They heard Whittaker's voice, the sound of blows, and the woman's cries.

I lay these facts beforè you with the knowledge that you will be glad to have the fullest possible information given you concerning the institution for whose administration you as Commissioner of the District of Columbia are responsible.

Very respectfully yours,

(Signed)   LUCY BURNS.

Mrs. Bovee, a matron, was discharged from the workhouse because she tried to be kind to the suffrage prisoners. She also gave them warnings to guide them past the possible contamination of hideous diseases. As soon as she was discharged from the workhouse she went to the headquarters of the Woman's Party and volunteered to make an affidavit. The affidavit of Mrs. Bovee follows:

I was discharged yesterday as an officer of Occoquan workhouse. For eight months I acted as night officer, with no complaint as to my performance of my duties. Yesterday Superintendent Whittaker told me I was discharged and gave me two hours in which to get out. I demanded the charges from the matron, Mrs. Herndon, and I was told that it was owing to something that Senator Lewis has said.

I am well acquainted with the conditions at Occoquan. I have had charge of all the suffragist prisoners who have been there. I know that their mail has been withheld from them. Mrs. Herndon, the matron, reads the mail, and often discussed it with us at the officers' table. She said of a letter sent to one of the suffragist pickets now in the workhouse, "They told her to keep her eyes open and notice everything. She will never get that letter," said Mrs. Herndon. Then she corrected herself, and added, "Not until she goes away." Ordinarily the mail not given the prisoners is destroyed. The mail for the suffragists is saved for them until they are ready to go away. I have seen three of the women have one letter each, but that is all. The three were Mrs. Watson, Miss Ewing, and I think Miss Flanagan.

The blankets now being used in the prison have been in use since December without being washed or cleaned. Blankets are washed once a year. Officers are warned not to touch any of the bedding. The one officer who handles it is compelled by the regulations to wear rubber gloves while she does so. The sheets for the ordinary prisoners are not changed completely, even when one is gone and another takes her bed. Instead the top sheet is put on the bottom, and one fresh sheet is given them. I was not there when these suffragists arrived, and I do not know how their bedding was arranged. I doubt whether the authorities would have dared to give them one soiled sheet.

The prisoners with disease are not always isolated, by any means. In the colored dormitory there are two women in the advanced stages of consumption. Women suffering from syphilis, who have open sores, are put in the hospital. But those whose sores are temporarily healed are put in the same dormitory with the others. There have been several such in my dormitory.

When the prisoners come they must undress and take a shower bath. For this they take a piece of soap from a bucket in the store room. When they are finished they throw the soap back in the bucket. The suffragists are permitted three showers a week and have only these pieces of soap which are common to all inmates. There is no soap at all in wash rooms.

The beans, hominy, rice, cornmeal (which is exceedingly coarse, like chicken feed) and cereal have all had worms in them. Sometimes the worms float on top of the soup. Often they are found in the cornbread. The first suffragists sent the worms to Whittaker on a spoon. On the farm is a fine herd of Holsteins. The cream is made into butter and sold to the tuberculosis hospital in Washington. At the officers' table we have very good milk. The prisoners do not have any butter or sugar, and no milk except by order of the doctor.

Prisoners are punished by being put on bread or water, or by being beaten. I know of one girl who has been kept seventeen days on only water this month in the "booby house." The same was kept nineteen days on water last year because she beat Superintendent Whittaker when he tried to beat her.

Superintendent Whittaker or his son are the only ones who beat the girls. Officers are not allowed to lay a hand on them in punishment. I know of one girl beaten until the blood had to be scrubbed from her clothing and from the floor of the "booby house." I have never actually seen a girl beaten, but I have seen her afterwards and I have heard the cries and blows. Dorothy Warfield was beaten and the suffragists heard the beating.

(Signed)   MRS. VIRGINIA BOVEE.

Subscribed and sworn to before
me this day of August, 1917.

JOSEPH H. BATT, *Notary Public.*

While the Administration was planning an investigation of the conditions in the workhouse, which made it difficult for women to sustain health through a thirty day sentence, it was, through its police court, sentencing more women to *sixty day sentences*, under the same conditions. The Administration was giving some thought to its plan of procedure, but not enough to master the simple fact that women would not stop going to prison until something had been done which promised passage of the amendment through Congress.

New forms of intimidation and hardship were offered by Superintendent Whittaker.

Mrs. Frederick Kendall of Buffalo, New York, a frail and highly sensitive woman, was put in a "punishment cell" on bread and water, under a charge of "impudence." Mrs. Kendall says that her impudence consisted of "protesting to the matron that scrubbing floors on my hands and knees was too severe work for me as I had been unable for days to eat the prison food. My impudence further consisted in asking for lighter work."

Mrs. Kendall was refused the clean clothing she should have had the day she was put in solitary confinement and was thus forced to wear the same clothing eleven days. She was refused a nightdress or clean linen for the cot. Her only toilet accommodations was an open pail. For four days she was allowed no water for toilet purposes. Her diet consisted of three thin slices of bread and three cups of water, carried to her in a paper cup which frequently leaked out half the meagre supply before it got to Mrs. Kendall's cell.

Representative and Mrs. Charles Bennet Smith, of Buffalo, friends of Mrs. Kendall, created a considerable disturbance when they learned of this cruel treatment, with the result that Mrs. Kendall was finally given clean clothing and taken from her confinement. When she walked from her cell to greet Mrs. Genevieve Clark Thompson, daughter of Champ Clark, Speaker of the House, and Miss Roberta Bradshaw, other friends, who, through the Speaker's influence, had obtained special permission to see Mrs. Kendall, she fell in a dead faint. It was such shocking facts as these that the Commissioners and their investigating board were vainly trying to keep from the country for the sake of the reputation of the Administration.

For attempting to speak to Mrs. Kendall through her cell door, to inquire as to her health, while in solitary, Miss Lucy Burns was placed on a bread and water diet.

Miss Jeannette Rankin of Montana, the only woman member of Congress, was moved by these and similar revelations to introduce a resolution [1] calling for a Congressional investigation of the workhouse.

There were among the suffrage prisoners women of all shades of social opinion.

The following letter by Miss Gvinter, the young Russian worker, was smuggled out of the workhouse. This appeal to Meyer London was rather pathetic, since not even he, the only Socialist member in Congress, stood up to denounce the treatment of the pickets.

Comrade Meyer London:
I am eight years in this movement, three and a half years a member of the Socialist Party, Branches 2 and 4 of the Bronx, and I have been an active member of the Waist Makers' Union since 1910. I am from New York, but am now in Balti-

[1] For text of Miss Rankin's resolution see Appendix 3.

more, where I got acquainted with the comrades who asked me to picket the White House, and of course I expressed my willingness to help the movement. I am now in the workhouse. I want to get out and help in the work as I am more revolutionary than the Woman's Party, yet conditions here are so bad that I feel I must stay here and help women get their rights. We are enslaved here. I am suffering very much from hunger and nearly blind from bad nourishment. The food is chiefly soup, cereal with worms, bread just baked and very heavy. Even this poor food, we do not get enough. I do not eat meat. When I told the doctor that he said, "You must eat, and if you don't like it here, you go and tell the judge you won't picket any more, and then you can get out of here." But I told him that I could not go against my principles and my belief. He asked, "Do you believe you should break the law?" I replied, "I have picketed whenever I had a chance for eight years and have never broken the law. Picketing is legal."

Please come here as quickly as possible, as we need your help.

Will you give the information in this letter to the newspapers?

Please pardon this scrap of paper as I have nothing else to write on. I would write to other comrades, to Hillquit or Paulsen, but you are in the Congress and can do more.

Yours for the Cause,

(Signed)   ANNA GVINTER.

OCCOQUAN WORKHOUSE, Friday, Sept. 21.

Miss Gvinter swore to an affidavit when she came out in which she said in part:

. . . The days that we had to stand on scaffolds and ladders to paint the dormitories, I was so weak from lack of food I was dizzy and in constant danger of falling.

. . . When they told me to *scrub the floors of the lavatories* I refused, because I have to work for my living and I could not afford to get any of the awful diseases that women down there have.

I obeyed all the rules of the institution. The only times I stopped working was because I was too sick to work.

(Signed)   ANNA GVINTER.

Sworn to before me and subscribed in my presence this 13th day of October, 1917.

(Signed)   C. LARIMORE KEELEY,
Notary Public, D. C.

Half a hundred women was the government's toll for one month. Continuous arrests kept the issue hot and kept people who cared in constant protest. It is impossible to give space to the countless beautiful messages which were sent to the women, or the fervent protests which went to government officials. Among the hundreds of thousands of protests was a valuable one by Dr. Harvey Wiley, the celebrated food expert, in a letter to Dr. George M. Kober, member of the Board in control of the jail and workhouse, and a well-known sanitarian. Dr. Wiley wrote:

November 3, 1917.

Dear Dr. Kober:
I am personally acquainted with many of the women who have been confined at Occoquan, and at the District jail, and have heard from their own lips an account of the nutrition and sanitary conditions prevailing at both places.

I, therefore, feel constrained to make known to you the conditions as they have been told to me, and as I believe them actually to exist.

As I understand it, there is no purpose in penal servitude of lowering the vitality of the prisoner, or in inviting disease. Yet both of these conditions prevail both at Occoquan and at the District jail. First of all, the food question. The diet furnished the prisoners at Occoquan especially is of a character to invite all kinds of infections that may prevail, and to lower the vitality so that the resistance to disease is diminished. I have fortunately come into possession of samples of the food actually given to these women. I have kept samples of the milk religiously for over two weeks to see if I could detect the least particle of fat, and have been unable to perceive any. The fat of milk is universally recognized by dieticians as its most important nutritive character. I understand that a dairy is kept on the farm at Occoquan, and yet it is perfectly certain that no whole milk is served or ever has been served to one of the so-called "picketers" in that jail. I have not had enough of the sample to make a chemical analysis, but being somewhat experienced in milk, I can truthfully say that it seems to me to be watered skimmed milk. I also have a sample of the pea soup served. The pea grains are coarsely broken, often more than half of a pea being served in one piece. They never have been cooked, but are in a perfectly raw state, and found to be inedible by the prisoners.

I have also samples of the corn bread which is most unattractive and repellant to the eye and to the taste. All of these witnesses say that the white bread apparently is of good quality, but the diet in every case is the cause of constipation, except in the case of pea soup, which brings on diarrhœa and vomiting. As nutrition is the very foundation of sanitation, I wish to call to your special attention, as a sanitarian, the totally inadequate sustenance given to these prisoners.

The food at the county jail at Washington is much better than the food at Occoquan, but still bad enough. This increased excellence of food is set off by the miserable ventilation of the cells, in which these noble women are kept in solitary confinement. Not only have they had a struggle to get the windows open slightly, but also at the time of their morning meal, the sweeping is done. The air of the cells is filled with dust and they try to cover their coffee and other food with such articles as they can find to keep the dust out of their food. Better conditions for promoting tuberculosis could not be found.

I appeal to you as a well-known sanitarian to get the Board of Charities to make such rules and regulations as would secure to prisoners of all kinds, and especially to political prisoners, as humane an environment as possible.

I also desire to ask that the Board of Charities would authorize me to make inspections of food furnished to prisoners at Occoquan and at the District Jail, and to have physical and chemical analysis made without expense to the Board, in

order to determine more fully the nutritive environment in
which the prisoners live.

Sincerely,

(Signed)   HARVEY WILEY.

This striking telegram from Richard Bennett, the distinguished actor, must have arrested the attention of the Administration.

September 22, 1917.

Hon. Newton Baker,
Secretary of War,
War Department,
Washington, D. C.

I have been asked to go to France personally, with the
film of "Damaged Goods," as head of a lecture corps to the
American army.   On reliable authority I am told that American women, because they have dared demand their political
freedom, are held in vile conditions in the Government workhouse in Washington; are compelled to paint the negro toilets
for eight hours a day; are denied decent food and denied communication with counsel.   Why should I work for democracy
in Europe when our American women are denied democracy at
home?   If I am to fight for social hygiene in France, why not
begin at Occoquan workhouse?

RICHARD BENNETT.

Mr. Bennett never received a reply to this message.

Charming companionships grew up in prison.   Ingenuity at
lifting the dull monotony of imprisonment brought to light
many talents for camaraderie which amused not only the suffrage prisoners but the "regulars."   Locked in separate cells,
as in the District Jail, the suffragists could still communicate
by song.   The following lively doggerel to the tune of "Captain
Kidd" was sung in chorus to the accompaniment of a hair comb.
It became a saga.   Each day a new verse was added, relating
the day's particular controversy with the prison authorities.

We worried Woody-wood,
As we stood, as we stood,
We worried Woody-wood,
As we stood.
We worried Woody-wood,
And we worried him right good;
We worried him right good as we stood.

We asked him for the vote,
As we stood, as we stood,
We asked him for the vote
As we stood,
We asked him for the vote,
But he'd rather write a note,
He'd rather write a note—so we stood.

We'll not get out on bail,
Go to jail, go to jail—
We'll not get out on bail,
We prefer to go to jail,
We prefer to go to jail—we're not frail.

We asked them for a brush,
For our teeth, for our teeth,
We asked them for a brush
For our teeth.
We asked them for a brush,
They said, "There ain't no rush,"
They said, "There ain't no rush—darn your teeth."

We asked them for some air,
As we choked, as we choked,
We asked them for some air
As we choked.
We asked them for some air
And they threw us in a lair,
They threw us in a lair, so we choked.

We asked them for our nightie,
As we froze, as we froze,
We asked them for our nightie
As we froze.
We asked them for our nightie,
And they looked—hightie-tightie—
They looked hightie-tightie—so we froze.

Now, ladies, take the hint,
As ye stand, as ye stand,
Now, ladies, take the hint,
As ye stand.
Now, ladies, take the hint,
Don't quote the Presidint,
Don't quote the Presidint, as ye stand.

Humor predominated in the poems that came out of prison. There was never any word of tragedy.

Not even an intolerable diet of raw salt pork, which by actual count of Miss Margaret Fotheringham, a teacher of Domestic Science and Dietetics, was served the suffragists *sixteen times in eighteen days,* could break their spirit of gayety. And when a piece of fish of unknown origin was slipped through the tiny opening in the cell door, and a specimen carefully preserved for Dr. Wiley—who, by the way, was unable to classify it—they were more diverted than outraged.

Sometimes it was a "prayer" which enlivened the evening hour before bedtime. Mary Winsor of Haverford, Pennsylvania, was the master prayer-maker. One night it was a Baptist prayer, another a Methodist, and still another a stern Presbyterian prayer. The prayers were most disconcerting to the matron for the "regulars" became almost hysterical with laughter, when they should be slipping into sleep. It was trying also to sit in the corridor and hear your daily cruelties narrated to God and punishment asked. This is what happened to the embarrassed warden and jail attendants if they came to protest.

Sometimes it was the beautiful voice of Vida Milholland which rang through the corridors of the dreary prison, with a stirring Irish ballad, a French love song, or the Woman's Marseillaise.

Again the prisoners would build a song, each calling out from cell to cell, and contributing a line. The following song to the tune of "Charlie Is My Darling" was so written and sung with Miss Lucy Branham leading:

SHOUT THE REVOLUTION OF WOMEN

> Shout the revolution
>   Of women, of women,
> Shout the revolution
>   For liberty.
> Rise, glorious women of the earth,
>   The voiceless and the free
> United strength assures the birth
>   Of true democracy.

Refrain

> Invincible our army,
>   Forward, forward,
> Triumphant daughters pressing
>   To victory.

> Shout the revolution
>   Of women, of women,
> Shout the revolution
>   For liberty.
> Men's revolution born in blood,
>   But ours conceived in peace,
> We hold a banner for a sword,
>   Till all oppression cease.

Refrain

> Prison, death, defying,
>   Onward, onward,
> Triumphant daughters pressing
>   To victory.

The gayety was interspersed with sadness when the suffragists learned of new cruelties heaped upon the helpless ones, those who were without influence or friends. They learned of that barbarous punishment known as "the greasy pole" used upon girl prisoners. This method of punishment consisted of strapping girls with their hands tied behind them to a greasy pole from which they were partly suspended. Unable to keep themselves in an upright position, because of the grease on the pole, they slipped almost to the floor, with their arms all but severed from the arm sockets, suffering intense pain for long periods of time. This cruel punishment was meted out to prisoners for slight infractions of the prison rules.

The suffrage prisoners learned also of the race hatred which the authorities encouraged. It was not infrequent that the jail officers summoned black girls to attack white women, if the latter disobeyed. This happened in one instance to the suffrage prisoners who were protesting against the warden's forcibly taking a suffragist from the workhouse without telling her or her comrades whither she was being taken. Black girls were called and commanded to physically attack the suffragists. The negresses, reluctant to do so, were goaded to deliver blows upon the women by the warden's threats of punishment.

And as a result of our having been in prison, our headquarters has never ceased being the mecca of many discouraged "inmates," when released. They come for money. They come for work. They come for spiritual encouragement to face life after the wrecking experience of imprisonment. Some regard us as "fellow prisoners." Others regard us as "friends at court."

Occasionally we meet a prison associate in the workaday world. Long after Mrs. Lawrence Lewis' imprisonment, when she was working on ratification of the amendment in Delaware, she was greeted warmly by a charming young woman who came forward at a meeting. "Don't you remember me?" she asked, as

Mrs. Lewis struggled to recollect. "Don't you remember me? I met you in Washington."

"I'm sorry but I seem to have forgotten where I met you," said Mrs. Lewis apologetically.

"In jail," came the answer hesitantly, whereupon Mrs. Lewis listened sympathetically while her fellow prisoner told her that she had been in jail at the time Mrs. Lewis was, that *her* crime was bigamy and that she was one of the traveling circus troupe then in Dover.

"She brought up her husband, also a member of the circus," said Mrs. Lewis in telling of the incident, "and they both joined enthusiastically in a warm invitation to come and see them in the circus."

As each group of suffragists was released an enthusiastic welcome was given to them at headquarters and at these times, in the midst of the warmth of approving and appreciative comrades, some of the most beautiful speeches were delivered. I quote a part of Katharine Fisher's speech at a dinner in honor of released prisoners:

Five of us who are with you to-night have recently come out from the workhouse into the world. A great change? Not so much of a change for women, disfranchised women. In prison or out, American women are not free. Our lot of physical freedom simply gives us and the public a new and vivid sense of what our lack of political freedom really means.

Disfranchisement is the prison of women's power and spirit. Women have long been classed with criminals so far as their voting rights are concerned. And how quick the Government is to live up to its classification the minute women determinedly insist upon these rights. Prison life epitomizes all life under undemocratic rule. At Occoquan, as at the Capitol and the White House, we faced hypocrisy, trickery and treachery on the part of those in power. And the constant appeal to us to "coöperate" with the workhouse authorities sounded wonderfully like the exhortation addressed to all women to "support the Government."

"Is that the law of the District of Columbia?" I asked Superintendent Whittaker concerning a statement he had made to me. "It is the law," he answered, "because it is the rule I make." The answer of Whittaker is the answer Wilson makes to women every time the Government, of which he is the head, enacts a law and at the same time continues to refuse to pass the Susan B. Anthony amendment. . . .

We seem to-day to stand before you free, but I have no sense of freedom because I have left comrades at Occoquan and because other comrades may at any moment join them there. . . .

While comrades are there what is our freedom? It is as empty as the so-called political freedom of women who have won suffrage by a state referendum. Like them we are free only within limits. . . .

We must not let our voice be drowned by war trumpets or cannon. If we do, we shall find ourselves, when the war is over, with a peace that will only prolong our struggle, a democracy that will belie its name by leaving out half the people.

The Administration continued to send women to the workhouse and the District Jail for thirty and sixty day sentences.

CHAPTER 7

DUDLEY FIELD MALONE was known to the country as sharing the intimate confidence and friendship of President Wilson. He had known and supported the President from the beginning of the President's political career. He had campaigned twice through New Jersey with Mr. Wilson as Governor; he had managed Mr. Wilson's campaigns in many states for the nomination before the Baltimore Convention; he had toured the country with Mr. Wilson in 1912; and it was he who led to victory President Wilson's fight for California in 1916.

So when Mr. Malone went to the White House in July, 1917, to protest against the Administration's handling of the suffrage question, he went not only as a confirmed suffragist, but also as a confirmed supporter and member of the Wilson Administration—the one who had been chosen to go to the West in 1916 to win women voters to the Democratic Party.

Mr. Malone has consented to tell for the first time, in this record of the militant campaign, what happened at his memorable interview with President Wilson in July, 1917, an interview which he followed up two months later with his resignation as Collector of the Port of New York. I quote the story in his own words:

Frank P. Walsh, Amos Pinchot, Frederic C. Howe, J. A. H. Hopkins, Allen McCurdy and I were present throughout the trial of the sixteen women in July. Immediately after the police court judge had pronounced his sentence of sixty days in the Occoquan workhouse upon these "first offenders," on the alleged charge of a traffic violation, I went over to Anne Martin, one of the women's counsel, and offered to act as attorney on the appeal of the case. I then went to the court clerk's office and telephoned to President Wilson at the White House, asking him to see me at once. It was three o'clock. I called a taxicab, drove direct to the executive offices and met him.

I began by reminding the President that in the seven years and a half of our personal and political association we had never had a serious difference. He was good enough to say that my loyalty to him had been one of the happiest circumstances of his public career. But I told him I had come to place my resignation in his hands as I could not remain a member of any administration which dared to send American women to prison for demanding national suffrage. I also informed him that I had offered to act as counsel for the suffragists on the appeal of their case. He asked me for full details of my complaint and attitude. I told Mr. Wilson everything I had witnessed from the time we saw the suffragists arrested in front of the White House to their sentence in the police court. I observed that although we might not agree with the "manners" of picketing, citizens had a right to petition the President or any other official of the government for a redress of grievances. He seemed to acquiesce in this view, and reminded me that the women had been unmolested at the White House gates for over five months, adding that he had even ordered the head usher to invite the women on cold days to come into the White House and warm themselves and have coffee.

"If the situation is as you describe it, it is shocking," said the President. "The manhandling of the women by the police was outrageous and the entire trial (before a judge of your own appointment) was a perversion of justice," I said. This seemed to annoy the President and he replied with asperity, "Why do you come to me in this indignant fashion for things which have been done by the police officials of the city of Washington?"

"Mr. President," I said, "the treatment of these women is the result of carefully laid plans made by the District Commissioners of the city of Washington, who were appointed to office by you. Newspaper men of unquestioned information and integrity have told me that the District Commissioners have been in consultation with your private secretary, Mr. Tumulty, and that the Secretary of the Treasury, Mr. McAdoo, sat in at a conference when the policy of these arrests was being determined."

The President asserted his ignorance of all this.

"Do you mean to tell me," he said, "that you intend to resign, to repudiate me and my Administration and sacrifice me for your views on this suffrage question?"

His attitude then angered me and I said, "Mr. President, if there is any sacrifice in this unhappy circumstance, it is I who am making the sacrifice. I was sent twice as your spokesman in the last campaign to the Woman Suffrage States of the West. You have since been good enough to say publicly and privately that I did as much as any man to carry California for you. After my first tour I had a long conference with you here at the White House on the political situation in those states. I told you that I found your strength with women voters lay in the fact that you had with great patience and statesmanship kept this country out of the European war. But that your great weakness with women voters was that you had not taken any step throughout your entire Administration to urge the passage of the Federal Suffrage Amendment, which Mr. Hughes was advocating and which alone can enfranchise all the women of the nation. You asked me then how I met this situation, and I told you that I promised the women voters of the West that if they showed the political sagacity to choose you as against Mr. Hughes, I would do everything in my power to get your Administration to take up and pass the suffrage amendment. You were pleased and approved of what I had done. I returned to California and repeated this promise, and so far as I am concerned, I must keep my part of that obligation."

I reiterated to the President my earlier appeal that he assist suffrage as an urgent war measure and a necessary part of America's program for world democracy, to which the President replied: "The enfranchisement of women is not at all necessary to a program of democracy and I see nothing in the argument that it is a war measure unless you mean that American women will not loyally support the war unless they are given the vote." I firmly denied this conclusion of the President and told him that while American women with or without the vote would support the United States Government against German militarism, yet it seemed to me a great opportunity of his leadership to remove this grievance which women generally felt against him and his administration. "Mr. President," I urged, "if you, as the leader, will persuade the administration to pass the Federal Amendment you will release from the suffrage fight the energies of thousands of women which will be given with redoubled zeal to the support of your program for international justice." But the President absolutely refused to admit the validity of my appeal, though it was as a "war measure" that the President some months later demanded that the Senate pass the suffrage amendment.

The President was visibly moved as I added, "You are the President now, reëlected to office. You ask if I am going to sacrifice you. You sacrifice nothing by my resignation. But I lose much. I quit a political career. I give up a powerful office in my own state. I, who have no money, sacrifice a lucrative salary, and go back to revive my law practice. But most of all I sever a personal association with you of the deepest affection which you know has meant much to me these past seven years. But I cannot and will not remain in office and see women thrown into jail because they demand their political freedom."

The President earnestly urged me not to resign, saying, "What will the people of the country think when they hear that the Collector of the Port of New York has resigned because of an injustice done to a group of suffragists by the police officials of the city of Washington?"

My reply to this was, "With all respect for you, Mr. President, my explanation to the public will not be as difficult as yours, if I am compelled to remind the public that you have appointed to office and can remove all the important officials of the city of Washington."

The President ignored this and insisted that I should not resign, saying, "I do not question your intense conviction about this matter as I know you have always been an ardent suffragist; and since you feel as you do I see no reason why you should not become their counsel and take this case up on appeal without resigning from the Administration."

"But," I said, "Mr. President, that arrangement would be impossible for two reasons; first, these women would not want me as their counsel if I were a member of your Administration, for it would appear to the public then as if your Administration was not responsible for the indignities to which they have been subjected, and your Administration *is* responsible; and, secondly, I cannot accept your suggestion because it may be necessary in the course of the appeal vigorously to criticize and condemn members of your cabinet and others close to you, and I could not adopt this policy while remaining in office under you." The President seemed greatly upset and finally urged me as a personal service to him to go at once and perfect the case on appeal for the suffragists, but not to resign until I had thought it over for a day, and until he had had an opportunity to investigate the facts I had presented to him. I agreed to this, and we closed the interview with the President saying, "If you consider my personal request and do not resign, please do not leave Washington without coming to see me." I left the executive offices and never saw him again.

There was just a day and a half left to perfect the exceptions for the appeal under the rules of procedure. No stenographic record of the trial had been taken, which put me under the greatest legal difficulties. I was in the midst of these preparations for appeal the next day when I learned to my surprise that the President had pardoned the women. He had not even consulted me as their attorney. Moreover, I was amazed that since the President had said he considered the treatment of the women "shocking," he had pardoned them without stating that he did so to correct a grave injustice. I felt certain that the high-spirited women in the workhouse would refuse to accept the pardon as a mere "benevolent" act on the part of the President.

I at once went down to the workhouse in Virginia. My opinion was confirmed. The group refused to accept the President's pardon. I advised them that as a matter of law no one could compel them to accept the pardon, but that as a matter of fact they would have to accept it, for the Attorney

General would have them all put out of the institution bag and baggage. So as a solution of the difficulty and in view of the fact that the President had said to me that their treatment was "shocking" I made public the following statement:

"The President's pardon is an acknowledgment by him of the grave injustice that has been done." This he never denied.

Under this published interpretation of his pardon the women at Occoquan accepted the pardon and returned to Washington. The incident was closed. I returned to New York. During the next two months I carefully watched the situation. Six or eight more groups of women in that time were arrested on the same false charges, tried and imprisoned in the same illegal way. Finally a group of women was arrested in September under the identical circumstances as those in July, was tried in the same lawless fashion and given the same sentence of "sixty days in the workhouse." The President may have been innocent of responsibility for the first arrests, but he was personally and politically responsible for all the arrests that occurred after his pardon of the first group. Under this development it seemed to me that self-respect demanded action, so I sent my resignation to the President, publicly stated my attitude and regretfully left his Administration."

Mr. Malone's resignation in September, 1917, came with a sudden shock, because the entire country and surely the Administration thought him quieted and subdued by the President's personal appeal to him in July.

Mr. Malone was shocked that the policy of arrests should be continued. Mr. Wilson and his Administration were shocked that any one should care enough about the liberty of women to resign a lucrative post in the Government. The nation was shocked into the realization that this was not a street brawl between women and policemen, but a controversy between suffragists and a powerful Administration. We had said so but it would have taken months to convince the public that the President was in any way responsible. Mr. Malone did what we could only have done with the greatest difficulty and after more prolonged sacrifices. He laid the responsibility squarely and dramatically where it belonged. It is impossible to over-emphasize what a tremendous acceleration Mr. Malone's fine, solitary and generous act gave to the speedy break-down of the Administration's resistance. His sacrifice lightened ours.

Women ought to be willing to make sacrifices for their own liberation, but for a man to have the courage and imagination to make such a sacrifice for the liberation of women is unparalleled. Mr. Malone called to the attention of the nation the true cause of the obstruction and suppression. He reproached the President and his colleagues after mature consideration, in the most honorable and vital way,—by refusing longer to associate himself with an Administration which backed such policies.

And Mr. Malone's resignation was not only welcomed by the militant group. The conservative suffrage leaders, although they heartily disapproved of picketing, were as outspoken in their gratitude.

Alice Stone Blackwell, the daughter of Lucy Stone, herself a pioneer suffrage leader and editor, wrote to Mr. Malone:

"May I express my appreciation and gratitude for the excellent and manly letter that you have written to President Wilson on woman suffrage? I am sure that I am only one of many women who feel thankful to you for it.

"The picketing seems to me a very silly business, and I am sure it is doing the cause harm instead of good; but the picketers are being shamefully and illegally treated, and it is a thousand pities, for President Wilson's own sake, that he ever allowed the Washington authorities to enter on this course of persecution. It was high time for some one to make a protest, and you have made one that has been heard far and wide. . . ."

Mrs. Carrie Chapman Catt, the President of the National American Woman Suffrage Association, wrote:

"I was in Maine when your wonderful letter announcing your resignation came out. It was the noblest act that any man ever did on behalf of our cause.   The letter itself was a high minded appeal. . . ."

Mrs. Norman de R. Whitehouse, the President of the New York State Woman Suffrage Party, with which Mr. Malone had worked for years, wired:

"Although we disagree with you on the question of picketing every suffragist must be grateful to you for the gallant support you are giving our cause and the great sacrifice you are making."

Mrs. James Lees Laidlaw, Vice Chairman of the New York Suffrage Party, said:

"No words of mine can tell you how our hearts have been lifted and our purposes strengthened in this tremendous struggle in New York State by the reading of your powerful and noble utterances in your letter to President Wilson. There flashed through my mind all the memories of Knights of chivalry and of romance that I have ever read, and they all paled before your championship, and the sacrifice and the high-spirited leadership that it signifies. Where you lead, I believe, thousands of other men will follow, even though at a distance, and most inadequately. . . ."

And from the women voters of California with whom Mr. Malone had kept faith came the message:

"The liberty-loving women of California greet you as one of the few men in history who have been willing to sacrifice material interests for the liberty of a class to which they themselves do not belong. We are thrilled by your inspiring words. We appreciate your sympathetic understanding of the viewpoint of disfranchised women. We are deeply grateful for the incalculable benefit of your active assistance in the struggle of American women for political liberty and for a real Democracy."

I reprint Mr. Malone's letter of resignation which sets forth in detail his position.

The President,   September 7, 1917.
    The White House,
        Washington, D. C.
Dear Mr. President:
    Last autumn, as the representative of your Administration,
I went into the woman suffrage states to urge your reëlection.
The most difficult argument to meet among the seven million
voters was the failure of the Democratic party, throughout
four years of power, to pass the federal suffrage amendment
looking toward the enfranchisement of all the women of the
country. Throughout those states, and particularly in California, which ultimately decided the election by the votes of
women, the women voters were urged to support you, even
though Judge Hughes had already declared for the federal
suffrage amendment, because you and your party, through
liberal leadership, were more likely nationally to enfranchise
the rest of the women of the country than were your opponents.
    And if the women of the West voted to reëlect you, I prom-
ised them that I would spend all my energy, at any sacrifice
to myself, to get the present Democratic Administration to
pass the federal suffrage amendment.
    But the present policy of the Administration, in permitting
splendid American women to be sent to jail in Washington, not
for carrying offensive banners, not for picketing, but on the
technical charge of obstructing traffic, is a denial even of their
constitutional right to petition for, and demand the passage
of, the federal suffrage amendment. It, therefore, now becomes
my profound obligation actively to keep my promise to the
women of the West.
    In more than twenty states it is a practical impossibility
to amend the state constitutions; so the women of those States
can only be enfranchised by the passage of the federal suffrage
amendment. Since England and Russia, in the midst of the
great war, have assured the national enfranchisement of their
women, should we not be jealous to maintain our democratic
leadership in the world by the speedy national enfranchisement
of American women?
    To me, Mr. President, as I urged upon you in Washington
two months ago, this is not only a measure of justice and
democracy, it is also an urgent war measure. The women of

the nation are, and always will be, loyal to the country, and the passage of the suffrage amendment is only the first step toward their national emancipation. But unless the government takes at least this first step toward their enfranchisement, how can the government ask millions of American women, educated in our schools and colleges, and millions of American women, in our homes, or toiling for economic independence in every line of industry, to give up by conscription their men and happiness to a war for democracy in Europe, while these women citizens are denied the right to vote on the policies of the Government which demands of them such sacrifice?

For this reason many of your most ardent friends and supporters feel that the passage of the federal suffrage amendment is a war measure which could appropriately be urged by you at this session of Congress. It is true that this amendment would have to come from Congress, but the present Congress shows no earnest desire to enact this legislation for the simple reason that you, as the leader of the party in power, have not yet suggested it.

For the whole country gladly acknowledges, Mr. President, that no vital piece of legislation has come through Congress these five years except by your extraordinary and brilliant leadership. And what millions of men and women to-day hope is that you will give the federal suffrage amendment to the women of the country by the valor of your leadership now. It will hearten the mothers of the nation, eliminate a just grievance, and turn the devoted energies of brilliant women to a more hearty support of the Government in this crisis.

As you well know, in dozens of speeches in many states I have advocated your policies and the war. I was the first man of your Administration, nearly five years ago, to publicly advocate preparedness, and helped to found the first Plattsburg training camp. And if, with our troops mobilizing in France, you will give American women this measure for their political freedom, they will support with greater enthusiasm your hope and the hope of America for world freedom.

I have not approved all the methods recently adopted by women in pursuit of their political liberty; yet, Mr. President, the Committee on Suffrage of the United States Senate was formed in 1883, when I was one year old; this same federal suffrage amendment was first introduced in Congress in 1878, brave women like Susan B. Anthony were petitioning Congress for the suffrage before the Civil War, and at the time of the Civil War men like William Lloyd Garrison, Horace Greeley, and Wendell Phillips assured the suffrage leaders that if they abandoned their fight for suffrage, when the war was ended the men of the nation "out of gratitude" would enfranchise the women of the country.

And if the men of this country had been peacefully demanding for over half a century the political right or privilege to vote, and had been continuously ignored or met with evasion by successive Congresses, as have the women, you, Mr. President, as a lover of liberty, would be the first to comprehend and forgive their inevitable impatience and righteous indignation. Will not this Administration, reëlected to power by the hope and faith of the women of the West, handsomely reward that faith by taking action now for the passage of the federal suffrage amendment?

In the Port of New York, during the last four years, billions of dollars in the export and import trade of the country have been handled by the men of the customs service; their treatment of the traveling public has radically changed, their vigilance supplied the evidence of the Lusitania note; the neutrality was rigidly maintained; the great German fleet guarded, captured, and repaired—substantial economies and reforms have been concluded and my ardent industry has been given to this great office of your appointment.

But now I wish to leave these finished tasks, to return to my profession of the law, and to give all my leisure time to fight as hard for the political freedom of women as I have always fought for your liberal leadership.

It seems a long seven years, Mr. President, since I first campaigned with you when you were running for Governor of New Jersey. In every circumstance throughout those years I have served you with the most respectful affection and unshadowed devotion. It is no small sacrifice now for me, as a member of your Administration, to sever our political relationship. But I think it is high time that men in this generation, at some cost to themselves, stood up to battle for the national enfranchisement of American women. So in order effectively to keep my promise made in the West and more freely to go into this larger field of democratic effort, I hereby resign my office as Collector of the Port of New York, to take effect at once, or at your earliest convenience.

Yours respectfully,

(Signed)   DUDLEY FIELD MALONE.

The President's answer has never before been published:

THE WHITE HOUSE   U. S. S. MAYFLOWER,
WASHINGTON   12 September, 1917.

My dear Mr. Collector:

Your letter of September 7th reached me just before I left home and I have, I am sorry to say, been unable to reply to it sooner.

I must frankly say that I cannot regard your reasons for resigning your position as Collector of Customs as convincing, but it is so evidently your wish to be relieved from the duties of the office that I do not feel at liberty to withhold my acceptance of your resignation. Indeed, I judge from your letter that any discussion of the reasons would not be acceptable to you and that it is your desire to be free of the restraints of public office. I, therefore, accept your resignation, to take effect as you have wished.

I need not say that our long association in public affairs makes me regret the action you have taken most sincerely.

Very truly yours,

(Signed)   WOODROW WILSON.

Hon. Dudley Field Malone,
Collector of Customs,
New York City.

To this Mr. Malone replied:

New York, N. Y.,
September 15th, 1917.

The President,
The White House,
    Washington, D. C.

Dear Mr. President:

Thank you sincerely for your courtesy, for I knew you were on a well-earned holiday and I did not expect an earlier reply to my letter of September 7th, 1917.

After a most careful re-reading of my letter, I am unable to understand how you could judge that any discussion by you of my reasons for resigning would not be acceptable to me since my letter was an appeal to you on specific grounds for action now by the Administration on the Federal Suffrage amendment.

However, I am profoundly grateful to you for your prompt acceptance of my resignation.

Yours respectfully,

(Signed)   DUDLEY FIELD MALONE.

It may have been accidental but it is interesting to note that the first public statement of Mr. Byron Newton, appointed by the Administration to succeed Mr. Malone as Collector of the Port of New York, was a bitter denunciation of all woman suffrage whether by state or national action.

CHAPTER 8

IMMEDIATELY after Mr. Malone's sensational resignation the Administration sought another way to remove the persistent pickets without passing the amendment. It yielded on a point of machinery. It gave us a report in the Senate and a committee in the House and expected us to be grateful.

The press had turned again to more sympathetic accounts of our campaign and exposed the prison régime we were undergoing. We were now for a moment the object of sympathy; the Administration was the butt of considerable hostility. Sensing their predicament and fearing any loss of prestige, they risked a slight advance.

Senator Jones, Chairman of the Suffrage Committee, made a visit to the workhouse. Scarcely had the women recovered from the surprise of his visit when the Senator, on the following day, September 15th, filed the favorable report which had been lying with his Committee since May 15th, exactly six months.

The Report, which he had so long delayed because he wanted [he said] to make it a particularly brilliant and elaborate one, read:

"The Committee on Woman Suffrage, to which was referred the joint resolution proposing an amendment to the Constitution of the United States, conferring upon women the right of suffrage, having the same under consideration, beg leave to report it back to the Senate with the recommendation that the joint resolution do pass."

This report to the Senate was immediately followed by a
vote of 181 to 107 in the House of Representatives in favor of
creating a Committee on Woman Suffrage in the House. This
vote was indicative of the strength of the amendment in the
House. The resolution was sponsored by Representative Pou,
Chairman of the Rules Committee and Administration leader,
himself an anti-suffragist.

It is an interesting study in psychology to consider some
of the statements made in the peculiarly heated debate the day
this vote was taken.

Scores of Congressmen, anxious to refute the idea that the
indomitable picket had had anything to do with their action,
revealed naïvely how surely it had.

Of the 291 men present, not one man stood squarely up for
the right of the hundreds of women who petitioned for justice.
Some indirectly and many, inadvertently, however, paid eloquent tribute to the suffrage picket.

From the moment Representative Pou in opening the debate
spoke of the nation-wide request for the committee, and the
President's sanction of the committee, the accusations and
counter-accusations concerning the wisdom of appointing it in
the face of the pickets were many and animated.

Mr. Meeker of Missouri, Democrat, protested against Congress "yielding to the nagging of a certain group."

Mr. Cantrill of Kentucky, Democrat, believed that "millions
of Christian women in the nation should not be denied the right
of having a Committee in the House to study the problem of
suffrage because of the mistakes of some few of their sisters."

"One had as well say," he went on, "that there should be no
police in Washington because the police force of this city permitted daily thousands of people to obstruct the streets and
impede traffic and permitted almost the mobbing of the women
without arresting the offenders. There was a lawful and peaceful way in which the police of this city could have taken charge

of the banners of the pickets without permitting the women carrying them to be the objects of mob violence. To see women roughly handled by rough men on the streets of the capital of the nation is not a pleasing sight to Kentuckians and to red-blooded Americans, and let us hope the like will never again be seen here."

Mr. Walsh, an anti-suffrage Democrat from Massachusetts, deplored taking any action which would seem to yield to the demand of the pickets who carried banners which "if used by a poor workingman in an attempt to get his rights would speedily have put him behind the bars for treason or sedition, and these poor, bewildered, deluded creatures, after their disgusting exhibition can thank their stars that because they wear skirts they are now incarcerated for misdemeanors of a minor character. . . . To supinely yield to a certain class of women picketing the gates of the official residence,—yes, even posing with their short skirts and their short hair within the view of this 'very capitol and our office buildings,' with banners which would seek to lead the people to believe that because we did not take action during this war session upon suffrage, if you please, and grant them the right of the ballot that we were traitors to the American Republic, would be monstrous."

The subject of the creation of a committee on suffrage was almost entirely forgotten. The Congressmen were utterly unable to shake off the ghosts of the pickets. The pickets had not influenced their actions! The very idea was appalling to Representative Stafford of Wisconsin, anti-suffrage Republican, who joined in the Democratic protests. He said:

"If a Suffrage Committee is created the militant class will exclaim, 'Ah, see how we have driven the great House of Representatives to recognize our rights. If we keep up this sort of practices, we will compel the House, when they come to vote on the constitutional amendment, to surrender obediently likewise'."

He spoke the truth, and finished dramatically with:

"Gentlemen, there is only one question before the House to-day and that is, if you look at it from a political aspect, whether you wish to approve of the practices of these women who have been disgracing their cause here in Washington for the past several months."

Representative Volstead, of Minnesota, Republican, came the closest of all to real courage in his protest:—

"In this discussion some very unfair comments have been made upon the women who picketed the White House. While I do not approve of picketing, I disapprove more strongly of the hoodlum methods pursued in suppressing the practice. I gather from the press that this is what took place. Some women did in a peaceable, and perfectly lawful manner, display suffrage banners on the public street near the White House. To stop this the police allowed the women to be mobbed, and then because the mob obstructed the street, the women were arrested and fined, while the mob went scot-free. . . ."

The Suffrage Committee in the House was appointed. The creation of this committee, which had been pending since 1913, was now finally granted in September, 1917. To be sure this was accomplished only after an inordinate amount of time, money and effort had been spent on a sustained and relentless campaign of pressure. But the Administration had yielded.

As a means to remove the pickets, however, this yielding had failed. "We ask no more machinery; we demand the passage of the amendment," said the pickets as they lengthened their line.

CHAPTER 9

FINDING that a Suffrage Committee in the House and a report in the Senate had not silenced our banners, the Administration cast about for another plan by which to stop the picketing. This time they turned desperately to longer terms of imprisonment. They were indeed hard pressed when they could choose such a cruel and stupid course.

Our answer to this policy was more women on the picket line, on the outside, and a protest on the inside of prison.

We decided, in the face of extended imprisonment, to demand to be treated as political prisoners. We felt that, as a matter of principle, this was the dignified and self-respecting thing to do, since we had offended politically, not criminally. We believed further that a determined, organized effort to make clear to a wider public the political nature of the offense would intensify the Administration's embarrassment and so accelerate their final surrender.

It fell to Lucy Burns, vice chairman of the organization, to be the leader of the new protest. Miss Burns is in appearance the very symbol of woman in revolt. Her abundant and glorious red hair burns and is not consumed—a flaming torch. Her body is strong and vital. It is said that Lucy Stone had the "voice" of the pioneers. Lucy Burns without doubt possessed the "voice" of the modern suffrage movement. Musical, appealing, persuading—she could move the most resistant person. Her talent as an orator is of the kind that makes for instant

175

intimacy with her audience. Her emotional quality is so powerful that her intellectual capacity, which is quite as great, is not
always at once perceived.

I find myself wanting to talk about her as a human being
rather than as a leader of women. Perhaps it is because she has
such winning, lovable qualities. It was always difficult for her
to give all of her energy and power to a movement. She
yearned to play, to read, to study, to be luxuriously indolent,
to revel in the companionship of her family, to which she is
ardently devoted; to do any one of a hundred things more pleasant than trying to reason with a politician or an unawakened
member of her own sex. But for these latter labors she had a
most gentle and persuasive genius, and she would not shrink
from hours of close argument to convince a person intellec-
tually and emotionally.

Unlike Miss Paul, however, her force is not nonresistant.
Once in the combat she takes delight in it; she is by nature a
rebel. She is an ideal leader for the stormy and courageous
attack—reckless and yet never to the point of unwisdom.

From the time Miss Burns and Miss Paul met for the first
time in Cannon Row Police Station, London, they have been
constant co-workers in suffrage. Both were students abroad at
the time they met. They were among the hundred women arrested for attempting to present petitions for suffrage to Parliament. This was the first time either of them had participated
in a demonstration. But from then on they worked together
in England and Scotland organizing, speaking, heckling members of the government, campaigning at bye-elections; going to
Holloway Prison together, where they joined the Englishwomen
on hunger strike. Miss Burns remained organizing in Scotland
while Miss Paul was obliged to return to America after serious
illness following a thirty day period of imprisonment, during
all of which time she was forcibly fed.

Miss Burns and she did not meet again until 1913—three

years having intervened—when they undertook the national work on Congress. Throughout the entire campaign Miss Burns and Miss Paul counseled with one another on every point of any importance. This combination of the cool strategist and passionate rebel—each sharing some of the attributes of the other—has been a complete and unsurpassed leadership.

You have now been introduced, most inadequately, to Lucy Burns, who was to start the fight inside the prison.

She had no sooner begun to organize her comrades for protest than the officials sensed a "plot," and removed her at once to solitary confinement. But they were too late. Taking the leader only hastened the rebellion. A forlorn piece of paper was discovered, on which was written their initial demand. It was then passed from prisoner to prisoner through holes in the wall surrounding leaden pipes, until a finished document had been perfected and signed by all the prisoners.

This historic document—historic because it represents the first organized group action ever made in America to establish the status of political prisoners—said:

To the Commissioners of the District of Columbia:

As political prisoners, we, the undersigned, refuse to work while in prison. We have taken this stand as a matter of principle after careful consideration, and from it we shall not recede.

This action is a necessary protest against an unjust sentence. In reminding President Wilson of his pre-election promises toward woman suffrage we were exercising the right of peaceful petition, guaranteed by the Constitution of the United States, which declares peaceful picketing is legal in the District of Columbia. That we are unjustly sentenced has been well recognized—when President Wilson pardoned the first group of suffragists who had been given sixty days in the workhouse, and again when Judge Mullowny suspended sentence for the last group of picketers. We wish to point out the inconsistency and injustice of our sentences—some of us have been given sixty days, a later group thirty days, and another group given a suspended sentence for exactly the same action.

Conscious, therefore, of having acted in accordance with the highest standards of citizenship, we ask the Commissioners of the District to grant us the rights due political prisoners. We ask that we no longer be segregated and confined under locks and bars in small groups, but permitted to see each other, and that Miss Lucy Burns, who is in full sympathy with this letter, be released from solitary confinement in another building and given back to us.

We ask exemption from prison work, that our legal right to consult counsel be recognized, to have food sent to us from outside, to supply ourselves with writing material for as much correspondence as we may need, to receive books, letters, newspapers, our relatives and friends.

Our united demand for political treatment has been delayed, because on entering the workhouse we found conditions so very bad that before we could ask that the suffragists be treated as political prisoners, it was necessary to make a stand for the ordinary rights of human beings for all the inmates. Although this has not been accomplished we now wish to bring the important question of the status of political prisoners to the attention of the commissioners, who, we are informed, have full authority to make what regulations they please for the District prison and workhouse.

The Commissioners are requested to send us a written reply so that we may be sure this protest has reached them.

Signed by,

Mary Winsor, Lucy Branham, Ernestine Hara, Hilda Blumberg, Maud Malone, Pauline F. Adams, Eleanor A. Calnan, Edith Ainge, Annie Arneil, Dorothy J. Bartlett, Margaret Fotheringham.

The Commissioners' only answer to this was a hasty transfer of the signers and the leader, Miss Burns, to the District Jail, where they were put in solitary confinement. The women were not only refused the privileges asked but were denied some of the usual privileges allowed to ordinary criminals.

Generous publicity was given to these reasonable demands,

and a surprisingly wide-spread protest followed the official denial of them. Scores of committees went to the District Commissioners. Telegrams backing up the women's demand again poured in upon all responsible administrators, from President Wilson down. Not even foreign diplomats escaped protest or appeal.

Miss Vera Samarodin sent to the Russian Ambassador the following touching letter, concerning her sister, which is translated from the Russian:—

The Russian Ambassador,
    Washington, D. C.
Excellency:
    I am appealing to you to help a young Russian girl imprisoned in the workhouse near Washington. Her name is Nina Samarodin. I have just come from one of the two monthly visits I am allowed to make her, as a member of her family.

The severity and cruelty of the treatment she is receiving at Occoquan are so much greater than she would have to suffer in Russia for the simple political offense she is accused of having committed that I hope you will be able to intercede with the officials of this country for her.

Her offense, aside from the fact that she infringed no law nor disturbed the peace, had only a political aim, and was proved to be political by the words of the judge who sentenced her, for he declared that because of the innocent inscription on her banner he would make her sentence light.

Since her imprisonment she has been forced to wear the dress of a criminal, which she would not in Russia; she has had to eat only the coarse and unpalatable food served the criminal inmates, and has not been allowed, as she would in Russia, to have other food brought to her; nor has she, as she would be there been under the daily care of a physician. She is not permitted to write letters, nor to have free access to books and other implements of study. Nina Samarodin has visibly lost in weight and strength since her imprisonment, and she has a constant headache from hunger.

Her motive in holding the banner by the White House, I

feel, cannot but appeal to you, Excellency, for she says it was
the knowledge that her family were fighting in Russia in this
great war for democracy, and that she was cut off from serving with them that made her desire to do what she could to
help the women of this nation achieve the freedom her own
people have.

Will you, if it is within your power, attempt to have her
recognized as a political prisoner, and relieve the severity of
the treatment she is receiving for obeying this impulse born of
her love of liberty and the dictates of her conscience?

I have, Excellency, the honor to be,
             Respectfully, your countrywoman,
                          (Signed) VERA SAMARODIN,
                                    Baltimore, Maryland.

Another Russian, Maria Moravsky, author and poet, who
had herself been imprisoned in Czarist Russia and who was touring America at the time of this controversy, expressed her surprise that our suffrage prisoners should be treated as common
criminals. She wrote:[1] "I have been twice in the Russian
prison; life in the solitary cell was not sweet; but I can assure
you it was better than that which American women suffragists
must bear.

"We were permitted to read and write; we wore our own
clothes; we were not forced to mix with the criminals; we did
no work. (Only a few women exiled to Siberia for extremely
serious political crimes were compelled to work.) And our
guardians and even judges respected us; they felt we were victims, because we struggled for liberty."

The Commissioners, who had to bear the responsibility of an
answer to these protests and to the demand of the prisoners,
contended to all alike that political prisoners did not exist.

"We shall be happy to establish a precedent," said the
women.

"But in America," stammered the Commissioners, "there is
no need for such a thing as political prisoners."

[1] Reprinted from The Suffragist, Feb. 8, 1919.

"The very fact that we can be sentenced to such long terms for a political offense shows that there does exist, in fact, a group of people who have come into conflict with state power for dissenting from the prevailing political system," our representatives answered.

We cited definitions of political offenses by eminent criminologists, penologists, sociologists, statesmen and historians. We declared that all authorities on political crime sustained our contention and that we clearly came under the category of political, if any crime. We pointed as proof to James Bryce, George Sigerson, Maurice Parmelee and even to Clemenceau, who defined the distinction between political offenses and common law crimes thus: " . . . theoretically a crime committed in the interest of the criminal is a common law crime, while an offense committed in the public interest is a political crime." [1]

We called to their attention the established custom of special treatment of political prisoners in Russia, France, Italy and even Turkey. [2]

We told them that as early as 1872 the International Prison Congress meeting in London recommended a distinction in the treatment of political and common law criminals and the resolution of recommendation was "agreed upon by the representatives of *all the Powers of Europe and America*—with the tacit concurrence of British and Irish officials." [3]

Mr. John Koren, International Prison Commissioner [4] for the United States, was throughout this agitation making a study of this very problem. As chairman of a Special Commit-

[1] Speech before the French Chamber of Deputies May 16, 1876, advocating amnesty for those who participated in the Commune of 1871. From the Annales de la Chambre des Députés, 1876, v. 2, pp. 44-48.

[2] Those interested in the question of political prisoners and their treatment abroad may want to read *Concerning Political Prisoners,* Appendix 6.

[3] Siegerson, *Political Prisoners at Home and Abroad,* p. 10.

[4] Appointed and sponsored by the Department of State as delegate to the International Prison Congress.

tee of the American Prison Association, empowered to investigate the problem of political prisoners for America, he made a
report at the annual meeting of the American Prison Association in New York, October, 1919, entitled "The Political Offenders and their Status in Prison" [1] in which he says:

"The political offender . . . must be measured by a different rule, and . . . is a creature of extraordinary and temporary conditions. . . .

"There are times in which the tactics used in the pursuit of
political recognition may result in a technical violation of the
law for which imprisonment ensues, as witness the suffragist
cases in Washington. . . . These militants were completely out
of place in a workhouse, . . . they could not be made to submit
to discipline fashioned to meet the needs of the derelicts of
society, and . . . they therefore destroyed it for the entire
institution."

There was no doubt in the official mind but that our claim
was just. But the Administration would not grant this demand, as such, of political prisoners. It must continue to persuade public opinion that our offense was not of a political
nature; that it was nothing more than unpleasant and unfortunate riotous conduct in the capital. The legend of "a few
slightly mad women seeking notoriety" must be sustained. Our
demand was never granted, but it was kept up until the last
imprisonment and was soon reinforced by additional protest
tactics. Our suffrage prisoners, however, made an important
contribution toward establishing this reform which others will
consummate. They were the first in America to organize and
sustain this demand over a long period of time. In America
we maintain a most backward policy in dealing with political
prisoners. We have neither regulation nor precedent for special
treatment of them. Nor have we official flexibility.

[1] Mr. Koren discusses the political offender from the penological, not the
social, point of view.

This controversy was at its height in the press and in the public mind when President Wilson sent the following message, through a New York State suffrage leader, on behalf of the approaching New York referendum on state woman suffrage:

"May I not express to you my very deep interest in the campaign in New York for the adoption of woman suffrage, and may I not say that I hope no voter will be influenced in his decision with regard to the great matter by anything the so-called pickets may have done here in Washington. However justly they may have laid themselves open to serious criticism, their action represents, I am sure, so small a fraction of the women of the country who are urging the adoption of woman suffrage that it would be most unfair and argue a narrow view to allow their actions to prejudice the cause itself. I am very anxious to see the great state of New York set a great example in this matter."

This statement showed a political appreciation of the growing power of the movement. Also it would be difficult to prove that the "small fraction" had not shown political wisdom in injecting into the campaign the embarrassment of a controversy which was followed by the above statement of the President. In the meantime he continued to imprison in Washington the "so-called pickets" whom he hoped would not influence the decision of the men voters of New York. It will be remembered, in passing, that the New York voters adopted suffrage at this time, although they had rejected it two years earlier. If the voters of New York were influenced at all by the "so-called pickets," could even President Wilson himself satisfactorily prove that it had been an adverse influence?

CHAPTER 10

THE HUNGER STRIKE——A WEAPON

WHEN the Administration refused to grant the demand of the prisoners and of that portion of the public which supported them, for the rights of political prisoners, it was decided to resort to the ultimate protest-weapon inside prison. A hunger strike was undertaken, not only to reinforce the verbal demand for the rights of political prisoners, but also as a final protest against unjust imprisonment and increasingly long sentences. This brought the Administration face to face with a more acute embarrassment. They had to choose between more stubborn resistance and capitulation. They continued for a while longer on the former path.

Little is known in this country about the weapon of the hunger strike. And so at first it aroused tremendous indignation. "Let them starve to death," said the thoughtless one, who did not perceive that that was the very thing a political administration could least afford to do. "Mad fanatics," said a kindlier critic. The general opinion was that the hunger strike was "foolish."

Few people realize that this resort to the refusal of food is almost as old as civilization. It has always represented a passionate desire to achieve an end. There is not time to go into the religious use of it, which would also be pertinent, but I will cite a few instances which have tragic and amusing likenesses to the suffrage hunger strike.

According to the Brehon Law,[1] which was the code of

[1] Joyce, *A Social History of Ancient Ireland,* Vol. I, Chapter VIII.

ancient Ireland by which justice was administered under ancient
Irish monarchs (from the earliest record to the 17th century),
it became the duty of an injured person, when all else failed,
to inflict punishment directly, for wrong done. "The plaintiff
'fasted on' the defendant." He went to the house of the defendant and sat upon his doorstep, remaining there without food to
force the payment of a debt, for example. The debtor was
compelled by the weight of custom and public opinion not to let
the plaintiff die at his door, and yielded. Or if he did not yield,
he was practically outlawed by the community, to the point of
being driven away. A man who refused to abide by the custom
not only incurred personal danger but lost all character.

If resistance to this form of protest was resorted to it had
to take the form of a counter-fast. If the victim of such a protest thought himself being unjustly coerced, he might fast in
opposition, "to mitigate or avert the evil."

"Fasting on a man" was also a mode of compelling action
of another sort. St. Patrick fasted against King Trian to
compel him to have compassion on his [Trian's] slaves.[1] He
also fasted against a heretical city to compel it to become or-
thodox.[2] He fasted against the pagan King Loeguire to
"constrain him to his will."[3]

This form of hunger strike was further used under the Brehon Law as compulsion to obtain a request. For example, the
Leinstermen on one occasion fasted on St. Columkille till they
obtained from him the promise that an extern King should never
prevail against them.

It is interesting to note that this form of direct action was
adopted because there was no legislative machinery to enforce
justice. These laws were merely a collection of customs attaining the force of law by long usage, by hereditary habit, and by

---

[1] *Tripartite Life of St. Patrick,* CLXXVII, p. 218.
[2] *Ibid.* CLXXVII, p. 418.
[3] *Ibid.* CLXXVII, p. 556.

public opinion. Our resort to this weapon grew out of the same situation. The legislative machinery, while empowered to give us redress, failed to function, and so we adopted the fast.

The institution of fasting on a debtor still exists in the East. It is called by the Hindoos "sitting dharna."

The hunger strike was continuously used in Russia by prisoners to obtain more humane practices toward them. Kropotkin [1] cites an instance in which women prisoners hunger struck to get their babies back. If a child was born to a woman during her imprisonment the babe was immediately taken from her and not returned. Mothers struck and got their babies returned to them.

He cites another successful example in Kharkoff prison in 1878 when six prisoners resolved to hunger strike to death if necessary to win two things—to be allowed exercise and to have the sick prisoners taken out of chains.

There are innumerable instances of hunger strikes, even to death, in Russian prison history. But more often the demands of the strikers were won. Breshkovsky [2] tells of a strike by 17 women against outrage, which elicited the desired promises from the warden.

As early as 1877 members of the Land and Liberty Society [3] imprisoned for peaceful and educational propaganda, in the Schlusselburg Fortress for political prisoners, hunger struck against inhuman prison conditions and frightful brutalities and won their points.

During the suffrage campaign in England this weapon was used for the double purpose of forcing the release of imprisoned militant suffragettes, and of compelling the British government to act.

Among the demonstrations was a revival of the ancient Irish

[1] See *In Russian and French Prisons,* P. Kropotkin.
[2] *For Russia's Freedom,* by Ernest Poole,—An Interview with Breshkovsky.
[3] See *The Russian Bastille,* Simon O. Pollock.

custom by Sylvia Pankhurst, who in addition to her hunger strikes within prison, "fasted on" the doorstep of Premier Asquith to compel him to see a deputation of women on the granting of suffrage to English women. She won.

Irish prisoners have revived the hunger strike to compel either release or trial of untried prisoners and have won. As I write, almost a hundred Irish prisoners detained by England for alleged nationalist activities, but not brought to trial, hunger struck to freedom. As a direct result of this specific hunger strike England has promised a renovation of her practices in dealing with Irish rebels.

And so it was that when we came to the adoption of this accelerating tactic, we had behind us more precedents for winning our point than for losing. We were strong in the knowledge that we could "fast on" President Wilson and his powerful Administration, and compel him to act or "fast back."

Among the prisoners who with Alice Paul led the hunger strike was a very picturesque figure, Rose Winslow (Ruza Wenclawska) of New York, whose parents had brought her in infancy from Poland to become a citizen of "free" America. At eleven she was put at a loom in a Pennsylvania mill, where she wove hosiery for fourteen hours a day until tuberculosis claimed her at nineteen. A poet by nature she developed her mind to the full in spite of these disadvantages, and when she was forced to abandon her loom she became an organizer for the Consumers' League, and later a vivid and eloquent power in the suffrage movement.

Her group preceded Miss Paul's by about a week in prison.

These vivid sketches of Rose Winslow's impressions while in the prison hospital were written on tiny scraps of paper and smuggled out to us, and to her husband during her imprisonment. I reprint them in their original form with cuts but no editing.

"If this thing is necessary we will naturally go through with it. Force is so stupid a weapon. I feel so happy doing my bit for decency—for *our* war, which is after all, real and fundamental."

*   *   *   *

"The women are all so magnificent, so beautiful. Alice Paul is as thin as ever, pale and large-eyed. We have been in solitary for five weeks. There is nothing to tell but that the days go by somehow. I have felt quite feeble the last few days—faint, so that I could hardly get my hair brushed, my arms ached so. But to-day I am well again. Alice Paul and I talk back and forth though we are at opposite ends of the building and a hall door also shuts us apart. But occasionally—thrills—we escape from behind our iron-barred doors and visit. Great laughter and rejoicing!"

*   *   *   *

To her husband:—

"My fainting probably means nothing except that I am not strong after these weeks. I know you won't be alarmed.

"I told about a syphilitic colored woman with one leg. The other one was cut off, having rotted so that it was alive with maggots when she came in. The remaining one is now getting as bad. They are so short of nurses that a little colored girl of twelve, who is here waiting to have her tonsils removed, waits on her. This child and two others share a ward with a syphilitic child of three or four years, whose mother refused to have it at home. It makes you absolutely ill to see it. I am going to break all three windows as a protest against their confining Alice Paul with these!

"Dr. Gannon is chief of a hospital. Yet Alice Paul and I found we had been taking baths in one of the tubs here, in which this syphilitic child, an incurable, who has his eyes bandaged all the time, is also bathed. He has been here a year. Into the room where he lives came yesterday two children to be operated on for tonsillitis. They also bathed in the same tub. The syphilitic woman has been in that room seven months. Cheerful mixing, isn't it? The place is alive with roaches, crawling all over the walls, everywhere. I found one in my bed the other day. . . ."

* * * *

"There is great excitement about my two syphilitics. Each nurse is being asked whether she told me. So, as in all institutions where an unsanitary fact is made public, no effort is made to make the wrong itself right. All hands fall to, to find the culprit, who made it known, and he is punished."

* * * *

"Alice Paul is in the psychopathic ward. She dreaded forcible feeding frightfully, and I hate to think how she must be feeling. I had a nervous time of it, gasping a long time afterward, and my stomach rejecting during the process. I spent a bad, restless night, but otherwise I am all right. The poor soul who fed me got liberally besprinkled during the process. I heard myself making the most hideous sounds. . . . One feels so forsaken when one lies prone and people shove a pipe down one's stomach."

* * * *

"This morning but for an astounding tiredness, I am all right. I am waiting to see what happens when the President realizes that brutal bullying isn't quite a statesmanlike method for settling a demand for justice at home. At least, if men are supine enough to endure, women—to their eternal glory—are not.

"They took down the boarding from Alice Paul's window yesterday, I heard. It is so delicious about Alice and me. Over in the jail a rumor began that I was considered insane and would be examined. Then came Doctor White, and said he had come to see 'the thyroid case.' When they left we argued about the matter, neither of us knowing which was considered 'suspicious.' She insisted it was she, and, as it happened, she was right. Imagine any one thinking Alice Paul needed to be 'under observation!' The thick-headed idiots!"

*   *   *   *

"Yesterday was a bad day for me in feeding. I was vomiting continually during the process. The tube has developed an irritation somewhere that is painful.

"Never was there a sentence [1] like ours for such an offense as ours, even in England. No woman ever got it over there even for tearing down buildings. And during all that agitation *we* were busy saying that never would such things happen in the United States. The men told us they would not endure such frightfulness."

*   *   *   *

"Mary Beard and Helen Todd were allowed to stay only a minute, and I cried like a fool. I am getting over that habit, I think.

"I fainted again last night. I just fell flop over in the bathroom where I was washing my hands and was led to bed when I recovered, by a nurse. I lost consciousness just as I got there again. I felt horribly faint until 12 o'clock, then fell asleep for awhile."

*   *   *   *

"I was getting frantic because you seemed to think Alice was with me in the hospital. She was in the psychopathic ward. The same doctor feeds us both, and told me. Don't let them tell you we take this well. Miss Paul vomits much. I do, too, except when I'm not nervous, as I have been every time against my will. I try to be less feeble-minded. It's the nervous reaction, and I can't control it much. I don't imagine bathing one's food in tears very good for one.

"We think of the coming feeding all day. It is horrible.

---

[1] Sentence of seven months for "obstructing traffic."

The doctor thinks I take it well. I hate the thought of Alice Paul and the others if I take it well."

*   *   *   *

"We still get no mail; we are 'insubordinate.' It's strange, isn't it; if you ask for food fit to eat, as we did, you are 'insubordinate'; and if you refuse food you are 'insubordinate.' Amusing. I am really all right. If this continues very long I perhaps won't be. I am interested to see how long our so-called 'splendid American men' will stand for this form of discipline.

"All news cheers one marvelously because it is hard to feel anything but a bit desolate and forgotten here in this place.

"All the officers here know we are making this hunger strike that women fighting for liberty may be considered political prisoners; we have told them. God knows we don't want other women ever to have to do this over again."

*   *   *   *

There have been sporadic and isolated cases of hunger strikes in this country but to my knowledge ours was the first to be organized and sustained over a long period of time. We shall see in subsequent chapters how effective this weapon was.

CHAPTER 11

THE Administration tried in another way to stop picketing. It sentenced the leader, Alice Paul, to the absurd and desperate sentence of seven months in the Washington jail for "obstructing traffic."

With the "leader" safely behind the bars for so long a time, the agitation would certainly weaken! So thought the Administration! To their great surprise, however, in the face of that reckless and extreme sentence, the longest picket line of the entire campaign formed at the White House in the late afternoon of November 10th. Forty-one women picketed in protest against this wanton persecution of their leader, as well as against the delay in passing the amendment. Face to face with an embarrassing number of prisoners the Administration used its wits and decided to reduce the number to a manageable size before imprisoning this group. Failing of that they tried still another way out. They resorted to imprisonment with terrorism.

In order to show how widely representative of the nation this group of pickets was, I give its personnel complete:

First Group

New York—Mrs. John Winters Brannan, Miss Belle Sheinberg, Mrs. L. H. Hornsby, Mrs. Paula Jakobi, Mrs. Cynthia Cohen, Miss M. Tilden Burritt, Miss Dorothy Day, Mrs. Henry Butterworth, Miss Cora Week, Mrs. P. B. Johns, Miss

Elizabeth Hamilton, Mrs. Ella O. Guilford, New York City; Miss Amy Juengling, Miss Hattie Kruger, Buffalo.

Second Group

Massachusetts—Mrs. Agnes H. Morey, Brookline; Mrs. William Bergen and Miss Camilla Whitcomb, Worcester; Miss Ella Findeisen, Lawrence; Miss L. J. C. Daniels, Boston.

New Jersey—Mrs. George Scott, Montclair.

Pennsylvania—Mrs. Lawrence Lewis, Miss Elizabeth McShane, Miss Katherine Lincoln, Philadelphia.

Third Group

California—Mrs. William Kent, Kentfield.

Oregon—Miss Alice Gram, Miss Betty Gram, Portland.

Utah—Mrs. R. B. Quay, Mrs. T. C. Robertson, Salt Lake City.

Colorado—Mrs. Eva Decker, Colorado Springs, Mrs. Genevieve Williams, Manitou.

Fourth Group

Indiana—Mrs. Charles W. Barnes, Indianapolis.

Oklahoma—Mrs. Kate Stafford, Oklahoma City.

Minnesota—Mrs. J. H. Short, Minneapolis.

Iowa—Mrs. A. N. Beim, Des Moines; Mrs. Catherine Martinette, Eagle Grove.

Fifth Group

New York—Miss Lucy Burns, New York City.

District of Columbia—Mrs. Harvey Wiley.

Louisiana—Mrs. Alice M. Cosu, New Orleans.

Maryland—Miss Mary Bartlett Dixon, Easton; Miss Julia Emory, Baltimore.

Florida—Mrs. Mary I. Nolan, Jacksonville.

There were exceptionally dramatic figures in this group. Mrs. Mary Nolan of Florida, seventy-three years old, frail in health but militant in spirit, said she had come to take her place with the women struggling for liberty in the same spirit that her revolutionary ancestor, Eliza Zane, had carried bullets to the fighters in the war for independence.

Mrs. Harvey Wiley looked appealing and beautiful as she said in court, "We took this action with great consecration of spirit, with willingness to sacrifice personal liberty for all the women of the country."

Judge Mullowny addressed the prisoners with many high-sounding words about the seriousness of obstructing the traffic in the national capital, and inadvertently slipped into a discourse on Russia, and the dangers of revolution. We always wondered why the government was not clever enough to eliminate political discourses, at least during trials, where the offenders were charged with breaking a slight regulation. But their minds were too full of the political aspect of our offense to conceal it. "The truth of the situation is that the court has not been given power to meet it," the judge lamented. "It is very, very puzzling—I find you guilty of the offense charged, but will take the matter of sentence under advisement."

And so the "guilty" pickets were summarily released.

The Administration did not relish the incarceration of forty-one women for another reason than limited housing accommodations. Forty-one women representing sixteen states in the union might create a considerable political dislocation. But these same forty-one women were determined to force the Administration to take its choice. It could allow them to continue their peaceful agitation or it could stand the reaction which was bound to come from imprisoning them. And so the forty-one women returned to the White House gates to resume their picketing. They stood guard several minutes before the police, taken unawares, could summon sufficient force to arrest them, and commandeer enough cars to carry them to police headquarters. As the Philadelphia *North American* pointed out: "There was no disorder. The crowd waited with interest and in a noticeably friendly spirit to see what would happen. There were frequent references to the pluck of the silent sentinels."

The following morning the women were ordered by Judge Mullowny to "come back on Friday. I am not yet prepared to try the case."

Logic dictated that either we had a right to stand at the gates with our banners or we did not have that right; but the Administration was not interested in logic. It had to stop picketing. Whether this was done legally or illegally, logically or illogically, clumsily or dexterously, was of secondary importance. Picketing must be stopped!

Using their welcome release to continue their protest, the women again marched with their banners to the White House in an attempt to picket. Again they were arrested. No one who saw that line will ever forget the impression it made, not only on friends of the suffragists, but on the general populace of Washington, to see these women force with such magnificent defiance the hand of a wavering Administration. On the following morning they were sentenced to from six days to six months in prison. Miss Burns received six months.

In pronouncing the lightest sentence upon Mrs. Nolan, the judge said that he did so on account of her age. He urged her, however, to pay her fine, hinting that jail might be too severe on her and might bring on death. At this suggestion, tiny Mrs. Nolan pulled herself up on her toes and said with great dignity: "Your Honor, I have a nephew fighting for democracy in France. He is offering his life for his country. I should be ashamed if I did not join these brave women in their fight for democracy in America. I should be proud of the honor to die in prison for the liberty of American women." Even the judge seemed moved by her beautiful and simple spirit.

In spite of the fact that the women were sentenced to serve

their sentences in the District Jail, where they would join Miss Paul and her companions, all save one were immediately sent to Occoquan workhouse.

It had been agreed that the demand to be treated as political prisoners, inaugurated by previous pickets, should be continued, and that failing to secure such rights they would unanimously refuse to eat food or do prison labor.

Any words of mine would be inadequate to tell the story of the prisoners' reception at the Occoquan workhouse. The following is the statement of Mrs. Nolan, dictated upon her release, in the presence of Mr. Dudley Field Malone:

It was about half past seven at night when we got to Occoquan workhouse. A woman [Mrs. Herndon] was standing behind a desk when we were brought into this office, and there were five or six men also in the room. Mrs. Lewis, who spoke for all of us, . . . said she must speak to Whittaker, the superintendent of the place.

"You'll sit here all night, then," said Mrs. Herndon.

I saw men begin to come upon the porch, but I didn't think anything about it. Mrs. Herndon called my name, but I did not answer. . . .

Suddenly the door literally burst open and Whittaker burst in like a tornado; some men followed him. We could see a crowd of them on the porch. They were not in uniform. They looked as much like tramps as anything. They seemed to come in—and in—and in. One had a face that made me think of an ourang-outang. Mrs. Lewis stood up. Some of us had been sitting and lying on the floor, we were so tired. She had hardly begun to speak, saying we demanded to be treated as political prisoners, when Whittaker said:

"You shut up. I have men here to handle you." Then he shouted, "Seize her!" I turned and saw men spring toward her, and then some one screamed, "They have taken Mrs. Lewis."

A man sprang at me and caught me by the shoulder. I am used to remembering a bad foot, which I have had for years, and I remember saying, "I'll come with you; don't drag me;

© *Harris & Ewing.*

Miss Matilda Young—Youngest Picket
Mrs. Mary Nolan—Oldest Picket

Left to Right

MISS MARION BURRITT   MRS. ALICE COSU
MRS. HARVEY W. WILEY   MRS. R. B. QUAY
MRS. JOHN WINTERS BRANNAN   MRS. A. N. BEIM
MRS. HENRY BUTTERWORTH   MRS. PHOEBE SCOTT
MRS. CYNTHIA COHEN

Left to Right

MRS. CATHERINE MARTINETTE   MISS CORA WEEK
MRS. WILLIAM KENT   MISS AMY JUENGLING
MISS MARY BARTLETT DIXON   MISS HATTIE KRUGER
MRS. C. T. ROBERTSON   MISS BELLE SHEINBERG
MISS JULIA EMORY

FACE JAIL

Left to Right

Mrs. Peggy Johns	Miss Alice Gram
Mrs. Mary Nolan	Mrs. W. Bergen
Miss Betty Gram	Miss Camilla Whitcomb
Miss Ella Findeisen	Mrs. Charles W. Barnes
Mrs. Kate Stafford	Mrs. Ella Guilford

Left to Right

Miss Elizabeth Hamilton	Miss Elizabeth McShane
Miss Catherine Lincoln	Mrs. Lawrence Lewis
Mrs. Eva Decker	Mrs. Paula Jakobi
Mrs. J. H. Short	Miss Dorothy Day
Mrs. Genevieve Williams	Mrs. L. H. Hornsby

Top—MISS ELIZABETH KALB ON STRETCHER*
Center—MISS KATE HEFFELFINGER BROUGHT TO HEADQUARTERS
BY JAIL ATTENDANT
Lower—MRS. LAWRENCE LEWIS ASSISTED FROM AMBULANCE
* © *Harris & Ewing.*

"Lafayette, We Are Here."

Wholesale Arrests

SUFFRAGISTS MARCH TO LAFAYETTE MONUMENT TO BURN
PRESIDENT WILSON'S WORDS

TORCHBEARER AND ESCORTS AT BASE OF MONUMENT.

SOME PUBLIC MEN WHO PROTESTED AGAINST
IMPRISONMENT OF SUFFRAGISTS

© *Underwood*
COL. WILLIAM BOYCE THOMPSON

© *Harris & Ewing*
GILSON GARDNER

© *Harris & Ewing*

J. A. H. HOPKINS

DR. HARVEY W. WILEY

I have a lame foot." But I was jerked down the steps and away into the dark. I didn't have my feet on the ground. I guess that saved me. I heard Mrs. Cosu, who was being dragged along with me, call, "Be careful of your foot."

Out of doors it was very dark. The building to which they took us was lighted up as we came to it. I only remember the American flag flying above it because it caught the light from a window in the wing. We were rushed into a large room that we found opened on a large hall with stone cells on each side. They were perfectly dark. Punishment cells is what they call them. Mine was filthy. It had no window save a slip at the top and no furniture but an iron bed covered with a thin straw pad, and an open toilet flushed from outside the cell. . . .

In the hall outside was a man called Captain Reems. He had on a uniform and was brandishing a thick stick and shouting as we were shoved into the corridor, "Damn you, get in here."

I saw Dorothy Day brought in. She is a frail girl. The two men handling her were twisting her arms above her head. Then suddenly they lifted her up and banged her down over the arm of an iron bench—twice. As they ran me past, she was lying there with her arms out, and we heard one of the men yell, "The —— suffrager! My mother ain't no suffrager. I'll put you through ——."

At the end of the corridor they pushed me through a door. Then I lost my balance and fell against the iron bed. Mrs. Cosu struck the wall. Then they threw in two mats and two dirty blankets. There was no light but from the corridor. The door was barred from top to bottom. The walls and floors were brick or stone cemented over. Mrs. Cosu would not let me lie on the floor. She put me on the couch and stretched out on the floor on one of the two pads they threw in. We had only lain there a few minutes, trying to get our breath, when Mrs. Lewis, doubled over and handled like a sack of something, was literally thrown in. Her head struck the iron bed. We thought she was dead. She didn't move. We were crying over her as we lifted her to the pad on my bed, when we heard Miss Burns call:

"Where is Mrs. Nolan?"

I replied, "I am here."

Mrs. Cosu called out, "They have just thrown Mrs. Lewis in here, too."

At this Mr. Whittaker came to the door and told us not to dare to speak, or he would put the brace and bit in our mouths and the straitjacket on our bodies. We were so terrified we kept very still. Mrs. Lewis was not unconscious; she was only stunned. But Mrs. Cosu was desperately ill as the night wore on. She had a bad heart attack and was then vomiting. We called and called. We asked them to send our own doctor, because we thought she was dying. . . . They [the guards] paid no attention. A cold wind blew in on us from the outside, and we three lay there shivering and only half conscious until morning.

"One at a time, come out," we heard some one call at the barred door early in the morning. I went first. I bade them both good-by. I didn't know where I was going or whether I would ever see them again. They took me to Mr. Whittaker's office, where he called my name.

"You're Mrs. Mary Nolan," said Whittaker.

"You're posted," said I.

"Are you willing to put on prison dress and go to the workroom?" said he.

I said, "No."

"Don't you know now that I am Mr. Whittaker, the superintendent?" he asked.

"Is there any age limit to your workhouse?" I said. "Would a woman of seventy-three or a child of two be sent here?"

I think I made him think. He motioned to the guard.

"Get a doctor to examine her," he said.

In the hospital cottage I was met by Mrs. Herndon and taken to a little room with two white beds and a hospital table.

"You can lie down if you want to," she said.

I took off my coat and hat. I just lay down on the bed and fell into a kind of stupor. It was nearly noon and I had had no food offered me since the sandwiches our friends brought us in the courtroom at noon the day before.

The doctor came and examined my heart. Then he examined my lame foot. It had a long blue bruise above the ankle, where they had knocked me as they took me across the night before. He asked me what caused the bruise. I said, "Those fiends when they dragged me to the cell last night." It was paining me. He asked if I wanted liniment and I said only hot water. They brought that, and I noticed they did not lock the door. A negro trusty was there. I fell back again into the same stupor.

The next day they brought me some toast and a plate of food, the first I had been offered in over 36 hours. I just looked at the food and motioned it away. It made me sick. . . . I was released on the sixth day and passed the dispensary as I came out. There were a group of my friends, Mrs. Brannan and Mrs. Morey and many others. They had on coarse striped dresses and big, grotesque, heavy shoes. I burst into tears as they led me away.

(Signed)   MARY I. NOLAN.

November 21, 1917.

The day following their commitment to Occoquan Mr. O'Brien, of counsel, was directed to see the women, to ascertain their condition. Friends and relatives were alarmed, as not a line of news had been allowed to penetrate to the world. Mr. O'Brien was denied admission and forced to come back to Washington without any report whatsoever.

The next day Mr. O'Brien again attempted to see his clients, as did also the mother of Miss Matilda Young, the youngest prisoner in Mr. Whittaker's care, and Miss Katherine Morey, who went asking to see her mother. Miss Morey was held under armed guard half a mile from the prison. Admission was denied to all of them.

The terrible anxiety at Headquarters was not relieved the third day by a report brought from the workhouse by one of the marines stationed at Quantico Station, Virginia, who had been summoned to the workhouse on the night the women arrived. He brought news that unknown tortures were going on. Mr. O'Brien immediately forced his way through by a court order, and brought back to Headquarters the astounding news of the campaign of terrorism which had started the moment the prisoners had arrived, and which was being continued at that moment. Miss Lucy Burns, who had asssumed responsibility for the welfare of the women, had managed to secrete small scraps of paper and a tiny pencil, and jot down briefly the day by day events at the workhouse.

This week of brutality, which rivaled old Russia, if it did not outstrip it, was almost the blackest page in the Administration's cruel fight against women.

Here are some of the scraps of Miss Burn's day-by-day log, smuggled out of the workhouse. Miss Burns is so gifted a writer that I feel apologetic for using these scraps in their raw form, but I know she will forgive me.

WEDNESDAY, NOVEMBER 14. Demanded to see Superintendent Whittaker. Request refused. Mrs. Herndon, the matron, said we would have to wait up all night. One of the men guards said he would "put us in sardine box and put mustard on us." Superintendent Whittaker came at 9 p. m. He refused to hear our demand for political rights. Seized by guards from behind, flung off my feet, and shot out of the room. All of us were seized by men guards and dragged to cells in men's part. Dorothy Day was roughly used—back twisted. Mrs. Mary A. Nolan (73-year-old picket from Jacksonville, Florida) flung into cell. Mrs. Lawrence Lewis shot past my cell. I slept with Dorothy Day in a single bed. I was handcuffed all night and manacled to the bars part of the time for asking the others how they were, and was threatened with a straitjacket and a buckle gag.

THURSDAY, NOVEMBER 16. . . . Asked for Whittaker, who came. He seized Julia Emory by the back of her neck and threw her into the room very brutally. She is a little girl. I asked for counsel to learn the status of the case. I was told to "shut up," and was again threatened with a straitjacket and a buckle gag. Later I was taken to put on prison clothes, refused and resisted strenuously. I was then put in a room where delirium tremens patients are kept.

On the seventh day, when Miss Lucy Burns and Mrs. Lawrence Lewis were so weak that Mr. Whittaker feared their
death, they were forcibly fed and taken immediately to the jail
in Washington. Of the experience Mrs. Lewis wrote:—

I was seized and laid on my back, where five people held
me, a young colored woman leaping upon my knees, which
seemed to break under the weight. Dr. Gannon then forced
the tube through my lips and down my throat, I gasping and
suffocating with the agony of it. I didn't know where to
breathe from and everything turned black when the fluid began
pouring in. I was moaning and making the most awful sounds
quite against my will, for I did not wish to disturb my friends
in the next room. Finally the tube was withdrawn. I lay
motionless. After a while I was dressed and carried in a chair
to a waiting automobile, laid on the back seat and driven into
Washington to the jail hospital. Previous to the feeding I
had been forcibly examined by Dr. Gannon, I struggling and
protesting that I wished a woman physician.

Of this experience, Miss Burns wrote on tiny scraps of
paper:

WEDNESDAY, 12 m. Yesterday afternoon at about four or
five, Mrs. Lewis and I were asked to go to the operating room.
Went there and found our clothes. Told we were to go to
Washington. No reason as usual. When we were dressed, Dr.
Gannon appeared, and said he wished to examine us. Both
refused. Were dragged through halls by force, our clothing
partly removed by force, and we were examined, heart tested,
blood pressure and pulse taken. Of course such data was of
no value after such a struggle. Dr. Gannon told me then I
must be fed. Was stretched on bed, two doctors, matron, four
colored prisoners present, Whittaker in hall. I was held down
by five people at legs, arms, and head. I refused to open
mouth. Gannon pushed tube up left nostril. I turned and
twisted my head all I could, but he managed to push it up. It
hurts nose and throat very much and makes nose bleed freely.
Tube drawn out covered with blood. Operation leaves one
very sick. Food dumped directly into stomach feels like a ball

of lead. Left nostril, throat and muscles of neck very sore all night. After this I was brought into the hospital in an ambulance. Mrs. Lewis and I placed in same room. Slept hardly at all. This morning Dr. Ladd appeared with his tube. Mrs. Lewis and I said we would not be forcibly fed. Said he would call in men guards and force us to submit. Went away and we were not fed at all this morning. We hear them outside now cracking eggs.

With Miss Burns and Mrs. Lewis, who were regarded as leaders in the hunger strike protest, removed to the district jail, Mr. Whittaker and his staff at Occoquan began a systematic attempt to break down the morale of the hunger strikers. Each one was called to the mat and interrogated.

"Will you work?"—"Will you put on prison clothes?"— "Will you eat?"—"Will you stop picketing?"—"Will you go without paying your fine and promise never to picket again?"

How baffled he must have been! The answer was definite and final. Their resistance was superb.

"One of the few warning incidents during the gray days of our imprisonment was the unexpected sympathy and understanding of one of the government doctors," wrote Miss Betty Gram of Portland, Oregon.

" 'This is the most magnificent sacrifice I have ever seen made for a principle [he said]. I never believed that American women would care so much about freedom. I have seen women in Russia undergo extreme suffering for their ideals, but unless I had seen this with my own eyes I never would have believed it. My sister hunger struck in Russia, where she was imprisoned for refusing to reveal the whereabouts of two of her friends indicted for a government offense. She was fed after three days. You girls are on your ninth day of hunger strike and your condition is critical. It is a great pity that such women should be subjected to this treatment. I hope that you will carry your point and force the hand of the government soon'."

The mother of Matilda Young, the youngest picket, anxiously appealed to Mr. Tumulty, Secretary to President Wilson, and a family friend, to be allowed to see the President and ask for a special order to visit her daughter. Failing to secure this, she went daily to Mr. Tumulty's office asking if he himself would not intercede for her. Mr. Tumulty assured her that her daughter was in safe hands, that she need give herself no alarm, the stories of the inhuman treatment at Occoquan were false, and that she must not believe them. Finally Mrs. Young pleaded to be allowed to send additional warm clothing to her daughter, whom she knew to be too lightly clad for the vigorous temperature of November. Mr. Tumulty assured her that the women were properly clothed, and refused to permit the clothing to be sent. The subsequent stories of the women showed what agonies they had endured, because they were inadequately clad, from the dampness of the cells into which they were thrown.

Mrs. John Winters Brannan was among the women who endured the "night of terror." Mrs. Brannan is the daughter of Charles A. Dana, founder of the New York *Sun* and that great American patriot of liberty who was a trusted associate and counselor of Abraham Lincoln. Mrs. Brannan, life-long suffragist, is an aristocrat of intellect and feeling, who has always allied herself with libertarian movements. This was her second term of imprisonment. She wrote a comprehensive affidavit of her experience. After narrating the events which led up to the attack, she continues:

Superintendent Whittaker . . . then shouted out in a loud tone of voice, "Seize these women, take them off, that one, that one,—take her off." The guards rushed forward and an almost indescribable scene of violent confusion ensued. I . . . saw one of the guards seize her [Lucy Burns] by the arms, twist or force them back of her, and one or two other guards seize her by the shoulders, shaking her violently. . . .

I then . . . took up my heavy sealskin coat, which was lying by, and put it on, in order to prepare myself if attacked. . . . I was trembling at the time and was stunned with terror at the situation as it had developed, and said to the superintendent, "I will give my name under protest," and started to walk towards the desk whereon lay the books. The superintendent shouted to me, "Oh, no, you won't; don't talk about protest; I won't have any of that nonsense."

I . . . saw the guards seizing the different women of the party with the utmost violence, the furniture being overturned and the room a scene of the utmost disturbance. I saw Miss Lincoln lying on the floor, with every appearance of having just been thrown down by the two guards who were standing over her in a menacing attitude. Seeing the general disturbance, I gave up all idea of giving my name at the desk, and instinctively joined my companions, to go with them and share whatever was in store for them. The whole group of women were thrown, dragged or herded out of the office on to the porch, down the steps to the ground, and forced to cross the road . . . to the Administration Building.

During all of this time, . . . Superintendent Whittaker was . . . directing the whole attack. . . .

. . . All of us were thrown into different cells in the men's prison, I being put in one with four other women, the cell containing a narrow bed and one chair, which was immediately removed. . . .

During the time that we were being forced into the cells the guards kept up an uproar, shouting, banging the iron doors, clanging bars, making a terrifying noise.

I and one of my companions were lying down on the narrow bed, on which were a blanket and one pillow. The door of the cell was opened and a mattress and a blanket being thrown in, the door was violently banged to. . . . My other . . . companions arranged the mattress on the floor and lay down, covering themselves with the blanket.

. . . I looked across the corridor and saw Miss Lincoln, . . . and asked her whether she was all right, being anxious to know whether she had been hurt by the treatment in the office building. . . . Instantly Superintendent Whittaker rushed forward, shouting at me, "Stop that; not another word from your mouth, or I will handcuff you, gag you and put you in a straitjacket. . . .

I wish to state again that the cells into which we were put were situated in the men's prison. There was no privacy for the women, and if any of us wished to undress we would be subject to the view or observation of the guards who remained in the corridor and who could at any moment look at us. . . . Furthermore, the water closets were in full view of the corridor where Superintendent Whittaker and the guards were moving about. The flushing of these closets could only be done from the corridor, and we were forced to ask the guards to do this for us,—the men who had shortly before attacked us. . . .

None of the matrons or women attendants appeared at any time that night. No water was brought to us for washing, no food was offered to us. . . .

I was exhausted by what I had seen and been through, and spent the night in absolute terror of further attack and of what might still be in store for us. I thought of the young girls who were with us and feared for their safety. The guards . . . acted brutal in the extreme, incited to their brutal conduct towards us, . . . by the superintendent. I thought of the offense with which we had been charged,—merely that of obstructing traffic,—and felt that the treatment that we had received was out of all proportion to the offense with which we were charged, and that the superintendent, the matron and guards would not have dared to act towards us as they had acted unless they relied upon the support of higher authorities. It seemed to me that everything had been done from the time we reached the workhouse to terrorize us, and my fear lest the extreme of outrage would be worked upon the young girls of our party became intense.

It is impossible for me to describe the terror of that night. . . .

The affidavit then continues with the story of how Mrs. Brannan was compelled the following morning to put on prison clothes, was given a cup of skimmed milk and a slice of toast, and then taken to the sewing room, where she was put to work sewing on the underdrawers of the male prisoners.

I was half fainting all of that day and . . . requested permission to lie down, feeling so ill. . . . I could not sleep, having a sense of constant danger. . . . I was almost paralyzed and in wretched physical condition.

On Friday afternoon Mrs. Herndon [matron] . . . led us through some woods nearby, for about three-quarters of a mile, seven of us being in the party. We were so exhausted and weary that we were obliged to stop constantly to rest. On our way back from the walk we heard the baying of hounds very near us in the woods. The matron said, "You must hurry, the bloodhounds are loose." One of the party, Miss Findeisen, asked whether they would attack us, to which the matron replied, "That is just what they would do," and hurried us along. The baying grew louder and nearer at times and then more distant, as the dogs rushed back and forth, and this went on until we reached the sewing room. The effect of this upon our nerves can better be imagined than described. . . .

Every conceivable lie was tried in an effort to force the women to abandon their various form of resistance. They were told that no efforts were being made from the outside to reach them, and that their attorney had been called off the case. Each one was told that she was the only one hunger striking. Each one was told that all the others had put on prison clothes and were working. Although they were separated from one another they suspected the lies and remained strong in their resistance. After Mr. O'Brien's one visit and the subsequent reports in the press he was thereafter refused admission to the workhouse.

The judge had sentenced these women to the jail, but the District Commissioners had ordered them committed to the workhouse. It was evident that the Administration was anxious to keep this group away from Alice Paul and her companions, as they counted on handling the rebellion more easily in two groups than one.

Meanwhile the condition of the prisoners in the workhouse grew steadily worse. It was imperative that we force the Administration to take them out of the custody of Superintendent Whittaker immediately. We decided to take the only course open—to obtain a writ of habeas corpus. A hurried journey by counsel to United States District Judge Waddill of Norfolk, Virginia, brought the writ. It compelled the government to bring the prisoners into court and show cause why they should not be returned to the district jail. This conservative Southern judge said of the petition for the writ, "It is shocking and blood-curdling."

There followed a week more melodramatic than the most stirring moving picture film. Although the writ had been applied for in the greatest secrecy, a detective suddenly appeared to accompany Mr. O'Brien from Washington to Norfolk, during his stay in Norfolk, and back to Washington. Telephone wires at our headquarters were tapped.

It was evident that the Administration was cognizant of every move in this procedure before it was executed. No sooner was our plan decided upon than friends of the Administration besought us to abandon the habeas corpus proceedings. One member of the Administration sent an emissary to our headquarters with the following appeal:

"If you will only drop these proceedings, I can absolutely guarantee you that the prisoners will be removed from the workhouse to the jail in a week."

"In a week? They may be dead by that time," we answered. "We cannot wait."

"But I tell you, you must not proceed."

"Why this mysterious week?" we asked. "Why not tomorrow? Why not instantly?"

"I can only tell you that I have a positive guarantee of the District Commissioners that the women will be removed," he said in conclusion. We refused to grant his request.

There were three reasons why the authorities wished for a week's time. They were afraid to move the women in their

weakened condition and before the end of the week they hoped
to increase their facilities for forcible feeding at the workhouse.
They also wished to conceal the treatment of the women, the
exposure of which would be inevitable in any court proceedings.
And lastly, the Administration was anxious to avoid opening up
the whole question of the legality of the very existence of the
workhouse in Virginia.

Persons convicted in the District for acts committed in
violation of District law were transported to Virginia—alien
territory—to serve their terms. It was a moot point whether
prisoners were so treated with sufficient warrant in law. Eminent jurists held that the District had no right to convict a person under its laws and commit that person to confinement in
another state. They contended that sentence imposed upon a
person for unlawful acts in the District should be executed in
the District.

Hundreds of persons who had been convicted in the District
of Columbia and who had served their sentences in Virginia had
been without money or influence enough to contest this doubtful
procedure in the courts. The Administration was alarmed.

We quickened our pace. A member of the Administration
rushed his attorney as courier to the women in the workhouse
to implore them not to consent to the habeas corpus proceedings. He was easily admitted and tried to extort from one prisoner at a time a promise to reject the plan. The women suspected his solicitude and refused to make any promise whatsoever without first being allowed to see their own attorney.

We began at once to serve the writ. Ordinarily this would
be an easy thing to do. But for us it developed into a very
difficult task. A deputy marshal must serve the writ. Counsel
sought a deputy. For miles around Washington, not one was
to be found at his home or lodgings. None could be reached
by telephone.

Meanwhile Mr. Whittaker had sped from the premises of

the workhouse to the District, where he kept himself discreetly hidden for several days. When a deputy was found, six attempts were made to serve the writ. All failed. Finally by a ruse, Mr. Whittaker was caught at his home late at night. He was aroused to a state of violent temper and made futile threats of reprisal when he learned that he must produce the suffrage prisoners at the Court in Alexandria, Virginia, on the day of November twenty-third.

CHAPTER 12

Great passions when they run through a whole population, inevitably find a great spokesman. A people cannot remain dumb which is moved by profound impulses of conviction; and when spokesmen and leaders are found, effective concert of action seems to follow as naturally. Men spring together for common action under a common impulse which has taken hold upon their very natures, and governments presently find that they have those to reckon with who know not only what they want, but also the most effective means of making governments uncomfortable until they get it. Governments find themselves, in short, in the presence of *Agitation*, of systematic movements of opinion, which do not merely flare up in spasmodic flames and then die down again, but burn with an accumulating ardor which can be checked and extinguished only by removing the grievances and abolishing the unacceptable institutions which are its fuel. Casual discontent can be allayed, but agitation fixed upon conviction cannot be. To fight it is merely to augment its force. It burns irrepressibly in every public assembly; quiet it there, and it gathers head at street corners; drive it thence, and it smoulders in private dwellings, in social gatherings, in every covert of talk, only to break forth more violently than ever because denied vent and air. It must be reckoned with. . . .

Governments have been very resourceful in parrying agitation, in diverting it, in seeming to yield to it, and then cheating it of its objects, in tiring it out or evading it. . . . But the end, whether it comes soon or late, is quite certain to be always the same.

—*"Constitutional Government in the United States."*
WOODROW WILSON, PH.D., LL.D.,
President of Princeton University.

THE special session of the 65th Congress, known as the "War Congress," adjourned in October, 1917, having passed every measure recommended as a war measure by the President.

In addition, it found time to protect by law migratory birds, to appropriate forty-seven million dollars for deepening rivers and harbors, and to establish more federal judgeships. No honest person would say that lack of time and pressure of war legislation had prevented its consideration of the suffrage measure. If one-hundredth part of the time consumed by its members in spreading the wings of the overworked eagle, and in uttering to bored ears "home-made" patriotic verse, had been spent in considering the liberty of women, this important legislation could have been dealt with. Week after week Congress met only for three days, and then often merely for prayer and a few hours of purposeless talking.

We had asked for liberty, and had got a suffrage committee appointed in the House to consider the pros and cons of suffrage, and a favorable report in the Senate from the Committee on Woman Suffrage, nothing more.

On the very day and hour of the adjournment of the special session of the War Congress, Alice Paul led eleven women to the White House gates to protest against the Administration's allowing its lawmakers to go home without action on the suffrage amendment.

Two days later Alice Paul and her colleagues were put on trial.

Many times during previous trials I had heard the District Attorney for the government shake his finger at Miss Paul and say, "We'll get you yet. . . . Just wait; and when we do, we'll give you a year!"

It was reported from very authentic sources that Attorney General Gregory had, earlier in the agitation, seriously considered arresting Miss Paul for the Administration, on the charge of conspiracy to break the law. We were told this plan was abandoned because, as one of the Attorney General's staff put it, "No jury would convict her."

However, here she was in their hands, in the courtroom.

Proceedings opened with the customary formality. The eleven prisoners sat silently at the bar, reading their morning papers, or a book, or enjoying a moment of luxurious idleness, oblivious of the comical movements of a perturbed court.

Nothing in the world so baffles the pompous dignity of a court as non-resistant defendants. The judge cleared his throat and the attendants made meaningless gestures.

"Will the prisoners stand up and be sworn?"

They will not.

"Will they question witnesses?"

They will not.

"Will they speak in their own behalf?"

The slender, quiet-voiced Quaker girl arose from her seat. The crowded courtroom pressed forward breathlessly. She said calmly and with unconcern: "We do not wish to make any plea before this court. We do not consider ourselves subject to this court, since as an unenfranchised class we have nothing to do with the making of the laws which have put us in this position."

What a disconcerting attitude to take! Miss Paul sat down as quietly and unexpectedly as she had arisen. The judge moved uneasily in his chair. The gentle way in which it was said was disarming. Would the judge hold them in contempt? He had not time to think. His part of the comedy he had expected to run smoothly, and here was this defiant little woman calmly stating that we were not subject to the court, and that we would therefore have nothing to do with the proceedings. The murmurs had grown to a babel of conversation. A sharp rap of the gavel restored order and permitted Judge Mullowny to say: "Unfortunately, I am here to support the laws that are made by Congress, and, of course, I am bound by those laws; and you are bound by them as long as you live in this country, notwithstanding the fact that you do not recognize the law."

Everybody strained his ears for the sentence. The Administration had threatened to "get" the leader. Would they dare?

Another pause!

"I shall suspend sentence for the time being," came solemnly from the judge.

Was it that they did not dare confine Miss Paul? Were they beginning actually to perceive the real strength of the movement and the protest that would be aroused if she were imprisoned? Again we thought perhaps this marked the end of the jailing of women.

But though the pickets were released on suspended sentences, there was no indication of any purpose on the part of the Administration of acting on the amendment. Two groups, some of those on suspended sentence, others first offenders, again marched to the White House gates. The following motto:

THE TIME HAS COME TO CONQUER OR SUBMIT; FOR
US THERE CAN BE BUT ONE CHOICE—WE HAVE
MADE IT.

a quotation from the President's second Liberty Loan appeal, was carried by Miss Paul.

Dr. Caroline E. Spencer of Colorado carried:

RESISTANCE TO TYRANNY IS OBEDIENCE TO GOD.

All were brought to trial again.

The trial of Miss Paul's group ran as follows:

MR. HART (Prosecuting Attorney for the Government): Sergeant Lee, were you on Pennsylvania Avenue near the White House Saturday afternoon?

SERGEANT LEE: I was.

MR. HART: At what time?

LEE: About 4:35 in the afternoon.

HART: Tell the court what you saw.

LEE: A little after half-past four, when the department clerks were all going home out Pennsylvania Avenue, I saw four suffragettes coming down Madison Place, cross the Avenue and continue on Pennsylvania Avenue to the gate of the White House, where they divided two on the right and two on the left side of the gate.

HART: What did you do?

LEE: I made my way through the crowd that was surrounding them and told the ladies *they were violating the law by standing at the gates,* and wouldn't they please move on?

HART: Did they move on?

LEE: They did not; and they didn't answer either.

HART: What did you do then?

LEE: I placed them under arrest.

HART: What did you do then?

LEE: *I asked the crowd to move on.*

Mr. Hart then arose and summing up said: "Your Honor, these women have said that *they will picket again.* I ask you to impose the maximum sentence."

Such confused legal logic was indeed drôle!

"You ladies seem to feel that we discriminate in making arrests and in sentencing you," said the judge heavily. "The result is that you force me to take the most drastic means in my power to compel you to obey the law."

More legal confusion!

"Six months," said the judge to the first offenders, "and then you will serve one month more," to the others.

Miss Paul's parting remark to the reporters who intercepted her on her way from the courtroom to begin her seven months' sentence was:

"We are being imprisoned, not because we obstructed traffic, but because we pointed out to the President the fact that he was obstructing the cause of democracy at home, while Americans were fighting for it abroad."

I am going to let Alice Paul tell her own story, as she related it to me one day after her release:

It was late afternoon when we arrived at the jail. There we found the suffragists who had preceded us, locked in cells.

The first thing I remember was the distress of the prisoners about the lack of fresh air. Evening was approaching, every window was closed tight. The air in which we would be obliged to sleep was foul. There were about eighty negro and white prisoners crowded together, tier upon tier, frequently two in a cell. I went to a window and tried to open it. Instantly a group of men, prison guards, appeared; picked me up bodily, threw me into a cell and locked the door. Rose Winslow and the others were treated in the same way.

Determined to preserve our health and that of the other prisoners, we began a concerted fight for fresh air. The windows were about twenty feet distant from the cells, and two sets of iron bars intervened between us and the windows, but we instituted an attack upon them as best we could. Our tin drinking cups, the electric light bulbs, every available article of the meagre supply in each cell, including my treasured copy of Browning's poems which I had secretly taken in with me, was thrown through the windows. By this simultaneous attack from every cell, we succeeded in breaking one window before our supply of tiny weapons was exhausted. The fresh October air came in like an exhilarating gale. The broken window remained untouched throughout the entire stay of this group and all later groups of suffragists. Thus was won what the "regulars" in jail called the first breath of air in their time.

The next day we organized ourselves into a little group for the purpose of rebellion. We determined to make it impossible to keep us in jail. We determined, moreover, that as long as we were there we would keep up an unremitting fight for the rights of political prisoners.

One by one little points were conceded to quiet resistance. There was the practice of sweeping the corridors in such a way that the dust filled the cells. The prisoners would be choking to the gasping point, as they sat, helpless, locked in the cells, while a great cloud of dust enveloped them from tiers above and below. As soon as our tin drinking cups, which were sacrificed in our attack upon the windows, were restored to us, we instituted a campaign against the dust. Tin cup after tin cup was filled and its contents thrown out into the corridor from every cell, so that the water began to trickle down from tier to tier. The District Commissioners, the Board of Charities, and other officials were summoned by the prison authorities. Hurried consultations were held. Nameless officials passed by in review and looked upon the dampened floor. Thereafter the corridors were dampened and the sweeping into the cells ceased. And so another reform was won.

There is absolutely no privacy allowed a prisoner in a cell. You are suddenly peered at by curious strangers, who look in at you all hours of the day and night, by officials, by attendants, by interested philanthropic visitors, and by prison reformers, until one's sense of privacy is so outraged that one rises in rebellion. We set out to secure privacy, but we did not succeed, for, to allow privacy in prison, is against all institutional thought and habit. Our only available weapon was our blanket, which was no sooner put in front of our bars than it was forcibly taken down by Warden Zinkhan.

Our meals had consisted of a little almost raw salt pork, some sort of liquid—I am not sure whether it was coffee or soup—bread and occasionally molasses. How we cherished the bread and molasses! We saved it from meal to meal so as to try to distribute the nourishment over a longer period, as almost every one was unable to eat the raw pork. Lucy Branham, who was more valiant than the rest of us, called out from her cell, one day, "Shut your eyes tight, close your mouth over the pork and swallow it without chewing it. Then you can do it." This heroic practice kept Miss Branham in fairly good health, but to the rest it seemed impossible, even with our eyes closed, to crunch our teeth into the raw pork.

However gaily you start out in prison to keep up a rebellious protest, it is nevertheless a terribly difficult thing to do in the face of the constant cold and hunger of undernourishment. Bread and water, and occasional molasses, is not a diet destined to sustain rebellion long. And soon weakness overtook us.

At the end of two weeks of solitary confinement, without any exercise, without going outside of our cells, some of the prisoners were released, having finished their terms, but five of us were left serving seven months' sentences, and two, one month sentences. With our number thus diminished to seven,

the authorities felt able to cope with us. The doors were un-
locked and we were permitted to take exercise. Rose Winslow
fainted as soon as she got into the yard, and was carried back
to her cell. I was too weak to move from my bed. Rose and I
were taken on stretchers that night to the hospital.

For one brief night we occupied beds in the same ward in
the hospital. Here we decided upon the hunger strike, as the
ultimate form of protest left us—the strongest weapon left
with which to continue within the prison our battle against the
Administration.

Miss Paul was held absolutely incommunicado in the prison
hospital. No attorney, no member of her family, no friend
could see her. With Miss Burns in prison also it became
imperative that I consult Miss Paul as to a matter of policy.
I was peremptorily refused admission by Warden Zinkhan, so
I decided to attempt to communicate with her from below her
window. This was before we had established what in prison
parlance is known as the "grape-vine route." The grape-vine
route consists of smuggling messages oral or written via a
friendly guard or prisoner who has access to the outside
world.

Just before twilight, I hurried in a taxi to the far-away
spot, temporarily abandoned the cab and walked past the
dismal cemetery which skirts the prison grounds. I had fortified myself with a diagram of the grounds, and knew which
entrance to attempt, in order to get to the hospital wing where
Miss Paul lay. We had also ascertained her floor and room.
I must first pick the right building, proceed to the proper
corner, and finally select the proper window.

The sympathetic chauffeur loaned me a very seedy looking
overcoat which I wrapped about me. Having deposited my hat
inside the cab, I turned up the collar, drew in my chin and
began surreptitiously to circle the devious paths leading to a
side entrance of the grounds. My heart was palpitating, for
the authorities had threatened arrest if any suffragists were

found on the prison grounds, and aside from my personal feelings, I could not at that moment abandon headquarters.

Making a desperate effort to act like an experienced and trusted attendant of the prison, I roamed about and tried not to appear roaming. I successfully passed two guards, and reached the desired spot, which was by good luck temporarily deserted. I succeeded in calling up loudly enough to be heard by Miss Paul, but softly enough not to be heard by the guards.

I shall never forget the shock of her appearance at that window in the gathering dusk. Everything in the world seemed black-gray except her ghost-like face, so startling, so inaccessible. It drove everything else from my mind for an instant. But as usual she was in complete control of herself. She began to hurl questions at me faster than I could answer. "How were the convention plans progressing?" . . . "Had the speakers been secured for the mass meeting?" . . . "How many women had signed up to go out on the next picket line?" And so on.

"Conditions at Occoquan are frightful," said I. "We are planning to . . ."

"Get out of there, and move quickly," shouted the guard, who came abruptly around the corner of the building. I tried to finish my message. "We are planning to habeas corpus the women out of Occoquan and have them transferred up here."

"Get out of there, I tell you. Damn you!" By this time he was upon me. He grabbed me by the arm and began shaking me. "You will be arrested if you do not get off these grounds." He continued to shake me while I shouted back, "Do you approve of this plan?"

I was being forced along so rapidly that I was out of range of her faint voice and could not hear the answer. I plead with the guard to be allowed to go back quietly and speak a few more words with Miss Paul, but he was inflexible. Once out of the grounds I went unnoticed to the cemetery and sat on a tombstone to wait a little while before making another attempt, hoping the guard would not expect me to come back. The lights were beginning to twinkle in the distance and it was now almost total darkness. I consulted my watch and realized that in forty minutes Miss Paul and her comrades would again be going through the torture of forcible feeding. I waited five minutes—ten minutes—fifteen minutes. Then I went back to the grounds again. I started through another entrance, but had proceeded only a few paces when I was forcibly evicted. Again I returned to the cold tombstone. I believe that I never in my life felt more utterly miserable and impotent. There were times, as I have said, when we felt inordinately strong. This was one of the times when I felt that we were frail reeds in the hands of cruel and powerful oppressors. My thoughts were at first with Alice Paul, at that moment being forcibly fed by men jailers and men doctors. I remembered then the man warden who had refused the highly reasonable request to visit her, and my thoughts kept right on up the scale till I got to the man-President—the pinnacle of power against us. I was indeed desolate. I walked back to the hidden taxi, hurried to headquarters, and plunged into my work, trying all night to convince myself that the sting of my wretchedness was being mitigated by activity toward a release from this state of affairs.

Later we established daily communication with Miss Paul through one of the charwomen who scrubbed the hospital floors. She carried paper and pencil carefully concealed upon her. On entering Miss Paul's room she would, with very comical stealth, first elaborately push Miss Paul's bed against the door, then crawl practically under it, and pass from this point of concealment the coveted paper and pencil. Then she would linger over the floor to the last second, imploring Miss Paul to hasten her writing. Faithfully every evening this silent, dusky messenger made her long journey after her day's work, and patiently waited while I wrote an answering note to be delivered to Miss Paul the following morning. Thus it was that while in the hospital Miss Paul directed our campaign, in spite of the Administration's most painstaking plans to the contrary.

Miss Paul's story continues here from the point where I interrupted it.

From the moment we undertook the hunger strike, a policy of unremitting intimidation began. One authority after another, high and low, in and out of prison, came to attempt to force me to break the hunger strike.

"You will be taken to a very unpleasant place if you don't stop this," was a favorite threat of the prison officials, as they would hint vaguely of the psycopathic ward, and St. Elizabeth's, the Government insane asylum. They alternately bullied and hinted. Another threat was "You will be forcibly fed immediately if you don't stop"—this from Dr. Gannon. There was nothing to do in the midst of these continuous threats, with always the "very unpleasant place" hanging over me, and so I lay perfectly silent on my bed.

After about three days of the hunger strike a man entered my room in the hospital and announced himself as Dr. White, the head of St. Elizabeth's. He said that he had been asked by District Commissioner Gardner to make an investigation. I later learned that he was Dr. William A. White, the eminent alienist.

Coming close to my bedside and addressing the attendant, who stood at a few respectful paces from him, Dr. White said: "Does this case talk?"

"Why wouldn't I talk?" I answered quickly.

"Oh, these cases frequently will not talk, you know," he continued in explanation.

"Indeed I'll talk," I said gaily, not having the faintest idea that this was an investigation of my sanity.

"Talking is our business," I continued, "we talk to any one on earth who is willing to listen to our suffrage speeches."

"Please talk," said Dr. White. "Tell me about suffrage;

why you have opposed the President; the whole history of your campaign, why you picket, what you hope to accomplish by it. Just talk freely."

I drew myself together, sat upright in bed, propped myself up for a discourse of some length, and began to talk. The stenographer whom Dr. White brought with him took down in shorthand everything that was said.

I may say it was one of the best speeches I ever made. I recited the long history and struggle of the suffrage movement from its early beginning and narrated the political theory of our activities up to the present moment, outlining the status of the suffrage amendment in Congress at that time. In short, I told him everything. He listened attentively, interrupting only occasionally, to say, "But, has not President Wilson treated you women very badly?" Whereupon, I, still unaware that I was being examined, launched forth into an explanation of Mr. Wilson's political situation and the difficulties he had confronting him. I continued to explain why we felt our relief lay with him; I cited his extraordinary power, his influence over his party, his undisputed leadership in the country, always painstakingly explaining that we opposed President Wilson merely because he happened to be President, not because he was President Wilson. Again came an interruption from Dr. White, "But isn't President Wilson directly responsible for the abuses and indignities which have been heaped upon you? You are suffering now as a result of his brutality, are you not?" Again I explained that it was impossible for us to know whether President Wilson was personally acquainted in any detail with the facts of our present condition, even though we knew that he had concurred in the early decision to arrest our women.

Presently Dr. White took out a small light and held it up to my eyes. Suddenly it dawned upon me that he was examining me personally; that his interest in the suffrage agitation and the jail conditions did not exist, and that he was merely interested in my reactions to the agitation and to jail. Even then I was reluctant to believe that I was the subject of mental investigation and I continued to talk.

But he continued in what I realized with a sudden shock, was an attempt to discover in me symptoms of the persecution mania. How simple he had apparently thought it would be, to prove that I had an obsession on the subject of President Wilson!

The day following he came again, this time bringing with him the District Commissioner, Mr. Gardner, to whom he asked me to repeat everything that had been said the day before. For the second time we went through the history of the suffrage movement, and again his inquiry suggested his persecution mania clue? When the narrative touched upon the President and his responsibility for the obstruction of the suffrage amendment, Dr. White would turn to his associate with the remark: "Note the reaction."

Then came another alienist, Dr. Hickling, attached to the psychopathic ward in the District Jail, with more threats and suggestions, if the hunger strike continued. Finally they departed, and I was left to wonder what would happen next. Doubtless my sense of humor helped me, but I confess I was not without fear of this mysterious place which they continued to threaten.

It appeared clear that it was their intention either to discredit me, as the leader of the agitation, by casting doubt upon my sanity, or else to intimidate us into retreating from the hunger strike.

After the examination by alienists, Commissioner Gardner, with whom I had previously discussed our demand for treatment as political prisoners, made another visit. "All these things you say about the prison conditions may be true," said Mr. Gardner, "I am a new Commissioner, and I do not know. You give an account of a very serious situation in the jail. The jail authorities give exactly the opposite. Now I promise you we will start an investigation at once to see who is right, you or they. If it is found you are right, we shall correct the conditions at once. If you will give up the hunger strike, we will start the investigation at once."

"Will you consent to treat the suffragists as political prisoners, in accordance with the demands laid before you?" I replied.

Commissioner Gardner refused, and I told him that the hunger strike would not be abandoned. But they had by no means exhausted every possible facility for breaking down our resistance. I overheard the Commissioner say to Dr. Gannon on leaving, "Go ahead, take her and feed her."

I was thereupon put upon a stretcher and carried into the psycopathic ward.

* * * *

There were two windows in the room. Dr. Gannon immediately ordered one window nailed from top to bottom. He then ordered the door leading into the hallway taken down and an iron-barred cell door put in its place. He departed with the command to a nurse to "observe her."

Following this direction, all through the day once every hour, the nurse came to "observe" me. All through the night, once every hour she came in, turned on an electric light sharp in my face, and "observed" me. This ordeal was the most terrible torture, as it prevented my sleeping for more than a few minutes at a time. And if I did finally get to sleep it was only to be shocked immediately into wide-awakeness with the pitiless light.

Dr. Hickling, the jail alienist, also came often to "observe" me. Commissioner Gardner and others—doubtless officials— came to peer through my barred door.

One day a young interne came to take a blood test. I protested mildly, saying that it was unnecessary and that I objected. "Oh, well," said the young doctor with a sneer and a supercilious shrug, "you know you're not mentally competent to decide such things." And the test was taken over my protest.

It is scarcely possible to convey to you one's reaction to such an atmosphere. Here I was surrounded by people on their way to the insane asylum. Some were waiting for their commitment papers. Others had just gotten them. And all the while everything possible was done to attempt to make me feel that I too was a "mental patient."

At this time forcible feeding began in the District Jail. Miss Paul and Miss Winslow, the first two suffragists to undertake the hunger strike, went through the operation of forcible feeding this day and three times a day on each succeeding day until their release from prison three weeks later. The hunger strike spread immediately to other suffrage prisoners in the jail and to the workhouse as recorded in the preceding chapter.

One morning [Miss Paul's story continues] the friendly face of a kindly old man standing on top of a ladder suddenly appeared at my window. He began to nail heavy boards across the window from the outside. He smiled and spoke a few kind words and told me to be of good cheer. He confided to me in a sweet and gentle way that he was in prison for drinking, that he had been in many times, but that he believed he had never seen anything so inhuman as boarding up this window and depriving a prisoner of light and air. There was only time for a few hurried moments of conversation, as I lay upon my bed watching the boards go up until his figure was completely hidden and I heard him descending the ladder.

After this window had been boarded up no light came into the room except through the top half of the other window, and almost no air. The authorities seemed determined to deprive me of air and light.

Meanwhile in those gray, long days, the mental patients in the psycopathic ward came and peered through my barred door. At night, in the early morning, all through the day there were cries and shrieks and moans from the patients. It was terrifying. One particularly melancholy moan used to keep up hour after hour, with the regularity of a heart beat. I said to myself, "Now I have to endure this. I have got to live through this somehow. I'll pretend these moans are the noise of an elevated train, beginning faintly in the distance and getting louder as it comes nearer." Such childish devices were helpful to me.

The nurses could not have been more beautiful in their spirit and offered every kindness. But imagine being greeted in the morning by a kindly nurse, a new one who had just come on duty, with, "I know you are not insane." The nurses explained the procedure of sending a person to the insane asylum. Two alienists examine a patient in the psycopathic ward, sign an order committing the patient to St. Elizabeth's Asylum, and there the patient is sent at the end of one week.

No trial, no counsel, no protest from the outside world! This was the customary procedure.

I began to think as the week wore on that this was probably their plan for me. I could not see my family or friends; counsel was denied me; I saw no other prisoners and heard nothing of them; I could see no papers; I was entirely in the hands of alienists, prison officials and hospital staff.

I believe I have never in my life before feared anything or any human being. But I confess I was afraid of Dr. Gannon, the jail physician. I dreaded the hour of his visit.

"I will show you who rules this place. You think you do. But I will show you that you are wrong." Some such friendly greeting as this was frequent from Dr. Gannon on his daily round. "Anything you desire, you shall not have. I will show you who is on top in this institution," was his attitude.

After nearly a week had passed, Dudley Field Malone finally succeeded in forcing an entrance by an appeal to court officials and made a vigorous protest against confining me in the psychopathic ward. He demanded also that the boards covering the window be taken down. This was promptly done and again the friendly face of the old man became visible, as the first board disappeared.

"I thought when I put this up America would not stand for this long," he said, and began to assure me that nothing dreadful would happen. I cherish the memory of that sweet old man.

The day after Mr. Malone's threat of court proceedings, the seventh day of my stay in the psychopathic ward, the attendants suddenly appeared with a stretcher. I did not know whither I was being taken, to the insane asylum, as threatened, or back to the hospital—one never knows in prison where one is being taken, no reason is ever given for anything. It turned out to be the hospital.

* * * *

After another week spent by Miss Paul on hunger strike in the hospital, the Administration was forced to capitulate. The doors of the jail were suddenly opened, and all suffrage prisoners were released.

With extraordinary swiftness the Administration's almost

incredible policy of intimidation had collapsed. Miss Paul had been given the maximum sentence of seven months, and at the end of five weeks the Administration was forced to acknowledge defeat. They were in a most unenviable position. If she and her comrades had offended in such degree as to warrant so cruel a sentence, (with such base stupidity on their part in administering it) she most certainly deserved to be detained for the full sentence. The truth is, every idea of theirs had been subordinated to the one desire of stopping the picketing agitation. To this end they had exhausted all their weapons of force.

From my conversation and correspondence with Dr. White, it is clear that as an alienist he did not make the slightest allegation to warrant removing Miss Paul to the psychopathic ward. On the contrary he wrote, "I felt myself in the presence of an unusually gifted personality" and . . . "she was wonderfully alert and keen . . . possessed of an absolute conviction of her cause . . . with industry and courage sufficient to avail herself of them [all diplomatic possibilities]. He praised the "most admirable, coherent, logical and forceful way" in which she discussed with him the purpose of our campaign.

And yet the *Administration put her in the psychopathic ward and threatened her with the insane asylum.*

An interesting incident occurred during the latter part of Miss Paul's imprisonment. Having been cut off entirely from outside communication, she was greatly surprised one night at a late hour to find a newspaper man admitted for an interview with her. Mr. David Lawrence, then generally accepted as the Administration journalist, and one who wrote for the various newspapers throughout the country defending the policies of the Wilson Administration, was announced. It was equally well known that this correspondent's habit was to ascertain the position of the leaders on important questions, keeping intimately in touch with opinion in White House circles at the same time.

Mr. Lawrence came, as he said, of his own volition, and not as an emissary from the White House. But in view of his close relation to affairs, his interview is significant as possibly reflecting an Administration attitude at that point in the campaign.

The conversation with Miss Paul revolved first about our fight for the right of political prisoners, Miss Paul outlining the wisdom and justice of this demand.

"The Administration could very easily hire a comfortable house in Washington and detain you all there," said Mr. Lawrence, "but don't you see that your demand to be treated as political prisoners is infinitely more difficult to grant than to give you the federal suffrage amendment? If we give you these privileges we shall have to extend them to conscientious objectors and to all prisoners now confined for political opinions. This the Administration cannot do."

The political prisoners protest, then, had actually encouraged the Administration to choose the lesser of two evils—some action on behalf of the amendment.

"Suppose," continued Mr. Lawrence, "the Administration should pass the amendment through one house of Congress next session and go to the country in the 1918 elections on that record and if sustained in it, pass it through the other house a year from now. Would you then agree to abandon picketing?"

"Nothing short of the passage of the amendment through Congress will end our agitation," Miss Paul quietly answered for the thousandth time.

Since Mr. Lawrence disavows any connection with the Administration in this interview, I can only remark that events followed exactly in the order he outlined; that is, the Admin-

istration attempted to satisfy the women by putting the amendment through the House and not through the Senate.

It was during Miss Paul's imprisonment that the forty-one
women went in protest to the picket line and were sent to the
workhouse, as narrated in the previous chapter. The terrorism
they endured at Occoquan ran simultaneously with the attempted intimidation of Miss Paul and her group in the jail.

CHAPTER 13

IN August, 1917, when it was clear that the policy of imprisoning suffragists would be continued indefinitely, and under longer sentences, the next three groups of pickets to be arrested asked for a decision from the highest court, the District Court of Appeals. Unlike other police courts in the country, there is no absolute right of appeal from the Police Court of the District of Columbia. Justice Robb, of the District Court of Appeals, after granting two appeals, refused to grant any more, upon the ground that he had discretionary power to grant or withhold an appeal. When further right of appeal was denied us, and when the Administration persisted in arresting us, we were compelled either to stop picketing or go to prison.

The first appealed case was heard by the Court of Appeals on January 8, 1918, and the decision [1] handed down in favor of the defendants on March 4, 1918. This decision was concurred in by all three judges, one of whom was appointed by President Wilson, a second by President Roosevelt and the third by President Taft.

In effect the decision declared that every one of the 218 suffragists arrested up to that time was illegally arrested, illegally convicted, and illegally imprisoned. The whole policy of the Administration in arresting women was by this decision held up to the world as lawless. The women could, if they had chosen, have filed suits for damages for false arrest and imprisonment at once.

[1] See Hunter vs. District of Columbia, 47 App. Cas. (D. C.) p. 406.

229

The appeal cases of the other pickets were ordered dismissed and stricken from the records. Dudley Field Malone was chief counsel in the appeal.

Another example of ethical, if not legal lawlessness, was shown by the Administration in the following incident. Throughout the summer and early autumn we had continued to press for an investigation of conditions at Occoquan, promised almost four months earlier.

October 2nd was the date finally set for an investigation to be held in the District Building before the District Board of Charities. Armed with 18 affidavits and a score of witnesses as to the actual conditions at Occoquan, Attorney Samuel C. Brent and Judge J. K. N. Norton, both of Alexandria, Virginia, acting as counsel with Mr. Malone, appeared before the Board on the opening day and asked to be allowed to present their evidence. They were told by the Board conducting the investigation that this was merely "an inquiry into the workhouse conditions and therefore would be held in secret without reporters or outsiders present." The attorneys demanded a public hearing, and insisted that the question was of such momentous importance that the public was entitled to hear both sides of it. They were told they might submit in writing any evidence they wished to bring before the Board. They refused to produce testimony for a "star chamber proceeding," and refused to allow their witnesses to be heard unless they could be heard in public.

Unable to get a public hearing, counsel left the following letter with the President of the Board:

Hon. John Joy Edson,
   President Board of Charities,
      Washington, D. C.
   Dear Sir:—We are counsel for a large group of citizens, men and women, who have in the past been associated with Occoquan work house as officials or inmates and who are ready

to testify to unspeakable conditions of mismanagement, graft, sanitary depravity, indignity and brutality at the institution.

We are glad you are to conduct this long-needed inquiry and shall coöperate in every way to get at the truth of conditions in Occoquan through your investigation, provided you make the hearings public, subpœna all available witnesses, including men and women now prisoners at Occoquan, first granting them immunity, and provided you give counsel an opportunity to examine and cross examine all witnesses so called.

We are confident your honorable board will see the justice and wisdom of a public inquiry. If charges so publicly made are untrue the management of Occoquan work house is entitled to public vindication, and if these charges are true, the people of Washington and Virginia should publicly know what kind of a prison they have in their midst, and the people of the country should publicly know the frightful conditions in this institution which is supported by Congress and the government of the United States.

We are ready with our witnesses and affidavits to aid your honorable board in every way, provided you meet the conditions above named. But if you insist on a hearing behind closed doors we cannot submit our witnesses to a star chamber proceeding and shall readily find another forum in which to tell the American public the vivid story of the Occoquan work house.

Respectfully yours,

(Signed) Dudley Field Malone,

J. K. N. Norton,

Samuel G. Brent.

Subsequently the District Board of Charities reported findings on their secret investigation. After a lengthy preamble, in which they attempted to put the entire blame upon the suffrage prisoners, they advised:

That the investigation directed by the Commissioners of the District of Columbia be postponed until the conditions of unrest, excitement, and disquiet at Occoquan have been overcome:

That the order relieving W. H. Whittaker as superintend-

ent, temporarily and without prejudice, be revoked, and Mr.
Whittaker be restored to his position as superintendent: [1]

That the members of the National Woman's Party now at
Occoquan be informed that unless they obey the rules of the
institution and discontinue their acts of insubordination and
riot, they will be removed from Occoquan to the city jail and
placed in solitary confinement.

In announcing the report to the press the District Commissioners stated that they approved the recommendations of
the Board of Charities "after most careful consideration," and
that "as a matter of fact, the District workhouse at Occoquan
is an institution of which the commissioners are proud, and is
a source of pride to every citizen of the nation's Capital."

That the Administration was in possession of the true facts
concerning Mr. Whittaker and his conduct in office there can
be no doubt.   But they supported him until the end of their
campaign of suppression.

Another example of the Administration's lawlessness appeared in the habeas corpus proceedings by which we rescued
the prisoners at the workhouse from Mr. Whittaker's custody.
The trial occurred on November 23rd.

No one present can ever forget the tragi-comic scene enacted in the little Virginia court room that cold, dark November morning.   There was Judge Waddill [2]—who had adjourned
his sittings in Norfolk to hasten the relief of the prisoners—a
mild mannered, sweet-voiced Southern gentleman.   There was
Superintendent Whittaker in his best Sunday clothes, which
mitigated very little the cruel and nervous demeanor which no
one who has come under his control will ever forget.   His
thugs were there, also dressed in their best clothes, which only
exaggerated their coarse features and their shifty eyes.   Mrs.
Herndon, the thin-lipped matron, was there, looking nervous

---

[1] Pending the investigation Mr. Whittaker was suspended, and his first
assistant, Alonzo Tweedale, served in the capacity of superintendent.
[2] Appointed to the bench by President Roosevelt.

and trying to seem concerned about the prisoners in her charge. Warden Zinkhan was there seeming worried at the prospect of the prisoners being taken from the care of Superintendent Whittaker and committed to him—he evidently unwilling to accept the responsibility.

Dudley Field Malone and Mr. O'Brien of counsel, belligerent in every nerve, were ready to try the case. The two dapper government attorneys, with immobile faces, twisted nervously in their chairs. There was the bevy of newspaper reporters struggling for places in the little courtroom, plainly sympathetic, for whatever they may have had to write for the papers they knew that this was a battle for justice against uneven odds. There were as many eager spectators as could be crowded into so small an area. Upon the whole an air of friendliness prevailed in this little court at Alexandria which we had never felt in the Washington courts. And the people there experienced a shock when the slender file of women, haggard, red-eyed, sick, came to the bar. Some were able to walk to their seats; others were so weak that they had to be stretched out on the wooden benches with coats propped under their heads for pillows. Still others bore the marks of the attack of the "night of terror." Many of the prisoners lay back in their chairs hardly conscious of the proceedings which were to free them. Mrs. Brannan collapsed utterly and had to be carried to a couch in an ante-room.

It was discovered just as the trial was to open that Miss Lucy Burns and Mrs. Lawrence Lewis, who it will be remembered had been removed to the jail before the writ had been issued, were absent from among the prisoners.

"They are too ill to be brought into court," Mr. Whittaker replied to the attorneys for the defense.

"We demand that they be brought into court at our risk," answered counsel for the defense.

The government's attorneys sustained Mr. Whittaker in

not producing them. It was clear that the government did not wish to have Miss Burns with the marks still fresh on her wrists from her manacling and handcuffing, and Mrs. Lewis with a fever from the shock of the first night, brought before the judge who was to decide the case.

"If it was necessary to handcuff Miss Burns to the bars of her cell, we consider her well enough to appear," declared Mr. O'Brien. "We consider we ought to know what has happened to all of these petitioners since these events. While I was at Occoquan Sunday endeavoring to see my clients, Mr. Whittaker was trying to induce the ladies, who, he says, are too sick to be brought here, to dismiss this proceeding. Failing in that, he refused to let me see them, though I had an order from Judge Mullowny, and they were taken back to the District of Columbia. From that time to this, though I had your Honor's order which you signed in Norfolk, the superintendent of the Washington jail also refused to allow me to see my clients, saying that your order had no effect in the District of Columbia."

"If there are any petitioners that you claim have not been brought here because they have been carried beyond the jurisdiction of the courts, I think we should know it," ruled the court. "Counsel for these ladies want them here; and they say that they ought to be here and are well enough to be here; that the respondent here has spirited them away and put them beyond the jurisdiction of the court. On that showing, unless there is some reason why they ought not to come, they should be here."

Miss Burns and Mrs. Lewis were accordingly ordered brought to court.

This preliminary skirmish over, the opening discussion revolved about a point of law as to whether the Virginia District Court had authority to act in this case.

After hearing both sides on this point, Judge Waddill said:

"These are not state prisoners; they are prisoners of the District of Columbia.   They are held by an order of the court claiming to have jurisdiction in the District of Columbia. But they are imprisoned in the Eastern District of Virginia, in Occoquan workhouse which, very much to our regret, is down here, and is an institution that we alone have jurisdiction over. No court would fail to act when such a state of affairs as is set forth in this petition is brought to its attention.

"Here was a case concerning twenty-five or thirty ladies. The statement as to their treatment was bloodcurdling; it was shocking to man's ideas of humanity if it is true.   They are here in court, and yet your answer denies all these facts which they submit.   It is a question whether you can do that and yet deny these petitioners the right of testimony."

Proceeding with this argument, the defense contended that the act itself of the District Commissioners in sending prisoners to the Occoquan workhouse was illegal; that no formal transfer from one institution to another had ever been made, the sentencing papers distinctly stating that all prisoners were committed to "the Washington Asylum and Jail."

"We deny that the records of the Commissioners of the District of Columbia can show that there was any order made by the Board for the removal of these women.   The liberty of a citizen cannot be so disregarded and trifled with that any police official or jailer may at his own volition, commit and hold him in custody and compel him to work.   The liberty of the people depends upon a broader foundation."

Repeated questions brought out from Mr. Zinkhan, Warden of the Jail, the fact that the directions given by the Commissioners to transfer prisoners from the jail to Occoquan rested entirely upon a verbal order given "five or six years ago."

"Do you really mean," interrupted the court, "that the only authority you have on the part of the Commissioners of

the District of Columbia to transfer parties down to Occoquan
is a verbal order made five or six years ago?"

Questions by the defense brought out the fact also that
Mr. Zinkhan could remember in detail the first oral orders he
had received for such a transfer, dating back to 1911, although
he could not remember important details as to how he had received the orders concerning the suffragists committed to his
care! He only knew that "orders were oral and explicit."

Q. [By defense in court] You say the three commissioners
were present?

A. Sure.

Q. Who else was present?

A. I am not sure just now who else was present. I remember somebody else was there, but I don't remember just
who. . . .

Q. Were the three commissioners present at the time Mr.
[Commissioner] Brownlow gave you this order?

A. Yes.

Q. You say it was a verbal order of the Commissioners?

A. Yes.

Q. Was the clerk of the Board present?

A. I think not.

Q. And you cannot remember who was present aside from
the three Commissioners?

A. No, I cannot remember just now.

Q. Try to recollect who was present at that meeting when
this order was given, aside from the Commissioners. There
was somebody else present?

A. It is my impression that there was some one other
person present, but I am not sure just now who it was.

Q. It was some official, some one well known, was it
not. . . . ?

A. I am not sure. . . .

[This conference was one in which Mr. McAdoo was reported to have participated.]

The gentle judge was distressed when in answer to a question by the government's attorney as to what Mr. Zinkhan did when the prisoners were given into his charge, the warden replied:

A. I heard early in the afternoon of the sentence, and I did not get away from the Commissioners' meeting until nearly 4 o'clock and I jumped in my machine and went down to the jail, and I think at that time six of them had been delivered there and were in the rotunda of the jail, and a few minutes after that a van load came. The remaining number of ten or twelve had not arrived, but inasmuch as the train had to leave at 5 o'clock and there would not be time enough to receive them in the jail and get them there in time for the train, I took the van that was there right over to the east end of the Union Station, and I think I took some of the others in my machine and another machine we had there carried some of the others over, and we telephoned the other van at Police Court to go direct to the east end of the Union Station and to deliver them to me. I had of course the commitments of those that were brought up to the jail—about 20 of them—and received from the officer of the court the other commitments of the last van load, and there I turned all of them except one that I kept back . . . over to the receiving and discharging officer representing the District Workhouse, and they were taken down there that evening.

There followed some questioning of the uneasy warden as to how he used this power to decide which prisoners should remain in jail and which should be sent to Occoquan. Warden Zinkhan stuttered something about sending "all the able bodied prisoners to Occoquan—women able to perform useful work"— and that "humanitarian motives" usually guided him in his selection. It was a difficult task for the warden for he had to conceal just *why* the suffrage prisoners were sent to Occoquan, and in so doing had to invent "motives" of his own.

Q. [By defense.] Mr. Zinkhan, were you or were you not actuated by humanitarian motives when you sent this group of women to the Occoquan Workhouse?

A. Yes.

Q. Were you actuated by humanitarian motives when you sent Mrs. Nolan, a woman of 73 years, to the workhouse? Did you think that she could perform some service at Occoquan that it was necessary to get her out of the District Jail and down there?

Warden Zinkhan gazed at the ceiling, shifted in his chair and hesitated to answer. The question was repeated, and finally the warden admitted uncomfortably that he believed he was inspired by "humanitarian motives."

"Mrs. Nolan, will you please stand up?" called out Mr. Malone.

All eyes turned toward the front row, where Mrs. Nolan slowly got to her feet. The tiny figure of a woman with pale face and snowy hair, standing out dramatically against her black bonnet and plain black dress, was answer enough.

Warden Zinkhan's answers after that came even more haltingly. He seemed inordinately fearful of trapping himself by his own words.

"The testimony has brought out the fact," the judge remarked at this point, "that two of these ladies were old and one of them is a delicate lady. Her appearance would indicate that she is not strong. Under this rule, if one of these ladies had been eighty years old and unable to walk she would have gone along with the herd and nobody would have dared to say 'ought this to be done?' Would the Commissioners in a case of that sort, if they gave consideration to it, think of sending such an individual there? Was not that what the law expected them to do, and not take them off in droves and inspect them at the Union Station and shoot them on down? Yet that is about what was done in this case."

In summing up this phase of the case in an eloquent appeal, Mr. Malone said:

"Can the Commissioners, with caprice and no order and no record except that orally given five or six years ago, and one which this warden now says was given 'oral and explicit,' transfer defendants placed in a particular institution, and under a particular kind of punishment arbitrarily to another institution, and add to their punishment?

"Even if we admit that the Commissioners had power, did Congress ever contemplate that any District Commissioners would dare to exercise power affecting the life and health of defendants in this fashion? Did Congress ever contemplate that, by mere whim, these things could be done? I am sure it did not, and even on the admission of the government that they had the power, they have exercised this power in such a scandalous fashion that it is worthy of the notice of the court and worthy of the remedy which we seek—the removal of the suffrage prisoners from the Occoquan workhouse."

After a brief recess, Judge Waddill rendered this decision: "The locking up of thirty human beings is an unusual sort of thing and judicial officers ought to be required to stop long enough to see whether some prisoners ought to go and some not; whether some might not be killed by going; or whether they should go dead or alive. *This class of prisoners* and this number of prisoners *should have been given special consideration.* There cannot be any controversy about this question . . . . You ought to lawfully lock them up instead of unlawfully locking them up—if they are to be locked up. . . . *The petitioners are, therefore, one and all, in the Workhouse without semblance of authority or legal process of any kind. . . . and they will accordingly be remanded to the custody of the Superintendent of the Washington Asylum and Jail."* . . .

It having been decided that the prisoners were illegally detained in the workhouse, it was not necessary to go into a discussion of the cruelties committed upon the prisoners while there.

The government's attorneys immediately announced that they would appeal from the decision of Judge Waddill. Pending such an appeal the women were at liberty to be paroled in the custody of counsel. But since they had come from the far corners of the continent and since some of them had served out almost half of their sentence, and did not wish in case of an adverse decision on the appeal, to have to return later to undergo the rest of their sentence, they preferred to finish their sentences.

These were the workhouse prisoners thus remanded to the jail who continued the hunger strike undertaken at the workhouse, and made a redoubtable reinforcement to Alice Paul and Rose Winslow and their comrades on strike in the jail when the former arrived.

CHAPTER 14

THE ADMINISTRATION OUTWITTED

WITH thirty determined women on hunger strike, of whom eight were in a state of almost total collapse, the Administration capitulated. It could not afford to feed thirty women forcibly and risk the social and political consequences; nor could it let thirty women starve themselves to death, and likewise take the the consequences. For by this time one thing was clear, and that was that the discipline and endurance of the women could not be broken. And so all the prisoners were unconditionally released on November 27th and November 28th.

On leaving prison Miss Paul said: "The commutation of sentences acknowledges them to be unjust and arbitrary. The attempt to suppress legitimate propaganda has failed.

"We hope that no more demonstrations will be necessary, that the amendment will move steadily on to passage and ratification without further suffering or sacrifice. But what we do depends entirely upon what the Administration does. We have one aim: the immediate passage of the federal amendment."

Running parallel to the protest made inside the prison, a public protest of nation-wide proportions had been made against continuing to imprison women. Deputations of influential women had waited upon all party leaders, cabinet officials, heads of the war boards, in fact every friend of the Administration, pointing out that we had broken no law, that we were unjustly held, and that the Administration would suffer politically for their handling of the suffrage agitation.

A committee of women, after some lively fencing with the Secretary of War, finally drove Mr. Baker to admit that women had been sent to prison for a political principle; that they were *not* petty disturbers but part of a great fundamental struggle. Secretary Baker said, "This [the suffrage struggle] is a revolution. There have been revolutions all through history. Some have been justified and some have not. The burden of responsibility to decide whether your revolution is justified or not is on you. The whole philosophy of your movement seems to be to obey no laws until you have a voice in those laws."

At least one member of the Cabinet thus showed that he had caught something of the purpose and depth of our movement. He never publicly protested, however, against the Administration's policy of suppression.

Mr. McAdoo, then Secretary of the Treasury, gave no such evidence of enlightenment as Mr. Baker. A committee of women endeavored to see him. He was reported "out. But we expect him here soon."

We waited an hour. The nervous private secretary returned to say that he had been mistaken. "The Secretary will not be in until after luncheon."

"We shall wait," said Mrs. William Kent, chairman of the deputation. "We have nothing more important to do to-day than to see Secretary McAdoo. We are willing to wait the whole day, if necessary, only it is imperative that we see him."

The private secretary's spirits sank. He looked as if he would give anything to undo his inadvertence in telling us that the Secretary was expected after luncheon! Poor man! We settled down comfortably to wait, a formidable looking committee of twenty women.

There was the customary gentle embarrassment of attendants whose chief is in a predicament from which they seem powerless to extricate him, but all were extremely courteous. The attendant at the door brought us the morning papers to read. Gradually groups of men began to arrive and cards were sent in the direction of the spot where we inferred the Secretary of the Treasury was safely hidden, hoping and praying for our early retirement.

Whispered conversations were held. Men disappeared in and out of strange doors. Still we waited.

Finally as the fourth hour of our vigil was dragging on, a lieutenant appeared to announce that the Secretary was very sorry but that he would not be able to see us "at all." We consulted, and finally sent in a written appeal, asking for "five minutes of his precious time on a matter of grave importance." More waiting! Finally a letter was brought to us directed to Mrs. William Kent, with the ink of the Secretary of the Treasury's signature still wet. With no concealment of contempt, he declared that under no circumstances could he speak with women who had conducted such an outrageous campaign in such an "illegal" way. We smiled as we learned from his pronouncement that "picketing" was "illegal," for we were not supposed to have been arrested for picketing. The tone of his letter, its extreme bitterness, tended to confirm what we had always been told, that Mr. McAdoo assisted in directing the policy of arrests and imprisonment.

I have tried to secure this letter for reproduction but unfortunately Mrs. Kent did not save it. We all remember its bitter passion, however, and the point it made about our "illegal picketing."

Congress convened on December 4th. President Wilson delivered a message, restating our aims in the war. He also recommended a declaration of a state of war against Austria; the control of certain water power sites; export trade-combination; railway legislation; and the speeding up of all necessary appropriation legislation. But he did not mention the suffrage amendment. Having been forced to release the prisoners, he again rested.

Immediately we called a conference in Washington of the Executive Committee and the National Advisory Council of the Woman's Party. Past activities were briefly reviewed and the political situation discussed. It is interesting to note that the Treasurer's report made at this conference showed that receipts in some months during the picketing had been double what they were the same month the previous year when there was no picketing. In one month of picketing the receipts went as high as six times the normal amount. For example in July of 1917, when the arrests had just begun, receipts for the month totalled $21,623.65 as against $3,690.62 for July of 1916. In November, 1917, when the militant situation was at its highest point, there was received at National Headquarters $31,117.87 as against $15,008.18 received in November, 1916. Still there were those who said we had no friends!

A rumor that the President would act persisted. But we could not rely on rumor. We decided to accelerate him and his Administration by filing damage suits amounting to $800,000 against the District Commissioners, against Warden Zinkhan, against Superintendent Whittaker and Captain Reams, a workhouse guard. [1] They were brought in no spirit of revenge, but merely that the Administration should not be allowed to forget its record of brutality, unless it chose to amend its conduct by passing the amendment. The suits were brought by the women who suffered the greatest abuse during the "night of terror" at the workhouse.

If any one is still in doubt as to the close relation between the Court procedure in our case and the President's actions,

[1] We were obliged to bring the suits against individuals, as we could not in the law bring them against the government.

this letter to one of our attorneys in January, 1918, must convince him.

My dear Mr. O'Brien:—

I wish you would advise me as soon as you conveniently can, what will be done with the suffragist cases now pending against Whittaker and Reams in the United States District Court at Alexandria.

I have heard rumors, the truth of which you will understand better than I, that *these cases will be dropped if the President comes out in favor of woman suffrage. This, I understand, he will do and certainly hope so,* as I am personally in favor of it and have been for many years. *But in case of his delay in taking any action, will you agree to continue these cases for the present?*

Very truly yours,
(Signed) F. H. STEVENS,
Assistant Corporation Counsel, D. C.

In order to further fortify themselves, the District Commissioners, when the storm had subsided, quietly removed Warden Zinkhan from the jail and Superintendent Whittaker resigned his post at the workhouse, presumably under pressure from the Commissioners.

The Woman's Party conference came to a dramatic close during that first week in December with an enormous mass meeting in the Belasco Theatre in Washington. On that quiet Sunday afternoon, as the President came through his gates for his afternoon drive, a passageway had to be opened for his motor car through the crowd of four thousand people who were blocking Madison Place in an effort to get inside the Belasco Theatre. Inside the building was packed to the rafters. The President saw squads of police reserves, who had been for the past six months arresting pickets for him, battling with a crowd that was literally storming the theatre in their eagerness to do honor to those who had been arrested. Inside there was a fever heat of enthusiasm, bursting cheers, and thundering applause which shook the building. America has never before nor since seen such a suffrage meeting.

Mrs. O. H. P. Belmont, chairman, opened the meeting by saying:

"We are here this afternoon to do honor to a hundred gallant women, who have endured the hardship and humiliation of imprisonment because they love liberty.

"The suffrage pickets stood at the White House gates for ten months and dramatized the women's agitation for political liberty. Self-respecting and patriotic American women will no longer tolerate a government which denies women the right to govern themselves. A flame of rebellion is abroad among women, and the stupidity and brutality of the government in this revolt have only served to increase its heat.

"As President Wilson wrote, 'Governments have been very successful in parrying agitation, diverting it, in seeming to yield to it and then cheating it, tiring it out or evading it. But the end, whether it comes soon or late, is quite certain to be the same.' While the government has endeavored to parry, tire, divert, and cheat us of our goal, the country has risen in protest against this evasive policy of suppression until to-day the indomitable pickets with their historic legends stand triumphant before the nation."

Mrs. William Kent, who had led the last picket line of forty-one women, was chosen to decorate the prisoners.

"In honoring these women, who were willing to go to jail for liberty," said Mrs. Kent, "we are showing our love of country and devotion to democracy." The long line of prisoners filed past her and amidst constant cheers and applause, received a tiny silver replica of a cell door, the same that appears in miniature on the title page of this book.

As proof of this admiration for what the women had done, the great audience in a very few moments pledged $86,326 to continue the campaign. Many pledges were made in honor of

Alice Paul, Inez Milholland, Mrs. Belmont, Dudley Field Malone, and all the prisoners. Imperative resolutions calling upon President Wilson and his Administration to act, were unanimously passed amid an uproar.

CHAPTER 15

IMMEDIATELY following the release of the prisoners and the magnificent demonstration of public support of them, culminating at the mass meeting recorded in the preceding chapter, political events happened thick and fast. Committees in Congress acted on the amendment. President Wilson surrendered and a date for the vote was set.

The Judiciary Committee of the House voted 18 to 2 to report the amendment to that body. The measure, it will be remembered, was reported to the Senate in the closing days of the previous session, and was therefore already before the Senate awaiting action. [1]

To be sure, the Judiciary Committee voted to report the amendment without recommendation. But soon after, the members of the Suffrage Committee, provision for which had also been made during the war session, were appointed. All but four members of this committee were in favor of national suffrage, and immediately after its formation it met to organize and decided to take the suffrage measure out of the hands of the Judiciary Committee and to press for a vote.

A test of strength came on December 18th.

On a trivial motion to refer all suffrage bills to the new suffrage committee, the vote stood 204 to 107. This vote, although unimportant in itself, clearly promised victory for the amendment in the House. In a few days, Representative Mon-

[1] See Chapter 8.

dell of Wyoming, Republican, declared that the Republican side
of the House would give more than a two-thirds majority of its
members to the amendment.

"It is up to our friends on the Democratic side to see
that the amendment is not defeated through hostility or indifference on their side," said Mr. Mondell.

Our daily poll of the House showed constant gains. Pledges
from both Democratic and Republican members came thick
and fast; cabinet members for the first time publicly declared
their belief in the amendment. A final poll, however, showed
that we lacked a few votes of the necessary two-thirds majority
to pass the measure in the House.

No stone was left unturned in a final effort to get the
President to secure additional Democratic votes to insure the
passage of the amendment. Finally, on the eve of the vote
President Wilson made his first declaration of support of the
amendment through a committee of Democratic Congressmen.
During the vote the following day Representative Cantrill of
Kentucky, Democrat, reported the event to the House. He
said in part:

It was my privilege yesterday afternoon to be one of a
committee of twelve to ask the President for advice and counsel
on this important measure (prolonged laughter and jeers).
Mr. Speaker, in answer to the sentiment expressed by part of
the House, I desire to say that at no time and upon no occasion
am I ever ashamed to confer with Woodrow Wilson upon any
important question (laughter, applause, and jeers) and that
part of the House that has jeered that statement before it
adjourns to-day will follow absolutely the advice which he
gave this committee yesterday afternoon. (Laughter and applause.) After conference with the President yesterday afternoon he wrote with his own hands the words which I now read
to you, and each member of the committee was authorized by
the President to give full publicity to the following:

*"The committee found that the President had not felt at
liberty to volunteer his advice to Members of Congress in this*

important matter, but when we sought his advice (laughter)
*he very frankly and earnestly advised us to vote for the amend-
ment as an act of right and justice to the women of the country
and of the world."*

. . . To my Democratic brethren who have made these halls
ring with their eloquence in their pleas to stand by the President, I will say that now is your chance to stand by the President and vote for this amendment, "as an act of right and
justice to the women of the country and of the world" . . .

Do you wish to do that which is right and just toward the
women of your own country? If so, follow the President's
advice and vote for this amendment. It will not do to follow
the President in this great crisis in the world's history on those
matters only which are popular in your own districts. The
true test is to stand by him, even though your own vote is unpopular at home. The acid test for a Member of Congress is
for him to stand for right and justice even if misunderstood
at home at first. In the end, right and justice will prevail
everywhere.

. . . No one thing connected with the war is of more
importance at this time than meeting the reasonable demand
of millions of patriotic and Christian women of the Nation
that the amendment for woman suffrage be submitted to the
States. . . .

The amendment passed the House January 10, 1918, by a
vote of 274 to 136—a two-thirds majority with one vote to
spare—*exactly forty years to a day from the time the suffrage
amendment was first introduced into Congress, and exactly one
year to a day from the time the first picket banner appeared at
the gates of the White House.*

Eighty-three per cent of the Republicans voting on the
measure, voted in favor of it, while only fifty per cent of the
Democrats voting, voted for it. Even after the Republicans
had pledged their utmost strength, more than two-thirds of
their membership, votes were still lacking to make up the Democratic deficiency, and the President's declaration that the measure ought to pass the House, produced them from his own

party. Those who contend that picketing had "set back the clock,"—that it did "no good,"—that President Wilson would "not be moved by it"—have, we believe, the burden of proof on their side of the argument. It is our firm belief that the solid year of picketing, with all its political ramifications, did compel the President to abandon his opposition and declare himself for the measure. I do not mean to say that many things do not coöperate in a movement toward a great event. I do mean to say that picketing was the most vital force amongst the elements which moved President Wilson. That picketing had compelled Congress to see the question in terms of political capital is also true. From the first word uttered in the House debate, until the final roll-call, political expediency was the chief motif.

Mr. Lenroot of Wisconsin, Republican, rose to say:

"May I suggest that there is a distinction between the Democratic members of the Committee on Rules and the Republican members, in this, that all of the Republican members are for this proposition?" This was met with instant applause from the Republican side.

Representative Cantrill prefaced his speech embodying the President's statement, which caused roars and jeers from the opposition, with the announcement that he was not willing to risk another election, with the voting women of the West, and the amendment still unpassed.

Mr. Lenroot further pointed out that: "From a Republican standpoint—from a partisan standpoint, it would be an advantage to Republicans to go before the people in the next election and say that this resolution was defeated by southern Democrats."

An anti-suffragist tried above the din and noise to remind Mr. Lenroot that three years before Mr. Lenroot had voted "No," but a Republican colleague came suddenly to the rescue with "What about Mr. Wilson?" which was followed by, "He

kept us out of war," and the jeers on the Republican side became more pronounced.

This interesting political tilt took place when Representatives Dennison and Williams of Illinois, and Representative
Kearns of Ohio, Republicans, fenced with Representative Raker
of California, Democrat, as he attempted, with an evident note
of self-consciousness, to make the President's reversal seem less
sudden.

MR. DENNISON: It was known by the committee that went
to see the President that the Republicans were going to take
this matter up and pass it in caucus, was it not?

MR. RAKER: I want to say to my Republican friends upon
this question that I have been in conference with the President for over three years upon this question. . . .

MR. KEARNS: How did the women of California find out
and learn where the President stood on this thing just before
election last fall? Nobody else seemed to know it.

MR. RAKER: They knew it.

MR. KEARNS: How did they find it out?

MR. RAKER: I will take a minute or two—

MR. KEARNS: I wish the gentleman would.

MR. RAKER: The President went home and registered. The
President went home and voted for woman suffrage.

MR. KEARNS: He said he believed in it for the several
states. . . .

MR. RAKER: One moment——

MR. KEARNS: That is the only information they had upon
the subject, is it?

MR. WILLIAMS: . . . Will the gentleman yield?

MR. RAKER: I cannot yield.

MR. WILLIAMS: Just for a question.

MR. RAKER: I cannot yield. . . .

That the President's political speed left some overcome was
clear from a remark of Mr. Clark of Florida when he said:

"I was amused at my friend from Oklahoma, Mr. Ferris, who wants us to stand with the President. God knows I want to stand with him. I am a Democrat, and I want to follow the leader of my party, and I am a pretty good lightning-change artist myself sometimes (laughter) ; but God knows I cannot keep up with his performance. (Laughter.) Why, the President wrote a book away back yonder" . . . and he quoted generously from President Wilson's many statements in defense of state rights as recorded in his early writings.

Mr. Hersey of Maine, Republican, drew applause when he made a retort to the Democratic slogan, "Stand by the President." He said:

"Mr. Speaker, I am still 'standing with the President,' or, in other words, the President this morning is standing with me."

The resentment at having been forced by the pickets to the point of passing the amendment was in evidence throughout the debate.

Representative Gordon of Ohio, Democrat, said with bitterness: "We are threatened by these militant suffragettes with a direct and lawless invasion by the Congress of the United States of the rights of those States which have refused to confer upon their women the privilege of voting. This attitude on the part of some of the suffrage Members of this House is on an exact equality with the acts of these women militants who have spent the last summer and fall, while they were not in the district jail or workhouse, in coaxing, teasing, and nagging the President of the United States for the purpose of inducing him, by coercion, to club Congress into adopting this joint resolution."

Shouts of "Well, they got him!" and "They got it!" from all sides, followed by prolonged laughter and jeers, interrupted the flow of his oratory.

Mr. Ferris of Oklahoma, Democrat, hoped to minimize the effectiveness of the picket.

"Mr. Speaker," he said, "I do not approve or believe in picketing the White House, the National Capitol, or any other station to bring about votes for women. I do not approve of wild militancy, hunger strikes, and efforts of that sort. I do not approve of the course of those women that . . . become agitators, lay off their womanly qualities in their efforts to secure votes. I do not approve of anything unwomanly anywhere, any time, and my course to-day in supporting this suffrage amendment is not guided by such conduct on the part of a very few women here or elsewhere." (Applause.)

Representative Langley of Kentucky, Republican, was able to see picketing in a fairer light:

"Much has been said pro and con about 'picketing',—that rather dramatic chapter in the history of this great movement. It is not my purpose to speak either in criticism or condemnation of that; but if it be true—I do not say that it is, because I do not know—but if it be true, as has been alleged, that certain promises were made, as a result of which a great campaign was won, and those promises were not kept, I wonder whether in that silent, peaceful protest that was against this broken faith, there can be found sufficient warrant for the indignities which the so-called 'pickets' suffered; and when in passing up and down the Avenue I frequently witnessed cultured, intellectual women arrested and dragged off to prison because of their method of giving publicity to what they believed to be the truth, I will confess that the question sometimes arose in my mind whether when the impartial history of this great struggle has been written their names may not be placed upon the roll of martyrs to the cause to which they were consecrating their lives in the manner that they deemed most effective."

Mr. Mays of Utah was one Democrat who placed the responsibility for militancy where it rightly belonged when he said:

"Some say to-day that they are ashamed of the action of the militants in picketing the Capitol. . . . But we should be more ashamed of the unreasonable stubbornness on the part of the men who refused them the justice they have so long and patiently asked."

And so the debate ran on. Occasionally one caught a glimmer of real comprehension amongst these men about to vote upon our political liberty; but more often the discussion stayed on a very inferior level.

And there were gems imperishable!

Even friends of the measure had difficulty not to romanticize about "Woman—God's noblest creature" . . . "man's better counterpart" . . . "humanity's perennial hope" . . . "the world's object most to be admired and loved" . . . and so forth.

Representative Elliott of Indiana, Republican, favored the resolution because—"A little more than four hundred years ago Columbus discovered America. Before that page of American history was written he was compelled to seek the advice and assistance of a woman. From that day until the present day the noble women of America have done their part in times of peace and of war. . . ."

If Queen Isabella was an argument in favor for Mr. Elliott of Indiana, Lady Macbeth played the opposite part for Mr. Parker of New Jersey, Republican. . . . "I will not debate the question as to whether in a time of war women are the best judges of policy. That great student of human nature, William Shakespeare, in the play of Macbeth, makes Lady Macbeth eager for deeds of blood until they are committed and war is begun and then just as eager that it may be stopped." . . .

Said Mr. Gray of New Jersey, Republican: "A nation will endure just so long as its men are virile. History, physiology, and psychology all show that giving woman equal political rights with man makes ultimately for the deterioration of manhood. It is, therefore, not only because I want our country to win this war but because I want our nation to possess the male virility necessary to guarantee its future existence that I am opposed to the pending amendment."

The hope was expressed that President Wilson's conversion would be like that of St. Paul, "and that he will become a master-worker in the vineyards of the Lord for this proposition." (Applause.)

Mr. Gallivan, Democrat, although a representative of Massachusetts, "the cradle of American liberty," called upon a great Persian philosopher to sustain him in his support. " 'Dogs bark, but the caravan moves on.' . . . Democracy cannot live half free and half female."

Mr. Dill of Washington, Democrat, colored his support with the following tribute: " . . . It was woman who first learned to prepare skins of animals for protection from the elements, and tamed and domesticated the dog and horse and cow. She was a servant and a slave. . . . To-day she is the peer of man."

Mr. Little of Kansas, Republican, tried to bring his colleagues back to a moderate course by interpolating:

"It seems to me, gentlemen, that it is time for us to learn that woman is neither a slave nor an angel, but a human being, entitled to be treated with ordinary common sense in the adjustment of human affairs. . . ."

But this calm statement could not allay the terror of Representative Clark of Florida, Democrat, who cried: "In the hearings before the committee it will be found that one of the leaders among the suffragettes declared that they wanted the ballot for 'protection', and when asked against whom she desired 'protection' she promptly and frankly replied, 'men.' My God, has it come to pass in America that the women of the land need to be protected from the men?" The galleries quietly nodded their heads, and Mr. Clark continued to predict either the complete breakdown of family life. . . . or "they [man and wife] must think alike, act alike, have the same ideals of life, and look forward with like vision to the happy consummation 'beyond the vale.' . . .

"God knows that . . . when you get factional politics limited to husband and wife, oh, what a spectacle will be presented, my countrymen. . . . Love will vanish, while hate ascends the throne. . . .

"To-day woman stands the uncrowned queen in the hearts of all right-thinking American men; to her as rightful sovereign we render the homage of protection, respect, love, and may the guiding hand of an all-wise Providence stretch forth in this hour of peril to save her from a change of relation which must bring in its train, discontent, sorrow, and pain," he concluded desperately, with the trend obviously toward "crowning" the queens.

There was the disturbing consideration that women know too much to be trusted. "I happen to have a mother," said Mr. Gray of New Jersey, Republican, "as most of us have, and incidentally I think we all have fathers, although a father does not count for much any more. My mother has forgotten more political history than he ever knew, and she knows more about the American government and American political economy than he has ever shown symptoms of knowing, and for the good of mankind as well as the country she is opposed to women getting into politics."

The perennial lament for the passing of the good old days was raised by Representative Welty of Ohio, Democrat, who said:

"The old ship of state has left her moorings and seems to be sailing on an unknown and uncharted sea. The government founded in the blood of our fathers is fading away. Last fall, a year ago, both parties recognized those principles in their platforms, and each candidate solemnly declared that he would abide by them if elected. But lo, all old things are passing away, and the lady from Montana has filed a bill asking that separate citizenship be granted to American women marrying foreigners."

Representative Greene of Massachusetts, Republican, all but shed tears over the inevitable amending of the Constitution:

"I have read it [the Constitution] many times, and there have been just 17 amendments adopted since the original Constitution was framed by the master minds whom God had inspired in the cabin of the Mayflower to formulate the Constitution of the Plymouth Colony which was made the basis of the Constitution of Massachusetts and subsequently resulted in the establishment of the Constitution of the United States under which we now live. . . ."

Fancy his shock at finding the pickets triumphant.

"Since the second session of the Sixty-fifth Congress opened," he said, "I have met several women suffragists from the State of Massachusetts. I have immediately propounded to them this one question: 'Do you approve or disapprove of the suffrage banners in front of the White House . . . ?' The answer in nearly every case to my question was: 'I glory in that demonstration' . . . the response to my question was very offensive, and I immediately ordered these suffrage advocates from my office."

And again the pickets featured in the final remarks of Mr. Small of North Carolina, Democrat, who deplored the fact that advocates of the amendment had made it an issue inducing party rivalry. "This is no party question, and such efforts will be futile. It almost equals in intelligence the scheme of that delectable and inane group of women who picketed the White House on the theory that the President could grant them the right to vote."

Amid su:h gems of intellectual delight the House of the great Amer.can Congress passed the national suffrage amendment.

We turned our entire attention then to the Senate.

CHAPTER 16

THE President had finally thrown his power to putting the amendment through the House. We hoped he would follow this up by insisting upon the passage of the amendment in the Senate. We ceased our acts of dramatic protest for the moment and gave our energies to getting public pressure upon him, to persuade him to see that the Senate acted. We also continued to press directly upon recalcitrant senators of the minority party who could be won only through appeals other than from the President.

There are in the Senate 96 members—2 elected from each of the 48 states. To pass a constitutional amendment through the Senate, 64 votes are necessary, a two-thirds majority. At this point in the campaign, 53 senators were pledged to support the measure and 43 were opposed. We therefore had to win 11 more votes. A measure passed through one branch of Congress must be passed through the other branch during the life of that Congress, otherwise it dies automatically and must be born again in a new Congress. We therefore had only the remainder of the first regular session of the 65th Congress and, failing of that, the short second session from December, 1918, to March, 1919, in which to win those votes.

Backfires were started in the states of the senators not yet committed to the amendment. Organized demand for action in the Senate grew to huge proportions.

We turned also to the leading influential members of the respective parties for active help.

Colonel Roosevelt did his most effective suffrage work at this period in a determined attack upon the few unconvinced Republican Senators. The Colonel was one of the few leaders in our national life who was never too busy to confer or to offer and accept suggestions as to procedure. He seemed to have imagination about women. He never took a patronizing attitude nor did he with moral unction dogmatically tell you how the fight should be waged and won. He presupposed ability among women leaders. He was not offended, morally or politically, by our preferring to go to jail rather than to submit in silence. In fact, he was at this time under Administration fire, because of his bold attacks upon some of their policies, and remarked during an interview at Oyster Bay:

"I may soon join you women in jail. One can never tell these days."

His sagacious attitude toward conservative and radical suffrage forces was always delightful and indicative of his appreciation of the political and social value of a movement's having vitality enough to disagree on methods. None of the banal philosophy that "you can never win until all your forces get together" from the Colonel. One day, as I came into his office for an interview, I met a member of the conservative suffragists just leaving, and we spoke. In his office the Colonel remarked, "You know, I contemplated having both you and Mrs. Whitney come to see me at the same time, since it was on a similar mission, but I didn't quite know whether the lion and the lamb would lie down together, and I thought I'd better take no chances. . . . But I see you're on speaking terms," he added. I answered that our relations were extremely amiable, but remarked that the other side might not like to be called "lambs."

"You delight in being the lions—on that point I am safe, am I not?" And he smiled his widest smile as he plunged into a vivid expository attack upon the Senatorial opponents of suffrage in his own party. He wrote letters to them. If this failed, he invited them to Oyster Bay for the week-end. Never did he abandon them until there was literally not a shadow of hope to bank on.

When the Colonel got into action something always happened on the Democratic side. He made a public statement to Senator Gallinger of New Hampshire, Republican leader in the Senate, in which he pointed to the superior support of the Republicans and urged even more liberal party support to ensure the passage of the amendment in the Senate. Action by the Democrats followed fast on the heels of this public statement.

The National Executive Committee of the Democratic party, after a referendum vote of the members of the National Committeemen, passed a resolution calling for favorable action in the Senate. Mr. A. Mitchell Palmer wrote to the Woman's Party saying that this resolution must be regarded as "an official expression of the Democratic Party through the only organization which can speak for it between national conventions."

The Republican National Committee meeting at the same time commended the course taken by Republican Representatives who had voted for the amendment in the House, and declared their position to be "a true interpretation of the thought of the Republican Party."

Republican and Democratic state, county and city committees followed the lead and called for Senate action.

State legislatures in rapid succession called upon the Senate to pass the measure, that they in turn might immediately ratify. North Dakota, New York, Rhode Island, Arizona, Texas and other states acted in this matter.

Intermittent attempts on the Republican side to force action, followed by eloquent speeches from time to time, piquing their opponents, left the Democrats bison-like across the path. The majority of them were content to rest upon the action taken in the House.

I was at this time Chairman of the Political Department of the Woman's Party, and in that capacity interviewed practically every national leader in both majority parties. I can not resist recording a few impressions.

Colonel William Boyce Thompson of New York, now Chairman of Ways and Means of the Republican National Committee, who with Raymond Robins had served in Russia as member of the United States Red Cross Mission, had just returned. The deadlock was brought to his attention. He immediately responded in a most effective way. In a brief but dramatic speech at a great mass meeting of the Woman's Party, at Palm Beach, Florida, he said:

"The story of the brutal imprisonment in Washington of women advocating suffrage is shocking and almost incredible. I became accustomed in Russia to the stories of men and women who served terms of imprisonment under the Czar, because of their love of liberty, but did not know that women in my own country had been subjected to brutal treatment long since abandoned in Russia.

"I wish now to contribute ten thousand dollars to the campaign for the passage of the suffrage amendment through the Senate, one hundred dollars for each of the pickets who went to prison because she stood at the gates of the White House, asking for the passage of the suffrage measure."

This was the largest single contribution received during the national agitation. Colonel Thompson had been a suffragist all his life, but he now became actively identified with the work for the national amendment. Since then he has continued to give generously of his money and to lend his political prestige as often as necessary.

Colonel House was importuned to use his influence to win additional Democratic votes in the Senate, or better still to urge the President to win them. Colonel House is an interesting but not unfamiliar type in politics. Extremely courteous, mild mannered, able, quickly sympathetic, he listens with undistracted attention to your request. His round bright eyes snap as he comes at you with a counter-proposal. It seems so reasonable. And while you know he is putting back upon you the very task you are trying to persuade him to undertake, he does it so graciously that you can scarcely resist liking it. He has the manner of having done what you ask without actually doing more than to make you feel warm at having met him. It is a kind of elegant statecraft which has its point of grace, but which is exasperating when effectiveness is needed. Not that Colonel House was not a supporter of the federal amendment. He was. But his gentle, soft and traditional kind of diplomacy would not employ high-powered pressure. "I shall be going to Washington soon on other matters, and I shall doubtless see the President. Perhaps he may bring up the subject in conversation, and if he does, and the opportunity offers itself, I may be able to do something." Some such gentle threat would come from the Colonel. He was not quite so tender, however, in dealing with Democratic senators, after the President declared for the amendment. He did try to win them.

Ex-President Taft, then joint Chairman of the National War Labor Board, was interviewed at his desk just after rendering an important democratic labor award.

"No, indeed! I'll do nothing for a proposition which adds more voters to our electorate. I thought my position on this question was well known," said Mr. Taft.

"But we thought you doubtless had changed your mind since the beginning of our war for democracy——" I started to answer.

"This is *not* a war for democracy," he said emphatically, looking quizzically at me for my assertion; "if it were, I

wouldn't be doing anything for it. . . . The trouble in this
country is we've got too many *men* voting as it is. Why, I'd
take the vote away from most of the men," he added. I wanted
to ask him what men he would leave voting. I wanted also to
tell him they were taking the vote away from one class of men
in Russia at that moment.

Instead, I said, "Well, I'm not quite sure whom we could
trust to sit in judgment"—while he looked smiling and serene,
as much as to say, "Oh, that would be a simple matter."

"However," I said, "we have no quarrel with you. You
are an avowed aristocrat, and we respect your candor. Our
quarrel is with democrats who will not trust their own doc-
trines." Again he smiled with as much sophistication as such
a placid face could achieve, and that was all. I believe Mr.
Taft has lately modified his attitude toward women voting.
I do not know how he squares that with his distaste of
democracy.

There was Samuel Gompers, President of the American
Federation of Labor, high in Administration confidence. It
was a long wait before Abby Scott Baker and I were allowed
into his sanctum.

"Well, ladies, what can I do for you?" was the opening
question, and we thought happily here is a man who will not
bore us with his life record on behalf of women. He comes to
the point with direction.

"Will you speak to the President on behalf of your organization, which has repeatedly endorsed national suffrage, to
induce him to put more pressure behind the Senate which is
delaying suffrage?" we asked with equal direction. We concealed a heavy sigh as a reminiscent look came into his shrewd,
wan eyes, and he began:

"Doubtless you ladies do not know that as long ago as
1888"—I believe that was the date—"my organization sent a
petition to the United States Congress praying for the adop-

tion of this very amendment and we have stood for it ever since. . . ."

"Don't you think it is about time that prayer was answered?" we ventured to interrupt. But his reverie could not be disturbed. He looked at us coldly, for he was living in the past, and continued to recount the patient, enduring qualities of his organization.

"I will speak to my secretary and see what the organization can do," he said finally. We murmured again that it was the President we wished him to speak to, but we left feeling reasonably certain that there would be no dynamic pressure from this cautious leader.

Herbert Hoover was the next man we sought. Here we encountered the well-groomed secretary who would not carry our cards into his chief.

"Mr. Hoover has appointments a week ahead," he said. "For example, his chart for to-day includes a very important conference with some grain men from the Northwest," . . . and he continued to recite the items of the chart, ending with "a dinner at the White House to-night."

"If we could see him for just five minutes," we persisted, "he could do what we ask this very night at the White House." But the trained-to-protect secretary was obdurate.

"We shall leave a written request for five minutes at Mr. Hoover's convenience," we said, and prepared the letter.

Time passed without answer. Mrs. Baker and I were compelled to go again to Mr. Hoover's office.

Again we were greeted by the affable secretary, who on this occasion recounted not only his chief's many pressing engagements, but his devoted family life—his Saturday and Sunday habits which were "so dreadfully cut into by his heavy work." We were sympathetic but firm. Would Mr. Hoover not be willing to answer our letter? Would he not be willing to state publicly that he thought the amendment ought to be passed in the Senate? Would the secretary, in short, please go to him to ascertain if he would be willing to say a single word in behalf of the political liberty of women? The secretary disappeared and returned to say, "Mr. Hoover wishes me to tell you ladies he can give no time whatever to the consideration of your question until after the war is over. This is final."

The Chief Food Administrator would continue to demand sacrifices of women throughout the war, but he would not give so much as a thought to their rights in return. Mr. Hoover was the only important man in public life who steadfastly refused to see our representatives. After announcing his candidacy for nomination to the Presidency he authorized his secretary to write us a letter saying he had always been for woman suffrage.

Mr. Bainbridge Colby, then member of the Emergency Fleet Corporation of the Shipping Board and member of the Inter-Allied Council which sat on shipping problems, now Secretary of State in President Wilson's Cabinet, was approached as a suffragist, known to have access to the President. Mr. Colby had just returned from abroad when I saw him. He is a cultivated gentleman, but he knows how to have superlative enthusiasm.

"In the light of the world events," he said, "this reform is insignificant. No time or energy ought to be diverted from the great program of crushing the Germans."

"But can we not do that," I asked, "without neglecting internal liberties?"

Mr. Colby is a strong conformist. He became grave. When I was indiscreet enough to reveal that I was inclined to pin my faith to the concrete liberty of women, rather than to a vague and abstract "human freedom," which was supposed to descend upon the world, once the Germans were beaten, I know he wanted to call me "seditious." But he is a gallant gentleman and he only frowned with distress. He continued with enthusiasm to plan to build ships.

Bernard Baruch, then member of the Advisory Committee of the Council of National Defense, later economic expert at the Peace Conference, was able to see the war and the women's problem at the same time. He is an able politician and was therefore sensitive to our appeal; he saw the passage of the amendment as a political asset. I do not know how much he believed in the principle. That was of minor importance. What was important was that he agreed to tell the President that he believed it wise to put more pressure on the measure in the Senate. Also I believe Mr. Baruch was one member of the Administration who realized in the midst of the episode that arresting women was bad politics, to say nothing of the doubtful chivalry of it.

George Creel, chairman of the Committee on Public Information, was also asked for help. We went to him many times, because his contact with the President was constant. A suffragist of long standing, he nevertheless hated our militant tactics, for he knew we were winning and the Administration was losing. He is a strange composite. Working at terrific tension and mostly under fire, he was rarely in calm enough mood to sit down and devise ways and means.

"But I talk to the President every day on this matter"— and—"I am doing all I can"—and—"The President is doing all he can"—he would drive at you—without stopping for breath.

"But if you will just ask him to get Senator ———"

"He is working on the Senator now. You people must give him time. He has other things to do," he would say, sweeping aside every suggestion. Familiar advice!

Charles D. Hilles, former Chairman of the Republican National Committee, was a leader who had come slowly to believe in national suffrage. But, once convinced, he was a faithful and dependable colleague who gave practical political assistance.

William Randolph Hearst in powerful editorials called upon the Senators to act. Mr. R. J. Caldwell of New York, life-long suffragist, financier and man of affairs, faithfully and persistently stood by the amendment and by the militants. A more generous contributer and more diligent ally could not be found. A host of public men were interviewed and the great majority of them did help at this critical juncture. It is impossible to give a list that even approaches adequacy, so I shall not attempt it.

Our pressure from below and that of the leaders from above began to have its effect. An attempt was made by Administration leaders to force a vote on May 19, 1918. Friends interceded when it was shown that not enough votes were pledged to secure passage. Again the vote was tentatively set for June 27th and again postponed.

The Republicans, led by Senator Gallinger, provided skirmishes from time to time. The Administration was accused on the floor of blocking action, to which accusation its leaders did not even reply.

Still unwilling to believe that we would be forced to resume our militancy we attempted to talk to the President again. A special deputation of women munition workers was sent to him under our auspices. The women waited for a week, hoping he would consent to see them among his receptions—to the Blue Devils of France, to a Committee of Indians, to a Committee of Irish Patriots, and so forth.

"No time," was the answer. And the munition workers were forced to submit their appeal in writing.

"We are only a few of the thousands of American women," they wrote the President, "who are forming a growing part of the army at home. The work we are doing is hard and dangerous to life and health, making detonators, handling TNT, the highest of all explosives. We want to be recognized by our country, as much her citizens as our soldiers are."

Mr. Tumulty replied for the President:

"The President asks me to say that nothing you or your associates could say could possibly increase his very deep interest in this matter and that he is doing everything that he could with honor and propriety do in behalf of the [suffrage] amendment."

An opportunity was given the President to show again his sympathy for a world-wide endeavor just after having ignored this specific opportunity at home. He hastened to accept the larger field. In response to a memorial transmitted through Mrs. Carrie Chapman Catt, President of the International Woman Suffrage Alliance, the French Union for Woman Suffrage urged the President to use his aid on their behalf "which will be a powerful influence for woman suffrage in the entire world." The memorial was endorsed by the suffrage committee of Great Britain, Italy, Belgium, and Portugal. The President took the occasion to say: "The democratic reconstruction of the world will not have been completely or adequately obtained until women are admitted to the suffrage. As for America it is my earnest hope that the Senate of the United States will give an unmistakable answer by passing the federal amendment before the end of this session."

Meanwhile four more Democratic Senators pledged their support to the amendment. Influenced by the President's declaration of support, and by widespread demands from their constituents, Senators Phelan of California, King of Utah, Gerry of Rhode Island, and Culberson of Texas abandoned the ranks of the opposition.

During this same period the Republican side of the Senate gave five more Republican Senators to the amendment. They were Senators McCumber of North Dakota, Kellogg of Minnesota, Harding of Ohio, Page of Vermont, and Sutherland of

West Virginia. All of these men except Senator McCumber [1] were won through the pressure from Republican Party leaders.

This gain of nine recruits reduced to two the number of votes to be won.

When at the end of seven months from the time the amendment had passed the House, we still lacked these two votes, and the President gave no assurance that he would put forth sufficient effort to secure them, we were compelled to renew our attacks upon the President.

[1] Senator McCumber, though opposed, was compelled to support the measure, by the action of the N. D. legislature commanding him to do so.

CHAPTER 17

T HE Senate was about to recess. No assurance was given by the majority that suffrage would be considered either before or after the recess. Alarmed and aroused, we decided upon a national protest in Washington August 6th, the anniversary of the birth of Inez Milholland.

The protest took the form of a meeting at the base of the Lafayette monument in the park, directly opposite the White House. Women from many states in the Union, dressed in white, hatless and coatless in the midsummer heat of Washington, marched to the monument carrying banners of purple, white and gold, led by a standard-bearer carrying the American flag. They made a beautiful mass of color as they grouped themselves around the statue, against the abundant green foliage of the park.

The Administration met this simple reasonable form of protest by further arrests.

Mrs. Lawrence Lewis of Philadelphia, the first speaker, began: "We are here because when our country is at war for liberty and democracy . . ." At that point she was roughly seized by a policeman and placed under arrest. The great audience stood in absolute and amazed silence.

Miss Hazel Hunkins of Montana took her place. "Here at the statue of Lafayette, who fought for the liberty of this country," she began, "and under the American flag, I am asking for . . ." She was immediately arrested.

Miss Vivian Pierce of California began: "President Wilson

has said . . ." She was dragged from the plinth to the waiting patrol.

One after another came forward in an attempt to speak, but no one was allowed to continue. Wholesale arrests followed. Just as the women were being taken into custody, according to the New York *Evening World* of August 13th, "the President walked out of the northeast gate of the White House and up Pennsylvania Avenue for a conference with Director General of Railroads McAdoo. The President glanced across the street and smiled."

Before the crowd could really appreciate what had happened, forty-eight women had been hustled to the police station by the wagon load, their gay banners floating from the backs of the somber patrols. They were told that the police had arrested them under the orders of Col. C. S. Ridley, the President's military aide, and assistant to the Chief Engineer attached to the War Department. All were released on bail and ordered to appear in court the following day.

When they appeared they were informed by the Government's attorney that he would have to postpone the trial until the following Tuesday so that he might examine witnesses to see "what offense, if any, the women would be charged with."

"I cannot go on with this case," he said, "*I have had no orders*. There are no precedents for cases like these. . . ."

The women demanded that their cases be dismissed, or else a charge made against them. They were merely told to return on the appointed day. Such was the indignation aroused against the Administration for taking this action that Senator Curtis of Kansas, Republican whip, could say publicly:

"The truth of this statement is made evident by the admission of the court that the forty-eight suffragists are arrested upon absolutely no charges, and that these women, among them munition workers and Red Cross workers, are held in Washington until next Tuesday, under arrest, while the United

States attorney for the District of Columbia decides for what offense, 'if any,' they were arrested.

"The meeting was called to make a justified protest against continued blocking of the suffrage amendment by the Democratic majority in the Senate. It is well known that three-fourths of the Republican membership in the Senate are ready to vote for the amendment, but under the control of the Democratic majority the Senate has recessed for six weeks without making any provision for action on this important amendment.

"In justice to the women who have been working so hard for the amendment it should be passed at the earliest date, and if action is not taken on it soon after the resumption of business in the Senate there is every possibility that it will not be taken during this Congress, and the hard-won victory in the House of Representatives will have been won for nothing."

When they finally came to trial ten days after their arrest, to face the charge of "holding a meeting in public grounds," and for eighteen of the defendants an additional charge of "climbing on a statue," the women answered the roll call but remained silent thereafter. The familiar farce ensued. Some were released for lack of identification. The others were sentenced to the District Jail—for ten days if they had merely assembled to hold a public meeting, for fifteen days if they had also "climbed on a statue."

The Administration evidently hoped by lighter sentences to avoid a hunger strike by the prisoners.

The women were taken immediately to a building, formerly used as a man's workhouse, situated in the swamps of the District prison grounds. This building, which had been declared unfit for human habitation by a committee appointed under President Roosevelt in 1909, and which had been uninhabited ever since, was now reopened, nine years later, to receive twenty-six women who had attempted to hold a meeting in a public park in Washington. The women protested in a body and demanded to be treated as political prisoners. This being refused, all save two very elderly women, too frail to do so, went on hunger strike at once.

This last lodgment was the worst. Hideous aspects which had not been encountered in the workhouse and jail proper were encountered here. The cells, damp and cold, were below the level of the upper door and entirely below the high windows. The doors of the cell were partly of solid steel with only a small section of grating, so that a very tiny amount of light penetrated the cells. The wash basins were small and unsightly; the toilet open, with no pretense of covering. The cots were of iron, without any spring, and with only a thin straw pallet to lie upon. The heating facilities were antiquated and the place was always cold. So frightful were the nauseating odors which permeated the place, and so terrible was the drinking water from the disused pipes, that one prisoner after another became violently ill.

"I can hardly describe that atmosphere," said Mrs. W. D. Ascough, of Connecticut. "It was a deadly sort of smell, insidious and revolting. It oppressed and stifled us. There was no escape."

As a kind of relief from these revolting odors, they took their straw pallets from the cells to the floor outside. They were ordered back to their cells but refused in a body to go. They preferred the stone floors to the vile odors within, which kept them nauseated.

Conditions were so shocking that Senators began to visit their constituents in this terrible hole. Many of them protested to the authorities. Protests came in from the country, too.

At the end of the fifth day the Administration succumbed to the hunger strike and released the prisoners, trembling with weakness, some of them with chills and some of them in a high

ABANDONED JAIL

PRISONERS ON STRAW PALLETS ON JAIL FLOOR

PICKETS AT CAPITOL

SENATE PAGES AND CAPITOL POLICE ATTACK PICKETS

THE URN GUARDED BY MISS BERTHE ARNOLD

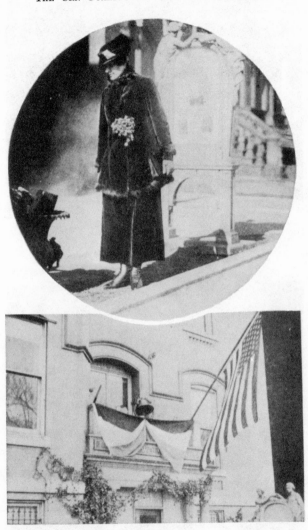

© Harris & Ewing.

THE BELL WHICH TOLLED THE CHANGE OF WATCH

WATCHFIRE "LEGAL."*

WATCHFIRE SCATTERED BY POLICE—DR. CAROLINE SPENCER
REBUILDING IT.

© *Harris & Ewing.*

One Hundred Women Hold Public Conflagration

PICKETS IN FRONT OF REVIEWING STAND, BOSTON

fever, scarcely able even to walk to the ambulance or motor car.

We had won from the Administration, however, a concession to our protest. Prior to the release of the prisoners we had announced that in spite of the previous arrests a second protest meeting would be held on the same spot. A permit to hold this second protest meeting was granted us.

"I have been advised [Col. Ridley wrote to Miss Paul] that you desire to hold a demonstration in Lafayette Square on Thursday, August 22d. By direction of the chief of engineers, U. S. Army, you are hereby *granted permission to hold this demonstration.* You are advised good order must prevail."

"We received yesterday [Miss Paul replied] your permit for a suffrage demonstration in Lafayette Park this afternoon, and are very glad that our meetings are no longer to be interfered with. Because of the illness of so many of our members, due to their treatment in prison this last week, and with the necessity of caring for them at headquarters, we are planning to hold our next meeting a little later. We have not determined on the exact date but we will inform you of the time as soon as it is decided upon."

It was reported on credible authority that this concession was the result of a conference at which the President, Secretary of War Baker and Colonel Ridley were present. It was said that Secretary Baker and Colonel Ridley persuaded the President to withdraw the orders to arrest us and allow our meetings to go on, even though they took the form of attacks upon the President.

Two days after the release of the women, the Republican Party, for the first time in the history of woman suffrage, caucused in the Senate in favor of forcing suffrage to a vote.

The resolution which was passed unanimously by the caucus determined to "insist upon consideration immediately" and "also to insist upon a final vote . . . at the earliest possible moment. . . . *Provided*, That this resolution shall not be construed as in any way binding the action or vote of any Member of the Senate upon the merits of the said woman suffrage amendment."

While not a direct attempt, therefore, to win more Republican Senators, this proved a very great tactical contribution to the cause. The Republicans were proud of their suffrage strength. They knew the Democrats were not. With the Congressional elections approaching the Republicans meant to do their part toward acquainting the country with the Administration's policy of vacillation and delay. This was not only helpful to the Republicans politically; it was also advantageous to the amendment in that it goaded the majority into action.

Nine months had passed since the vote in the House and we were perilously near the end of the session, when on the 16th of September, Senator Overman, Democrat, Chairman of the Rules Committee, stated to our Legislative Chairman that suffrage was "not on the program for this session" and that the Senate would recess in a few days for the election campaigns without considering any more legislation. On the same day Senator Jones, Chairman of the Suffrage Committee, announced to us that he would not even call his Committee together to consider taking a vote.

We had announced a fortnight earlier that another protest meeting would be held at the base of the Lafayette Monument that day, September 16th, at *four* o'clock. No sooner had this protest been announced than the President publicly stated that he would receive a delegation of Southern and Western women partisans on the question of the amendment at *two* o'clock the same day.

To this delegation he said, "I am, as I think you know, heartily in sympathy with you. I have endeavored to assist you in every way in my power, and I shall continue to do so.

I will do all I can to urge the passage of the amendment by an early vote."

Presumably this was expected to disarm us and perhaps silence our demonstration. However, it merely moved us to make another hasty visit to Senator Overman, Chairman of the Rules Committee, and to Senator Jones, Chairman of the Suffrage Committee, between the hours of two and four to see if the President's statement that he would do all he could to secure an early vote had altered their statements made earlier in the day.

These Administration leaders assured us that their statements stood; that no provision had been made for action on the amendment; that the President's statement did not mean that a vote would be taken this session; and that they did not contemplate being so advised by him.

Such a situation was intolerable. The President was uttering more fine words, while his Administration leaders interpreted them to mean nothing, because they were not followed up by action on his part.

We thereupon changed our demonstration at four o'clock to a more drastic form of protest. We took these words of the President to the base of Lafayette Monument and burned them in a flaming torch.

A throng gathered to hear the speakers. Ceremonies were opened with the reading of the following appeal by Mrs. Richard Wainwright, wife of Rear-Admiral Wainwright:

"Lafayette, we are here!

"We, the women of the United States, denied the liberty which you helped to gain, and for which we have asked in vain for sixty years, turn to you to plead for us.

"Speak, Lafayette, dead these hundred years but still living in the hearts of the American people. Speak again to plead for us like the bronze woman at your feet, condemned like us to a silent appeal. She offers you a sword. Will you not use for us the sword of the spirit, mightier far than the sword she holds out to you?

"Will you not ask the great leader of democracy to look upon the failure of our beloved country to be in truth the place where every one is free and equal and entitled to a share in the government? Let that outstretched hand of yours pointing to the White House recall to him his words and promises, his trumpet call for all of us, to see that the world is made safe for democracy.

"As our army now in France spoke to you there, saying here we are to help your country fight for liberty, will you not speak here and now for us, a little band with no army, no power but justice and right, no strength but in our Constitution and in the Declaration of Independence; and win a great victory again in this country by giving us the opportunity we ask,—to be heard through the Susan B. Anthony amendment.

"Lafayette, we are here!"

Before the enthusiastic applause for Mrs. Wainwright's appeal had died away, Miss Lucy Branham of Baltimore stepped forward with a flaming torch, which she applied to the President's latest words on suffrage. The police looked on and smiled, and the crowd cheered as she said:

"The torch which I hold symbolizes the burning indignation of the women who for years have been given words without action. . . .

"For five years women have appealed to this President and his party for political freedom. The President has given words, and words, and words. To-day women receive more words. We announce to the President and the whole world to-day, by this act of ours, our determination that words shall not longer be the only reply given to American women—our determination that this same democracy for whose establishment abroad we are making the utmost sacrifice, shall also prevail at home.

"We have protested to this Administration by banners; we have protested by speeches; we now protest by this symbolic act.

"As in the ancient fights for liberty, the crusaders for freedom symbolized their protest against those responsible for injustice by consigning their hollow phrases to the flames, so we, on behalf of thousands of suffragists, in this same way to-day protest against the action of the President and his party in delaying the liberation of American women."

Mrs. Jessie Hardy Mackaye of Washington, D. C., then came forward to the end of the plinth to speak, and as she appeared, a man in the crowd handed her a twenty-dollar bill for the campaign in the Senate. This was the signal for others. Bills and coins were passed up. Instantly marshals ran hither and thither collecting the money in improvised baskets while the cheers grew louder and louder. Many of the policemen present were among the donors.

Burning President Wilson's words had met with popular approval from a large crowd!

The procession of women was starting back to headquarters, the police were eagerly clearing the way for the line; the crowd was dispersing in order; the great golden banner, "Mr. President, what will you *do* for woman suffrage?" was just swinging past the White House gate, when President Wilson stepped into his car for the afternoon drive.

CHAPTER 18

THE next day the Administration completely reversed its policy. Almost the first Senate business was an announcement on the floor by Senator Jones, Chairman of the Suffrage Committee, that the suffrage amendment would be considered in the Senate September 26th. And Senator Overman, Chairman of the Rules Committee, rather shyly remarked to our legislative chairman that he had been "mistaken yesterday." It was "now in the legislative program." The Senate still stood 62 votes for and 34 against the amendment—2 votes lacking. The President made an effort among individual Democrats to secure them. But it was too feeble an effort and he failed.

Chairman Jones took charge of the measure on the floor. The debate opened with a long and eloquent speech by Senator Vardaman of Mississippi, Democrat, in support of the amendment. "My estimate of woman," said he, in conclusion, "is well expressed in the words employed by a distinguished author who dedicated his book to a 'Little mountain, a great meadow, and a woman,' 'To the mountain for the sense of time, to the meadow for the sense of space, and to the woman for the sense of everything.'"

Senator McCumber of North Dakota, Republican, followed with a curious speech. His problem was to explain why, although opposed to suffrage, he would vote for the amendment. Beginning with the overworked "cave man" and "beasts of the forests," and down to the present day, "the male had always protected the female." He always would! Forgetting recent events in the Capital, he went so far as to say, " . . . In our courts she ever finds in masculine nature an asylum of protection, even though she may have committed great wrong. While the mind may be convinced beyond any doubt, the masculine heart finds it almost impossible to pronounce the word 'guilty' against a woman." Scarcely had the galleries ceased smiling at this idea when he treated them to a novel application of the biological theory of inheritance. "The political field," he declared, "always has been and probably always will be an arena of more or less bitter contest. The political battles leave scars as ugly and lacerating as the physical battles, and the more sensitive the nature the deeper and more lasting the wound. And as no man can enter this contest or be a party to it and assume its responsibilities without feeling its blows and suffering its wounds, much less can woman with her more emotional and more sensitive nature.

"But . . . you may ask why should she be relieved from the scars and wounds of political contest? Because they do not affect her alone but are *transmitted through her to generations yet to come. . . .*"

The faithful story of the sinking ship was invoked by the Senator from North Dakota. One might almost imagine after listening to Congressional debates for some years that traveling on sinking ships formed a large part of human experience. "Fathers, sons, and brothers," said the Senator in tearful voice, "guarding the lifeboats until every woman from the highest to the lowest has been made safe, waving adieu with a smile of cheer on their lips, while the wounded vessel slowly bears them to a strangling death and a watery tomb, belie the charge . . ." that woman needs her citizenship as a form of protection.

In spite of these opinions, however, the Senator was obliged to vote for the amendment because his state had so ordered.

Senator Hardwick of Georgia, Democrat, felt somewhat betrayed that the suffrage plank in the platform of his party in 1916, recommending state action, should be so carelessly set aside. "There is not a Democratic Senator present," said Mr. Hardwick, "who does not know the history that lies back of the adoption of that plank. There is not a Democratic Senator who does not know that the plank was written here in Washington and sent to the convention and represented the deliberate voice of the administration and of the party on this question, which was to remit this question to the several States for action. . . .

"The President of the United States . . . was reported . . . to have sent this particular plank . . . from Washington, supposedly by the hands of one of his Cabinet officers." The fact that his own party and the Republican party were both advancing on suffrage irritated him into denouncing the alacrity with which "politicians and senators are trying to get on the band wagon first."

Senator McKellar of Tennessee, Democrat, reduced the male superiority argument to simple terms when he said: " . . . Taking them by and large, there are brainy men and brainy women, and that is about all there is to the proposition."

Our armies were sweeping victorious toward Germany. There was round on round of eloquence about the glories of war. Rivers of blood flowed. And always the rôle of woman was depicted as a contented binding of wounds. There were those who thought woman should be rewarded for such service. Others thought she ought to do it without asking anything in return. But all agreed that this was her rôle. There was no woman's voice in that body to protest against the perpetuity of such a rôle.

The remarks of Senator Reed of Missouri, anti-suffrage Democrat, typify this attitude. " . . . Women in my state believe in the old-fashioned doctrine that men should fight the battles on the red line; that men should stand and bare their bosoms to the iron hail; and that back of them, if need be, there shall be women who may bind up the wounds and whose tender hands may rest upon the brow of the valiant soldier who has gone down in the fight.

"But, sir, that is woman's work, and it has been woman's work always. . . . The woman who gave her first born a final kiss and blessed him on his way to battle," had, according to the Senator from Missouri, earned a "crown of glory . . . gemmed with the love of the world."

And with Senator Walsh of Montana, Democrat, "The women of America have already written a glorious page in the history of the greatest of wars that have vexed the world. They, like Cornelia, have given, and freely given their jewels to their country."

Some of us wondered.

Senator McLean of Connecticut, anti-suffrage Republican, flatly stated "that all questions involving declarations of war and terms of peace should be left to that sex which must do the fighting and the dying on the battlefield." And he further said that until boys between 18 and 21 who had just been called to the colors should ask for the vote, "their mothers should be and remain both proud and content" without it. He concluded with an amusing account of the history of the ballot box. "This joint resolution," he said, "goes beyond the seas and above the clouds. It attempts to tamper with the ballot box, over which mother nature always has had and always will have supreme control; and such attempts always have ended and always will end in failure and misfortune."

Senator Phelan of California, Democrat, made a straightforward, intelligent speech.

Senator Beckham of Kentucky, Democrat, deplored the idea that man was superior to woman. He pleaded "guilty to the charge of Romanticism." He said, "But I look upon woman as superior to man." Therefore he could not trust her with a vote. He had the hardihood to say further, with the men of the world at each other's throats, . . . "Woman is the civilizing, refining, elevating influence that holds man from barbarism." We charged him with ignorance as well as romanticism when he said in closing, "It is the duty of man to work and labor for woman; to cut the wood, to carry the coal, to go into the fields in the necessary labor to sustain the home where the woman presides and by her superior nature elevates him to higher and better conceptions of life."

Meanwhile Senator Shafroth of Colorado, Democrat, life-long advocate of suffrage, was painstakingly asking one senator after another, as he had been for years, "Does not the Senator believe that the just powers of government are derived from the consent of the governed?" and then—"But if you have the general principle acknowledged that the just powers of government are derived from the consent of the governed." . . . and so forth. But the idea of applying the Declaration of Independence to modern politics fairly put them to sleep.

These samples of senatorial profundity may divert, outrage, or bore us, but they do not represent the real battle. It is not that the men who utter these sentiments do not believe them. More is the pity, they do. But they are smoke screens—mere skirmishes of eloquence or foolishness. They do not represent the motives of their political acts.

The real excitement began when Senator Pittman of Nevada, Democrat, attempted to reveal to the senators of his party the actual seriousness of the political crisis in which the Democrats were now involved. He also attempted to shift the blame for threatened defeat of the amendment to the Republican side of the chamber. There was a note of desperation in his voice, too, since he knew that President Wilson had not up to that moment won the two votes lacking. The gist of Senator Pittman's remarks was this: The Woman's Party has charged the Senate Woman Suffrage Committee, which is in control of the Democrats, and the President himself, with the responsibility for obstructing a vote on the measure. "I confess," said he, that this is "having its effect as a campaign argument" in the woman suffrage states.

Senator Wolcott of Delaware, Democrat, interrupted him to ask if this was "the party that has been picketing here in Washington?" Senator Pittman, having just paid this tribute to our campaign in the West, hastened to say that it was, but that there was another association, the National American Woman Suffrage Association, which had always conducted its campaign in a "lady-like—modest—and intelligent way" and which had "never mixed in politics."

Waving a copy of the *Suffragist* in the air, Senator Pittman began his attempt to shift responsibility to the Republican side, for the critical condition of the amendment. He denounced the Republicans for caucusing on the amendment and deciding unanimously to press for a vote, when they [the Republicans] knew there were two votes lacking. He scored us for having given so much publicity to the action of the caucus and declared with vehemence that a "trick" had been executed through Senator Smoot which he would not allow to go unrevealed. Senator Pittman charged that the Republicans had promised enough votes to pass the amendment and that upon that promise the Democrats had brought the measure on the floor; that the Republicans thereupon withdrew enough votes to cause the defeat of the amendment. Whether or not this was true, at any rate, as Senator Smoot pointed out, the Democratic Chairman in charge of the measure could at any moment send the measure back to Committee, safe from immediate defeat. This was true, but not exactly a suggestion to be welcomed by the Democrats.

"Yes," replied Senator Pittman, "and then if we move to refer it back to the committee, the Senator from Utah would say again, 'The Democrats are obstructing the passage of this amendment. . . . We told you all the time they wanted to kill it.' . . . If we refer it back to the committee, then we will be charged, as we have been all the time in the suffrage states, with trying to prevent a vote on it, and still the Woman's Party campaign will go on as it is going on now; and if we vote on it they will say: 'We told you the Democrats would kill it, because the President would not make 32 on his side vote for it'."

That was the crux of the whole situation. The Democrats had been manœuvered into a position where they could neither afford to move to refer the amendment back to the committee, nor could they afford to press it to a losing vote. They were indeed in an exceedingly embarrassing predicament.

Throughout hours of debate, Senator Pittman could not get away from the militants. Again and again, he recited our deeds of protest, our threats of reprisal, our relentless strategy of holding his party responsible for defeat or victory.

"I should like the Senator," interpolated Senator Poindexter of Washington, Republican, "so long as he is discussing the action of the pickets, to explain to the Senate whether or not it is the action of the pickets . . . the militant . . . woman's party, that caused the President to change his attitude on the subject. Was he coerced into supporting this measure—after he had for years opposed it—because he was picketed? When did the President change his attitude? If it was not because he was picketed, will the Senator explain what was the cause of the change in the President's attitude?"

Mr. Pittman did not reply directly to these questions.

Senator Reed of Missouri, anti-Administration Democrat, consumed hours reading into the Congressional Record various press reports of militant activities.   He dwelt particularly upon the news headlines, such as,

"Great Washington Crowd Cheers Demonstration at White House by National Woman's Party." . . .

"Suffragists Burn Wilson 'Idle Words' . . ."

"Money Instead of Jeers Greet Marchers and Unique Protest Against Withholding Vote" . . .

"Apply Torch to President's Words . . . Promise to Urge Passage of Amendment Not Definite Enough for Militants."

"Suff's Burn Speech . . . Apply Torch to Wilson's Words During Demonstration—Symbol of 'Indignation'—Throngs Witnessing Doings in Lafayette Square Orderly and Contribute to Fund—President Receives Delegation of American Suffrage Association Women."

Senator McKellar of Tennessee, Democrat, asked Mr. Reed if he did not believe that we had a right peaceably to assemble under the "first amendment to our Constitution which I shall read: Congress shall make no law . . . abridging . . . the right of the people peaceably to assemble, and to petition the Government for a redress of grievances."   Mr. Reed made no direct answer.

Lest the idea get abroad from the amount of time they spent in discussing the actions of the "wicked militants," that we *had* had something to do with the situation which had resulted in Democratic despair, Senator Thomas of Colorado, the one Democrat who had never been able to conceal his hostility to us for having reduced his majority in 1914, arose to pay a tribute to the conservative suffrage association of America. Their "escutcheon," he said, "is unstained by mob methods or appeals to violence.   It has neither picketed Presidents nor populated prisons. . . . It has carried no banners flaunting insults to the Executive," while the militants on the other hand have indulged in "much tumult and vociferous braying, all for notoriety's sake." . . . The galleries smiled as he counseled the elder suffrage leaders "not to lose courage nor yet be faint-hearted," for this "handicap" would soon be overcome. It would have taken an abler man than Senator Thomas, in the face of the nature of this debate, to make any one believe that we had been a "handicap" in forcing them to their position. He was the only one hardy enough to try. After this debate the Senate adjourned, leaving things from the point of view of party politics, tangled in a hopeless knot. It was to untie this knot that the President returned hastily from New York in answer to urgent summons by long distance telephone, and went to the Capitol to deliver his memorable address.

Mr. Vice President and Gentlemen of the Senate: The unusual circumstances of a world war in which we stand and are judged in the view not only of our own people and our own consciences but also in view of all nations and all peoples will, I hope, justify in your thought, as it does in mine, the message I have come to bring you. I regard the concurrence of the Senate in the constitutional amendment proposing the extension of the suffrage to women as vitally essential to the successful prosecution of the great war of humanity in which we are engaged. I have come to urge upon you the considerations which have led me to that conclusion. It is not only my privilege, it is also my duty to appraise you of every circumstance and element involved in this momentous struggle which seems to me to affect its very processes and its outcome. It is my duty to win the war and to ask you to remove every obstacle that stands in the way of winning it.

I had assumed that the Senate would concur in the amendment because no disputable principle is involved but only a question of the method by which the suffrage is to be extended to women. There is and can be no party issue involved in it. Both of our great national parties are pledged, explicitly pledged, to equality of suffrage for the women of the country. Neither party, therefore, it seems to me, can justify hesitation as to the method of obtaining it, can rightfully hesitate to substitute federal initiative for state initiative, if the early adoption of the measure is necessary to the successful prosecution of the war and if the method of state action proposed in party platforms of 1916 is impracticable within any reasonable length of time, if practicable at all. And its adoption is, in my judgment, clearly necessary to the successful prosecution of the war and the successful realization of the objects for which the war is being fought.

That judgment, I take the liberty of urging upon you with solemn earnestness for reasons which I shall state very frankly and which I shall hope will seem as conclusive to you as they have seemed to me.

This is a peoples' war, and the peoples' thinking constitutes its atmosphere and morale, not the predilections of the drawing room or the political considerations of the caucus. If we be indeed democrats and wish to lead the world to democracy, we can ask other peoples to accept in proof of our sincerity and our ability to lead them whither they wish to be led nothing less persuasive and convincing than our actions. Our professions will not suffice. Verification must be forthcoming when verification is asked for. And in this case verification is asked for, asked for in this particular matter. You ask by whom? Not through diplomatic channels; not by Foreign Ministers, not by the intimations of parliaments. It is asked for by the anxious, expectant, suffering peoples with whom we are dealing and who are willing to put their destinies in some measure in our hands, if they are sure that we wish the same things that they wish. I do not speak by conjecture. It is not alone the voices of statesmen and of newspapers that reach me, *and the voices of foolish and intemperate agitators do not reach me at all!* Through many, many channels I have been made aware what the plain, struggling, workaday folk are thinking upon whom the chief terror and suffering of this tragic war falls. They are looking to the great, powerful, famous democracy of the West to lead them to the new day for which they have so long waited; and they think, in their logical simplicity, that democracy means that women shall play their part in affairs alongside men and upon an equal footing with them. If we reject measures like this, in ignorance or defiance of what a new age has brought forth, of what they have seen but we have not, they will cease to follow or to trust us. They have seen their own governments accept this inter-

pretation of democracy,—seen old governments like Great
Britain, which did not profess to be democratic, promise readily and as of course this justice to women, though they had
before refused it, the strange revelations of this war having
made many things new and plain to governments as well as to
peoples.

Are we alone to refuse to learn the lesson? Are we alone to
ask and take the utmost that women can give,—service and
sacrifice of every kind,—and still say that we do not see what
title that gives them to stand by our sides in the guidance of
the affairs of their nation and ours? We have made partners of the women in this war; shall we admit them only to a
partnership of sacrifice and suffering and toil and not to a
partnership of privilege and of right? This war could not
have been fought, either by the other nations engaged or by
America, if it had not been for the services of the women,—
services rendered in every sphere,—not only in the fields of
effort in which we have been accustomed to see them work,
but wherever men have worked and upon the very skirts and
edges of the battle itself. We shall not only be distrusted but
shall deserve to be distrusted if we do not enfranchise them
with the fullest possible enfranchisement, as it is now certain
that the other great free nations will enfranchise them. We
cannot isolate our thought or our action in such a matter
from the thought of the rest of the world. We must either
conform or deliberately reject what they propose and resign
the leadership of liberal minds to others.

The women of America are too noble and too intelligent and
too devoted to be slackers whether you give or withhold this
thing that is mere justice; but I know the magic it will work
in their thoughts and spirits if you give it them. I propose it
as I would propose to admit soldiers to the suffrage, the men
fighting in the field for our liberties and the liberties of the
world, were they excluded. The tasks of the women lie at the
very heart of the war, and I know how much stronger that
heart will beat if you do this just thing and show our women
that you trust them as much as you in fact and of necessity
depend upon them.

Have I said that the passage of this amendment is a vitally
necessary war measure, and do you need further proof? Do

you stand in need of the trust of other peoples and of the trust of our women? Is that trust an asset or is it not? I tell you plainly, as commander-in-chief of our armies and of the gallant men in our fleets, as the present spokesman of this people in our dealings with the men and women throughout the world who are now our partners, as the responsible head of a great government which stands and is questioned day by day as to its purposes, its principles, its hopes, whether they be serviceable to men everywhere or only to itself, and who must himself answer these questionings or be shamed, as the guide and director of forces caught in the grip of war and by the same token in need of every material and spiritual resource this great nation possesses,—I tell you plainly that this measure which I urge upon you is vital to the winning of the war and to the energies alike of preparation and of battle.

And not to the winning of the war only. It is vital to the right solution of the great problems which we must settle, and settle immediately, when the war is over. We shall need then a vision of affairs which is theirs, and, as we have never needed them before, the sympathy and insight and clear moral instinct of the women of the world. The problems of that time will strike to the roots of many things that we have not hitherto questioned, and I for one believe that our safety in those questioning days, as well as our comprehension of matters that touch society to the quick, will depend upon the direct and authoritative participation of women in our counsels. We shall need their moral sense to preserve what is right and fine and worthy in our system of life as well as to discover just what it is that ought to be purified and reformed. Without their counselings we shall be only half wise.

That is my case. This is my appeal. Many may deny its validity, if they choose, but no one can brush aside or answer the arguments upon which it is based. The executive tasks of this war rest upon me. I ask that you lighten them and place in my hands instruments, spiritual instruments, which I do not now possess, which I sorely need, and which I have daily to apologize for not being able to employ. (Applause).

It was a truly beautiful appeal.

When the applause and the excitement attendant upon the occasion of a message from the President had subsided, and the floor of the chamber had emptied itself of its distinguished visitors, the debate was resumed.

"If this resolution fails now," said Senator Jones of Washington, ranking Republican member of the Suffrage Committee, "it fails for lack of Democratic votes."

Senator Cummins of Iowa, Republican, also a member of the Suffrage Committee, reminded opponents of the measure of the retaliatory tactics used by President Wilson when repudiated by senators on other issues. "I sincerely hope," he said tauntingly, "that the President may deal kindly and leniently with those who are refusing to remove this obstacle which stands in his way. It has not been very long since the President retired the junior Senator from Mississippi [Mr. Vardaman] from public life. Why? Because he refused at all times to obey the commands which were issued for his direction. The junior Senator from Georgia [Mr. Hardwick] suffered the same fate. How do you hope to escape? . . . My Democratic friends are either proceeding upon the hypothesis that the President is insincere or that they may be able to secure an immunity from him that these other unfortunate aspirants for office failed to secure."

Senator Cummins chided Senator Reed for denouncing "the so-called militants who sought to bring their influence to bear upon the situation in rather a more forcible and decisive method than was employed by the national association. . . . I did not believe in the campaign they were pursuing (not one senator was brave enough to say outright that he did). . . .

"But that was simply a question for them to determine; and if they thought that in accordance with the established custom the President should bring his influence to bear more effectively than he had, they had a perfect right to burn his message; they had a perfect right to carry banners in Lafayette Park, in front of the White House, or anywhere else; they had a perfect right to bring their banners into the Capitol and display them with all the force and vigor which they could command. I did not agree with them; but they also were making a campaign for an inestimable and a fundamental right.

"What would you have done, men, if you had been deprived of the right to vote? What would you have done if you had been deprived of the right of representation? Have the militants done anything worse than the revolutionary forces who gathered about the tea chests and threw them into the sea? . . .

"I do not believe they [the militants] committed any crime; and while I had no particle of sympathy with the manner in which they were conducting their campaign, I think their arrest and imprisonment and the treatment which they received while in confinement are a disgrace to the civilized world, and much the more a disgrace to the United States, which assumes to lead the civilized world in humane endeavor. They disturbed nobody save that disturbance which is common to the carrying forward of all propaganda by those who are intensely and vitally interested in it. I wish they had not done it, but I am not to be the judge of their methods so long as they confine themselves to those acts and to those words which are fairly directed to the accomplishment of their purposes. I cannot accept the conclusion that because these women burned a message in Lafayette Park or because they carried banners upon the streets in Washington therefore they are criminals."

The time had come to take the vote, but we knew we had not won. The roll was called and the vote stood 62 to 34 [Oct. 1, 1918], counting all pairs. We had lost by 2 votes.

Instantly Chairman Jones, according to his promise to the women, changing his vote from "yea" to "nay," moved for a reconsideration of the measure, and thus automatically kept it on the calendar of the Senate. That was all that could be done.

The President's belief in the power of words had lost the amendment. Nor could he by a speech, eloquent as it was, break down the opposition in the Senate which he had so long protected and condoned.

Our next task was to secure a reversal of the Senate vote. We modified our tactics slightly.

CHAPTER 19

OUR immediate task was to compel the President to secure a reversal of two votes in the Senate. It became necessary to enter again the Congressional elections which were a month away.

By a stroke of good luck there were two senatorial contests—in New Jersey and New Hampshire—for vacancies in the short term. That is, we had an opportunity to elect two friends who would take their seats in time to vote on the amendment before the end of this session. It so happened that the Democratic candidates were pledged to vote for the amendment if elected, and that the Republican candidates were opposed to the amendment. We launched our campaign in this instance for the election of the Democratic candidates. We went immediately to the President to ask his assistance in our endeavor. We urged him personally to appeal to the voters of New Jersey and New Hampshire on behalf of his two candidates. As Party leader he was at the moment paying no attention whatever to the success of these two suffragists. Both of the Democratic candidates themselves appealed to President Wilson for help in their contests, on the basis of their suffrage advocacy. His speech to the Senate scarcely cold, the President refused to lend any assistance in these contests, which with sufficient effort might have produced the last two votes.

At the end of two weeks of such pressure upon the President we were unable to interest him in this practical endeavor. It was clear that he would move again only under attack. We went again, therefore, to the women voters of the West and asked them to withhold their support from the Democratic Senatorial candidates in the suffrage states in order to compel the President to assist in the two Eastern contests. This campaign made it clear to the President that we were still holding him and his party to their responsibility.

And as has been pointed out, our policy was to oppose the Democratic candidates at elections so long as their party was responsible for the passage of the amendment and did not pass it. Since there is no question between individuals in suffrage states—they are all suffragists—this could not increase our numerical strength. It could, however, and did demonstrate the growing and comprehensive power of the women voters.

Shortly before election, when our campaign was in full swing in the West, the President sent a letter appealing to the voters of New Jersey to support Mr. Hennessey, the Democratic candidate for the Senate. He subsequently appealed to the voters of New Hampshire to elect Mr. Jameson, candidate for Democratic Senator in New Hampshire.

We continued our campaign in the West as a safeguard against relaxation by the President after his appeal. There were seven senatorial contests in the western suffrage states. In all but two of thse contests—Montana and Nevada—the Democratic Senatorial candidates were defeated. In these two states the Democratic majority was greatly reduced.

Republicans won in New Jersey and New Hampshire and a Republican Congress was elected to power throughout the country.

The election campaign had had a wholesome effect, however, on both parties and was undoubtedly one of the factors in persuading the President to again appeal to the Senate.

Immediately after the defeat in the Senate, and throughout the election campaign, we attempted to hold banners at the Capitol to assist our campaign and in order to weaken the resistance of the senators of the opposition. The mottoes on the banners attacked with impartial mercilessness both Democrats and Republicans. One read:

> SENATOR WADSWORTH'S REGIMENT IS FIGHTING FOR
> DEMOCRACY ABROAD.
> SENATOR WADSWORTH LEFT HIS REGIMENT AND IS
> FIGHTING AGAINST DEMOCRACY IN THE SENATE.
> SENATOR WADSWORTH COULD SERVE HIS COUNTRY
> BETTER BY FIGHTING WITH HIS REGIMENT ABROAD
> THAN BY FIGHTING WOMEN AT HOME.

Another read:

> SENATOR SHIELDS TOLD THE PEOPLE OF TENNESSEE
> HE WOULD SUPPORT THE PRESIDENT'S POLICIES.
> THE ONLY TIME THE PRESIDENT WENT TO THE SEN-
> ATE TO ASK ITS SUPPORT SENATOR SHIELDS VOTED
> AGAINST HIM.
> DOES TENNESSEE BACK THE PRESIDENT'S WAR PRO-
> GRAM OR SENATOR SHIELDS?

And still a third:

> GERMANY HAS ESTABLISHED "EQUAL, UNIVERSAL, SE-
> CRET, DIRECT FRANCHISE."
> THE SENATE HAS DENIED EQUAL, UNIVERSAL, SE-
> CRET SUFFRAGE TO AMERICA.
> WHICH IS MORE OF A DEMOCRACY, GERMANY OR
> AMERICA?

As the women approached the Senate, Colonel Higgins, the Sergeant at Arms of the Senate, ordered a squad of Capitol policemen to rush upon them. They wrenched their banners from them, twisting their wrists and manhandling them as they took them up the steps, through the door, and down

into the guardroom,—their banners confiscated and they themselves detained for varying periods of time. When the
women insisted on knowing upon what charges they were held,
they were merely told that "peace and order must be maintained on the Capitol grounds," and further, "It don't make
no difference about the law, Colonel Higgins is boss here, and
he has taken the law in his own hands."

Day after day this performance went on. Small detach-
ments of women attempted to hold banners outside the United
States Senate, as the women of Holland had done outside the
Parliament in the Hague. It was difficult to believe that
American politicians could be so devoid of humor as they
showed themselves. The panic that overwhelms our official
mind in the face of the slightest irregularity is appalling!
Instead of maintaining peace and order, the squads of police
managed to keep the Capitol grounds in a state of confusion.
They were assisted from time to time by Senate pages, small
errand boys who would run out and attack mature women
with impunity. The women would be held under the most rigid
detention each day until the Senate had safely adjourned.
Then on the morrow the whole spectacle would be repeated.

While the United States Senate was standing still under our
protest world events rushed on. German autocracy had collapsed. The Allies had won a military victory. The Kaiser
had that very week fled for his life because of the uprising of
his people.

"We are all free voters of a free republic now," was the
message sent by the women of Germany to the women of the
United States through Miss Jane Addams. We were at that
moment heartily ashamed of our government. German women
voting! American women going to jail and spending long
hours in the Senate guardhouse without arrests or charges.
The war came to an end. Congress adjourned November 21st.

When the 65th Congress reconvened for its short and final

session, December 2nd, 1918 [less than a month after our election campaign], President Wilson, for the first time, included suffrage in his regular message to Congress, the thing that we had asked of him at the opening of every session of Congress since March, 1913.

There were now fewer than a hundred days in which to get action from the Senate and so avoid losing the benefit of our victory in the House.

In his opening address to Congress, the President again appealed to the Senate in these words:

"And what shall we say of the women—of their instant intelligence, quickening every task that they touched; their capacity for organization and coöperation, which gave their action discipline and enhanced the effectiveness of everything they attempted; their aptitude at tasks to which they had never before set their hands; their utter self-sacrifice alike in what they did and in what they gave? Their contribution to the great result is beyond appraisal. They have added a new luster to the annals of American womanhood.

"The least tribute we can pay them is to make them the equals of men in political rights, as they have proved themselves their equals in every field of practical work they have entered, whether for themselves or for their country. These great days of completed achievement would be sadly marred were we to omit that act of justice. Besides the immense practical services they have rendered, the women of the country have been the moving spirits in the systematic economies in which our people have voluntarily assisted to supply the suffering peoples of the world and the armies upon every front with food and everything else we had, that might serve the common cause. The details of such a story can never be fully written but we carry them at our hearts and thank God that we can say that we are the kinsmen of such."

Again we looked for action to follow this appeal. Again

we found that the President had uttered these words but had made no plan to translate them into action.

And so his second appeal to the Senate failed, coming as it did after the hostility of his party to the idea of conferring freedom on women nationally, had been approved and fostered by President Wilson for five solid years. He could not overcome with additional eloquence the opposition which he himself had so long formulated, defended, encouraged and solidified, especially when that eloquence was followed by either no action or only half-hearted efforts.

It would now require a determined assertion of his political power as the leader of his party. We made a final appeal to him as leader of his party and while still at the height of his world power, to make such an assertion and to demand the necessary two votes.

CHAPTER 20

N O sooner had we set ourselves to a brief, hot campaign to compel President Wilson to win the final votes than he sailed away to France to attend the Peace Conference, sailed away to consecrate himself to the program of liberating the oppressed peoples of the whole world. He cannot be condemned for aiming to achieve so gigantic a task. But we reflected that again the President had refused his specific aid in an humble aspiration, for the rosy hope of a more boldly conceived ambition.

It was positively impossible for us, by our own efforts, to win the last 2 votes. We could only win them through the President. That he had left behind him his message urging the Senate to act, is true. That Administration leaders did not consider these words a command, is also true. It must be realized that even after the President had been compelled to publicly declare his support of the measure, it was almost impossible to get his own leaders to take seriously his words on suffrage. And so again the Democratic Chairman of the Rules Committee, in whose keeping the program lay, had no thought of bringing it to a vote. The Democratic Chairman of the Woman Suffrage Committee assumed not the slightest responsibility for its success, nor could he produce any plan whereby the last votes could be won. They knew, as well as did we, that the President only could win those last 2 votes. They made it perfectly clear that until he had done so, they could do nothing.

Less than fifty legislative days remained to us. Something had to be done quickly, something bold and offensive enough to threaten the prestige of the President, as he was riding in sublimity to unknown heights as a champion of world liberty; something which might penetrate his reverie and shock him into concrete action. We had successfully defied the full power of his Administration, the odds heavily against us. We must now defy the popular belief of the world in this apostle of liberty. This was the feeling of the four hundred officers of the National Woman's Party, summoned to a three days' conference in Washington in December, 1918. It was unanimously decided to light a fire in an urn, and, on the day that the President was officially received by France, to burn with fitting public ceremonies all the President's past and present speeches or books concerning "liberty", "freedom" and "democracy."

It was late afternoon when the four hundred women proceeded solemnly in single file from headquarters, past the White House, along the edge of the quiet and beautiful Lafayette Park, to the foot of Lafayette's statue. A slight mist added beauty to the pageant. The purple, white and gold banners, so brilliant in the sunshine, became soft pastel sails. Half the procession carried lighted torches; the other half banners. The crowd gathered silently, somewhat awe-struck by the scene. Massed about that statue, we felt a strange strength and solidarity, we felt again that we were a part of the universal struggle for liberty.

The torch was applied to the pine-wood logs in the Grecian Urn at the edge of the broad base of the statue. As the flames began to mount, Vida Milholland stepped forward and without accompaniment sang again from that spot of beauty, in her own challenging way, the Woman's Marseillaise. Even the small boys in the crowd, always the most difficult to please, cheered and clapped and cried for more.

Mrs. John Rogers, Jr., chairman of the National Advisory Council, said, as president of the ceremony:

"We hold this meeting to protest against the denial of liberty to American women. All over the world to-day we see surging and sweeping irresistibly on, the great tide of democracy, and women would be derelict in their duty if they did not see to it that it brings freedom to the women of this land. . . .

"Our ceremony to-day is planned to call attention to the fact that President Wilson has gone abroad to establish democracy in foreign lands when he has failed to establish democracy at home. We burn his words on liberty to-day, not in malice or anger, but in a spirit of reverence for truth.

"This meeting is a message to President Wilson. We expect an answer. If the answer is more words we will burn them *again*. The only answer the National Woman's Party will accept is the instant passage of the amendment in the Senate."

The few hoots and jeers which followed all ceased, when a tiny and aged woman stepped from her place to the urn in the brilliant torch light. The crowd recognized a veteran. It was the most dramatic moment in the ceremony. Reverend Olympia Brown of Wisconsin, one of the first ordained women ministers in the country, then in her eighty-fourth year, gallant pioneer, friend and colleague of Susan B. Anthony, said, as she threw into the flames the speech made by the President on his arrival in France:

" . . . I have fought for liberty for seventy years, and I protest against the President's leaving our country with this old fight here unwon."

The crowd burst into applause and continued to cheer as she was assisted from the plinth of the statue, too frail to dismount by herself. Then came the other representative women, from Massachusetts to California, from Georgia to Michigan, each one consigning to the flames a special declaration of the

President's on freedom. The flames burned brighter and brighter and leapt higher as the night grew black.

The casual observer said, "They must be crazy. Don't they know the President isn't at home? Why are they appealing to him in the park opposite the White House when he is in France?"

The long line of bright torches shone menacingly as the women marched slowly back to headquarters, and the crowd dispersed in silence. The White House *was* empty. But we knew our message would be heard in France.

CHAPTER 21

DECEMBER came to an end with no plan for action on the amendment assured. This left us January and February only before the session would end. The President had not yet won the necessary 2 votes. We decided therefore to keep a perpetual fire to consume the President's speeches on democracy as fast as he made them in Europe.

And so on New Year's Day, 1919, we light our first watchfire of freedom in the Urn dedicated to that purpose. We place it on the sidewalk in a direct line with the President's front door. The wood comes from a tree in Independence Square, Philadelphia. It burns gaily. Women with banners stand guard over the watchfire. A bell hung in the balcony at headquarters tolls rhythmically the beginning of the watch. It tolls again as the President's words are tossed to the flames. His speech to the workingmen of Manchester; his toast to the King at Buckingham Palace: "We have used great words, all of us. We have used the words 'right' and 'justice' and now we are to prove whether or not we understand these words;" his speech at Brest; all turn into ignominious brown ashes.

The bell tolls again when the watch is changed. All Washington is reminded hourly that we are at the President's gate, burning his words. From Washington the news goes to all the world.

People gather to see the ceremony. The omnipresent small boys and soldiers jeer, and some tear the banners. A soldier rushes to the scene with a bucket of water which does not extinguish the flames. The fire burns as if by magic. A policeman arrives and uses a fire extinguisher. But the fire burns on! The flames are as indomitable as the women who guard them! Rain comes, but all through the night the watchfire burns. All through the night the women stand guard.

Day and night the fire burns. Boys are permitted by the police to scatter it in the street, to break the urn, and to demolish the banners. But each time the women rekindle the fire. A squad of policemen tries to demolish the fire. While the police are engaged at the White House gates, other women go quietly in the dusk to the huge bronze urn in Lafayette Park and light another watchfire. A beautiful blaze leaps into the air from the great urn. The police hasten hither. The burning contents are overturned. Alice Paul refills the urn and kindles a new fire. She is placed under arrest. Suddenly a third blaze is seen in a remote corner of the park. The policemen scramble to that corner. When the watchfires have been continued for four days and four nights, in spite of the attempts by the police to extinguish them, general orders to arrest are sent to the squad of policemen.

Five women are taken to the police station. The police captain is outraged that the ornamental urn valued at $10,000 should have been used to hold a fire which burned the President's words! His indignation leaves the defendants unimpressed, however, and he becomes conciliatory. Will the "ladies" promise to be good and light no more fires in the park?"

Instead, the "ladies" inquire on what charge they are held. Not even the police captain knows. They wait at the police station to find out, refusing to give bail unless they are told. Meanwhile other women address the crowd lingering about the watchfire. The crowd asks thoughtful questions. Little knots of men can be seen discussing "what the whole thing is about anyway."

Miss Mildred Morris, one of the participants, overheard

the following discussion in one group composed of an old man, a young sailor and a young soldier.

"But whatever you think of them," the sailor was telling the soldier, "you have to admire their sincerity and courage. They've got to do this thing. They want only what's their right and real men want to give it to them."

"But they've got no business using a sidewalk in front of the White House for a bonfire," declared the soldier. "It's disloyal to the President, I tell you, and if they weren't women I'd slap their faces."

"Listen, sonny," said the old man, patting the soldier's arm, "I'm as loyal to the President as any man alive, but I've got to admit that he ain't doing the right thing towards these women. He's forced everything else he's wanted through Congress, and if he wanted to give these women the vote badly enough he could force the suffrage amendment through. If you and I were in these women's places, sonny, we'd act real vicious. We'd want to come here and clean out the whole White House."

"But if the President doesn't want to push their amendment through, it's his right not to," argued the soldier. "It's nobody's business how he uses his power."

"Good God!" the sailor burst out. "Why don't you go over and get a job shining the Kaiser's boots?"

The women were released without bail, since no one was able to supply a charge. But a thorough research was instituted and out of the dusty archives some one produced an ancient statute that would serve the purpose. It prohibits the building of fires in a public place in the District of Columbia between sunset and sunrise. And so the beautiful Elizabethan custom of lighting watchfires as a form of demonstration was forbidden!

In a few days eleven women were brought to trial. There was a titter in the court room as the prosecuting attorney read with heavy pomposity the charge against the prisoners "to wit: That on Pennsylvania Avenue, Northwest, in the District of Columbia they did aid and abet in setting fire to certain combustibles consisting of logs, paper, oil, etc., *between the setting of the sun in the said District of Columbia on the fifth day of January and the rising of the sun in the said District of Columbia of the sixth day of January,* 1919, *A. D.*"

The court is shocked to hear of this serious deed. The prisoners are unconcerned.

"Call the names of the prisoners," the judge orders.

The clerk calls, "Julia Emory."

No answer!

"Julia Emory," he calls a second time.

Dead silence!

The clerk tries another name, a second, a third, a fourth. Always there is silence!

In a benevolent tone, the judge asks the policeman to identify the prisoners. They identify as many as they can. An attempt is made to have the prisoners rise and be sworn. They sit.

"We will go on with the testimony," says the judge.

The police testify as to the important details of the crime. They were on Pennsylvania Avenue—they looked at their watch—they learned it was about 5:30—they saw the ladies in the park putting wood on fires in urns. "I threw the wood on the pavement; they kept putting it back," says one policeman. "Each time I tried to put out the fire they threw on more wood," says another. "They kept on lighting new fires, and I'd keep putting them out," says a third with an injured air.

The prosecuting attorney asks an important question, "Did you command them to stop?"

Policeman—"I did sir, and I said, 'You ladies don't want to be arrested do you?' They made no answer but went on attending to their fires."

The statute is read for the second time. Another witness is called. This time the district attorney asks the policeman,— "Do you know what time the sun in the District of Columbia set on January 5th and rose on January 6th?"

At this profound question, the policeman hesitates, looks abashed, then says impressively, "The sun in the District of Columbia set at 5 o'clock January 5th, and rose at 7:28 o'clock January 6th."

The prosecutor is triumphant. He looks expectantly at the judge.

"How do you know what time the sun rose and set on those days?" asks the judge.

"From the weather bureau," answers the policeman.

The judge is perplexed.

"I think we should have something more official," he says.

The prosecutor suggests that perhaps an almanac would settle the question. The judge believes it would. The government attorney disappears to find an almanac.

Breathless, the prisoners and spectators wait to hear the important verdict of the almanac. The delay is interminable. The court room is in a state of confusion. The prisoners, especially, are amused at the proceedings. It is clear their fate may hang upon a minute or two of time. An hour goes by, and still the district attorney has not returned. Another half hour! Presently he returns to read in heavy tones from the almanac. The policeman looks embarrassed. His information from the weather bureau differs from that of the almanac. His sun rose two minutes too early and continued to shine twelve minutes too long! However, it doesn't matter. The sun shone long enough to make the defendants guilty.

The judge looks at the prisoners and announces that they are "guilty" and "shall pay a fine of $5.00 or serve five days in jail." The Administration has learned its lesson about hunger strikes and evidently fears having to yield to another strike. And so it seeks safety in lighter sentences. The judge pleads almost piteously with them not to go to jail at all, and says that he will put them on probation if they will promise to be good and not light any more fires in the District of Columbia. The prisoners make no promise. They have been found guilty according to the almanac and they file through the little gate into the prisoners' pen.

Somehow they did not believe that whether the sun rose at 7:26 or 7:28 was the issue which had decided whether they should be convicted or not, and it was not in protest against the almanac that they straightway entered upon a hunger strike.

Meanwhile the watchfires continued in the capital. January thirteenth, the day the great world Peace Conference under the President's leadership, began to deliberate on the task of administering "right" and "justice" to all the oppressed of the earth, twenty-three women were arrested in front of the White House.

Another trial! More silent prisoners! They were to be tried this time in groups. A roar of applause from friends in the courtroom greeted the first four as they came in. The judge said that he could not possibly understand the motive for this outburst, and added, "If it is repeated, I shall consider it contempt of court." He then ordered the bailiff to escort the four prisoners out and bring them in again.—Shades of school days!

"And if there is any applause *this time* . . ."

With this threat still in the air, the prisoners reëntered and the applause was louder than before. Great Confusion! The judge roared at the bailiff. The bailiff roared at the prisoners and their friends.

Finally they rushed to the corners of the courtroom and evicted three young women.

"Lock the doors, and see that they do not return," shouted

the angry judge. Thus the dignity of the court was restored. But the group idea had to be abandoned. The prisoners were now brought in one at a time, and one policeman after another testified that, "she kep' alightin' and alightin' fires."

Five days' imprisonment for each woman who "kep' alightin' " watchfires!

On January 25th, in Paris, President Wilson received a delegation of French working women who urged woman suffrage as one of the points to be settled at the Peace Conference. The President expressed admiration for the women of France, and told them of his deep personal interest in the enfranchisement of women. He was 'honored' and 'touched' by their tribute. It was a great moment for the President. He had won the position in the eyes of the world of a devout champion of the liberty of women, but at the very moment he was speaking to these French women American women were lying in the District of Columbia jail for demanding liberty at his gates.

Mrs. Mary Nolan, the eldest suffrage prisoner, took to the watchfire those vain words of the President to the French women. The flames were just consuming—"All sons of freedom are under oath to see that freedom never suffers," when a whole squadron of police dashed up to arrest her. There was a pause when they saw her age. They drew back for an instant. Then one amongst them, more "dutiful" than the rest, quietly placed her under arrest. As she marched along by his side, cheers for her went up from all parts of the crowd.

"Say what you think about them, but that little old lady has certainly got pluck," they murmured.

At the bar Mrs. Nolan's beautiful speech provoked irrepressible applause. The judge ordered as many offenders as could be recognized brought before him. Thirteen women were hastily produced. The trial was suspended while the judge

sentenced these thirteen to "forty-eight hours in jail for contempt of court."

And so, throughout January and the beginning of February, 1919, the story of protest continued relentlessly.
Watchfires—arrests—convictions—hunger strikes — release — until again the nation rose in protest against imprisoning the
women and against the Senate's delay. Peremptory cables
went to the President at the Peace Conference, commanding him to act. News of our demonstrations were well reported in the Paris press. The situation must have again
seemed serious to him, for although reluctantly and perhaps
unwillingly, he did begin to cable to Senate leaders, who in turn
began to act. On February 2d, the Democratic Suffrage Senators called a meeting at the Capitol to "consider ways and
means." On February 3d, Senator Jones announced in the
Senate that the amendment would be•brought up for discussion
February 10th. The following evening, February 4th, a caucus of all Democratic Senators was called together at the Capitol by Senator Martin of Virginia, Democratic floor leader in
the Senate. This was the first Democratic caucus held in the
Senate since war was declared, which would seem to point to
the anxiety of the Democrats to marshal two votes.

Several hours of very passionate debate occurred, during
which Senator Pollock of South Carolina announced for the
first time his support of the measure.

Senator Pollock had yielded to pressure by cable from the
President as well as to the caucus. This gain of one vote had
reduced the number of votes lacking to one.

Many Democratic leaders now began to show alarm lest
the last vote be not secured. William Jennings Bryan was one
leader who, rightly alarmed over such a situation, personally
consulted with the Democratic opponents. The argument
which he presented to them he subsequently gave to the press.

"Woman suffrage is coming to the country and to the world. It will be submitted to the states by the next Congress, if it is not submitted by the present Congress.

"I hope the Democrats of the South will not handicap the Democrats of the North by compelling them to spend the next twenty-five years explaining to the women of the country why their party prevented the submission of the suffrage amendment to the states.

"This is our last chance to play an important part in bringing about this important reform, and it is of vital political concern that the Democrats of the Northern Mississippi Valley should not be burdened by the charge that our party prevented the passage of the suffrage amendment, especially when it is known that it is coming in spite of, if not with the aid of, the Democratic Party."

As we grew nearer the last vote the President was meeting what was perhaps his most bitter resistance from within. It was a situation which he could have prevented. His own early hostility, his later indifference and negligence, his actual protection given to Democratic opponents of the measure, his own reversal of policy practically at the point of a pistol, the half-hearted efforts made by him on its behalf, were all coming to fruition at the moment when his continued prestige was at stake. His power to get results on this because of belated efforts was greatly weakened. This also undermined his power in other undertakings essential to his continued prestige. Whereas more effort, at an earlier time, would have brought fairer results, now the opponents were solidified in their opposition, were through their votes publicly committed to the nation as opponents, and were unwilling to sacrifice their heavy dignity to a public reversal of their votes. This presented a formidable resistance, indeed.

Therefore the Democratic blockade continued.

And so did the watchfires!

CHAPTER 22

BURNED IN EFFIGY

T HE suffrage score now stood as follows: One vote lacking in the Senate, 15 days in which to win it, and President Wilson across the sea! The Democrats set February 10 as the date on which the Senate would again vote on the amendment, without any plan as to how the last vote would be won.

We were powerless to secure the last vote. That was still the President's problem. Knowing that he always put forth more effort under fire of protest from us than when not pressed, we decided to make as a climax to our watchfire demonstrations a more drastic form of protest. We wanted to show our contempt for the President's inadequate support which promised so much in words and which did so little in deeds to match the words.

And so on the day preceding the vote we burned in effigy a portrait of President Wilson even as the Revolutionary fathers had burned a portrait of King George. [1]

[1] This is the inscription on a tablet at the State House, Dover Green, Dover, in commemoration of Delaware's revolutionary leaders.

Signers of the Declaration of Independence.

Caeser Rodney—Thomas McKain—George Read

At the urgent request of Thomas McKain, Caesar Rodney being then in Delaware, rode post haste on horseback to Philadelphia and reached Independence Hall July 4, 1776.

The following day news of the adoption of the Declaration of Independence reaching Dover a portrait of King George was burned on Dover Green at the order of the Committee of Safety. The following historic words being uttered by the chairman:

"Compelled by strong necessity thus we destroy even the shadow of that king who refused to reign over a free people."

A hundred women marched with banners to the center of the sidewalk opposite the White House. Mingling with the party's tri-colored banners were two lettered ones which read:

ONLY FIFTEEN LEGISLATIVE DAYS ARE LEFT IN THIS
CONGRESS.
FOR MORE THAN A YEAR THE PRESIDENT'S PARTY HAS
BLOCKED SUFFRAGE IN THE SENATE.
IT IS BLOCKING IT TO-DAY.
THE PRESIDENT IS RESPONSIBLE FOR THE BETRAYAL
OF AMERICAN WOMANHOOD.

And—

WHY DOES NOT THE PRESIDENT INSURE THE PASSAGE
OF SUFFRAGE IN THE SENATE TO-MORROW?
WHY DOES HE NOT WIN FROM HIS PARTY THE ONE
VOTE NEEDED?
HAS HE AGREED TO PERMIT SUFFRAGE AGAIN TO BE
PUSHED ASIDE?
PRESIDENT WILSON IS DECEIVING THE WORLD.
HE PREACHES DEMOCRACY ABROAD AND THWARTS
DEMOCRACY HERE.

As the marchers massed their banners, and grouped themselves about the urn, a dense crowd of many thousand people closed in about them, a crowd so interested that it stood almost motionless for two hours while the ceremonies continued. The fire being kindled, and the flames leaping into the air, Miss Sue White of Tennessee and Mrs. Gabrielle Harris of South Carolina dropped into the fire in the urn a figure of President Wilson sketched on paper in black and white—a sort of effigy de luxe, we called it, but a symbol of our contempt none the less.

Mrs. Henry O. Havemeyer of New York, life-long suffragist and woman of affairs, said as master of the ceremonies, "Every

Anglo-Saxon government in the world has enfranchised its women. In Russia, in Hungary, in Austria, in Germany itself, the women are completely enfranchised, and thirty-four women are now sitting in the new Reichstag. We women of America are assembled here to-day to voice our deep indignation that . . . American women are still deprived of a voice in their government at home. We mean to show that the President. . . ." She was caught by the arm, placed under arrest, and forced into the waiting patrol wagon.

Thereupon the police fell upon the ceremonies, and indiscriminate arrests followed. Women with banners were taken; women without banners were taken. Women attempting to guard the fire; women standing by doing nothing at all; all were seized upon and rushed to the patrol. While this uproar was going on, others attempted to continue the speaking where Mrs. Havemeyer had left it, but each was apprehended as she made her attempt. Some that had been scheduled to speak, but were too shy to utter a word in the excitement, were also taken. When the "Black Marias" were all filled to capacity, nearby automobiles were commandeered, and more patrols summoned. And still not even half the women were captured.

The police ceased their raids suddenly. Orders to arrest no more had evidently been given. Some one must have suggested that a hundred additions to the already overcrowded jail and workhouse would be too embarrassing. Perhaps the ruse of arresting some, and hoping the others would scamper away at the sight of authority, was still in their minds.

After a brief respite they turned their attention to the fascinated crowd. They succeeded in forcing back these masses of people half way across Pennsylvania Avenue, and stationed an officer every two feet in front of them. But still women came to keep the fire burning. Was there no end of this battalion of women? The police finally declared a "military zone" between the encircling crowd and the remaining women, and no person was allowed to enter the proscribed area. For another hour, then, the women stood on guard at the urn, and as night fell, the ceremonies ended. Sixty of them marched back to headquarters. Thirty-nine had been arrested.

The following morning, February 10th, saw two not unrelated scenes in the capital. Senators were gathering in their seats in the senate chamber to answer to the roll call on the suffrage amendment. A few blocks away in the courthouse, thirty-nine women were being tried for their protest of the previous day.

There was no uncertainty either in the minds of the galleries or of the senators. Every one knew that we still lacked *one* vote. The debate was confined to two speeches, one for and one against.

When the roll was called, there were voting and paired in favor of the amendment, 63 senators; there were voting and paired against the amendment 33 senators. The amendment lost therefore, by one vote. Of the 63 favorable votes 32 were Republicans and 31 Democrats. Of the 33 adverse votes 12 were Republicans and 21 Democrats. This means that of the 44 Republicans in the Senate, 32 or 73 per cent voted for the amendment. Of the 52 Democrats in the Senate 31 or 60 per cent voted for it. And so it was again defeated by the opposition of the Democratic Administration, and by the failure of the President to put behind it enough power to win.

Meanwhile another burlesque of justice dragged wearily on in the dim courtroom. The judge was sentencing thirty-nine women to prison. When the twenty-sixth had been reached, he said wearily, "How many more are out there?"

When told that he had tried only two-thirds of the defendants, he dismissed the remaining thirteen without trial!

They were as guilty as their colleagues. But the judge was tired. Twenty-six women sent to jail is a full judicial day's work, I suppose.

There was some rather obvious shame and unhappiness in the Senate because of the petty thing they had done. The prisoners in the courtroom were proud because they had done their utmost for the principle in which they believed.

Senator Jones of New Mexico, Chairman of the Committee, and his Democratic colleagues refused to reintroduce the Susan B. Anthony amendment in the Senate immediately after this defeat. But on Monday, February 17, Senator Jones of Washington, ranking Republican on the Suffrage Committee, obtained unanimous consent and reintroduced it, thereby placing it once more on its way to early reconsideration.

CHAPTER 23

IT was announced that the President would return to America on February 24th. That would leave seven days in which he could act before the session ended on March 3d. We determined to make another dramatic effort to move him further.

Boston was to be the President's landing place. Boston, where ancient liberties are so venerated, and modern ones so abridged! No more admirable place could have been found to welcome the President home in true militant fashion.

Wishing the whole world to know that women were greeting President Wilson, why they were greeting him, and what form of demonstration the greetings would assume, we announced our plans in advance. Upon his arrival a line of pickets would hold banners silently calling to the President's attention the demand for his effective aid. In the afternoon they would hold a meeting in Boston Common and there burn the parts of the President's Boston speech which should pertain to democracy and liberty. These announcements were met with official alarm of almost unbelievable extent. Whereas front pages had been given over heretofore to publishing the elaborate plans for the welcome to be extended to the President, eulogies of the President, and recitals of his great triumph abroad, now the large proportion of this space was devoted to clever plans of the police to outwit the suffragists. The sustained publicity of this demonstration was unprecedented. It actually filled the Boston papers for all of two weeks.

A "deadline," a diagram of which appeared in the press, was to be established beyond which no suffragist, no matter how enterprising, could penetrate to harass the over-worked President with foolish ideas about the importance of liberty for women. Had not this great man the cares of the world on his shoulders? This was no time to talk about liberty for women! The world was rocking and a great peace conference was sitting, and the President was just returning to report on the work done so far. The Boston descendants of the early revolutionists would do their utmost to see that no untoward event should mar the perfection of their plans. They would see to it that the sacred soil of the old Boston Common should not be disgraced.

It was a perfect day. Lines of marines whose trappings shone brilliantly in the clear sunshine were in formation to hold back the crowds from the Reviewing stand where the President should appear after heading the procession in his honor. It seemed as if all Boston were on hand for the welcome. A slender file of twenty-two women marched silently into the sunshine, slipped through the "deadline," and made its way to the base of the Reviewing stand. There it unfurled its beautiful banners and took up its post directly facing the line of marines which was supposed to keep all suffragists at bay. Quite calmly and yet triumphantly, they stood there, a pageant of beauty and defiant appeal, which not even the most hurried passerby could fail to see and comprehend.

There were consultations by the officials in charge of the ceremonies. The women looked harmless enough, but had they not been told that they must not come there? They were causing no riot, in fact they were clearly adding much beauty—people seemed to take them as part of the elaborate ceremony—but officials seldom have sense of humor enough or adaptability enough to change quickly, especially when they have made threats. It would be a taint on their honor, if they did not "pick up" the women for the deed.

One could hear the people reading slowly the large lettered banner:

MR. PRESIDENT, YOU SAID IN THE SENATE ON SEPTEMBER 20 "WE SHALL NOT ONLY BE DISTRUSTED BUT WE SHALL DESERVE TO BE DISTRUSTED IF WE DO NOT ENFRANCHISE WOMEN." YOU ALONE CAN REMOVE THIS DISTRUST NOW BY SECURING THE ONE VOTE NEEDED TO PASS THE SUFFRAGE AMENDMENT BEFORE MARCH 4.

The American flag carried by Miss Katherine Morey of Brookline held the place of honor at the head of the line and there were the familiar, "Mr. President, how long must women wait for liberty?" and "Mr. President, what will you do for woman suffrage?" The other banners were simply purple, white and gold.

"When we had stood there about three quarters of an hour," said Katherine Morey, "Superintendent Crowley came to me and said, 'We want to be as nice as we can to you suffragette ladies, but you cannot stand here while the President goes by, so you might as well go back now.' I said I was sorry, but as we had come simply to be there at that very time, we would not be able to go back until the President had gone by. He thereupon made a final appeal to Miss Paul, who was at headquarters, but she only repeated our statement. The patrol wagons were hurried to the scene and the arrests were executed in an exceedingly gentlemanly manner. But the effect on the crowd was electric. The sight of 'ladies' being put into patrols, seemed to thrill the Boston masses as nothing the President subsequently said was able to.

"We were taken to the House of Detention and there charged with 'loitering more than seven minutes'."

As Mrs. Agnes H. Morey, Massachusetts Chairman of the Woman's Party, later remarked:

"It is a most extraordinary thing. Thousands loitered from curiosity on the day the President arrived. Twenty-two loitered for liberty, and only those who loitered for liberty were arrested."

Realizing that the event of the morning had diverted public attention to our issue, and undismayed by the arrests, other women entered the lists to sustain public attention upon our demand to the President.

The ceremony on the Common began at three o'clock. Throngs of people packed in closely in an effort to hear the speakers, and to catch a glimpse of the ceremony, presided over by Mrs. Louise Sykes of Cambridge, whose late husband was President of the Connecticut College for Women. From three o'clock until six, women explained the purpose of the protest, the status of the amendment, and urged those present to help. At six o'clock came the order to arrest. Mrs. C. C. Jack, wife of Professor Jack of Harvard University, Mrs. Mortimer Warren of Boston, whose husband was head of a base hospital in France, and Miss Elsie Hill, daughter of the late Congressman Hill, were arrested and were taken to the House of Detention, where they joined their comrades.

"Dirty, filthy hole under the Court House," was the general characterization of the House of Detention. "Jail was a Paradise compared to this depraved place," said Miss Morey. "We slept in our clothes, four women to a cell, on iron shelves two feet wide. In the cell was an open toilet. The place slowly filled up during the night with drunks and disorderlies until pandemonium reigned. In the evening, Superintendent Crowley and Commissioner Curtis came to call on us. I don't believe they had ever been there before, and they were painfully embarrassed. Superintendent Crowley said to me, "If you were drunk we could release you in the morning, but unfortunately since you are not we have got to take you into court."

When the prisoners were told next morning the decision of Chief Justice Bolster to try each prisoner separately and in closed court, they all protested against such proceedings. But guards took the women by force to a private room. "The Matron, who was terrified," said Miss Morey, "shouted to the guards, 'You don't handle the drunks that way. You know you don't.' But they continued to push, shove and shake the women while forcing them to the ante room."

"As an American citizen under arrest, I demand a public trial," was the statement of each on entering the judge's private trial room.

While the trial was proceeding without the women's co-operation,—some were tried under wrong names, some were tried more than once under different names, but most of them under the name of Jane Doe—vigorous protests were being made to all the city officials by individuals among the throngs who had come to the court house to attend the trial. This protest was so strong that the last three women were tried in open court. The judge sentenced everybody impartially to eight days in jail in lieu of fines, with the exception of Miss Wilma Henderson, who was released when it was learned that she was a minor.

The women were taken to the Charles Street Jail to serve their sentences. "The cells were immaculately clean," said Miss Morey, "but there was one feature of this experience which obliterated all its advantages. The cells were without modern toilet facilities. The toilet equipment consisted of a heavy wooden bucket, about two and a half feet high and a foot and a half in diameter, half filled with water. No one of us will ever forget that foul bucket. It had to be carried to the lower floor—we were on the third and fourth floors—every morning. I could hardly lift mine off the floor, to say nothing of getting it down stairs (Miss Morey weighs 98 pounds), so there it stayed. Berry Pottier managed to get hers down, but was so exhausted she was utterly unable to get it back to her cell.

"The other toilet facility provided was a smaller bucket of water to wash in, but it was of such a strangely unpleasant odor that we did not dare use it."

The Boston reporters were admitted freely—and they wrote columns of copy. There was the customary ridicule, but there were friendly light touches such as, "Militant Highlights—To be roommates at Vassar College and then to meet again as cell-mates was the experience of Miss Elsie Hill and Mrs. Lois Warren Shaw." . . . "Superintendent Kelleher didn't know when he was in Congress with Elsie Hill's father he would some day have Congressman Hill's daughter in his jail."

And there were friendly serious touches in these pages of sensational news—such as this excerpt from the front page of the Boston *Traveler* of February 25, 1919. "The reporter admired the spirit of the women. Though weary from loss of sleep, the fire of a great purpose burned in their eyes. . . .

"It was a sublime forgetting of self for the goal ahead, and whether the reader is in sympathy with the principle for which these women are ready to suffer or not, he will be forced to admire the spirit which leads them on."

Photographs of the women were printed day by day— giving their occupations, if any, noting their revolutionary ancestors, ascertaining the attitude of husbands and fathers. Mrs. Shaw's husband's telegram was typical of the support the women got. "Don't be quitters," he wired, "I have competent nurses to look after the children." Mr. Shaw is a Harvard graduate and a successful manufacturer in Manchester, New Hampshire.

Telegrams of protest from all over the country poured in upon all the Boston officials who had had any point of contact with the militants. All other work was for the moment suspended. Such is the quality of Mrs. Morey's organizing genius that she did not let a solitary official escape. Telegrams also went from Boston, and especially from the jail, to President Wilson.

Official Boston was in the grip of this militant invasion when suddenly a man of mystery, one E. J. Howe, appeared and paid the women's fines. It was later discovered that the mysterious E. J. Howe alleged to have acted for a "client." Whether the "client" was a part of Official Boston, no one ever knew. There were rumors that the city wished to end its embarrassment.

Sedate Boston had been profoundly shaken. Sedate Boston gave more generously than ever before to militant finances. And when the "Prison Special" arrived a few days later a Boston theatre was filled to overflowing with a crowd eager to hear more about their local heroines, and to cheer them while they were decorated with the already famous prison pin.

Something happened in Washington, too, after the President's safe journey thither from Boston.

CHAPTER 24

DEMOCRATIC CONGRESS ENDS

I T would be folly to say that President Wilson was not at this time aware of a very damning situation.

The unanswerable "Prison Special"—a special car of women prisoners—was touring the country from coast to coast to keep the public attention, during the closing days of the session, fixed upon the suffrage situation in the Senate. The prisoners were addressing enormous meetings and arousing thousands, especially in the South, to articulate condemnation of Administration tactics. It is impossible to calculate the number of cables which, as a result of this sensational tour, reached the President during his deliberations at the Peace Table. The messages of protest which did not reach the President at the Peace Conference were waiting for him on his desk at the White House.

Even if some conservative Boston suffragists did present him with a beautiful bouquet of jonquils tied with a yellow ribbon, as their welcome home, will any one venture to say that that token of trust was potent enough to wipe from his consciousness the other welcome which led his welcomers to jail? Will any one contend that President Wilson upon his arrival in Washington, and after changing his clothes, piously remarked:

"By the way, Tumulty, I want to show you some jonquils tied with a yellow ribbon that were presented to me in Boston. I am moved, I think I may say deeply moved by this sincere tribute, to do something this morning for woman suffrage.

Just what is the state of affairs? And does there seem to be any great demand for it?" We do not know what, if anything, he did say to Secretary Tumulty, but we know what he did. He hurried over to the Capitol, and there made his first official business a conference with Senator Jones of New Mexico, Chairman of the Senate Suffrage Committee. After expressing chagrin over the failure of the measure in the Senate, the President discussed ways and means of getting it through.

An immediate result of the conference was the introduction in the Senate, February 28th, by Senator Jones, of another resolution on suffrage. Senator Jones had refused to reintroduce the original suffrage resolution immediately after the Senate defeat, February 10th. Now he came forward with this one, a little differently worded, but to the same purpose as the original amendment. [1]

This resolution was a concession to Senator Gay of Louisiana, Democrat, who had voted against the measure on February 10th, but who immediately pledged his vote in favor of the new resolution. Thus the sixty-fourth and last vote was won. The majority instantly directed its efforts toward getting a vote on the new resolution.

On March 1st Senator Jones attempted to get unanimous consent to consider it. Senator Wadsworth, of New York, Republican anti-suffragist, objected. When consent was again asked, the following day, Senator Weeks of Massachusetts, Republican anti-suffragist, objected. On the last day of the session, Senator Sherman of Illinois, Republican suffragist, objected. And so the Democratic Congress ended without passing the amendment.

On the face of it, these parliamentary objections from Republicans prevented action, when the Democrats had finally

[1] This amendment, although to the same purpose as the original amendment, was not as satisfactory because of possible controversial points in the enforcement article. The original amendment is of course crystal clear in this regard.

secured the necessary votes. As a matter of fact, however, the President and his party were responsible for subjecting the amendment to the tactical obstruction of individual anti-suffrage Senators. They waited until the last three days to make the supreme effort. That the President did finally get the last vote even at a moment when parliamentary difficulties prevented it from being voted upon, proved our contention that he could pass the amendment at any time he set himself resolutely to it. This last ineffective effort also proved how hard the President had been pushed by our tactics.

But it seems to me that President Wilson has a pathetic aptitude for acting a little too late. The fact that the majority of the Southern contingent in his party stood stubbornly against him on woman suffrage, was of course a real obstacle. But we contended that the business of a statesman who declared himself to be a friend of a measure was to remove even real obstacles to the success of that measure. Perhaps our standard was too high. It must be confessed that people in general are distressingly patient, easily content with pronouncements, and shockingly inert about seeing to it that political leaders act as they speak.

We had seen the President overcome far greater obstacles than stood in his way on this issue. We had seen him lead a country which had voted to stay out of the European war into battle almost immediately after they had so voted. We had seen him conscript the men of the same stubborn South, which had been conspicuously opposed to conscription. We had seen him win mothers to his war point of view after they had fought passionately for him and his peace program at election time. He had taken pains to lead men and women—influential and obscure—to his way of thinking. I do not condemn him—I respect him for being able to do this. The point is that he *did* overcome obstacles when his heart and head were set to the task.

Since our problem was neither in his head nor his heart, it was our task to put it there. Having got it there, it was our responsibility to see that it churned and churned there, until he had to act. We did our utmost.

For six full years, through three Congresses under President Wilson's power, the continual Democratic resistance, meandering, delays, deceits had left us still disfranchised. A world war had come and gone during this span of effort. Vast millions had died in pursuit of liberty. A Czar and a Kaiser had been deposed. The Russian people had revolutionized their whole social and economic system. And here in the United States of America we couldn't even wrest from the leader of democracy and his poor miserable associates the first step toward our political liberty—the passage of an amendment through Congress, submitting the question of democracy to the states!

What a magnificent thing it was for those women to rebel! Their solitary steadfastness to their objective stands out in this world of confused ideals and half hearted actions, clear and lonely and superb!

CHAPTER 25

A FAREWELL TO PRESIDENT WILSON

THE Republican Congress elected in November, 1918, would not sit until December, 1919—such is our unfortunate system—unless called together by the President in a special session. We had polled the new Congress by personal interviews and by post, and found a safe two-thirds majority for the amendment in the House. In the new Senate we still lacked a fateful one vote.

Our task was, therefore, to induce the President to call a special session of Congress at the earliest possible moment, and to see that he did not relax his efforts toward the last vote.

"He won't do it!" . . ."President Wilson will never let the Republican Congress come together until the regular time." . . . "Especially with himself in Europe!" The usual points of objection were raised. But we persisted. We felt that the President could win this last vote. And the fear that a Republican Congress might, if he did not, was an accelerating factor.

One feature of the campaign to force a special session was a demonstration in New York, on the eve of President Wilson's return to Europe, at the time he addressed a mass meeting in the Metropolitan Opera House on behalf of his proposed League of Nations. The plan of demonstration was to hold outside of the Opera House banners addressed to President Wilson, and to consign his speech to the flames of a torch at a public meeting nearby.

It was a clear starry night in March when the picket line of 25 women proceeded with tri-colored banners from New York headquarters in Forty-first street to the Opera House. As we neared the corner of the street opposite the Opera House and before we could cross the street a veritable battalion of policemen in close formation rushed us with unbelievable ferocity. Not a word was spoken by a single officer of the two hundred policemen in the attack to indicate the nature of our offense. Clubs were raised and lowered and the women beaten back with such cruelty as none of us had ever witnessed before.

The women clung to their heavy banner poles, trying to keep the banners above the maelstrom. But the police seized them, tore the pennants, broke the poles, some of them over our backs, trampled them underfoot, pounded us, dragged us, and in every way behaved like frantic beasts. It would have been so simple quietly to detain our little handful until after the President's speech, if that seemed necessary. But to launch this violent attack under the circumstances was madness. Not a pedestrian had paid any except friendly attention to the slender file of women. But the moment this happened an enormous crowd gathered, made up mostly of soldiers and sailors, many of whom had just returned from abroad and were temporarily thronging the streets of New York. They joined forces with the police in the attack.

Miss Margaretta Schuyler, a beautiful, fragile young girl, was holding fast a silken American flag which she had carried at the head of the procession when a uniformed soldier jumped upon her, twisted her arms until she cried in pain, cursed, struggled until he had torn her flag from its pole, and then broke the pole across her head, exulting in his triumph over his frailer victim.

When I appealed to the policeman, who was at the moment occupied solely with pounding me on the back, to intercept the soldier in his cruel attack, his only reply was: "Oh, he's helping me." He thereupon resumed his beating of me and I cried, "Shame, shame! Aren't you ashamed to beat American women in this brutal way?" I offered no other resistance. "If we are breaking any law, arrest us! Don't beat us in this cowardly fashion!"

"We'll rush you like bulls," was his vulgar answer, "we've only just begun."

Another young woman, an aviatrice, was seized by the coat collar and thrown to the pavement for trying to keep hold of her banner. Her fur cap was the only thing that saved her skull from serious injury. As it was, she was trampled under foot and her face severely cut before we could rescue her with the assistance of a sympathetic member of the crowd. The sympathetic person was promptly attacked by the policeman for helping his victim to her feet. There were many shouts of disapproval of the police conduct and many cheers for the women from the dense crowd.

By this time the crowd had massed itself so thickly that we could hardly move an inch. It was perfectly apparent that we could neither make our way to the Opera House nor could we extricate ourselves. But the terrors continued. Women were knocked down and trampled under foot, some of them almost unconscious, others bleeding from the hands and face; arms were bruised and twisted; pocketbooks were snatched and wrist-watches stolen.

When it looked as if the suffocating mêlée would result in the death or permanent injury to some of us, I was at last dragged by a policeman to the edge of the crowd. Although I offered not the slightest resistance, I was crushed continuously in the arm by the officer who walked me to the police station, and kept muttering: "You're a bunch of cannibals,—cannibals,—Bolsheviks."

Upon arriving at the police station I was happily relieved

to find five of my comrades already there. We were all impartially cursed at; told to stand up; told to sit down; forbidden to speak to one another; forbidden even to smile at one another. One by one we were called to the desk to give our name, age, and various other pieces of information. We stood perfectly silent before the station lieutenant as he coaxingly said, "You'd better tell."—"You'd better give us your name." —"You'd better tell us where you live—it will make things easier for you." But we continued our silence.

Disorderly conduct, interfering with the police, assaulting the police (Shades of Heaven! assaulting the police!), were the charges entered against us.

We were all locked in separate cells and told that we would be taken to the Woman's Night Court for immediate trial.

While pondering on what was happening to our comrades and wondering if they, too, would be arrested, or if they would just be beaten up by the police and mob, a large, fat jail matron came up and began to deliver a speech, which ran something like this:

"Now, shure and you ladies must know that this is goin' a bit too far. Now, I'm for suffrage alright, and I believe women ought to vote, but why do you keep botherin' the President? Don't you know he has got enough to think about with the League of Nations, the Peace Conference and fixin' up the whole world on his mind?"

In about half an hour we were taken from our cells and brought before the Lieutenant, who now announced, "Well, you ladies may go now,—I have just received a telephone order to release you."

We accepted the news and jubilantly left the station house, returning at once to our comrades. There the battle was still going on, and as we joined them we were again dragged and cuffed about the streets by the police and their aids, but there were no more arrests. Elsie Hill succeeded in speaking from a balcony above the heads of the crowd:

"Did you men turn back when you saw the Germans coming? What would you have thought of any one who did? Did you expect us to turn back? We never turn back, either—and we won't until democracy is won! Who rolled bandages for you when you were suffering abroad? Who bound your wounds in your fight for democracy? Who spent long hours of the night and the day knitting you warm garments? There are women here to-night attempting to hold banners to remind the President that democracy is not won at home, who have given their sons and husbands for your fight abroad. What would they say if they could see you, their comrades in the fight over there, attacking their mothers, their sisters, their wives over here? Aren't you ashamed that you have not enough sporting blood to allow us to make our fight in our own way? Aren't you ashamed that you accepted the help of women in your fight, and now to-night brutally attack them?"

And they did listen until the police, in formation—looking now like wooden toys—advanced from both sides of the street and succeeded in entirely cutting off the crowd from Miss Hill.

The meeting thus broken up, we abandoned a further attempt that night. As our little, bannerless procession filed slowly back to headquarters, hoodlums followed us. The police of course gave us no protection and just as we were entering the door of our own building a rowdy struck me on the side of the head with a heavy banner pole. The blow knocked me senseless against the stone building; my hat was snatched from my head, and burned in the street. We entered the building to find that soldiers and sailors had been periodically rushing it in our absence, dragging out bundles of our banners, amounting to many hundreds of dollars, and burning them in the street, without any protest from the police.

One does not undergo such an experience without arriving

at some inescapable truths, a discussion of which would interest me deeply but which would be irrelevant in this narrative.

"Two hundred maddened women try to see the President." . . . "Two hundred women attack the police," and similar false headlines, appeared the next morning in the New York papers. It hurt to have the world think that we had attacked the police. That was a slight matter, however, for that morning at breakfast, aboard the *George Washington*, the President also read the New York papers. He saw that we were not submitting in silence to his inaction. It seems reasonable to assume that on sailing down the harbor that morning past the Statue of Liberty the President had some trouble to banish from his mind the report that "two hundred maddened women" had tried to "make the Opera House last night."

CHAPTER 26

THE "Prison Special," which was nearing the end of its dramatic tour, was arousing the people to call for a special session of Congress, as the President sailed away.

Although a Republican Congress had been elected, President Wilson, as the head of the Administration, was still responsible for initiating and guiding legislation. We had to see to it that, with his Congress out of power, he did not relax his efforts on behalf of the amendment.

There was this situation which we were able to use to our advantage. Two new Democratic Senators, Senator Harrison of Mississippi and Senator Harris of Georgia, had been elected to sit in the incoming Congress through the President's influence. He, therefore, had very specific power over these two men, who were neither committed against suffrage by previous votes nor were they yet won to the amendment.

We immediately set ourselves to the task of getting the President to win one of these men. From the election of these two men in the autumn to early spring, constant pressure was put upon the President to this end. When we could see no activity on the part of the President to secure the support of one of them, we again threatened publicly to resume dramatic protests against him. We kept the idea abroad that he was still responsible, and that we would continue to hold him so, until the amendment was passed.

Such a situation gave friends of the Administration considerable alarm. They realized that the slightest attack on the President at that moment would jeopardize his many other endeavors. And so these friends of the President undertook to acquaint him with the facts.

Senator Harris was happily in Europe at the time. A most anxious cable, signed by politicians in his own party, was sent to the President in Paris explaining the serious situation and urging him to do his utmost to secure the vote of the Senator at once.

Senator Harris was in Italy when he received an unexpected telegram asking him to come to Paris. He journeyed with all speed to the President, perhaps even thinking that he was about to be dispatched to some foreign post, to learn that the conference was for the purpose of securing his vote on the national suffrage amendment.

Senator Harris there and then gave his vote, the 64th vote.

On that day the passage by Congress of the original Susan B. Anthony amendment was assured.

Instantly a cable was received at the White House carrying news to the suffragists of the final capture of the elusive last vote. Following immediately on the heels of this cable came another cable calling the new Congress into special session May 19th.

In the light of the President's gradual yielding and final surrender to our demand, it will not be out of place to summarize briefly just what happened.

President Wilson began his career as President of the United States an anti-suffragist. He was opposed to suffrage for women both by principle and political expediency. Sometimes I think he regarded suffragists as a kind of sect—good women, no doubt, but tiresome and troublesome. Whether he has yet come to see the suffrage battle as part of a great movement embracing the world is still a question. It is not an important question, for in any case it was not inward conviction but political necessity that made him act.

Believing then that suffragists were a sect, he said many things to them at first with no particular care as to the bearing of these things upon political theory or events. He offered, successively, "consideration," an "open mind," a "closed mind," and "age-long conviction deeply matured," party limitations, party concert of action, and what not. He saw in suffrage the "tide rising to meet the moon," but waited and advised us to wait with him. But we did not want to wait, and we proceeded to try to make it impossible for him to wait, either. We determined to make action upon this issue politically expedient for him.

When the President began to perceive the potential political power of women voters, he first declared, as a "private citizen," that suffrage was all right for the women of his home state, New Jersey, but that it was altogether wrong to ask him as President to assist in bringing it about for all the women of the nation. He also interested himself in writing the suffrage plank in the Democratic Party's national platform, specifically relegating action on suffrage to the states. Then he calmly announced that he could not act nationally, "even if I wanted to," because the platform had spoken otherwise.

The controversy was lengthened. The President's conspicuous ability for sitting still and doing nothing on a controversial issue until both sides have exhausted their ammunition was never better illustrated than in this matter. He allowed the controversy to continue to the point of intellectual sterility. He buttressed his delays with more evasions, until finally the women intensified their demand for action. They picketed his official gates. But the President still recoiled from action. So mightily did he recoil from it that he was willing to imprison women for demanding it.

It is not extraordinary to resent being called upon to act,

for it is only the exceptional person who springs to action, even when action is admitted to be desirable and necessary. And the President is *not* exceptional. He is surprisingly ordinary.

While the women languished in prison, he fell back upon words—beautiful words, too—expressions of friendliness, good wishes, hopes, and may-I-nots. In this, too, he was acting like an ordinary human being, not like the statesman he was reputed to be. He had habituated himself to a belief in the power of words, and every time he uttered them to us he seemed to refortify himself in his belief in their power.

It was the women, not the President, who were exceptional. They refused to accept words. They persisted in demanding acts. Step by step under terrific gunfire the President's resistance crumbled, and he yielded, one by one, every minor facility to the measure, always withholding from us, however, the main objective. Not until he had exhausted all minor facilities, and all possible evasions, did he publicly declare that the amendment should pass the House, and put it through. When he had done that we rested from the attack momentarily, in order to let him consummate with grace, and not under fire, the passage of the amendment in the Senate. He rested altogether. We were therefore compelled to renew the attack. He countered at first with more words. But his reliance upon them was perceptibly shaken when we burned them in public bonfires. He then moved feebly but with a growing concern toward getting additional votes in the Senate. And when, as an inevitable result of his policy—and ours—the political embarrassment became too acute, calling into question his honor and prestige, he covertly began to consult his colleagues. We pushed him the harder. He moved the faster toward concrete endeavor. He actually undertook to win the final votes in the Senate.

There he found, however, that quite an alarming situation

had developed—a situation which he should have anticipated, but for which he was totally unprepared. Opposition in his own party had been growing more and more rigid and cynical. His own opposition to the amendment, his grant of immunity to those leaders in his party who had fought the measure, his isolating himself from those who might have helped—all this was coming to fruition among his subordinates at a time when he could least afford to be beaten on anything. What would have been a fairly easy race to win, if he had begun running at the pistol shot, had now become most difficult.

Perceiving that he had now not only to move himself, but also to overcome the obstacle which he had allowed to develop, we increased the energy of our attack. And finally the President made a supreme assertion of his power, and secured the last and 64th vote in the Senate. He did this too late to get the advantage—if any advantage is to be gained from granting a just thing at the point of a gun—for this last vote arrived only in time for a Republican Congress to use it.

It seems to me that Woodrow Wilson was neither devil nor God in his manner of meeting the demand of the suffragists. There has persisted an astounding myth that he is an extraordinary man. Our experience proved the contrary. He behaved toward us like a very ordinary politician. Unnecessarily cruel or weakly tolerant, according as you view the justice of our fight, but a politician, not a statesman. He did not go out to meet the tide which he himself perceived was "rising to meet the moon." That would have been statesmanship. He let it all but engulf him before he acted. And even as a politician he failed, for his tactics resulted in the passage of the amendment by a Republican Congress.

CHAPTER 27

THE Republican Congress convened in Special Session May 19.

Instantly Republican leaders in control of the 66th Congress caucussed and organized for a prompt passage of the amendment. May 21st the Republican House of Representatives passed the measure by a vote of 304 to 89—the first thing of any importance done by the new House. This was 42 votes above the required two-thirds majority, whereas the vote in the House in January, 1918, under Democratic control had given the measure only one vote more than was required.

Immediately the Democratic National Committee passed a resolution calling on the legislatures of the various states to hold special legislative sessions where necessary, to ratify the amendment as soon as it was through Congress, in order to "enable women to vote in the national elections of 1920."

When the 64th vote was assured two more Republican Senators announced their support, Senator Keyes of New Hampshire and Senator Hale of Maine, and on June 4th the measure passed the Senate by a vote of 66 to 30,—2 votes more than needed.[1] Of the 49 Republicans in the Senate, 40 voted for the amendment, 9 against. Of the 47 Democrats in the Senate, 26 voted for it and 21 against.

And so the assertion that "the right of citizens of the United States to vote shall not be denied or abridged by the

---

[1] These figures include all voting and paired.

United States or by any state on account of sex," introduced
into Congress by the efforts of Susan B. Anthony in 1878,
was finally submitted to the states for ratification [1] on June
4th, 1919.

I do not need to explain that the amendment was not won
from the Republican Congress between May 19th and June
4th, 1919. The Republican Party had been gradually coming
to appreciate this opportunity throughout our entire national
agitation from 1913 to date. And our attack upon the party
in power, which happened to be President Wilson's party, had
been the most decisive factor in stimulating the opposition
party to espouse our side. It is perhaps fortunate for the
Republican Party that it was their political opponents who
inherited this lively question in 1913. However, the political
advantage is theirs for having promptly and ungrudgingly
passed the amendment the moment they came into power. But
it will not be surprising to any one who has read this book
that I conclude by pointing out that the real triumph belongs
to the women.

Our objective was the national enfranchisement of women.
A tiny step, you may say. True! But so long as we know
that this is but the first step in the long struggle of women
for political, economic and social emancipation, we need not be
disturbed. If political institutions as we know them to-day in
their discredited condition break down, and another kind of
organization—perhaps industrial—supplants them, women
will battle for their place in the new system with as much
determination as they have shown in the struggle just ended.

That women have been aroused never again to be content
with their subjection there can be no doubt. That they will
ultimately secure for themselves equal power and responsibility

[1] When a constitutional amendment has passed Congress it must be
ratified by a majority vote of 36 state legislatures and thereupon proclaimed
operative by the Secretary of State of the United States before it becomes
the law of the land. For ratification data see Appendix 1.

in whatever system of government is evolved is positive. How revolutionary will be the changes when women get this power and responsibility no one can adequately foretell. One thing is certain. They will not go back. They will never again be good and willing slaves.

It has been a long, wearying struggle. Although drudgery has persisted throughout, there have been compensatory moments of great joy and beauty. The relief that comes after a great achievement is sweet. There is no residue of bitterness. To be sure, women have often resented it deeply that so much human energy had to be expended for so simple a right. But whatever disillusionments they have experienced, they have kept their faith in women. And the winning of political power by women will have enormously elevated their status.

*1. Mrs. Lawrence Lewis; 2. Mrs. George Roewer; 3. Mrs. Jessica Henderson; 4. Mrs. Naomi Barrett; 5. Miss Elizabeth Huff; 6. Dr. Caroline E. Spencer; *7. Miss Ruth Crocker; 8. Miss Rose Winslow; 9. Miss Berry Pottier; *10. Miss Julia Hurbut; 11. Miss Ernestine Hara; 12. Mrs. Betsey Reyneau.

* © Harris & Ewing.

1. Mrs. Kate Winston; *2. Miss Hazel Hunkins; 3. Miss Mary H. Ingham; *4. Miss Elizabeth Kalb; 5. Miss Maud Jamison; *6. Mrs. Louise Mayo; 7. Mrs. Annie J. McGee; 8. Miss Nell Mercer; *9. Mrs. Bertha C. Moller; *10. Miss Katherine C. Morey; 11. Mrs. Agnes H. Morey; 12. Miss Maud Malone; 13. Mrs. Elsie Vervane; †14. Mrs. John Rogers, Jr.

*© Harris & Ewing; †© Underwood.

1. Miss Eleanor Calnan;   2. Mrs. W. D. Ascough;   3.
Miss Julia Emory; 4. Mrs. Dorothy Bartlett; 5. Mrs.
Abby Scott Baker; 6. Miss Louise Bryant; *7. Miss
Mary Gertrude Fendall; *8. Miss Katharine Fisher; 9.
Miss Alice Gram; 10. Dr. Sarah H. Lockrey; 11. Mrs.
Frederick W. Kendall; 12. Mrs. Elizabeth Walmsley;
13. Miss Sue White; 14. Mrs. Iris Calderhead Walker.

1. MISS EDNA DIXON; 2. MISS GERTRUDE L. CROCKER;
*3. MISS CLARA WOLD; 4. MISS JENNIE BRONENBERG; 5.
MISS LUCY BRANHAM; 6. MRS. MARY E. BROWN; †7. MRS.
KATE J. BOECKH; 8. MRS. PAULA JAKOBI; *9. MISS MARY
DUBROW; 10. MRS. PAULINE ADAMS; 11. MRS. REBECCA
WINSOR EVANS; ‡12. MISS VIRGINIA ARNOLD; *13. MRS. A.
R. COLVIN; 14. MISS EDITH AINGE.

*© *Harris & Ewing;* †*Clinedinst;* ‡*Edmonston.*

1. Miss Lavinia L. Dock; 2. Miss Rose Fishstein; 3. Mrs. Wm. F. Dowell; 4. Miss Reba Gomborov; 5. Mrs. Lucy Branham; 6. Mrs. Annie Arneil; 7. Miss Cora Crawford; *8. Mrs. Gilson Gardner; *9. Miss Elsie Hill; *10. Miss Natalie Gray; 11. Mrs. J. Irving Gross; 12. Mrs. Lucille Calmes; 13. Mrs. H. E. Russian; 14. Mrs. Ruby E. Koenig.

1. Miss Margaret Fotheringham; *2. Miss Anne Martin; 3. Mrs. Martha Reed Shoemaker; *4. Mrs. M. Toscan Bennett; 5. Miss Lucy Ewing; 6. Miss Betty Gram; 7. Miss Gladys Greiner; 8. Mrs. H. O. Havemeyer; *9. Miss Kate Heffelfinger; 10. Mrs. Rosa Fishstein; †11. Mrs. Florence Bayard Hilles; 12. Mrs. Effie M. Main; 13. Mrs. Margaret Oaks; 14. Miss Vida Milholland.

*1. Mrs. Harvey W. Wiley; 2. Mrs. Phoebe C. Munnecke;
†3. Miss Nina Samarodin; 4. Miss Mary Winsor; 5. Miss
Rhoda Kellogg; 6. Mrs. Lois Warren Shaw; 7. Miss
Ruth Small; 8. Mrs. Alexander Shields; †9. Mrs.
Helena Hill Weed; *10. Miss Mabel Vernon; 11. Mrs.
Robert H. Walker; 12. Miss Margaret F. Whittemore;
13. Miss Martha W. Moore; 14. Miss Ellen Winsor.

*ⓒ *Edmonston;* †*Harris & Ewing.*

MRS. LOUISE SYKES BURNING PRESIDENT WILSON's SPEECH ON BOSTON COMMON

APPENDICES

APPENDIX 1

Text of the National Suffrage Amendment

Proposing an amendment to the Constitution of the United States extending the right of suffrage to women.

Resolved by the Senate and House of Representatives of the United States of America in Congress assembled (two-thirds of each House concurring therein), That the following articles be proposed to the legislatures of the several States as an amendment to the Constitution of the United States, which when ratified by three-fourths of the said legislatures, shall be valid as part of said Constitution, namely:

"ARTICLE—SEC. 1.   The right of citizens of the United States to vote shall not be denied or abridged by the United States or by any State on account of sex.

"SEC. 2.   Congress shall have power, by appropriate legislation, to enforce the provisions of this article."

Record of Action on National Suffrage Amendment

In Congress

Drafted

By Susan B. Anthony in 1875

First Introduced

January 10, 1878, by Hon. A. A. Sargent, in the Senate

Reported from Committee

In the Senate
1878, Adverse majority.
1879, Favorable minority.
1882, Favorable majority,
    adverse minority.
1884, Favorable majority,
    adverse minority.
1886, Favorable majority.
1890, Favorable majority.
1892, Favorable majority,
    adverse minority.
1896, Adverse majority.
1913, Favorable majority.
1914, Favorable majority.
1917, Favorable majority.
1919, Unanimously favorably.

In the House
1883, Favorable majority.
1884, Adverse majority,
    favorable minority.
1886, Favorable minority.
1890, Favorable majority.
1894, Adverse majority.
1914, Without recommendation.
1916, Without recommendation.
1917, Without recommendation.
1918, Favorable majority.
1919, Favorable majority.

Voted Upon

In the Senate
January 25, 1887. Yeas 16, nays 34. Absent 25 (of whom 4 were announced as for and 2 against).
March 19, 1914. Yeas 35, nays 34, failing by 11 of the necessary two-thirds vote.
October 1, 1918. Yeas 54, nays 30, failing by 2 of the two-thirds vote.
February 10, 1919. Yeas 55, nays 29, failing by 1 of the necessary two-thirds vote.
June 4, 1919. Yeas 56, nays 25, passing by 2 votes over necessary two-thirds majority.

In the House
January 12, 1915. Yeas 174, nays 204, failing by 78 of the necessary two-thirds vote.
January 10, 1918. Yeas 274, nays 136, passing by 1 vote over necessary two-thirds majority.
May 21, 1919. Yeas 304, nays 89, passing by 42 votes over necessary two-thirds majority.

In the States

	State	Date of Ratification	VOTE Senate	VOTE House	Party of Governor	Party Controlling Legislature
1	Wisconsin	June 10, 1919	24–1	54–2	Rep.	Rep.
2	*Michigan	June 10, 1919	Unan.	Unan.	Rep.	Rep.
3	*Kansas	June 16, 1919	Unan.	Unan.	Rep.	Rep.
4	*Ohio	June 16, 1919	27–3	73–6	Dem.	Rep.
5	*New York	June 16, 1919	Unan.	Unan.	Dem.	Rep.
6	Illinois	June 17, 1919	Unan.	133–4	Rep.	Rep.
7	Pennsylvania	June 24, 1919	32–6	153–44	Rep.	Rep.
8	Massachusetts	June 25, 1919	34–5	184–77	Rep.	Rep.
9	*Texas	June 29, 1919	Unan.	96–21	Dem.	Dem.
10	*Iowa	July 2, 1919	Unan.	95–5	Rep.	Rep.
11	*Missouri	July 3, 1919	28–3	125–4	Dem.	Div'd.
12	*Arkansas	July 20, 1919	20–2	76–17	Dem.	Dem.
13	*Montana	July 30, 1919	38–1	Unan.	Dem.	Rep.
14	*Nebraska	Aug. 2, 1919	Unan.	Unan.	Rep.	Rep.
15	*Minnesota	Sept. 8, 1919	60–5	120–6	Rep.	Rep.
16	*New Hampshire	Sept. 10, 1919	14–10	212–143	Rep.	Dem.
17	*Utah	Sept. 30, 1919	Unan.	Unan.	Dem.	Rep.
18	*California	Nov. 1, 1919	Unan.	73–2	Rep.	Rep.
19	*Maine	Nov. 5, 1919	24–5	72–68	Rep.	Rep.
20	*North Dakota	Dec. 1, 1919	38–4	103–6	Rep.	Rep.
21	*South Dakota	Dec. 4, 1919	Unan.	Unan.	Rep.	Rep.
22	*Colorado	Dec. 12, 1919	Unan.	Unan.	Rep.	Rep.
23	Rhode Island	Jan. 6, 1920	37–1	89–3	Rep.	Div'd.
24	Kentucky	Jan. 6, 1920	30–8	72–25	Rep.	Rep.
25	*Oregon	Jan. 12, 1920	Unan.	Unan.	Rep.	Rep.
26	*Indiana	Jan. 16, 1920	43–3	Unan.	Rep.	Rep.
27	*Wyoming	Jan. 27, 1920	Unan.	Unan.	Dem.	Div'd.
28	*Nevada	Feb. 7, 1920	Unan.	Unan.	Dem.	Div'd.
29	New Jersey	Feb. 10, 1920	18–2	34–24	Dem.	Rep.
30	*Idaho	Feb. 11, 1920	29–6	Unan.	Rep.	Rep.
31	*Arizona	Feb. 12, 1920	Unan.	Unan.	Dem.	Dem.
32	*New Mexico	Feb. 19, 1920	17–5	36–10	Rep.	Rep.
33	*Oklahoma	Feb. 27, 1920	24–15	84–12	Dem.	Dem.
34	*West Virginia	Mar. 10, 1920	15–14	47–40	Rep.	Dem.
35	*Washington	Mar. 22, 1920	Unan.	Unan.	Rep.	Rep.
36	*Tennessee	Aug. 18, 1920	25–4	49–47	Dem.	Dem.

*States ratifying at Special Session.

APPENDIX 2

Countries in Which Women Vote

Azerbaijain (Moslem)
   Republic 1919
Australia 1902
Austria 1918
[1]Belgium 1919
British East Africa... 1919
Canada 1918
Czecho Slovakia 1918
Denmark 1915
[2]England 1918
Finland 1906
Germany 1918
Holland 1919
Hungary 1918

Iceland 1919
Ireland 1918
Isle of Man.......... 1881
Luxembourg 1919
[3]Mexico 1917
New Zealand 1893
Norway 1907
Poland 1918
Rhodesia 1919
Russia 1917
Scotland 1918
[4]Sweden 1919
United States 1920
Wales 1918

[1] *Electoral Reform Bill as passed granted suffrage to widows who have not remarried and mothers of soldiers killed in battle or civilians shot by Germans.*

[2] *Women over age of 30—Bill to reduce age to 21 has passed its second reading.*

[3] *No sex qualification for voting in constitution. Women have so far not availed themselves of their right to vote, but are expected to do so in the coming elections.*

[4] *To be confirmed in 1920.*

APPENDIX 3

Resolution (171) to authorize an Investigation of the District of Columbia Workhouse.

Introduced in the House by Miss Jeannette Rankin, Representative from Montana.

October 5, 1917.

Text of Resolution:

Resolved, That a select committee of seven Members of the House of Representatives be appointed by the Speaker to investigate the administration of the District of Columbia Workhouse at Occoquan, Virginia, and to report thereon as early as possible during the second session of the Sixty-fifth Congress. Said committee is authorized to sit during the recess in Washington, District of Columbia and elsewhere, to subpœna witnesses, and to call for records relating to the said workhouse. To defray the necessary expenses of such investigation, including the employment of clerical assistance, the committee is authorized to expend not to exceed $1,000 from the contingent fund of the House.

Resolution (130) to authorize an Investigation of Mob Attacks on Suffragists.

Introduced in the House by John Baer, Representative from North Dakota.

August 17, 1917.

Text of Resolution:

Whereas, in the city of Washington, D. C., about 350 feet from the White House premises is a building known as the Cameron House, in which is located headquarters and main offices of a woman's organization at which is continually congregated women of character, courage and intelligence, who come from various sections of the United States, and

Whereas, on three successive days, to wit: the 14th, 15th and 16th days of August, 1917, on said days immediately following the closing of the day's work by the clerks and employees of the Executive Departments, hundreds of these clerks and employees, acting with sailors, then and now in the service of the United States Navy and in uniform at the time, and soldiers, then and now in the service of the United States Army, also in their uniforms at the time,—and these clerks, employees, sailors and soldiers, and others, formed themselves into mobs and deliberately, unlawfully and violently damaged the said headquarters and offices of the said woman's organization by pelting rotten eggs through the doors and windows, shooting a bullet from a revolver through a window, and otherwise damaging said Cameron House, and also violently and unlawfully did strike, choke, drag and generally mistreat and injure and abuse the said women when they came defenseless upon the streets adjoining as well as when they were in the said building; and

Whereas, the organized police of the City of Washington, District of Columbia, made no attempt to properly safeguard the property and persons of the said defenseless women, but, on the contrary, said police even seemed to encourage the lawless acts of the mob; and

Whereas, such lawlessness is in the Capital of the United States and within a few hundred feet of the Executive Mansion and offices of the President of the United States; and

Whereas, these attacks upon defenseless women are not only an outrage and crime in themselves, that prove the perpetrators and those lending aid to the same to be cowards, but in addition, create throughout the world contempt for the United States and set a vicious example to the people throughout the United States and the world at large, of lawlessness and violence; and encourage designing cowards and manipulators everywhere to form mobs to molest the innocent and defenseless under any pretext whatever; and

WHEREAS, there seems to be no activity or attempt on the part of any one in authority in the City of Washington, District of Columbia, nor by the government officials to apprehend, arrest or punish those perpetrating the violence, on account of which the same may occur indefinitely unless Congress acts in the premises; and

WHEREAS, the legal status upon the premises stated would excuse the occupants of the Cameron House if they were so disposed in firing upon the mobs aforesaid, and thus create a state of greater violence and unlawry, to further injure the prestige and good name of the United States for maintaining law and order and institutions of democracy; therefore be it

Resolved, that the Speaker appoint a Committee of seven members to investigate into all the facts relating to the violence and unlawful acts aforesaid, and make the earliest possible report upon the conditions, with the purpose in view of purging the army and navy of the United States and other official departments, of all lawless men who bring disgrace upon the American flag by participating in mob violence, and also to inquire regarding the conduct of all government employees and the police of the city of Washington, District of Columbia, with a view to maintaining law and order.

APPENDIX 4

SUFFRAGE PRISONERS

NOTE:—Scores of women were arrested but never brought to trial; many others were convicted and their sentences suspended or appealed. It has been possible to list below only those women who actually served prison sentences although more than five hundred women were arrested during the agitation.

MINNIE D. ABBOTT, Atlantic City, N. J., officer of the N.W.P. [National Woman's Party]. Arrested picketing July 14, 1917, sentenced to 60 days in Occoquan workhouse.

MRS. PAULINE ADAMS, Norfolk, Va., wife of leading physician, prominent clubwoman and Congressional District Chairman of the N.W.P. Arrested picketing Sept. 4, 1917. Sentenced to 60 days in Occoquan workhouse. Arrested watchfire demonstration Feb. 9, 1919, but released on account of lack of evidence.

EDITH AINGE, Jamestown, N. Y., native of England, came to America when a child, and has brought up family of nine brothers and sisters. Worked for state suffrage in N. Y. 1915. Served five jail sentences. Sentenced to 60 days in Occoquan for picketing Sept., 1917, 15 days in Aug., 1918, Lafayette Sq. meeting, and three short terms in District Jail in Jan., 1919, watchfire demonstrations.

HARRIET U. ANDREWS, Kansas City, Mo., came to Washington as war worker. Arrested watchfire demonstration and sentenced to 5 days in District Jail Jan., 1919.

MRS. ANNIE ARNEIL, Wilmington, Del., did picket duty from beginning in 1917. One of first six suffrage prisoners. Served eight jail sentences. 3 days, June, 1917; 60 days in Occoquan, Aug.-Sept., 1917, picketing; 15 days, Aug., 1918, Lafayette Sq. meeting, and five sentences of 5 days each in Jan. and Feb., 1919, watchfire demonstrations.

BERTHE ARNOLD, Colorado Springs, Colo., daughter of prominent physician. Educated at Colo. State Univ. Student of music Phila.; member of D.A.R.; kindergarten teacher. Arrested Jan., 1919, watchfire demonstration, sentenced to 5 days in District Jail.

VIRGINIA ARNOLD, North Carolina, student George Washington and Columbia Univs., school teacher, later organizer and executive secretary N.W.P. in Washington. Served 3 days June, 1917, with first pickets sentenced.

354

Mrs. W. D. Ascough, Detroit, Mich. Former Conn. State Chairman, N.W.P. Studied for concert stage London and Paris. Abandoned concert stage to devote time to suffrage. Sentenced to 15 days Aug., 1918, Lafayette Sq. meeting, and 5 days Feb., 1919, in watchfire demonstration. Member "Prison Special" which toured country in Feb., 1919.

Mrs. Abby Scott Baker, Washington, D. C., wife of Dr. Robert Baker, and descendant long line of army officers. Three sons in service during World War. Known as the diplomat of the N.W.P., and as such has interviewed practically every man prominent in political life. Member executive committee of N.W.P. and has been political chairman since 1918. Arrested picketing and sentenced to 60 days in Occoquan, Sept., 1917.

Mrs. Charles W. Barnes, Indianapolis, Ind., officer of Ind. Branch, N.W.P. Arrested picketing Nov., 1917, sentenced to 15 days in jail.

Mrs. Naomi Barrett, Wilmington, Del., arrested watchfire demonstration Jan. 13, 1919. Sentenced to 5 days in District Jail.

Mrs. W. J. Bartlett, Putnam, Conn., leader Conn. State Grange. Arrested Aug., 1917, picketing, sentenced to 60 days.

Mrs. M. Toscan Bennett, Hartford, Conn., wife of lawyer and writer, member D.A.R. and Colonial Dames, has been active in state suffrage work for many years. Member National Advisory Council, N.W.P. and Conn. state treasurer. Arrested Jan., 1919, watchfire demonstration. Sentenced to 5 days in District Jail.

Hilda Blumberg, New York City, native of Russia, one of youngest prisoners. Educated and taught school in this country. Arrested picketing, Sept., 1917; sentenced to 30 days in Occoquan; arrested again Nov. 10, sentenced to 15 days.

Mrs. Kate Boeckh, Washington, D. C., native of Canada, one of first women aeroplane pilots. Arrested picketing Aug., 1917, case appealed. Arrested applauding in court Jan., 1919, served 3 days.

Mrs. Catherine Boyle, Newcastle, Del., munitions worker during World War. Arrested Jan., 1919, watchfire demonstration, sentenced to 5 days in jail.

Lucy G. Branham, Baltimore, Md., organizer N.W.P., graduate Washington College, Md.; M. A., Johns Hopkins; graduate student Univ. of Chicago and Ph.D. Columbia. Won Carnegie hero medal for rescuing man and woman from drowning at St. Petersburg, Fla. Arrested picketing Sept., 1917, sentenced to 60 days in Occoquan and District Jail.

Mrs. Lucy G. Branham, Baltimore, Md., mother of Miss Lucy Branham, widow of Dr. John W. Branham who lost his life fighting a yellow fever epidemic in Ga. Arrested watchfire demonstration Jan., 1919; sentenced to 3 days in District Jail.

Mrs. John Winters Brannan, New York City, daughter of the late Charles A. Dana, founder and editor N. Y. *Sun*, trusted counselor of President Lincoln; wife of Dr. Brannan, Pres. Board of Trustees Bellevue Hospital; member executive committee N.W.P., state chairman New York Branch. Did brilliant state suffrage work as officer of Woman's Political Union in N. Y. Arrested picketing July 14, 1917, sentenced to 60 days in Occoquan; pardoned by President after serving 3 days. Again arrested picketing Nov. 10, 1917, sentenced to 45 days.

JENNIE BRONENBERG, Philadelphia, Pa. Student Wharton School, Univ. of Pa. Arrested Feb., 1919, sentenced to 5 days in District Jail.

MRS. MARY E. BROWN, Wilmington, Del., state press chairman, N.W.P. Father member First Del. regiment; mother field nurse, Civil War. Descendant Captain David Porter, of Battleship Essex, War of 1812. Arrested watchfire demonstration Jan. 13, 1919, sentenced to 5 days in District Jail.

LOUISE BRYANT, New York City, formerly of Portland, Ore., author, poet and journalist, wife of John Reed. Correspondent for Phila. Public Ledger in Petrograd for six months during Russian revolution. Arrested watchfire demonstration Feb., 1919, sentenced to 5 days in District Jail.

LUCY BURNS, New York City, graduate Vassar College, student of Yale Univ. and Univ. of Bonn, Germany. High School teacher. Joined English militant suffrage movement 1909, where she met Alice Paul, with whom she joined in establishing first permanent suffrage headquarters in Washington in Jan., 1913; helped organize parade of March 3, 1913; vice chairman and member of executive committee Congressional Union for Woman Suffrage [later the N.W.P.], for a time editor of *The Suffragist.* Leader of most of the picket demonstrations and served more time in jail than any other suffragist in America. Arrested picketing June, 1917, sentenced to 3 days; arrested Sept., 1917, sentenced to 60 days; arrested Nov. 10, 1917, sentenced to six months; in January, 1919, arrested watchfire demonstrations for which she served one 3 day and two 5 day sentences. She also served 4 prison terms in England.

MRS. HENRY BUTTERWORTH, New York City, comes of an old Huguenot family. Active in civic and suffrage work in N. Y. for past 20 years. Charter member National Society of Craftsmen. Arrested picketing Nov., 1917, sentenced to 30 days in Occoquan.

MRS. LUCILLE A. CALMES, Princeton, Ia. Great-granddaughter of George Fowler, founder of New Harmony, Ind. Government worker during World War. Arrested watchfire demonstration Jan. 13, 1919, sentenced to 5 days in District Jail.

ELEANOR CALNAN, Methuen, Mass. Congressional district chairman of Mass. Branch N.W.P. Arrested picketing July 14, 1917, sentenced to 60 days in Occoquan, pardoned by President after 3 days; arrested Sept., 1917, sentenced to 60 days in Occoquan. Arrested in Boston, Feb., 1919, for participation in Boston demonstration at home coming of President; sentenced to 8 days in Charles St. Jail.

MRS. AGNES CHASE, Washington, D. C., formerly of Ill.; engaged in scientific research work for U. S. Dept. of Agriculture. Arrested Lafayette Sq. meeting August, 1918, sentenced to 10 days. Arrested watchfire demonstration Jan., 1919, sentenced to 5 days.

Mrs. PALYS L. CHEVRIER, New York City, arrested watchfire demonstration Jan., 1919, sentenced to 5 days. Member "Prison Special" which toured country in Feb., 1919.

Mrs. HELEN CHISASKI, Bridgeport, Conn., munition worker and member of Machinists' Union. Arrested watchfire demonstration Jan. 13, 1919; sentenced to 5 days in jail.

Mrs. WILLIAM CHISHOLM, Huntington, Pa., now deceased; arrested picketing Sept. 4, 1917, sentenced to 60 days in Occoquan.

JOSEPHINE COLLINS, Framingham, Mass., owns and manages the village store at Framingham Center. She encountered serious opposition from some of her customers on account of her militant activities; one of first members N.W.P.; arrested in Boston Feb., 1919, for taking part in welcome to the President; sentenced to 8 days in Charles St. Jail.

Mrs. SARAH TARLETON COLVIN, St. Paul, Minn., member famous Tarleton family of Alabama, wife of Dr. A. R. Colvin, Major in the Army, and Acting Surgical Chief at Fort McHenry during World War; graduate nurse Johns Hopkins training school, Red Cross nurse in this country during war; Minnesota state chairman N.W.P. Member "Prison Special." Arrested watchfire demonstrations Jan., 1919; sentenced to 2 terms of 5 days each.

BETTY CONNOLLY, West Newton, Mass., household assistant, arrested in Boston, Feb., 1919, demonstration of welcome to President Wilson; sentenced to 8 days in Charles St. Jail.

Mrs. ALICE M. COSU, New Orleans, La., vice chairman La. state branch N.W.P. Arrested picketing Nov., 1917, and sentenced to 30 days in Occoquan workhouse.

CORA CRAWFORD, Philadelphia, Pa., business woman. Marched in 1913 suffrage parade in Washington. Arrested watchfire demonstration Jan., 1919; sentenced to 5 days in District Jail.

GERTRUDE CROCKER, Washington, D. C., formerly of Ill., educated at Vassar College and Univ. of Chicago. National Treasurer N.W.P. 1916; government worker, 1917. Served 3 jail sentences: 30 days for picketing in 1917, 10 days for assisting Lafayette Sq. meeting 1918, and 5 days for participating watchfire 1919.

RUTH CROCKER, Washington, D. C., formerly of Ill., sister of Gertrude Crocker. Came to Washington for suffrage, later government worker. Served 30 days at Occoquan for picketing in 1917 and 3 days in District Jail for watchfire demonstration Jan., 1919.

MISS L. J. C. DANIELS, Grafton, Vt., and Boston. Arrested picketing Nov. 10, 1917, sentenced to 15 days. Took part in Capitol picketing Nov., 1918; arrested watchfire demonstration Jan. 9, 1919, sentenced to 5 days in District Jail. Arrested in Boston for participation in welcome demonstration to President, sentenced to 8 days in Charles St. Jail.

DOROTHY DAY, New York City, member of the "Masses" [now the "Liberator"] staff. Arrested picketing Nov. 10, 1917, sentenced to 30 days in Occoquan workhouse.

EDNA DIXON, Washington, D. C., daughter of physician; teacher in public schools. Arrested picketing Aug., 1917, sentenced to 30 days in Occoquan workhouse.

LAVINIA L. DOCK, Fayetteville, Pa., associated with the founders of American Red Cross nursing service; secretary of American Federation of Nurses and member of International Council of Nurses. Assisted in relief work during Johnstown flood and during Fla. yellow fever epidemic; army nurse during Spanish-American War, author of "The History of Nursing," "The Tuberculosis Nurse," and a number of other text books on nursing. One of early workers of Henry St. Settlement in N. Y., and founder of visiting nurse movement in N. Y. On staff of American Journal of Nursing. One of first six pickets to serve prison sentence of 3 days in June, 1917. Later that summer she served 25 days in Occoquan; and in Nov. 15 days.

MRS. MARY CARROLL DOWELL, Philadelphia, Pa., wife of William F. Dowell, magazine editor and writer with whom she has been associated in business. Active club and suffrage worker in Pa. and N. J., state officer Pa. branch N.W.P. Arrested watchfire demonstration Jan. 20, 1919, and served 5 days in District Jail.

MARY DUBROW, Passaic, N. J.; student Univ. of N. Y.; teacher in N. J. until she joined suffrage ranks as organizer and speaker. Arrested watchfire demonstration Jan. 6, 1919, sentenced to 10 days.

JULIA EMORY, Baltimore, Md.; daughter of late state senator, D. H. Emory. Gave up work for Trade Union League to work for suffrage in 1917. Sentenced to 30 days in Occoquan for picketing Nov., 1917. After her release became organizer N.W.P. Aug., 1918, arrested and sentenced to 10 days Lafayette Sq. meeting. Jan. 7, 1919, sentenced to 10 days, and later in that month to 5 days for watchfire demonstrations. Led Capitol picket Oct. and Nov., 1919, and suffered many injuries at hands of police.

MRS. EDMUND C. EVANS, Ardmore, Pa., one of three Winsor sisters who served prison terms for suffrage. Member of prominent Quaker family. Arrested watchfire demonstration Jan., 1919, and sentenced to 5 days in District Jail.

LUCY EWING, Chicago, Ill., daughter of Judge Adlai Ewing, niece of James Ewing, minister to Belgium under Cleveland; niece also of Adlai Stevenson, Vice-President under Cleveland. Officer Ill. Branch N.W.P. Arrested picketing Aug. 17, 1917, sentenced to 30 days in Occoquan workhouse.

MRS. ESTELLA EYLWARD, New Orleans, La. Business woman. Came to Washington to take part in final watchfire demonstration Feb., 1919; arrested and sentenced to 5 days in District Jail.

MARY GERTRUDE FENDALL, Baltimore, Md., graduate of Bryn Mawr College; campaigned for N.W.P. in West 1916; national treasurer of organization June, 1917, to December, 1919. Arrested and sentenced to 3 days, Jan., 1919, for applauding in court.

ELLA FINDEISEN, Lawrence, Mass. Arrested picketing Nov. 10, 1917, sentenced to 30 days at Occoquan.

KATHARINE FISHER, Washington, D. C., native of Mass. Great-great-granddaughter of Artemas Ward, ranking Major General in Revolutionary War. Teacher, social worker and later employee of U. S. War Risk Bureau. Written prose and verse on suffrage and feminist topics. Arrested picketing Sept. 13, 1917, sentenced to 30 days 'at Occoquan workhouse.

MRS. ROSE GRATZ FISHSTEIN, Philadelphia, Pa., native of Russia. Came to America at 15. Had been imprisoned for revolutionary activities in Russia and fled to this country following release on bail. Operator in shirt factory; later union organizer; factory inspector for N. Y. State Factory Commission. Feb. 9, 1919 arrested watchfire demonstration and sentenced to 5 days in District Jail.

ROSE FISHSTEIN, Philadelphia, Pa., sister-in-law of Mrs. Rose G. Fishstein, born in Russia, educated in N. Y. and Phila. Student of Temple Univ., business woman. Arrested watchfire demonstration, Feb., 1919, sentenced to 5 days in District Jail.

CATHERINE M. FLANAGAN, Hartford, Conn., state and national organizer for N.W.P.; formerly secretary for Conn. Woman Suffrage Association. Father came to this country as Irish exile because of his efforts in movement for Irish freedom. Arrested picketing August, 1917, sentenced to 30 days in Occoquan workhouse.

MARTHA FOLEY, Dorchester, Mass., active worker in Mass. labor movement. Arrested in demonstration at homecoming of President in Boston, Feb., 1919; sentenced to 8 days in Charles St. Jail.

MRS. T. W. FORBES, Baltimore, Md., officer of Just Government League of Md.; arrested watchfire demonstration Feb. 9, 1919, sentenced to 5 days in District Jail.

JANET FOTHERINGHAM, Buffalo, N. Y., teacher of physical culture. Arrested picketing July 14, 1917, sentenced to 60 days in workhouse. but pardoned by President after 3 days.

MARGARET FOTHERINGHAM, Buffalo, N. Y., Red Cross dietician, stationed at military hospital at Waynesville, N. C., during war. Later dietician at Walter Reid Military Hospital, Washington, D. C. Arrested picketing Aug., 1917, sentenced to 60 days.

FRANCIS FOWLER, Brookline, Mass., sentenced to 8 days in Charles St. Jail for participation in demonstration of welcome to President, Boston, Feb., 1919.

MRS. MATILDA HALL GARDNER, Washington, D. C., formerly of Chicago, daughter of late Frederick Hall, for many years editor of Chicago *Tribune,* and wife of Gilson Gardner, Washington representative of Scripps papers. Educated Chicago, Paris and Brussels. Associated with Alice Paul and Lucy Burns when they came to Washington to begin agitation for federal suffrage and member of national executive committee of N.W.P. since 1914. Arrested July 14, 1917, sentenced to 60 days in Occoquan; Jan. 13, 1919, sentenced to 5 days in District Jail.

ANNA GINSBERG, New York City; served 5 days in District jail for watchfire demonstration Feb., 1919.

REBA GOMBOROV, Philadelphia, Pa.; born in Kiev, Russia. Educated in U. S. public schools; social worker; assistant secretary and visitor for Juvenile Aid Society of Phila. President Office Workers' Association; secretary of Penn. Industrial Section for Suffrage; member N.W.P., Trade Union League. Sentenced to 5 days in District Jail Jan., 1919, for watchfire demonstration.

ALICE GRAM, Portland, Ore., graduate Univ. of Ore., came to Washington to take part in picket Nov. 10, 1917. Arrested and sentenced to 30 days in Occoquan workhouse. Following release assistant in press dept. N.W.P.

BETTY GRAM, Portland, Ore., graduate Univ. of Ore. Abandoned stage career to take part in picket demonstration of Nov. 10, 1917. Worker in Juvenile courts of Portland. Sentenced to 30 days in Occoquan workhouse; later arrested in Boston demonstration of Feb., 1919, and sentenced to 8 days in Charles St. Jail. Business manager of *The Suffragist* and national organizer for N.W.P.

NATALIE GRAY, Col. Springs, Col., daughter of treasurer Col. Branch N. W. P. Arrested picketing Aug. 17, 1917, sentenced to 30 days in Occoquan workhouse.

MRS. FRANCIS GREEN, New York City, one of second group of women to serve prison sentences for suffrage in this country. Served 3 days in District Jail following picket demonstration of July 4, 1917.

GLADYS GREINER, Baltimore, Md., daughter of John E. Greiner, engineering expert, member of Stevens Railway Commission to Russia in 1917. Graduate of Forest Glen Seminary, Md.; did settlement work in mountain districts of Ky.; has held tennis and golf championships of Md., and for 3 years devoted all time to suffrage. Arrested picketing July 4, 1917, sentenced to 3 days in District Jail; arrested Oct. 20, 1917, sentenced to 30 days in District Jail; arrested Lafayette Sq. meeting Aug., 1918, sentenced to 15 days in District Jail. Recently taken up work in labor movement.

MRS. J. IRVING GROSS. Boston, Mass., charter member of Mass. Branch N.W.P. Father and husband both fought in Civil War. Arrested 5 times Lafayette Sq. meetings Aug., 1918, and sentenced to 15 days in District Jail. Arrested in Boston demonstration on Common following landing of President and sentenced to 8 days in Charles St. Jail.

ANNA GWINTER, New York City, arrested for picketing Nov. 10, 1917, and sentenced to 30 days in Occoquan workhouse.

ELIZABETH HAMILTON, New York City, arrested for picketing Nov. 10, 1917, and sentenced to 30 days in Occoquan workhouse.

ERNESTINE HARA, New York City, young Roumanian, arrested for picketing Sept., 1917, and sentenced to 30 days in Occoquan workhouse.

REBECCA HARRISON, Joplin, Mo., arrested final watchfire demonstration Feb. 10, 1919; sentenced to 5 days in District Jail.

Mrs. H. O. Havemeyer, New York City; widow of late H. O. Havemeyer; leader of suffrage movement for many years; one of its most eloquent speakers, and generous contributor to its funds; active in Liberty Loan campaigns, in the Land Army movement of N. Y. State, and in working for military rank for nurses. As member of "Prison Special" spoke for suffrage in the large cities. Arrested Feb. 10, 1919, for taking part in final watchfire demonstration; sentenced to 5 days in District Jail.

Kate Heffelfinger, Shamokin, Pa.; art student; sentenced to 6 months in District Jail for picketing Oct. 15, 1917; another month later added for previous offense. Aug., 1918, sentenced to 15 days for participating in Lafayette Sq. meeting; Jan., 1919, sentenced to 5 days for participation in watchfire demonstration.

Mrs. Jessica Henderson, Boston, Mass., wife of prominent Bostonian, one of liberal leaders of Boston; identified with many reform movements. Mother of 6 children, one of whom, Wilma, aged 18, was arrested with her mother, spent night in house of detention, and was released as minor. Sentenced to 8 days in Charles St. Jail Feb., 1919, for participation in Boston demonstration of welcome to President.

Minnie Hennesy, Hartford, Conn.; business woman, having supported herself all her life; arrested for picketing Oct. 6, 1917, and sentence suspended. Rearrested Oct. 8, 1917, and sentenced to 6 months.

Anne Herkimer, Baltimore, Md., Child Labor inspector for U. S. Children's Bureau. Arrested Feb., 1919, and sentenced to 5 days in District Jail for participating watchfire demonstration.

Elsie Hill, Norwalk, Conn.; daughter of late Ebenezer J. Hill, 21 years Congressman from Conn.; graduate Vassar College and student abroad. Taught French in District of Columbia High School. Lately devoted all her time to suffrage. Member of executive committee of Congressional Union 1914-1915; President D.C. Branch College Equal Suffrage League, and later national organizer for N.W.P. Aug., 1918, sentenced to 15 days in District Jail for speaking at Lafayette Sq. meeting. Feb., 1919, sentenced to 8 days in Boston for participation in welcome demonstration to President.

Mrs. George Hill, Boston, Mass.; sentenced to 8 days in Boston, Feb., 1919, for participation in welcome to President.

Mrs. Florence Bayard Hilles, Newcastle, Del.; daughter of late Thomas Bayard, first American ambassador to Great Britain and secretary of state under Cleveland. Munitions worker during World War. After the war engaged in reconstruction work in France. Chairman Del. Branch N.W.P. and member of national executive committee. Arrested picketing July 14, 1917, sentenced to 60 days in Occoquan workhouse; pardoned by President after 3 days.

Mrs. J. A. H. Hopkins (Allison Turnbull), Morristown, N. J., state chairman N.W.P., member executive committee N.W.P. 1917, and president and officer of various women's clubs. Her husband was leader Progressive Party and later supported President Wilson, serving on Democratic National Campaign Committee in 1916. At present Chairman Committee of

48. Mrs. Hopkins arrested July 14, 1917, for picketing, sentenced to 60 days in workhouse; pardoned by President after 3 days.

Mrs. L. H. Hornsby, New York City, formerly of Ill., one of first women aviators in this country. Arrested for picketing Nov. 10, 1917; sentenced to 30 days in District Jail.

Elizabeth Huff, Des Moines, Ia.; came to Washington to work for war department during war; later with Red Cross. Sentenced to 5 days in jail, Jan., 1919, for watchfire demonstration.

Eunice Huff, Des Moines, Ia.; sister of Elizabeth; also engaged in war work in Washington. Sentenced to 3 days in jail Jan., 1919, for applauding suffrage prisoners in court.

Hazel Hunkins, Billings, Mont.; graduate Vassar College; later instructor in Chemistry, Univ. of Mo. Joined suffrage movement as organizer for N.W.P. Later investigator for War Labor Board. Active in all picketing campaigns. Aug. 1918, sentenced to 15 days for participation in Lafayette Sq. meeting.

Julia Hurlbut, Morristown, N. J., vice chairman N. J. Branch N.W.P. In 1916 assisted in Washington state campaign. Arrested picketing July 14, 1917, sentenced to 60 days in Occoquan workhouse; pardoned by President after 3 days. Engaged in war work in France during war.

Mary Ingham, Philadelphia, Pa.; graduate Bryn Mawr College; Pa. chairman of N.W.P.; secretary of National Progressive League 1912. Has held offices of vice president of Pa. Women's Trade Union League, director of Bureau of Municipal Research of Phila., member of board of corporators of Woman's Medical College of Pa., where she was former student. For several years manager woman's department of Bonbright and Co., investment brokers. Arrested for picketing July 14, 1917; sentenced to 60 days in Occoquan, pardoned by President after 3 days.

Mrs. Mark Jackson, Baltimore, Md., arrested picketing Aug., 1917, sentenced to 30 days.

Paula Jakobi, New York City; playwright, author of "Chinese Lily." Once matron of Framingham reformatory for purpose of studying prison conditions. Arrested picketing Nov. 10, 1917, and sentenced to 30 days in Occoquan workhouse.

Maud Jamison, Norfolk, Va.; came to Washington in 1916 as volunteer worker of N.W.P. Later became assistant in treasurer's department. Had been school teacher and business woman before joining N.W.P. Took active part in picketing from the beginning; one of first group arrested, June, 1917; served 3 days in District Jail; later served 30 days in District Jail; Oct., 1917, sentenced to 7 months. Released by Government after 44 days. Jan., 1919, served 5 days in jail for participation in watchfire demonstration.

Mrs. Peggy Baird Johns, New York City, formerly of St. Louis, newspaper woman and magazine writer. Sentenced to 30 days in Occoquan workhouse Aug., 1917; and 30 days in Nov., 1917, for picketing.

WILLIE GRACE JOHNSON, Shreveport, La., state officer, N.W.P. and prominent in civic work. Successful business woman. Arrested in final watchfire demonstration Feb., 1919. Sentenced to 5 days in District Jail.

AMY JUENGLING, Buffalo, N. Y.; of Swiss and German ancestry. Graduated with honors from Univ. of N. Y. Has lived in Porto Rico and North Carolina, in latter state doing educational work among mountaineers. At present engaged in Americanization work. Nov., 1917, sentenced to 30 days in Occoquan workhouse for picketing.

ELIZABETH GREEN KALB, Houston, Texas; graduate Rice Institute, 1916; student Univ. Chicago, 1916. Won Carnegie Peace Prize in Texas state intercollegiate oratory contest in 1915. In 1918 became active worker for N.W.P., taking part in Capitol picket. Arrested watchfire demonstration Jan., 1919, sentenced to 5 days in District Jail. In charge of literature and library dept. of N.W.P. at national headquarters.

RHODA KELLOGG, Minneapolis, Minn.; graduate Univ. of Minn. and Pres. of Univ. Equal Suffrage Club. Sentenced to 24 hours for applauding suffrage prisoners in Court Jan., 1919, sentenced to 5 days in District Jail for participation in watchfire demonstration same month.

MRS. FREDERICK W. KENDALL, Hamburg, N. Y.; wife of one of editors of Buffalo Express; writer, public speaker and club leader. Arrested for picketing, Aug., 1917, and sentenced to 30 days in Occoquan workhouse.

MARIE ERNST KENNEDY, Philadelphia, Pa.; formerly state chairman N.W.P. Arrested Feb., 1919, in watchfire demonstration, sentenced to 5 days in jail.

MRS. MARGARET WOOD KESSLER, Denver, Col.; vice president Woman's Progressive Club of Col. Sept., 1917, sentenced to 30 days in Occoquan for picketing.

ALICE KIMBALL, New York City. Has been engaged in Y.W.C.A. work, and as librarian in N. Y. Public Library, and later as labor investigator. Sentenced to 15 days in District Jail for taking part in Lafayette Sq. meeting Aug. 10, 1918.

MRS. BEATRICE KINKEAD, Montclair, N. J., active member of N.W.P. in N. J. Joined picket of July 14, 1917. Sentenced to 60 days in Occoquan, but pardoned by President after 3 days.

MRS. RUBY E. KOENIG, Hartford, Conn. Took part in Lafayette Sq. meeting of Aug., 1918, and suffered sprained arm from rough treatment by police. Arrested and sentenced to 15 days in District Jail.

HATTIE KRUGER, Buffalo, N. Y. Trained nurse; ran for Congress on Socialist ticket in 1918. Worker in Lighthouse Settlement, Philadelphia, and for time probation officer of Juvenile Court of Buffalo. Nov. 10, 1917, sentenced to 30 days in Occoquan workhouse for picketing.

DR. ANNA KUHN, Baltimore, Md., physician. Arrested picketing Nov. 10, 1917, sentenced to 30 days.

Mrs. Lawrence Lewis, Philadelphia, Pa., maternal ancestor of family which took possession 1660 land grant in Conn. from King, paternal ancestor Michael Hillegas who came Phila. 1727, a founder of Phila. Academy Fine Arts, Assembly, etc. Son of Hillegas was first U. S. treasurer; sister of Dr. Howard A. Kelly, well-known surgeon, formerly professor Johns Hopkins Hospital, author of many medical books; sister of Mrs. R. R. P. Bradford, founder and Pres. of Lighthouse Settlement, Phila.; member executive committee of N.W.P. since 1913; chairman of finance 1918; national treasurer, 1919; chairman ratification committee 1920; active in state suffrage work many years; served 3 days in jail for picketing July, 1917; arrested Nov. 10, 1917, sentenced to 60 days; arrested Lafayette Sq. meeting, Aug., 1918, sentenced to 15 days; arrested watchfire demonstration Jan., 1919, sentenced to 5 days in jail.

Katharine Lincoln, New York City, formerly of Philadelphia. Was working for Traveler's Aid when she came to picket Nov. 10, 1917. Sentenced to 30 days in Occoquan workhouse. Worked for N.W.P. for several months; later campaigned for Anne Martin, candidate for U. S. Senate from Nev.

Dr. Sarah H. Lockrey, Philadelphia, Pa.; graduate Woman's Medical College of Pa. Served as interne Woman's Hospital in Phila., and later head of gynecological clinic of same hospital. Surgeon on West Phila. Hospital for Women and Children. Received degree of Fellow of American College of Surgery 1914. Chairman of her Congressional District for the N.W.P. Aug., 1918, sentenced to 15 days in District Jail for taking part in Lafayette Sq. meeting.

Elizabeth McShane, Philadelphia, Pa., graduate Vassar College; principal of school near Indianapolis, later business woman. Assisted in Pa. health survey, working with the American Medical Association. Aug., 1918, sentenced to 15 days in jail for participation in Lafayette Sq. meeting. Jan., 1919, served 5 days for participating in watchfire demonstration. Member of "Prison Special" 1919.

Mrs. Annie J. Magee, Wilmington, Del., one of first Del. supporters of N.W.P. Took part in many pickets. Arrested watchfire demonstration Jan., 1919, and sentenced to 5 days in District Jail.

Mrs. Effie B. Main, Topeka, Kan., arrested for taking part in Lafayette Sq. meeting Aug. 10, 1918; sentenced to 10 days in District Jail.

Maud Malone, New York City, librarian in N. Y. Lifelong suffragist; arrested for picketing, Sept. 4, 1917, and served sentence of 60 days at Occoquan workhouse.

Anne Martin, Reno, Nev.; graduate Leland Stanford Univ.; studied in English Univs. Professor of history in Univ. of Nev. As Pres. of Nev. Woman's Civic League led successful fight for state suffrage in 1914. Served as legislative chairman for Congressional Union, and N.W.P. and member of executive committee. When N.W.P. was formed, in 1916, elected its chairman. When it combined with Congressional Union, she became vice chairman. In 1918 ran on independent ticket for U. S. Senate. July 14, 1917, sentenced to 60 days at Occoquan workhouse for picketing. Pardoned by President after 3 days.

Mrs. Louise Parker Mayo, Framingham, Mass., of Quaker descent. Taught school for five years before marriage to William I. Mayo, grandson of Chief Justice Isaac Parker of Mass. Mother of 7 children. Arrested for picketing July 14, 1917; sentenced to 60 days in Occoquan workhouse; pardoned by President after 3 days.

Nell Mercer, Norfolk, Va.; member of Norfolk Branch, N.W.P. Business woman. Feb., 1919, sentenced to 5 days in District Jail for participation in final watchfire demonstration.

Vida Milholland, New York City; daughter of Mr. and Mrs. John E. Milholland and sister of Inez Milholland Boissevain. Student at Vassar where won athletic championships and dramatic honors. Studied singing here and abroad, but on death of sister gave up career of promise to devote herself to suffrage work. July 4, 1917, arrested and served 3 days in District Jail for picketing. In 1919 toured the country with "Prison Special," singing at all meetings.

Mrs. Bertha Moller, Minneapolis, Minn., campaigned for state suffrage before joining N.W.P. Interested in industrial problems. Of Swedish descent, one of ancestors served on staff of Gustavus-Adolphus, and 2 uncles are now members of Swedish parliament. She served 2 jail sentences, one of 24 hours for applauding suffragists in court, and another of 5 days for participation in watchfire demonstration, Jan., 1919.

Martha W. Moore, Philadelphia, Pa., of Quaker ancestry, student at Swarthmore College; charter member of Congressional Union; has devoted herself to social service work, Children's Aid, Traveler's Aid, etc. Arrested and sentenced to 5 days in District Jail Jan., 1919, for participation in watchfire demonstration.

Mrs. Agnes H. Morey, Brookline, Mass., comes of line of Colonial ancestors who lived in Concord. Following picket of Nov. 10, 1917, sentenced to 30 days at District Jail and Occoquan. Chairman of Mass. Branch N.W.P., of which she was one of founders, and member of National Advisory Council N.W.P. Member of "Suffrage Special" of 1916, and a gifted speaker and organizer.

Katharine A. Morey, Brookline, Mass., daughter of Mrs. A. H. Morey; also officer State Branch N.W.P. Organizer election campaign 1916 in Kansas and has many times assisted at national headquarters. One of first group pickets sentenced, served 3 days, June, 1917; Feb., 1919, arrested in Boston demonstration of welcome to President and sentenced to 8 days in Charles St. Jail.

Mildred Morris, Denver, Col., well-known newspaper woman of Denver. Came to Washington for Bureau of Public Information during war. Later investigator for War Labor Board. Now Washington correspondent International News Service. In Jan., 1919, served 5 day sentence in District Jail for lighting watchfire.

Mrs. Phoebe C. Munnecke, Detroit, Mich.; assisted with meetings and demonstrations in Washington winter of 1918-19. Jan., 1919, arrested for lighting watchfire, sentenced to 10 days in jail. Later sentenced to 3 days in jail for applauding suffrage prisoners in court,

GERTRUDE MURPHY, Minneapolis, Minn., superintendent of music in Minn. public schools. Jan., 1919, served 24-hour sentence for applauding suffragists in court. Later served 5 days in District Jail for participation in watchfire demonstration.

MRS. MARY A. NOLAN, Jacksonville, Fla., born in Va.; descended from family of Duffy, Cavan, Ireland. Educated at convent of Mont de Chantal in W. Va. As young woman was teacher and leader in Southern library movement. Suffrage pioneer; prominent in Confederate organizations of South. In 1917 joined N.W.P., came to Washington to picket. Arrested Nov. 10, 1917, sentenced to 6 days in District Jail, but sent to Occoquan workhouse. January, 1919, arrested many times in watchfire demonstrations; sentenced to 24 hours in jail. Oldest suffrage prisoner.

MRS. MARGARET OAKES, Idaho; arrested Lafayette Sq. meeting Aug., 1918, and sentenced to 10 days in District Jail.

ALICE PAUL, Moorestown, N. J. English Quaker ancestor imprisoned for Quaker beliefs died in English prison; born of Quaker parentage and brought up in this small Quaker town. Received her A.B. degree from Swarthmore College, and her M.A. and Ph.D. from Univ. of Pa. Graduate of N. Y. School of Philanthropy, and studied at Universities of London and Birmingham, specializing in economics and sociology. While in England took part in militant campaign under Mrs. Pankhurst. On return to America, she was appointed chairman in 1913 of the Congressional Committee of the National American Woman Suffrage Association. Founded Congressional Union for Woman Suffrage; made chairman. When this became an independent organization reappointed chairman. When it merged with the N.W.P. in 1917, she was chosen chairman of the combined organizations, and has continued in this office to the present date. Has served 6 prison terms for suffrage, 3 in England and 3 in United States. In Oct., 1919, she was sentenced to 7 months for picketing and served 5 weeks before released on account of hunger strike. While in jail suffered the severest treatment inflicted upon any suffrage prisoner. In Aug., 1918, sentenced to 10 days for participation in Lafayette Sq. meeting. In Jan., 1919, sentenced to 5 days for lighting a watchfire.

BERRY POTTIER, Boston, Mass., of French descent; art student; participated in Boston demonstration at home-coming of President, and sentenced to 8 days in Charles St. Jail.

EDNA M. PARTELL, Hartford, Conn., sentenced to 5 days in District Jail for participation in Lafayette Sq. meeting Aug., 1918.

MRS. R. B. QUAY, Salt Lake City, Utah; arrested in Nov. 10, 1917, picket; sentenced to 30 days in District Jail, but sent to Occoquan workhouse.

MRS. BETSY REYNEAU, Detroit, Mich., wife of Paul Reyneau; portrait painter. Arrested picketing July 14, 1917. Sentenced to 60 days in Occoquan, but pardoned by the President after 3 days.

MRS. C. T. ROBERTSON, Salt Lake City, Utah; active worker for reforms affecting women. Arrested in Nov. 10, 1917, picket; sentenced to 30 days in District Jail, but sent to Occoquan workhouse.

Mrs. George E. Roewer, Belmont, Mass., graduate of Radcliffe, active suffragist since college days; wife of well known attorney of Boston and granddaughter of prominent figures in German Revolution of 1848 who were exiled to the United States. Sentenced to 8 days in Boston Charles St. Jail following participation in welcome demonstration to the President, Feb. 1919.

Mrs. John Rogers, Jr., New York City, wife of Dr. John Rogers, Jr., celebrated thyroid expert, is a descendant of Roger Sherman, signer of the Declaration of Independence. A pioneer worker for state suffrage before taking up national work. Before entering suffrage movement active in improving conditions in New York public schools. Chairman Advisory Council of the N.W.P., and one of the most forceful speakers in the suffrage ranks. In 1916 and 1919 as member of "Suffrage Special" and "Prison Special" toured the country speaking for suffrage. July 14, 1917, sentenced to 60 days in Occoquan workhouse for picketing, but was pardoned by the President after 3 days.

Marguerite Rossette, Baltimore, Md., young artist, and niece of Dr. Joshua Rossette, well known social worker. Took part in N.W.P. demonstrations, served 5 days in District Jail for participation in final watchfire demonstration, Feb., 1919.

Mrs. Elise T. Russian, Detroit, Mich., born in Constantinople of Armenian parentage. Educated in this country. Taught school in Mass. until marriage. State officer N.W.P. Sentenced to 5 days in District Jail for participation in Jan., 1919, watchfire demonstration; and 8 days in Boston in the Charles St. Jail for participation in welcome demonstration to President in Feb., 1919.

Nina Samarodin, born in Kiev, Russia, graduate of Kiev University. In 1914 came to America on visit, but entered industrial fight, becoming, first, worker and then union organizer. Teacher Rand School of Social Science, New York. Sentenced to 30 days in Occoquan for picketing September, 1917.

Mrs. Phoebe Persons Scott, Morristown, New Jersey, graduate of Smith College where she specialized in biology and botany. Did settlement work at New York Henry St. Settlement. Worked for state suffrage before joining N.W.P. and becoming one of its officers. Sentenced to 30 days in District Jail for picketing Nov. 10, 1917, but sent to Occoquan workhouse.

Ruth Scott, Bridgeport, Conn., munitions worker. Sentenced to 5 days in District Jail for participation in watchfire demonstration Jan., 1919.

Belle Sheinberg, New York City; of Russian descent; student of New York Univ., who left her studies to picket in Washington Nov. 10, 1917. Sentenced to 30 days in Occoquan workhouse.

Mrs. Lucille Shields, Amarillo, Texas. Picketed regularly during 1917. July 4, 1917, served 3 days in District Jail for picketing; served 5 days Jan. 13, 1919, for participation in watchfire demonstration. Soon after release sentenced to 3 days for applauding suffrage prisoners in Court.

Mrs. Martha Reed Shoemaker, Philadelphia, Pa., graduate of Vassar College. Served 5 days in District Jail for participation in final watchfire demonstration of Feb. 9, 1919.

Mrs. Mary Short, Minneapolis, Minn., state officer N.W.P. Sentenced to 30 days in Occoquan workhouse for picketing November 10, 1917.

Mrs. Lois Warren Shaw, Manchester, N. H., student of Vassar and Radcliffe, mother of six children. Wife of V. P. and General Manager McElwain Shoe Co., N. H., chairman N.W.P. Sentenced to 8 days in Charles St. Jail after participation in Boston demonstration to welcome President Feb., 1919.

Ruth Small, Boston, Mass., participant in several state suffrage campaigns before taking up national work. In charge of Boston headquarters of N.W.P. for a time. For taking part in Boston demonstration on the return of the President in Feb., 1919, sentenced to 8 days in Charles St. Jail.

Dr. Caroline E. Spencer, Colorado Springs, Col., formerly of Philadelphia. Secretary Col. Branch, N.W.P. Graduate Woman's Medical College of Pa. October 20, 1917, arrested for picketing and sentenced to 7 months' imprisonment. For participating in watchfire demonstration Jan. 13, 1919, sentenced to 5 days in District Jail.

Mrs. Kate Stafford, Oklahoma City, Okla., active worker for reforms affecting women and children in her own state. Mother of six children. Picketed Nov. 10, 1917, and was sentenced to 30 days in District Jail.

Doris Stevens, Omaha, Neb., now resident New York City. Graduate of Oberlin College; social worker and teacher; organized and spoke for state suffrage campaigns in Ohio and Michigan; joined Congressional Union in 1913. Organized first Convention of women voters at Panama Pacific Exposition in 1915; managed 1916 election campaign in Cal. for N.W.P. Has acted successively as executive secretary, organizer, legislative chairman, political chairman, and executive committee member of N.W.P. Arrested for picketing July 14, 1917; sentenced to 60 days in Occoquan workhouse; pardoned by President after 3 days. Arrested N. Y. Mar., 1919, picket demonstration Metropolitan Opera House, but not sentenced.

Elizabeth Stuyvesant, New York City, formerly of Cincinnati; dancer by profession; active in settlement work and in campaign for birth-control. July 4, 1917, arrested for picketing and sentenced to 3 days in District Jail.

Elsie Unterman, Chicago, Ill., social worker who took week's vacation in January, 1919, to come to Washington to picket. She served 3 days in District Jail for applauding suffragists in court.

Mabel Vernon, Wilmington, Del., Secretary N.W.P., graduate Swarthmore College. Fellow student with Alice Paul. Gave up position as high school teacher when Congressional Union was founded to become organizer and speaker. With remarkable gifts as a speaker, has addressed large meetings in every part of the country. As brilliant organizer has had charge of many important organization tasks of N.W.P. Organized the transcontinental trip of voting envoys to the President. Campaigned in Nev. 1914 and 1916. Became national organization chairman N.W.P. Organized the Washington picket line for several months. One of the first six women to serve prison sentence for suffrage in District Jail. For picketing June, 1917, served 3 days.

Mrs. Elsie Vervane, Bridgeport, Conn., munitions worker and President of Woman's Machinist Union of Bridgeport. In Jan., 1919, came to Washington with group of union women and took part in watchfire demonstration; arrested and served 5 days in District Jail.

Iris Calderhead [now wife of John Brisben Walker], Marysville, Kansas, now resident of Denver, Colo., daughter of former-Representative Calderhead of Kansas. Graduate of Univ. of Kansas and student at Bryn Mawr. Abandoned school teaching to work for suffrage; became organizer and speaker for N.W.P. July 4, 1917, arrested for picketing and served 3 days in District Jail.

Mrs. Robert Walker, Baltimore, Md., officer Md. Branch N.W.P. A Quaker and graduate of Swarthmore College; wife of a captain in the late war and mother of 3 children. Arrested July 14, 1917, for picketing and sentenced to 60 days in Occoquan workhouse. Pardoned by President after 3 days.

Bertha Wallerstein, New York City, student of Barnard College; served 5 days in District Jail Jan., 1919, for watchfire demonstration.

Mrs. Bertha Walmsley, Kansas City, Mo., holding government position at time arrested for applauding suffragists in court; served 3 days in District Jail.

Mrs. William Upton Watson, Chicago, Ill., treasurer state branch, N.W.P. Sentenced to 30 days Occoquan workhouse for picketing Aug. 17, 1917. Aug., 1918, sentenced to 5 days for participation in Lafayette Sq. meeting.

Mrs. C. Weaver, Bridgeport, Conn., worked during war in munitions factory. Came to Washington for watchfire demonstration of Jan. 13, 1919; arrested and sentenced to 5 days in District Jail.

Eva Weaver, Bridgeport, Conn., daughter of Mrs. C. Weaver, also worked in munitions factory; arrested with mother Jan. 13, 1919, and served 5 days in District Jail.

Mrs. Helena Hill Weed, Norwalk, Conn., graduate of Vassar and Montana School of Mines. One of few qualified women geologists of country. Daughter of late Congressman Ebenezer Hill. At one time vice-president general of D.A.R. Prominent member of Congressional Union and N.W.P. from early days. One of first pickets arrested, July 4, 1917; served 3 days in District Jail. Aug., 1918, arrested for participation in Lafayette Sq. meeting; sentenced to 15 days. Jan., 1918, sentenced to 24 hours for applauding in court.

Cora A. Week, New York City, of Norse descent; parents Wisconsin pioneers; studied art in Boston; became member Art Student's League of New York; helped organize Oliver Merson Atelier in Paris; exhibited Paris Salon. Arrested for picketing Nov. 10, 1917; sentenced to 30 days in District Jail. Member of "Prison Special" 1919.

CAMILLA WHITCOMB, Worcester, Mass., chairman 4th Congressional District Mass. N.W.P. Nov. 10, 1917, sentenced to 30 days in jail for picketing.

SUE WHITE, Jackson, Tenn., state chairman N.W.P.; recently edited *The Suffragist;* organizer and research chairman. Belongs to prominent pioneer families of Tenn. and Ky. and is descendant of Marshall and Jefferson families of Va. Court and convention reporter for ten years; 1918 appointed by Governor, Secretary of Tenn. State Commission for the Blind. Identified with U.D.C. and D.A.R.; the Federation of Women's Clubs and Parent Teachers' Association. Has done much to organize suffrage sentiment in her state. Feb. 9, 1919, arrested and served 5 days in District Jail for participating in final watchfire demonstration.

MARGARET FAY WHITTEMORE, Detroit, Mich. Her grandmother, a Quaker, started suffrage work in Michigan. Daughter of one of leading patent attorneys of country. N.W.P. organizer since 1914. Imprisoned 3 days for picketing July 4, 1917. Jan., 1919, served 24 hours in jail for applauding in court.

MRS. HARVEY W. WILEY, Washington, D. C., daughter of General Kelton, and wife of Dr. Harvey Wiley, food expert and ex-director of the pure food department of U. S. Government. Member of national advisory council of N.W.P. Has done lobbying, political work and picketing for N.W.P. Nov. 10, 1917, sentenced to 15 days in District Jail; appealed her case; later sustained by higher court.

ROSE WINSLOW, New York City, born in Poland and brought to this country when child. Began work at age of 11 in Philadelphia; for many years worked in hosiery factory in Pittsburg; later employed in shop in Philadelphia. Recently has won success as an actress. Has brilliant gifts; 1916 spoke throughout West in suffrage campaign of N.W.P. Oct. 15, 1917, sentenced to 7 months in District Jail for picketing.

MARY WINSOR, Haverford, Pa.; comes of family of pioneer Quaker descent. Educated at Drexel Institute of Philadelphia, at Bryn Mawr and abroad. At request of American Academy of Political and Social Science made survey of English suffrage movement. Founder and Pres. of Pa. Limited Suffrage Society. Sept., 1917, sentenced to 60 days at Occoquan workhouse for picketing. Later sentenced to 10 days for participation in Lafayette Sq. meeting. Has worked and spoken for suffrage in many parts of the country. Member "Prison Special" Feb., 1919.

ELLEN WINSOR, Haverford, Pa., sister of Mary Winsor and of Mrs. Edmund C. Evans, both of whom served prison sentences. Jan., 1919, sentenced to 5 days in District Jail for participation in watchfire demonstration.

MRS. KATE WINSTON, Chevy Chase, Md., wife of Prof. A. P. Winston, formerly Professor of economics at Univ. of Col. and at Univ. of Tokio. Jan., 1919, arrested and sentenced to 5 days in District Jail for participation in watchfire demonstration.

CLARA WOLD, Portland, Ore., newspaper writer. Of Norwegian parentage; her family closely related to Henrik Ibsen. Graduate of Univ. of Ore. Took part in Lafayette Sq. meeting of Aug., 1918; sentenced to 15 days. Jan., 1919, arrested for participation in watchfire demonstration and sentenced to 5 days. For several months acted as editor of *The Suffragist*.

JOY YOUNG, New York City, formerly of Washington, D. C., wife of Merrill Rogers. Former assistant on *The Suffragist* and later organizer for N.W.P. in various parts of the country. Served 3 days in District Jail for picketing July 4, 1917.

MATILDA YOUNG, Washington, D. C., sister of Joy Young; has devoted all her time to suffrage for several years. Youngest picket arrested, being 19 years old when she first served a prison term. For picketing Nov. 10, 1917, sentenced to 15 days in District Jail; served two terms in jail in Jan., 1919; 5 days for watchfire demonstration; 3 days for applauding suffrage prisoners in court.

APPENDIX 5

DIRECTORS OF NATIONAL CAMPAIGN
EXECUTIVE COMMITTEES LISTED BY YEARS

——o——

CONGRESSIONAL COMMITTEE

EXECUTIVE COMMITTEE 1913

Miss Alice Paul, N. J., Chairman
Miss Lucy Burns, N. Y., Vice-chairman
Mrs. Mary R. Beard, N. Y.
Miss Crystal Eastman, N. Y.
Mrs. Lawrence Lewis, Pa.

CONGRESSIONAL UNION FOR WOMAN SUFFRAGE

EXECUTIVE COMMITTEE 1914

Miss Alice Paul, N. J., Chairman
Miss Lucy Burns, N. Y., Vice-chairman
Mrs. Mary R. Beard, N. Y.
Mrs. O. H. P. Belmont, N. Y.
Miss Crystal Eastman, N. Y.
Mrs. Gilson Gardner, D. C.
Miss Elsie Hill, Conn.
Mrs. William Kent, Cal.
Mrs. Lawrence Lewis, Pa.

EXECUTIVE COMMITTEE 1915

Miss Alice Paul, N. J., Chairman
Miss Lucy Burns, N. Y., Vice-chairman
Mrs. Mary R. Beard, N. Y.
Mrs. O. H. P. Belmont, N. Y.
Miss Crystal Eastman, N. Y.
Mrs. Gilson Gardner, D. C.
Miss Elsie Hill, Conn.
Mrs. Donald R. Hooker, Md.
Mrs. William Kent, Cal.
Mrs. Lawrence Lewis, Pa.

EXECUTIVE COMMITTEE 1916

Miss Alice Paul, N. J., Chairman
Miss Lucy Burns, N. Y., Vice-chairman

Mrs. O. H. P. Belmont, N. Y.
Mrs. John Winters Brannan, N. Y.
Mrs. Gilson Gardner, D. C.
Mrs. Donald R. Hooker, Md.
Mrs. William Kent, Cal.
Mrs. Lawrence Lewis, Pa.
Miss Anne Martin, Nevada
Mrs. Harriot Stanton Blatch, N. Y.

WOMAN'S PARTY (*Formed June,* 1916)

EXECUTIVE COMMITTEE

Miss Anne Martin, Nev., Chairman
Mrs. Phoebe Hearst, Cal., 1st Vice-chairman
Judge Mary M. Bartelme, Ill., 2nd Vice-chairman
Miss Mabel Vernon, Nev., Secretary
Miss Alice Paul, N. J., ex-officio

NATIONAL WOMAN'S PARTY

(*After Amalgamation of Congressional Union and Woman's Party*)

EXECUTIVE COMMITTEE 1917

Miss Alice Paul, N. J., Chairman
Miss Anne Martin, Nev., Vice-chairman
Miss Mabel Vernon, Del., Secretary
Miss Gertrude L. Crocker, Ill., Treasurer
Mrs. Abby Scott Baker, D. C.
Mrs. O. H. P. Belmont, N. Y.
Mrs. John Winters Brannan, N. Y.
Miss Lucy Burns, N. Y.
Mrs. Gilson Gardner, D. C.
Mrs. Florence Bayard Hilles, Del.
Mrs. Donald R. Hooker, Md.
Mrs. J. A. H. Hopkins, N. J.
Mrs. William Kent, Cal.
Mrs. Lawrence Lewis, Pa.
Miss Doris Stevens, N. Y.
Miss Maud Younger, Cal.

EXECUTIVE COMMITTEE 1918

Miss Alice Paul, N. J., Chairman
Miss Anne Martin, Nev., Vice-chairman
Miss Mabel Vernon, Del., Secretary
Miss Mary Gertrude Fendall, Md., Treasurer
Mrs. Abby Scott Baker, D. C.
Mrs. O. H. P. Belmont, N. Y.
Mrs. John Winters Brannan, N. Y.
Miss Lucy Burns, N. Y.
Mrs. Gilson Gardner, D. C.
Mrs. Thomas N. Hepburn, Conn.
Mrs. Florence Bayard Hilles, Del.

Mrs. Donald R. Hooker, Md.
Mrs. Lawrence Lewis, Pa.
Miss Doris Stevens, N. Y.
Miss Maud Younger, Cal.

Executive Committee 1919-1920

Miss Alice Paul, N. J., Chairman
Miss Mabel Vernon, Del., Secretary
Miss Mary Gertrude Fendall, Md., Treasurer
Mrs. Abby Scott Baker, D. C.
Mrs. O. H. P. Belmont, N. Y.
Mrs. John Winters Brannan, N. Y.
Miss Lucy Burns, N. Y.
Mrs. Gilson Gardner, D. C.
Mrs. Thomas N. Hepburn, Conn.
Mrs. Florence Bayard Hilles, Del.
Mrs. Donald R. Hooker, Md.
Mrs. Henry G. Leach, N. Y.
Mrs. Lawrence Lewis, Pa.
Miss Doris Stevens. N. Y.
Mrs. Richard Wainwright, D. C.
Miss Maud Younger, Cal.

APPENDIX 6

CONCERNING POLITICAL PRISONERS

DEFINITIONS

James Bryce: [1]

"Perhaps we may say that whenever the moral judgment of the community at large does not brand an offence as sordid and degrading, and does not feel the offence to be one which destroys its respect for the personal character of the prisoner, it may there be held that prison treatment ought to be different from that awarded to ordinary criminals."

George Sigerson: [2]

"Men may differ, in thought and deed, on many questions without moral guilt. Forms of government and measures relating to the welfare and organization of society have been, in all ages and countries, questions on which men have entertained divergent convictions, and asserted their sincerity by conflicting action, often at grave personal sacrifice and the loss of life. On the other hand, all people are agreed in condemning certain acts, stigmatized as crimes, which offend against the well-being of the individual or the community.

"Hence, civilized states distinguish between actions concerning which good men may reasonably differ, and actions

---

[1] James Bryce made this distinction in 1889 between the two kinds of offenders. Letter Introductory to "Political Prisoners at Home and Abroad," Sigerson.

[2] "Political Prisoners at Home and Abroad."

which all good men condemn. The latter, if permitted to prevail, would disintegrate and destroy the social life of mankind;
the former, if successful, would simply reorganize it, on a
different basis. . . . The objects may, in one generation, be
branded as crimes, whilst in the next those who fail to make
them triumph and suffered as malefactors are exalted as
patriot martyrs, and their principles incorporated amongst
the foundation principles of the country's constitution.

"Attempts to effect changes by methods beyond the conventions which have the sanction of the majority of a community,
may be rash and blameworthy sometimes, but they are not
necessarily dishonorable, and may even occasionally be obliga-
tory on conscience."

As to the incumbency upon a government to differentiate
in punishments inflicted upon these two classes of offenders, he
further says: "When a Government exercises its punitive power,
it should, in awarding sentence, distinguish between the two
classes of offenders. To confound in a common degradation
those who violate the moral law by acts which all men condemn,
and those who offend against the established order of society
by acts of which many men approve, and for objects which
may sometime be accepted as integral parts of established
order, is manifestly wrong in principle. It places a Government
morally in the wrong in the eyes of masses of the population, a
thing to be sedulously guarded against."

George Clemenceau: [1]

"Theoretically a crime committed in the interest of the
criminal is a common law crime, while an offense committed in
the public interest is a political crime." He says further,
"That an act isolated from the circumstances under which it
was committed . . . may have the *appearance* of a common

[1] Clemenceau in a speech before the French Chamber of Deputies, May
16th, 1876, advocating amnesty for those who participated in the Commune
of 1871. From the Annals de la Chambre des Deputies, 1876, v. 2, pp. 44-48.

law crime . . . while viewed in connection with the circumstances under which it is committed (in connection with a movement) . . . it may take on a political character."

Maurice Parmelee: [1]

"Common crimes are acts contrary to the law committed in the interest of the individual criminal or of those personally related to the criminal. Political crimes are acts contrary to the law committed against an existing government or form of government in the interest of another government or form of government. . . . .

"Furthermore, there are other offenses against the law which are not common crimes, and yet are not political crimes in the usual criminological sense. . . . .

"Among these crimes, which are broader than the ordinary political crimes, are offenses in defense of the right to freedom of thought and belief, in defense of the right to express one's self in words in free speech, . . . and many illegal acts committed by conscientious objectors to the payment of taxes or to military service, the offenses of laborers in strikes and other labor disturbances, the violations of law committed by those who are trying to bring about changes in the relations between the sexes, etc.

"Common crimes are almost invariably anti-social in their nature, while offenses which are directly or indirectly political are usually social in their intent, and are frequently beneficial to society in their ultimate effect. We are, therefore, justified in calling them social crimes, as contrasted with the anti-social common crimes. . . . ."

[1] "Criminology" by Maurice Parmelee, Chap. XXVIII. Author also of "Poverty and Social Progress," "The Science of Human Behavior," "The Principles of Anthropology and Sociology in their relation to Criminal Procedure." During the late war Dr. Parmelee was a Representative of the U. S. War Trade Board stationed at the American Embassy, London; economic advisor to the State Department, and Chairman of the Allied Rationing Committee which administered the German Blockade.

Treatment Accorded Political Prisoners Abroad

It is interesting to note what other countries have done toward handling intelligently the problem of political offenders.

Russia was probably the first country in modern history to recognize political prisoners as a class,[1] although the treatment of different groups and individuals varied widely.

First of all, the political offender was recognized as a "political" not by law, but by custom. When sure of a verdict of guilty, either through damaging evidence or a packed jury, the offender was tried. When it was impossible to commit him to trial because there were no proofs against him, "Administrative Exile" was resorted to. These judgments or Administrative orders to exile were pronounced in secret on political offenders; one member of the family of the defendant was admitted to the trial under the law of 1881. Those exiled by Administrative order were transported in cars, but stopped en route at the *etapes*, political prisoners along with common law convicts. Since 1866 politicals condemned by the courts to hard labor or to exile, journeyed on foot with common law convicts.[1]

There were no hospitals for political exiles; doctors and surgeons among the exiled helped their sick comrades.

Families were permitted to follow the loved ones into exile, if they chose. For example, wives were allowed to stay at Lower Kara, and visit their husbands in the prison in Middle Kara twice a week and to bring them books.

When criminal convicts were freed in Siberia after serving a given sentence at hard labor, they received an allotment of land and agricultural implements for purposes of sustenance, and after two years the government troubled no more about

[1] Siberia received its first exiles [non-conformists] in the 17th Century.

them. They became settlers in some province of Southern Siberia. With political exiles it was quite different. When they had finished a seven, ten, or twelve year sentence, they were not liberated but transferred to the tundras within the Arctic Circle.

Fancy a young girl student exiled to a village numbering a hundred houses, with the government allowance of 8 to 10 shillings a month to live on. Occupations were closed to her, and there was no opportunity to learn a trade. She was forbidden to leave the town even for a few hours. The villagers were for the most part in fear of being suspected if seen to greet politicals in the street.

"Without dress, without shoes, living in the nastiest huts, without any occupation, they [the exiles] were mostly dying from consumption," said the *Golos* of February 2, 1881. They lived in constant fear of starvation. And the Government allowance was withdrawn if it became known that an exile received any monetary assistance from family or friends.

Those politicals condemned to hard labor in Siberia worked mostly in gold mines for three months out of twelve, during which period meat was added to their diet. Otherwise black bread was the main food of the diet.

When held in prisons awaiting trial or convicted and awaiting transfer into exile, politicals did no work whatever. Their only occupation was reading. Common criminals had to work in prison as well as in Siberia.

In the fortress of Sts. Peter and Paul,[1] Kropotkin was lodged in a cell big enough to shelter a big fortress gun (25 feet on the diagonal). The walls and floor were lined with felt to prevent communication with others. "The silence in these felt-covered cells is that of a grave," wrote Kropotkin. . . . "Here I wrote my two volumes on The Glacial Period." Here

---

[1] In the Trubeskoi bastion, one building in the fortress.

he also prepared maps and drawings. This privilege was only granted to him, however, after a strong movement amongst influential circles compelled it from the Czar.[1] The Geographical Society for whom he was writing his thesis also made many pleas on his behalf. He was allowed to buy tobacco, writing paper and to have books—but no extra food.

Kropotkin says that political prisoners were not subjected to corporal punishment, through official fear of bloodshed. But he must mean by corporal punishment actual beatings, for he says also, "The black holes, the chains, the riveting to barrows are usual punishments." And some politicals were alleged to have been put in *oubliettes* in the Alexis Ravelin [2] which must have been the worst feature of all the tortures. This meant immurement alive in cells, in a remote spot where no contact with others was possible, and where the prisoner would often be chained or riveted for years.

More recently there was some mitigation of the worst features of the prison régime and some additional privileges were extended to politicals.

All this applied to old Russia. There is no documentary proof available yet, as to how Soviet Russia treats its offenders against the present government. The Constitution of the Russian Socialist Federated Soviet Republic [3] does not provide a status for political prisoners, but it does provide for their release. It specifically deals with amnesty which is proof of the importance with which it regards the question of political offenders. It says: "The All-Russian Central Executive Committee deal with questions of state such as . . . the right to declare individual and general amnesty." [4]

France has had perhaps the most enlightened attitude of all the nations toward political offenders. She absolutely

[1] See *Memoirs of a Revolutionist,* Kropotkin.
[2] Another section of Sts. Peter and Paul Fortress.
[3] Adopted by the 5th All-Russian Congress of Soviets, July 10, 1918. Reprinted from *The Nation,* January 4, 1919.
[4] Article 3, Chapter 9 . . . 49 q.

guarantees special treatment, by special regulations, and does not leave it to the discretion of changing governments.

On August 7, 1834, Thiers, in a ministerial circular, laid down the fundamental principles upon which France has acted. The only obligation upon the defendant, according to this circular, was to prove the political nature of the offense,— "that it should be demonstrated and incontestable that they have acted under the influence of their opinions." [1] Theirs advocated superior diet for political prisoners and no work.

His edict was followed by special regulations issued for politicals under the Empire, February 9th, 1867, through M. Pietri, Prefect of the Seine. These regulations, illustrative of the care France exercised at an early date over her politicals, defined the housing conditions, diet, intercourse with comrades inside the prison and with family and friends from the outside. Their privacy was carefully guarded. No curious visitor was allowed to see a political unless the latter so desired.

Kropotkin wrote [2] of his incarceration in Clairvaux prison in 1883, to which he and twenty-two others were transferred from Lyons after being prosecuted for belonging to the International Workingmen's Association: "In France, it is generally understood that for political prisoners the loss of liberty and the forced inactivity are in themselves so hard that there is no need to inflict additional hardships."

In Clairvaux he and his comrades were given quarters in spacious rooms, not in cells. Kropotkin and Emile Gautier, the French anarchist, were given a separate room for literary work and the Academy of Sciences offered them the use of its library.

There was no intercourse with common law prisoners. The politicals were allowed to wear their own clothes, to smoke, to buy food and wine from the prison canteen or have it brought

[1] *Sigerson, Political Prisoners at Home and Abroad,* p. 89.
[2] *Memoirs of a Revolutionist,* Kropotkin.

in; they were free of compulsory work, but might, if they chose, do light work for which they were paid. Kropotkin mentions the extreme cleanliness of the prison and the "excellent quality" of the prison food.

Their windows looked down upon a little garden and also commanded a beautiful view of the surrounding country. They played nine-pins in the yard and made a vegetable and flower garden on the surface of the building's wall. For other forms of recreation, they were allowed to organize themselves into classes. This particular group received from Kropotkin lessons in cosmography, geometry, physics, languages and bookbinding. Kropotkin's wife was allowed to visit him daily and to walk with him in the prison gardens.

Sebastian Faure, the great French teacher and orator, was sentenced to prison after the anarchist terrorism in 1894 and while there was allowed to write his "La Douleur Universelle."

Paul La Fargue, son-in-law of Karl Marx, wrote his famous "The Right to be Lazy" in Sainte Pelagie prison.

France has continued this policy to date. Jean Grave, once a shoemaker and now a celebrated anarchist, was condemned to six months in La Sante prison for an offensive article in his paper, *Les Temps Nouveaux*. Such is the liberty allowed a political that while serving this sentence he was given paper and materials with which to write another objectionable article, called "La Société Mourante et l'Anarchie," for the publication of which he received another six months.

It is interesting to note the comparatively light sentences political offenders get in France. And then there is an established practice of amnesty. They rarely finish out their terms. Agitation for their release extends from the extreme revolutionary left to the members of the Chamber of Deputies, frequently backed by the liberal press.

Italy also distinguishes between political and common law

offenders. The former are entitled to all the privileges of *custodia honesta* [1] which means they are allowed to wear their own clothes, work or not, as they choose; if they do work, one half their earnings is given to them. Their only penal obligation is silence during work, meals, school and prayers. A friend of Sr. Serrati, the ex-editor of the Italian journal *Il Proletario*, tells me that Serrati was a political prisoner during the late war; that he was sentenced to three and a half years, but was released at the end of six months, through pressure from the outside. But while there, he was allowed to write an article a day for *Avanti*, of which paper he was then an editor.

Even before the Franco-Prussian War German principalities recognized political offenders as such. The practice continued after the federation of German states through the Empire and up to the overthrow of Kaiser Wilhelm. Politicals were held in "honorable custody" in fortresses where they were deprived only of their liberty.

For revolutionary activities in Saxony in 1849, Bakunin [2] was arrested, taken to a Cavalry Barracks and later to Koenigstein Fortress, where politicals were held. Here he was allowed to walk twice daily under guard. He was allowed to receive books, he could converse with his fellow prisoners and could write and receive numerous letters. In a letter to a friend [3] he wrote that he was occupied in the study of mathematics and English, and that he was "enjoying Shakespeare." And . . . "they treat me with extraordinary humaneness."

Another letter to the same friend a month later said he was writing a defense of his political views in "a comfortable room," with "cigars and food brought in from a nearby inn."

[1] Sigerson, pp. 154-5.
[2] The Life of Michael Bakunin—Eine Biographie von Dr. Max Nettlau. (Privately printed by the author. Fifty copies reproduced by the autocopyist, Longhaus.)
[3] To Adolph R—— (the last name illegible) October 15, 1849.

The death sentence was pronounced against him in 1850 but commuted to imprisonment for life. The same year he was extradited to Austria where the offense was committed, then to Russiá and on to Siberia in 1855, whence he escaped in 1860 in an American ship.

In 1869 Bebel[1] received a sentence of *three weeks* in Leipzig (contrast with Alice Paul's seven months' sentence) "for the propagation of ideas dangerous to the state." Later for high treason based upon Social-Democratic agitation he was sentenced to two years in a fortress. For *lèse majesté* he served nine months in Hubertusburg—a fortress prison (in 1871). Here politicals were allowed to pay for the cleaning of their cells, to receive food from a nearby inn, and were allowed to eat together in the corridors. They were only locked in for part of the time, and the rest of the time were allowed to walk in the garden. They were permitted lights until ten at night; books; and could receive and answer mail every day. Bebel received permission to share cell quarters with the elder Liebknecht (Wilhelm), then serving time for his internationalism. He says that political prisoners were often allowed a six weeks' leave of absence between sentences; when finishing one and beginning a second.

According to Sigerson, politicals in Austria also were absolved from wearing prison clothes, might buy their own food and choose their work. I am told the same régime prevailed in Hungary under Franz Joseph.

The new constitution of the German Republic adopted at Weimar July 31, 1919, provides that [2] "The President of the Republic shall exercise for the government the right of pardon. . . . Government amnesties require a national law."

In the Scandinavian countries there is no provision for special consideration of political prisoners, although a proposed

[1] *My Life*, August Bebel.
[2] Article 49.

change in Sweden's penal laws now pending includes special treatment for them, and in Denmark, although politicals are not recognized apart from other prisoners, the people have just won an amnesty for all prisoners convicted of political offense as I write. Neither Switzerland nor Spain makes separate provision for politicals, although there are many prisoners confined in their prisons for political offenses, especially in Spain, where there are nearly always actually thousands in *Monjuich*. Portugal also subjects political offenders to the same régime as criminals.

Concerning Turkey and Bulgaria, I appealed to George Andreytchine, a Bulgarian revolutionist who as protégé of King Ferdinand was educated at Sofia and Constantinople, knowing his knowledge on this point would be authentic. He writes: "Turkey, which is the most backward of all modern states, recognized the status of political prisoners before 1895, or shortly after the Armenian massacres. Thousands of Bulgarian, Greek, Armenian and Arabian insurgents, caught with arms in their hands, conspiring and actually in open rebellion against the Ottoman Empire, were sentenced to exile or hard labor, but were never confined in the same prisons with ordinary criminals and felons. They were put in more hygienical prisons where they were allowed to read and write and to breathe fresh air. Among some of my friends who were exiled to Turkish Africa for rebellion was a young scholar, Paul Shateff, by name, who while there wrote a remarkable monograph on the ethnology and ethnography of the Arabian Tribes in which he incidentally tells of the special treatment given him and his fellow exiles as political prisoners.

"There is something to be said for the political wisdom of the Sultans. Amnesty is an established practice, usually at the birthday of the Sultan or the coming to power of a new Sultan, or on Ramadan,[1] a national holiday.

"In 1908 when the young Turks assumed control of the government, all political prisoners were released and cared for by the state. My friend Paul Shateff was sent at state expense to Bruxelles to finish his studies.

"Bulgaria, another one of those 'backward countries,' established the political régime even earlier than Turkey. Politicals are allowed to read, to write books or articles for publication, to receive food from outside, and are periodically released on amnesty."

And now we come to England. In general England, too, gives political offenders much lighter sentences than does America, but, except in isolated cases, she treats them no better. She does not recognize them as political prisoners. If they are distinguished prisoners like Dr. Jamison, who was permitted to serve the sentence imposed upon him for leading an armed raid into the Transvaal in 1895, in a luxuriously furnished suite, to provide himself with books, a piano, and such food as he chose, and to receive his friends, special dispensation is allowed; or like William Cobbett, who was imprisoned for writing an alleged treasonable article in his journal, *The Register*, in 1809; or Leigh Hunt for maligning the Prince Regent who, he believed, broke his promise to the Irish cause; Daniel O'Connell and six associates in 1844 for "seditious activity"; John Mitchell, who in 1848 was sent to Bermuda and then to Van Dieman's Land.[2] These British prisoners, while not proclaimed as politicals, did receive special privileges.[3]

More recently Bertrand Russell, the distinguished man of letters who served sixty-one days in lieu of payment of fine for

[1] The month (the ninth in the Mohammedan year) in which the first part of the Koran is said to have been received.
[2] English penal colony in Tasmania.
[3] For details of their handsome treatment see Sigerson, pp. 19-20.

writing a pamphlet intended to arouse public indignation against the treatment of a certain conscientious objector, received special privileges. In England the matter of treatment rests largely with the will of the Prime Minister, who dictates the policy to the Home Secretary, who in turn directs the Chairman of the Board of Directors of Prisons. The Home Secretary may, however, of his own accord issue an order for special privileges if he so desires, or if there is a strong demand for such an order. Many government commissions and many distinguished British statesmen have recommended complete recognition and guarantee of the status of political prisoners, but the matter has been left to common law custom and precedent, and the character of the prime minister. In the case of Ireland the policy agreed upon is carried out by the Lord Lieutenant of Ireland.

It is difficult to generalize about England's treatment of Irish political offenders. From the earliest nationalist activities she has treated them practically all as common criminals, or worse, if such a thing is possible. She has either filled English prisons, or, as in the sixties, put them in convict ships and sent them to Bermuda and Australia for life sentences along with common convicts where they performed the hardest labor. Irish prisoners have fought with signal and persistent courage for the rights due political offenders. Lately, after militant demonstrations within the prisons and after deaths resulting from concerted hunger striking protests, some additional privileges have been extended. But these can be and are withheld at will. There is no guarantee of them.

As early as 1835 Canadian nationalists who had taken part in an insurrection in Upper Canada on behalf of self-government and who were sent to Van Dieman's Land in convict ships, entered a vigorous protest to Lord Russell, the Home Secretary, against not receiving the treatment due political prisoners.

England has to her credit, then, some flexibility about extending privileges to politicals. We have none. England has to her credit lighter sentences—Irish cases excepted. No country, not excluding imperial Germany, has ever given such cruelly long sentences to political offenders as did America during the late war.

I have incorporated this discussion in such a book for two reasons: first, because it seemed to me important that you should know what a tremendous contribution the suffrage prisoners made toward this enlightened reform. They were the first in America to make a sustained demand to establish this precedent which others will consummate. They kept up the demand to the end of the prison episode, reënforcing it by the hunger strike protest. The other reason for including this discussion here is that it seems to me imperative that America recognize without further delay the status of political offenders. As early as 1872 the International Prison Congress meeting in London recommended a distinction in the treatment of common law criminals and politicals, and the resolution was agreed upon by the representatives of *all the Powers of Europe and America* with the tacit concurrence of British and Irish officials. And still we are behind Turkey in adopting an enlightened policy. We have neither regulation, statute nor precedent. Nor have we the custom of official flexibility.

NOTE.—The most conspicuous political prisoner from the point of view of actual power the United States has ever held in custody was Jefferson Davis, the President of the Confederate States, during the rebellion of the South against the Union. He was imprisoned in Fortress Monroe and subjected to the most cruel and humiliating treatment conceivable. For details of his imprisonment see the graphic account given in "Jefferson Davis—A Memoir" by his wife, Vol. II, pp. 653-95.